D1154362

Closing Chapters

Closing Chapters

Urban Change, Religious Reform, and the Decline of Youngstown's Catholic Elementary Schools, 1960–2006

Thomas G. Welsh

LEXINGTON BOOKS
Lanham • Boulder • New York • Toronto • Plymouth, UK

Published by Lexington Books
A wholly owned subsidiary of The Rowman & Littlefield Publishing Group, Inc.
4501 Forbes Boulevard, Suite 200, Lanham, Maryland 20706
www.lexingtonbooks.com

Estover Road, Plymouth PL6 7PY, United Kingdom

British Library Cataloguing in Publication Information Available

Library of Congress Cataloging-in-Publication Data

Welsh, Thomas G., 1961–
  Closing chapters : urban change, religious reform, and the decline of Youngstown's Catholic elementary schools, 1960-2006 / Thomas G. Welsh.
    p. cm.
  Summary: "Closing Chapters attempts to explain the disintegration of urban parochial schools in Youngstown, Ohio, a onetime industrial center that lost all but one of its eighteen Catholic parochial elementary schools between 1960 and 2006. Through the examination of Youngstown, Welsh sheds light on a significant national phenomenon: the fragmentation of American Catholic identity"— Provided by publisher.
  ISBN 978-0-7391-6594-2 (hardback) — ISBN 978-0-7391-6596-6 (ebook)
  1. Catholic elementary schools—Ohio—Youngstown—History. 2. Urban education—Ohio—Youngstown—History. 3. Catholics—Religious identity—United States. I. Title.
  LC503.Y68W45 2011
  372.1042'71277139—dc23   2011032543

♾️ ™ The paper used in this publication meets the minimum requirements of American National Standard for Information Sciences—Permanence of Paper for Printed Library Materials, ANSI/NISO Z39.48-1992.

Printed in the United States of America

Contents

Acknowledgments

This project benefited from the guidance and support of numerous mentors, colleagues, friends, and relatives. Given that this manuscript had its origins in a dissertation project, I feel obliged to express my appreciation to former members of my dissertation committee at Kent State University, including co-advisors Natasha Levinson, Ph.D., and Averil McClelland, Ph.D. (Department of Educational Foundations and Special Services), and outside members Joanne Dowdy, Ph.D. (Department of Teaching Leadership and Curriculum Studies), and Paul McBride, Ph.D. (professor emeritus and former chair of the History Department at Ithaca College, Ithaca, New York). My interest in the transformation of urban parochial schools was largely inspired by Dr. Levinson, who highlighted this issue in a graduate course titled "Modern Philosophical Theories of Education." Dr. McClelland played a significant role in the development of a theoretical framework that enabled me to draw from literature on the topics of urban Catholic education and American Catholic identity. At the proposal stage, Dr. Dowdy suggested that I include a chapter devoted to the development of Immaculate Conception Elementary School—a recommendation that enabled me to provide a detailed account of the manner in which one parish school in Youngstown, Ohio, was affected by urban trends as well as the fragmentation of Catholic identity. Perhaps no one has done more to enrich this manuscript than Dr. McBride, who reviewed drafts of each chapter and generously shared his own insights on a range of issues related to the topic. As a native of Youngstown, and an alumnus of Catholic elementary and secondary schools, Dr. McBride was well positioned to comment on the accuracy of my characterizations and conclusions.

I am also grateful to Information Age Publishing for permitting the use of material that first appeared in volume 38, numbers 1 and 2, of the *American Educational History Journal*.

No less worthy of acknowledgment are the scores of Youngstown-area residents who assisted in this project. As I developed my proposal, I benefited from the valuable insights of Wallace Dunne, director of Government Programs, Resource Development, and Athletics for the Diocese of Youngstown. George H. Beelen, Ph.D., professor emeritus and former chair of Youngstown State University's History Department, kindly agreed to review several chapters of this manuscript and directed me to useful data on race relations in early twentieth-century Youngstown. Attorney Robert E. Casey agreed to share his memories of Immaculate Conception Elementary School and introduced me to his longtime friend, Dr. McBride. Attorney Casey was one of many Youngstown-area residents who agreed to be interviewed for this study. Other interviewees included Sister Julia Baluch, O.S.U.; Beverly Blackshear; Naomi Byrd; Ida Carter; James Gray Doran; Elizabeth Fleisher Fekety; the late Joseph Hill; Carla Haiser Hlavac; Sister Charlotte Italiano, O.S.U.; Joseph and Judith Magielski; the late Sister Virginia McDermott, O.S.U.; Paula McKinney; Bishop George V. Murry, S.J.; Father Edward P. Noga; Martin J. ("Jack") O'Connell; Father Kevin Peters; Fred and Josephine Ross; Father Joseph S. Rudjak; Richard S. Scarsella; Father Nicholas R. Shori; Father John R. Summers; Joan E. Welsh; T. Gordon Welsh; Sister Teresa Winsen, O.S.U.; and Hank and Kathleen Zimmerman.

While conducting research for this project, I benefited from the assistance of the following individuals: Debbie Bushmire, Sally Freaney, Hannah Moses, and Melissa Williams, reference librarians at Youngstown's Reuben-McMillan Public Library; Lou Jacquet, managing editor of *The Catholic Exponent*, the bi-weekly newspaper of the Diocese of Youngstown; William Lawson, executive director of the Mahoning Valley Historical Society; Sherry Linkon, Ph.D., co-director of the Center for Working Class Studies at Youngstown State University; Sister Bridget Nolan, O.S.U., archivist of the Ursuline Sisters Archives, in Canfield, Ohio; Pamela Speis, archivist at the Mahoning Valley Historical Society; and Nancy Yuhasz, chancellor of the Diocese of Youngstown. Throughout, I enjoyed the boundless support of my parents, the late Thomas G. Welsh, Sr., and Elaine M. Welsh. Finally, I owe a special word of appreciation to my aunt, Sister Marcia Welsh, O.S.U., a retired instructor and community service coordinator, who helped to arrange interviews with other members of the Ursuline religious community.

Thomas G. Welsh Jr.
June 8, 2011, Youngstown, Ohio

Dedication

This manuscript is dedicated to the memory of my father, Thomas G. Welsh Sr., who passed away on March 8, 2010, after a courageous two-year battle with cancer. An urban educator who was devoted to his church, he became involved in many issues addressed in this manuscript. In the 1960s and 1970s, he served as a lector at St. Brendan Church in Youngstown, a member of that parish's Vatican II committee, and a speaker for the Pre-Cana Conference for the Diocese of Youngstown. In retirement, he worked as a volunteer for charitable organizations including the St. Vincent de Paul Society, while assisting his older sibling, Sr. Marcia Welsh, O.S.U., with her work in the area of prison ministry. In various ways, my father's life reflected the spirit of social engagement that helped transform American Catholicism in the wake of the Second Vatican Council.

.

Chapter 1

Introduction

On June 4, 1943, an area of northeastern Ohio—including Stark, Columbiana, Mahoning, Portage, Trumbull, and Ashtabula counties—was "canonically erected" as the Diocese of Youngstown. The new diocese, which comprised 3,404 square miles, featured several major manufacturing and steel-production centers as well as large stretches of agricultural territory. In *The March of the Eucharist from Dungannon,* a commemorative volume published 8 years later, the Diocese of Youngstown claimed 110 churches, 3 hospitals, and 2 schools of nursing operated by religious orders. The volume's author, the Most Reverend James A. McFadden, bishop of Youngstown, wrote with evident conviction that "[t]he Diocese of Youngstown is well established and is developing a vigorous Catholic life in opposition to the evil forces which would destroy our country."[1] Among the instruments the diocese relied upon to develop this "vigorous Catholic life" was a parallel educational system comprising 50 parochial elementary schools with about 11,560 students enrolled.[2]

An especially vibrant pattern of parochial education could be found in the diocesan center of Youngstown, which alone boasted 18 parish elementary schools as well as a high school and junior high school. (A second Catholic high school opened in 1954.) In 1961, a local newspaper reported that "[o]ne out of every three children in Youngstown will attend a Catholic elementary school or high school in September, as school boards estimate 13,318 in Catholic schools in the city."[3] However, in Youngstown, as elsewhere, an era of expansion overseen by "builder bishops" gave way to a long period of contraction and uncertainty. Urban Catholic educators were confronted "with crisis after crisis that shook the very foundation of American Catholic education and caused Catholic educators to question the viability and survival of the parish schools they had worked so hard to preserve."[4] Hence, by spring 2006, the local media reported that the last

1

two Catholic elementary schools operating in Youngstown's center city were closing their doors, leaving only one parish school within the municipal limits.[5] Three years later, in 2009, the diocese, as a whole, retained no more than 36 parish schools, which were spread across Mahoning, Trumbull, Columbiana, Portage, Ashtabula, and Stark counties. In February 2009, Youngstown Bishop George V. Murry, SJ, reported that the Diocese of Youngstown had 40,000 fewer Catholics than it did in 2002 and called for an "orderly downsizing of the diocese." The bishop acknowledged that a "strategic plan" to deal with the situation would involve the closure of churches and schools throughout the diocese.[6]

The expansion and decline of Catholic elementary schools in this Midwestern industrial town is an example of a larger phenomenon that is related to the question of Catholic identity in the United States. Therefore, an examination of Youngstown's urban parish schools—from the post–World War II era to the present—will shed light on a significant national phenomenon: the fragmentation of American Catholic identity. While the fragmentation of U.S. Catholic identity has been addressed in general studies of American Catholicism, it has been discussed less frequently in research concerning the decline of one of the Catholic community's most iconic institutions: the urban parochial school. Hence, this examination of Youngstown's parochial schools will draw upon two distinct bodies of literature (dealing with American Catholic identity and American Catholic education, respectively) in an effort to identify and interpret factors that contributed to the decline of a once vibrant system of parochial education.

The so-called crisis in the American Catholic Church should be a familiar issue to any casual purveyor of the U.S. media. Over the past 20 years, it has been difficult to access a newspaper, television, or an online news outlet without encountering some instance of discord or scandal within the U.S. Catholic community. In recent years, the polarizing actions and statements of Pope Benedict XVI have underscored an overall impression of fragmentation. In 2006, the pope's decision to read aloud a fourteenth-century description of Islam as "evil and inhuman" drew criticism from Muslim leaders and raised questions about his commitment to interfaith dialogue.[7] Less than a year later, in July 2007, the pope angered many Protestants when he approved a document indicating that "other Christian communities are either defective or not true churches and Catholicism provides the only true path to salvation."[8] A *New York Times* editorial on Pope Benedict's earlier statements regarding Islam described him as "a doctrinal conservative" whose "greatest fear appears to be the loss of a uniform Catholic identity, not exactly the best jumping-off point for tolerance or interfaith dialogue."[9] Meanwhile, Pope Benedict's tendency to associate "Catholic activism with the specter of Communism," along with his "laissez-faire approach to economic and social justice," has simultaneously alienated liberal American Catholics and rallied conservative ones.[10]

Several years earlier, in 2002, polarization of opinion among U.S. Catholics was even more apparent, as the church was rocked by widespread allegations of sexual abuse by members of the clergy. Although revulsion over the nature of the allegations transcended ideological boundaries, liberals and conservatives responded differently to the crisis. Many liberals called for "dramatic change in church culture" and questioned the requirement of priestly celibacy and the ban on the ordination of women. Liberal reform groups "considered these changes essential if the church hoped to claim relevance in the lives of younger Catholics." Meanwhile, conservative Catholic organizations were inclined to attribute the abuse scandal to a supposed prevalence of homosexuals in the priesthood, and to call for their removal.[11] Conservative Catholics also railed against what they termed the permissive moral standards of mainstream U.S. society, citing them as a contributing factor in abuse cases. Overall, conservatives were more likely to accuse the U.S. media of anti-Catholic bias than to criticize the responses of bishops and other administrators who handled reports of abuse. "If a Presbyterian minister tries to seduce a young boy met on the Internet, it is reported as the story of an evil and depraved man, not of a troubled church," Philip Jenkins wrote. "If a priest is caught in the same circumstances, then this event is contextualized with other tales of 'pedophile priests.'"[12] In this climate of sometimes hostile disagreement, traditional images of a cohesive Catholic subculture appeared more remote than ever. Writing in 2001, Jay P. Dolan contended that "this scandal of abuse and cover-up has shaken to its foundation the sacred trust between priests and their parishioners."[13]

Amid the flurry of criticism directed at U.S. Catholic institutions in the wake of the clergy abuse scandal, many observers would have been surprised to learn that, five decades earlier, the U.S. media had generated almost exclusively positive images of U.S. Catholic culture. No less surprising is the fact that a large percentage of American Catholics accepted the authenticity of these idealized images. As historian and political analyst Garry Wills noted, "Nuns were played by the likes of Ingrid Bergman, Loretta Young, Celeste Holm, and Alida Valli. The priests were Barry Fitzgerald, Bing Crosby, Spencer Tracy, Frank Sinatra, and Montgomery Clift. The TV face of Catholicism was Fulton Sheen, complete with an angel as the eraser-boy for his blackboard." Within a decade, such positive characterizations had all but vanished. As Wills observed, "In the 1960s, this saccharine view of Catholic childhood yielded to new memories of Catholic childhood, peopled with coercive nuns and creepy priests, not a single Bing Crosby type among them."[14] It was as though the price of Catholic assimilation into mainstream culture involved a sweeping disavowal of the Catholic "ghetto" and all for which it had stood. That said, negative characterizations of the "old" Catholic subculture failed to resonate for all American Catholics. Even a critical observer like Wills mused: "It was a ghetto, undeniably. But not a bad ghetto to grow up in."[15] Indeed, the "ghetto," with its residual "Old World" values, often smoothed the path for European immigrants as they struggled to accommodate themselves to a radically different culture. Catholic writer James Flanigan, in a reflection on the controversial film *Doubt*, which deals with the issue of clerical abuse, noted that religious figures played a largely constructive role in the 1950s Bronx neighborhood of his upbringing. "The teachers [at neighboring Catholic schools] knew that their role was to bring their charges into the new land and the new society, 'secular' though that might be," Flanigan wrote. "It is poetic but accurate to say that the clergy and religious provided a passage to America for those students."[16]

For all its insularity, the traditional urban Catholic enclave reinforced among its inhabitants a strong sense of collective identity.[17] Through participation in a vast network of "parallel" institutions and organizations, Catholics were shielded from rapid (and potentially traumatic) assimilation into mainstream American culture. Among the Catholic subculture's most notable normative institutions was the urban parish school, which was occasionally praised but more often criticized by "ghetto" alumni. In more recent years, however, the steady decline of the urban parochial school has prompted a growing number of American Catholics to re-evaluate the importance of this institution. For many, the decline of urban parochial schools is merely one element in a demoralizing vista of institutional decay. "I think some of the anxieties and difficulties we see and feel express our sense that the infrastructure of the church, like that of the country, is going," observed *Commonweal* editor Margaret O'Brien Steinfels, writing more than a decade ago. "For the past twenty-five years, we have lived on all the good things that people have done for two centuries, and I think we are simply unclear whether we are maintaining that kind of patrimony to pass on to the next generation." For Catholics like Steinfels, the "identity question" has become central. "It has been raised about Catholic colleges and universities, about Catholic hospitals, about grammar schools where non-Catholic children are educated," she wrote. "It is raised when we look at the declining number of priests and women religious, the decline in religious orders, the appointment of bishops seemingly committed to restoring a notion of authority that is not likely to be successful, at least in this country."[18]

What led to this impasse? Liberals and conservatives, despite their strongly held differences, appear to agree on one thing: a turning point in U.S. Catholic history came with the reforms of the Second Vatican Council, which culminated in the banning of the Tridentine (Latin) mass and the weakening of longstanding cultural markers that sharply differentiated U.S. Catholics from other Americans. These reforms contributed to—or dovetailed with—a period characterized by divergent conceptions of Catholic identity and strong disagreement over the purposes, even the necessity, of Catholic education. Charles R. Morris, in his well-regarded journalistic treatment of U.S. Catholic history, noted that the "contested legacy" of Vatican II had profound implications for both Catholic identity and parochial education. Morris has argued that, while the council "expressly did *not* approve the use of the vernacular for the entire Mass," advocates of change took steps to ensure that "the use of the vernacular became general throughout the Church within just a few years of the Council's close." More significantly, and to the discomfort of many conservatives, "elementary school catechetics almost immediately reflected the most liberal versions of doctrinal and ethical teachings, as if they had been automatically endorsed by the Council."[19] Within a short period of time, the face of American Catholicism was transformed. Historian Philip Gleason, SJ, noted that the postconciliar reforms reflected a wholesale rejection of Catholic "medievalism," a development that influenced approaches to ethics, theology, and education as well as liturgical art, music, and architecture.[20]

Catholic intellectuals were especially divided on the religious impact of the postconciliar reforms. The liberal Wills, in his celebrated reflection on Catholic disunity, *Bare Ruined Choirs,* questioned whether the reforms went far enough and described pre–Vatican II religious practices and values as "pretense."[21] Wills criticized an approach to religion that, in his view, depended heavily on symbolism while leaving little room for a sophisticated understanding of theology. "Faith bound one's whole life up in ties of communal teaching, habits, discipline, authority, childhood assumptions, personal relationships," Wills wrote of the preconciliar church.[22] Meanwhile, the traditionalist James Hitchcock, in his *Decline and Fall of Radical Catholicism,* lamented a "weakening of belief" in the wake of the council.[23] Observers on both sides of the ideological divide, however, appeared to recognize that the reforms had contributed to the demise of a clearly defined Catholic subculture. "We spoke a different language from the rest of men—not only the actual Latin memorized when we learned to 'serve Mass' as altar boys," Wills wrote. "We also had odd bits of Latinized English that were not part of other six-year-olds' vocabulary—words like 'contrition' and 'transubstantiation.'" He added that, for young American Catholics, to "know the terms was to know the thing, to solve the problem."[24]

Such feelings of certainty were no longer evident among U.S. Catholic youth by the late 1960s. As Catholic scholar Chester Gillis noted, the "successful assimilation" of U.S. Catholics that came in the wake of Vatican II resulted in a "loss of group identity, lack of common vision, detachment from specific marks of identification, and appropriation of practices and values esteemed by the common culture, whether or not they adhere to Catholic principles."[25] Likewise, Wills observed that, while the council "removed some ugly excrescences from the church's long history," it also resulted in the elimination of "many of the things that gave Catholics their sense of identity—the Latin Mass, the Friday abstinence from meat, the morning fast before communion, mandatory Sunday church attendance, mandatory annual communion ('the Easter duty'), traditional liturgical music, the Legion of Decency (rating movies), the *Index of Forbidden Books.*"[26] Moreover, parish school classrooms themselves became ideological battlegrounds, as parents and educators argued over aspects of the curriculum. Catholic educators appeared bereft of what Gleason called a "distinctive vision of an alternative culture to which the modern world should be converted,"[27] and some educators promoted a "value-based curriculum" that failed to satisfy the requirements of traditionalists, who questioned whether parochial schools were "doing enough to insure that their students had specifically Catholic values."[28] Meanwhile, the council's general theme of social engagement encouraged some Catholic educators to envision urban parish schools as "instruments of social justice" that would alleviate inequalities arising from racism.[29] In time, this development fueled an internal debate over the ultimate purpose of Catholic education.

The debate over Vatican II was by no means the only controversy sending shock waves through the U.S. Catholic community in the wake of the 1960s. U.S. Catholics were deeply divided in their responses to the civil rights movement, the Vietnam War, the feminist movement, and the legalization of abortion. Catholic historian Mark S. Massa noted that rising levels of discord among Catholics represented a sharp departure from the atmosphere of the immediate postwar era. While the mainstream Protestant community "had undergone a series of traumatic identity crises during the first third of the twentieth century over its ability to remain the 'cultural faith,'" the U.S. Catholic Church maintained a "cultural 'innocence.'" Massa observed that the U.S. Catholic community "had weathered both the Great Depression and the traumas of the world wars with its self-confidence and corporate esprit intact, proclaiming itself (and being viewed by others) as far more self-assured, cohesive, and vibrant than the much larger and more established Protestant mainstream that had piped the cultural tune for three centuries." He attributed the "survival of innocence" he discerned within the Catholic community to the church's anomalous "sociological position." The U.S. Catholic Church, given its role as "*both* the largest religious group in the land" and "something of a distrusted outsider," was not obliged to "make sense of the great intellectual and social crises of the twentieth century as it made no claims to speak for the culture as a whole." Therefore, while American Protestants "fought like theological cats and dogs over evolution, biblical criticism, and the uniqueness of Jesus as savior," their Catholic counterparts "worried over who would speak at the next Communion breakfast and what Catholic team would win the city-wide parochial high school championship."[30]

Within two decades, however, debates over values and educational goals among Catholics reflected not only larger societal forces, but also those at play within the Catholic community itself. Furthermore, disagreement over fundamental aspects of Catholic identity became increasingly pronounced over time. "The Catholic Church is on a fateful journey and the gathering momentum is astonishing," wrote journalist John Cornwell. "Reminiscent of a river dividing at an estuary, the fragmentations, in a process of action and interaction, are reshaping the landscape of Catholicism." Cornwell attributed this development, in part, "to a profound cultural change and the collapse of traditions, the rapid adoption of ideas under the influence of mass media, the mobility of people and money, the disappearance of 'jobs for life,' and the alteration and erosion of values and principles."[31] Cornwell, a Briton, has been one of scores of international observers to comment on the apparent "identity crisis" facing Catholics worldwide. Others have focused specifically on the American scene. Writing in 2003, former *New York Times* correspondent and *Commonweal* editor Peter Steinfels observed that many younger Catholics "are distanced from parish life and church institutions, have little sense of church authority, and are not sufficiently versed in the distinctive symbols, narratives, and vocabulary of Catholicism to articulate to themselves a coherent Catholic identity."[32] More recently, in 2008, Kerry Kennedy, daughter of the late Senator Robert F. Kennedy, noted that the institutional church in America appears unable to inspire confidence among a large percentage of Catholics. "Religion today is at a time of enormous change," Kennedy wrote. "When addressing such issues as immigration, the mishandling of the pedophile crisis, the notion of a just war in the post-9/11 world, the suppression of women, the intolerance of homosexuality, birth control, abortion, euthanasia, stem cell research, along with a host of other issues . . . Catholics express anguish, disappointment, frustration, anger, and despair."[33] Frustration with Catholic leadership was exacerbated during the lead-up to the 2008 presidential election, when influential Catholics—including a number of bishops—criticized co-religionists who supported then presidential candidate Barack Obama. In May 2008, Kansas City Archbishop Joseph Naumann urgently recommended that Kansas Governor Kathleen Sebelius, a close advisor to candidate Obama, decline the sacrament of Communion—a statement that created a firestorm within the U.S. Catholic community.[34]

Any discussion of the fragmentation of U.S. Catholic identity, however, should include a brief overview of characteristics associated with the traditional model—one that held sway for nearly two decades after World War II, only to disintegrate in the mid-1960s. The following characteristics were among the more salient features of traditional U.S. Catholic identity: well-defined cultural markers, commonly shared values, clearly defined collective goals, common neighborhoods, common political affiliation, high levels of within-group altruism, united opposition to outside criticism, reluctance to engage with other religious organizations, and hierarchal notions of authority. This book does not argue for the resurrection of these characteristics of traditional Catholic identity, a project that is neither possible nor entirely desirable. Rather, it contends that a widely embraced model of U.S. Catholic identity became increasingly untenable. Furthermore, this book argues that the void created by the retreat of the previous model has not yet been filled by a model of identity capable of inspiring general acceptance among U.S. Catholics. Consequently, U.S. Catholic identity has become a matter of passionate debate within an increasingly pluralistic community.

The collapse of a more traditional model of American Catholicism was one of many developments that adversely affected Youngstown's pattern of urban parish schools. Therefore, this examination of declining urban parochial schools shows how controversies within the U.S. Catholic community synthesized with post–World War II trends that contributed to the erosion of a wide variety of urban institutions. It takes into account some of the major social, political, and economic trends of the postwar era, and their impact on Youngstown's urban parochial schools. These trends contributed to—and in some cases, were driven by—a steep decline in traditional Catholic identity. Although this study is limited to 18 urban parochial elementary schools that operated in Youngstown, the developments identified in this research are representative of those found in urban centers around the country. Such trends include demographic change, deindustrialization, and urban depopulation. If the trends examined in this book affected both urban parochial and public elementary schools, their impact on Catholic schools was compounded by deepening fissures within the Catholic community. Hence, this study describes how these trends adversely affected Youngstown's urban parish schools, while analyzing the ways in which they facilitated—and in some cases, reflected—the fragmentation of Catholic identity. Historical analysis of these urban trends, and their impact on Youngstown's parish schools, draws upon sources including census data, public records, diocesan and parish records, interviews, and secondary source material. Overall, this study has been designed to highlight the manner in which urban change and internal reform within the Catholic Church coincided to weaken a separatist model of U.S. Catholicism—a model that had inspired a "bold, expensive, and extremely successful strategy of creating a virtually self-contained urban Catholic social structure."[35]

To appreciate the severity of what happened to Youngstown's parochial school system, one must examine its earlier history of rapid expansion. Therefore, the second chapter, "Rise of a Parochial School System," offers a concise historical overview of the city's parochial schools. The chapter examines factors that led to the development of a robust pattern of Catholic parochial schools, including the prevalence of ethnic and religious tension within the city during the first half of the twentieth century. Among others, it shows how religious identity was often deeply entwined with ethnic identity among Youngstown's Catholics. This interdependence fueled the rise of so-called "national parishes" and contributed to the establishment of parochial schools that served the needs of specific ethnic groups. Although ethnic divisions within Youngstown's Catholic community could easily have prevented the rise of a system of shared values and goals, members of national parishes nevertheless participated in a broader "Catholic" culture. This culture was characterized by, among others, "public and unique religious practices" and adherence to Vatican teachings.[36] The Catholic community's remarkable capacity to act collectively (in spite of ethnic divisions) was reflected in its establishment of a powerful voting bloc and its development of parallel urban institutions, including parish schools. Unsurprisingly, these collective achievements reinforced the tendency of critical observers to view the U.S. Catholic community in monolithic terms. As late as the 1940s and early 1950s, warnings that Catholicism posed a threat to democratic institutions emanated from the U.S. liberal establishment. Naturally, such instances of anti-Catholic fervor reinforced the widely held perception that U.S. Catholics were "outsiders in the land of their birth."[37] As the chapter shows, the seemingly contradictory forces at play within Youngstown's Catholic community—along with external factors such as anti-Catholic sentiment—bolstered a broad commitment to urban parochial schools among local Catholics.

The third chapter, "'The Immaculate': One School's Experience," tracks the progress of Immaculate Conception Elementary School, from its inception in the late nineteenth century to its closure in 2006. Readers will follow the parish school's development as it moves from a vibrant, though insulated, Irish American institution to a "mission school" dependent on fund-raising initiatives to provide educational services to mainly nonwhite and non-Catholic students. A local newspaper reported that, by the early 1990s, the majority of Immaculate Conception's students were non-Catholic and from low-income families.[38] Significantly, as the chapter shows, the transformation of Immaculate Conception was made possible, in large part, by postconciliar reevaluations of Catholic education, which emphasized social justice initiatives that looked beyond the traditional borders of the Catholic community. Given its long history, and the variety of urban trends that affected the school, Immaculate Conception serves as an ideal choice for a case study intended to shed light on the rise and fall of the community's pattern of parochial schools. Taken together, "Rise of a Parochial School System" and "'The Immaculate': One School's Experience" highlight the unique circumstances in which Youngstown's parish schools developed and, eventually, declined.

The fourth chapter, "Urban Exodus: Depopulation and Urban Parish Schools," examines the impact of Youngstown's steep population losses upon the city's parish schools. Some observers have contended that, in other northeastern urban centers, the effects of depopulation were postponed by circumstances arising from the organizational structure of the U.S. Catholic diocese. Catholic historian John T. McGreevy, for instance, has argued that the geographical nature of the Catholic parish was responsible for the relatively small percentage of white Catholic urban dwellers who abandoned American cities in the postwar era. "Crucially, the parish was immovable," McGreevy wrote. "Where Jewish synagogues and Protestant churches could sell their buildings both to recover their equity and to relocate away from the expanding African-American ghetto, Catholic parishes and their property were registered in the name of the diocese and by definition served the people living within the parish boundaries." He noted that even national parishes "tended to have geographical boundaries" and operated "on the assumption that the vast majority of church members would live in the immediate area."[39] McGreevy claimed that the continuing presence of churches, parish schools, and other Catholic institutions in the center city encouraged urban Catholics to view their neighborhoods as sacred territory that required their participation and support.[40] In time, however, more and more Catholics found their way to the suburbs, leaving behind financially strapped urban parishes and parochial schools, many of which were eventually forced to close.

Given that urban depopulation in Youngstown was exacerbated by deindustrialization, the fourth chapter goes on to describe the ways in which the collapse of the urban industrial sector affected the city's parish schools. Youngstown, along with much of the industrial northeastern United States, witnessed a devastating economic downturn in the late 1970s and early 1980s. Some observers have contended that the community's overwhelming dependence on steel manufacturing practically ensured that Youngstown would be more severely affected by the "Rust Belt" phenomenon than most other industrial communities in northeastern Ohio. Indeed, the 1977 closure of the main plant of the community's dominant steel producer, Youngstown Sheet

& Tube Company, ruined the livelihoods of thousands of urban dwellers. At the same time, subsequent (and catastrophic) increases in unemployment compounded preexisting trends toward suburbanization and demographic change. In combination, these forces contributed to what many observers have described as the growing isolation of urban neighborhoods.

Urban economic decline had far-reaching consequences for urban parish schools. Overall, the city's Catholic institutions were hit especially hard, as depopulation and deindustrialization fueled the concurrent trend of shrinking enrollment and contributed to a steep decline in parish donations. Meanwhile, the loss of thousands of industry-related jobs depleted Youngstown's beleaguered white, ethnic, working-class neighborhoods—the ground upon which urban parish schools once flourished. McGreevy, among others, has argued that heavily Catholic urban neighborhoods once reinforced traditional religious and ethnic allegiances among urban dwellers. Whether conceived of as "sacred space" or as a re-creation of the European village in an American urban setting, the urban Catholic enclave is widely understood as a preserve of traditional social and religious values; and these neighborhoods were generally characterized by "an institutional structure of enormous magnitude." As McGreevy observed, most parishes in northern urban centers "included a church (often of remarkable scale), a parochial school, a convent, a rectory, and occasionally, ancillary gymnasiums or auditoriums."[41] Hence, the erosion of urban Catholic enclaves deprived U.S. Catholics of their traditional milieu, a development that helped weaken a longstanding model of U.S. Catholic identity.

The fifth chapter, "Demographic Change and Urban Parish Schools," examines the material and ideological consequences of demographic change as it pertained to urban parochial elementary schools. Many observers of Catholic education have argued that the sharp decline in the urban white population—and subsequent rise in the nonwhite population—that began in the wake of World War II affected urban Catholic elementary schools on a variety of levels. The fact that few African Americans were Roman Catholic sharply reduced the chances that blacks would play a dominant role in the financial maintenance of urban Catholic parishes. In addition, as more students from minority groups became clients of urban parish schools in cities throughout the United States, Catholic educators faced "the conflicting pressures of keeping tuition-paying enrollment up and remaining accessible to families from a broad range of social and economic backgrounds."[42] In Youngstown, relatively few African Americans were enrolled at urban parochial schools until the 1980s, and many black students eventually shifted to charter schools and Protestant denominational schools following a rise of urban educational alternatives. Hence, sweeping demographic change ensured that the majority of Youngstown's parish schools would lose their traditional (largely white) patrons, a development that contributed to their growing insolvency.

Significantly, a number of urban parish schools responded to demographic change by broadening their mission and reaching out (in unprecedented ways) to nonwhite and non-Catholic students. In Youngstown, two urban parish schools—Immaculate Conception and St. Patrick's—became associated with this trend. Members of the Catholic community, of course, differed in their responses to demographic change. In 1976, the diocesan school board, despite the vocal support of clerical leaders, narrowly defeated a proposal to implement a diocesan-wide tax that would benefit struggling center-city schools like Immaculate Conception, an institution that enrolled a large percentage of nonwhite and non-Catholic students.[43] Unsurprisingly, the hierarchy and laity were frequently at odds in their responses to this phenomenon. In communities throughout the country, episcopal leaders supported the church's continued institutional presence in the center city and voiced a commitment to the education of urban students, regardless of race or religion.[44] With the advent of school desegregation, the Diocese of Youngstown cautioned white urban residents against treating Catholic schools as "havens" from racially integrated public schools.[45] In other settings, similar public positions by church leaders—along with diocesan support for parish schools that served mainly nonwhite, non-Catholic students—inflamed some white members of the laity, who accused the hierarchy of being insensitive to their concerns. Ultimately, the local Catholic community failed to develop a unified response to urban demographic change.

The debate over support for urban parochial schools that no longer served traditional constituents became more complicated in the 1980s, when a series of high-profile empirical studies suggested that Catholic schools, especially those in urban settings, were more effective than public schools at boosting levels of academic achievement among students of minority and low-income backgrounds. Subsequent research suggested that urban Catholic schools fostered a sense of community that was conducive to lower dropout rates and the effective promotion of civic values. Taken as a whole, these conclusions raised questions about the public school system's capacity to achieve one of its fundamental goals: the establishment of a common civic space for students of diverse backgrounds. Many Catholic educators, however, have criticized the use of such findings to serve a conservative political agenda. Catholic educators James Youniss and John J. Convey, for instance, accused educational researchers of complicity "in allowing Catholic schools to be used for ulterior purposes," that is, the promotion of a "school choice" agenda.[46] Moreover, they contended, a "narrow focus on the Catholic versus public school achievement question directs attention away from more fundamental issues about the survival and future structure of Catholic schools."[47] Ironically, growing support for urban educational alternatives—a partial by-product of contested research that praised the effectiveness of urban Catholic schools—produced crippling challenges for urban parish schools that were already economically troubled.[48] In Youngstown, at least one urban pastor publicly drew a connection between the closing of a parish school in the late 1990s and the establishment of a charter school in the same neighborhood.[49]

The sixth chapter, "Out of These Ashes: Vatican II and Catholic Identity," explores the debate over the values and educational mission of parish schools, which arose among participants in Catholic education starting in the 1960s. American Catholics, as noted, were scarcely immune to changes that trans-formed—and polarized—mainstream U.S. society during the same period. Moreover, Catholics no longer had the luxury of retreating into a comfort-able sanctuary of traditional values and practices, given that the Catholic Church was in a state of flux. Although numerous factors contributed to the unraveling of what could be described as an "American Catholic consensus," this development was crystallized by the reforms of Vatican II. Anthony S. Bryk and his coauthors wrote that the Second Vatican Council "has been aptly described as a paradigm shift from medievalism to postmodernity in the images of the Church and its relationship with the world."[50] Indeed, the scope of issues addressed at the council was nothing less than breathtaking. As John W. O'Malley observed, the council dealt with the use of the organ in church services; the place of Thomas Aquinas in the curriculum of seminar-ies; the legitimacy of stocking nuclear weapons; the blessing of water used for baptisms; the role of the laity in the church's ministries; the relationship of bishops to the pope; the purposes of marriage; priests' salaries; the role of conscience in moral decision making; the proper clothing (or habit) for nuns; the church's relationship to the arts; marriage among deacons; translations of the Bible; the boundaries of dioceses; the legitimacy (or illegitimacy) of wor-shipping with non-Catholics; and so, almost, it might seem, into infinity."[51]

The most relevant of the conciliar documents for U.S. parochial educa-tion was *The Declaration on Christian Education*. While this document was largely a restatement of the church's traditional commitment to religious edu-cation, it nevertheless adopted "a position that is more open to the world at large."[52] The U.S. National Council of Catholic Bishops (NCCB), in response to the council's recommendations on education, issued a directive of its own. In 1972, the NCCB's statement, *To Teach as Jesus Did*, "fleshed out the council's theme of active, publicly engaged schools." Bryk and his coauthors have provided a useful overview of this directive, noting that it "articulated a threefold educational ministry: to teach the message of hope contained in the gospel; to build community 'not simply as a concept to be taught, but as a reality to be lived'; and 'service to all mankind which flows from a sense of Christian community.'" They concluded, "Schools, then, were reconceived as instruments of social justice that would embody this commitment in every detail of their educational philosophy."[53]

The "social justice" agenda advanced by Catholic educators in the post-conciliar era was not universally embraced, however. Morris noted that the liberal revamping of the mission and "catechetics" of U.S. parochial schools alienated many conservative Catholics, who constituted a substantial minority of parochial school subscribers. Traditionalists were no less concerned about the departure of teaching nuns from the classroom: a development that they feared would undermine the religious atmosphere of parish schools. Some observers have contended that liberalizing influences within religious orders inspired thousands of nuns to abandon teaching in favor of more fulfilling types of community service. As former *New York Times* religion editor Kenneth Briggs observed, many American nuns felt that the status of women religious had declined because of the council's emphasis on the role of the laity in the church.[54] Scores of these women chose to leave their religious orders to pursue marriage, a career, or both. This development not only dramatically altered the atmosphere of parochial elementary schools; it also exacerbated a preexisting pattern of rising costs. Lay teachers, who often supported families, were more inclined than members of teaching orders to demand higher salaries. In time, lay instructors began to demand a livable wage, and "the Church was suddenly the target of its own social justice rhetoric."[55]

The seventh (and final) chapter, "A House Divided: Conclusions," offers an overview of the controversies that swept the U.S. Catholic community in the decades following Vatican II. At the same time, the chapter describes the ways in which Catholic disunity weakened support for traditional institutions, especially schools. Furthermore, the chapter draws a strong link between the Catholic laity's disagreement with the church's official positions on controversial issues (e.g., birth control, legalized abortion, women's rights), and their conspicuously reduced levels of church-related giving. The chapter not only examines the fallout from the Second Vatican Council, but also the effects of the conservative retrenchment within the Catholic hierarchy, which became evident by the late 1970s. Finally, it outlines areas of future exploration for educational researchers. For instance, the U.S. church's understated approach to evangelizing within the black community during the post–Vatican II era, while it reflected a more ecumenical outlook,[56] may also have ensured that urban Catholic institutions remained a "foreign presence" in heavily African American neighborhoods.[57] The chapter also includes a brief description of steps that diocesan leaders have taken to preserve parochial elementary schools still operating within the six-county Diocese of Youngstown.

The seventh chapter is followed by an epilogue, "Last Mass," which provides an overview of recent developments within the Diocese of Youngstown, including the momentous closing of Immaculate Conception parish, which merged with its neighbor, Sacred Heart of Jesus parish, in January 2011. The ongoing consolidation (or reconfiguration) of diocesan parishes reflects the influence of trends that had earlier contributed to the decline of the city's system of parochial elementary schools, and at this writing, the depopulation of urban neighborhoods continues to bear down on the city's Catholic institutions. That said, it is worth noting that hopeful signs have emerged in the area of leadership. Interviews with diocesan leaders, including Youngstown Bishop George V. Murry, SJ, indicate the diocese is engaged in long-term planning that is designed to safeguard its remaining presence in urban neighborhoods—a move away from the seemingly piecemeal policies of the past, which postponed (rather than prevented) the collapse of Youngstown's pattern of parochial elementary schools.

Overall, this historical overview of Youngstown's Catholic elementary schools examines how fissures within the Catholic community contributed to the decline of urban parochial schools. Earlier explorations of this topic have argued persuasively that the social impact of Vatican II, along with certain Catholic responses to the controversies of the 1960s, set the stage for a model of Catholic schooling that was inclusive and civic-minded. This study shows, however, that the controversies that swept the Catholic community in the 1960s—including disagreement over the legacy of Vatican II—also had negative consequences for urban parochial schools. While the Second Vatican Council was, in many ways, a liberating influence that enabled U.S. Catholics to broaden their concept of "social justice," it left in its wake a deeply polarized community. In the decades following the 1960s, U.S. Catholics lost much of their cohesiveness as a community: a cohesiveness that once enabled them to establish and maintain a wide network of parallel institutions.[58] This period of fragmentation contributed to (and was shaped by) a host of internal trends that injured urban parochial schools. Such trends included a sharp decline in religious vocations, falling parish donations, and weakened support for the enterprise of Catholic parochial schools.

At the same time, this study takes into account the impact of larger urban trends on Catholic parochial schools. Naturally, changes in the urban landscape created myriad challenges for a variety of urban institutions, including public schools. Although the impact of these larger urban trends on parochial schools has been thoughtfully examined in previous studies, much of this research has downplayed the role that Catholic disunity played in the decline of urban parochial schools. A number of studies have examined the interrelationship between urban change and the collapse of traditional American

Catholic identity. These studies, however, tend to take a broader view of U.S. Catholic culture and institutional life, and they do not focus exclusively on urban parish schools. This book argues that the Catholic community's apparent inability to forge common goals that were rooted in broader societal commitments posed a serious threat to the church's longstanding institutional presence in urban centers. This trend was evident in Youngstown, where urban parochial schools have all but disappeared and urban parishes wage a daily struggle for survival. If this trend is allowed to progress to its natural conclusion, the U.S. Catholic Church may squander a valuable opportunity for engagement with urban minority groups—including African Americans, whose relations with the institution have often been informed by distrust. It seems especially ironic that the exodus of parochial schools from central cities coincides with the emergence of the (largely urban) Latino community as a locus of growth and vitality within the U.S. Catholic Church. This widening pattern of institutional retreat, as indicated above, owes much to the impact of larger urban trends. This book shows, however, that a fuller understanding of the phenomenon of declining urban parish schools can be obtained by examining the ways in which urban change intersected with rising levels of disharmony within the American Catholic community.

NOTES

1. James A. McFadden, *The March of the Eucharist from Dungannon* (Youngstown, OH: Diocese of Youngstown, 1951), 22.

2. Elaine Polomsky Soos, "Catholic Schools Prepare Students for Real World," *The Catholic Exponent,* 11, May 18, 1993, supplement marking the fiftieth anniversary of the Diocese of Youngstown.

3. "Catholic Schools to Have Third of City's Students,"*The Youngstown Vindicator,* 7, July 14, 1961.

4. Timothy Walch, *Parish School: American Catholic Parochial Education from Colonial Times to the Present* (Washington, DC: The National Catholic Educational Association, 2003), 169.

5. Harold Gwin, "Final Bell Tolls for Two Schools: There Were Some Long Faces As Children Left St. Matthias on Tuesday," *The Vindicator,* B-1, June 7, 2006.

6. Linda M. Linonis, "Bishop Murry Seeks Orderly Downsizing of the Diocese," *The Vindicator,* A-1, February 6, 2009.

7. Ian Fisher, "Some Muslim Leaders Want Pope to Apologize for Remarks," *The New York Times,* A-6, September 16, 2006.

8. The Associated Press, "Pope Angers Protestants with Reassertion of Primacy of Church," *The Vindicator,* A-4, July 11, 2007.

9. "The Pope's Words," *The New York Times,* September 16, 2006, A-14, editorial.

10. David Gibson, *The Rule of Benedict: Pope Benedict XVI and His Battle with the Modern World* (New York, NY: HarperSanFrancisco, 2006), 357–58.

11. David France, *Our Fathers: The Secret Life of the Catholic Church in an Age of Scandal* (New York, NY: Broadway Books, 2004), 258–60.

12. Philip Jenkins, *The New Anti-Catholicism: The Last Acceptable Prejudice* (Oxford, UK: Oxford University Press, 2003), 143.

13. Jay P. Dolan, *In Search of an American Catholicism: A History of Religion and Culture in Tension* (New York, NY: Oxford University Press, 2002), 257.

14. Garry Wills, *Why I Am a Catholic* (Boston, MA: Houghton Mifflin Company, 2002), 11–12.

15. Garry Wills, *Bare Ruined Choirs: Doubt, Prophecy, and Radical Religion* (Garden City, NY: Doubleday, 1972), 37.

16. James Flanigan, "The Priests, the Nuns and the People: Changes in the Church and Religious Life Are Reflected in the Bronx Neighborhood of 'Doubt,'" *National Catholic Reporter,* 14a, February 20, 2009.

17. Charles R. Morris, *American Catholic: The Saints and Sinners Who Built America's Most Powerful Church* (New York, NY: Vintage, 1997), ix.

18. Margaret O'Brien Steinfels, "Are Catholics Active Enough in Church?" in *American Catholic Identity: Essays in an Age of Change,* ed. Francis J. Butler (Kansas City, MO: Sheed & Ward, 1994), 37.

19. Morris, *American Catholic,* 324.

20. Philip Gleason, *Keeping the Faith: American Catholicism, Past and Present* (Notre Dame, IN: University of Notre Dame Press, 1987), 13–14.

21. Wills, *Bare Ruined Choirs,* 9.

22. Ibid., 32–33.

23. Ibid., 261.

24. Ibid., 16.

25. Chester Gillis, *Roman Catholicism in America* (New York, NY: Columbia University Press, 1999), 278–79.

26. Garry Wills, *Head and Heart: American Christianities* (New York, NY: The Penguin Press, 2007), 474.

27. Gleason, *Keeping the Faith,* 32.

28. Walch, *Parish School,* 231–32.

29. Anthony S. Bryk, Valerie E. Lee, and Peter B. Holland, *Catholic Schools and the Common Good* (Cambridge, MA: Harvard University Press, 1993), 51–52.

30. Mark S. Massa, *Catholics and American Culture: Fulton Sheen, Dorothy Day, and the Notre Dame Football Team* (New York, NY: W. W. Norton & Company, 1999), 7–8.

31. John Cornwell, *Breaking Faith: Can the Catholic Church Save Itself?* (New York, NY: Viking Press, 2001), 24–25.

32. Peter Steinfels, *A People Adrift: The Crisis of the Roman Catholic Church in America* (New York, NY: Simon & Schuster, 2003), 209.

33. Kerry Kennedy, *Being Catholic Now: Prominent Americans Talk About Change in the Church and the Quest for Meaning* (New York, NY: Crown Publishers, 2008), xvi–xvii.

34. Mary Barron, "The Return of the Communion Wars: Prominent Catholic Democrat Targeted for Obama Support," *National Catholic Reporter,* 10, May 30, 2008, findarticles.com/p/articles/mi_m1141/is_20_44/ai_n25495213/ (accessed June 7, 2010).

35. Morris, *American Catholic,* 257.

36. Gillis, *Roman Catholicism in America,* 2.

37. Dolan, *In Search of an American Catholicism,* 132–33.

38. Ron Cole, "Immaculate Redemption: Urban School Rebounds," *The Vindicator,* A-1, October 2, 1994.

39. John T. McGreevy, *Parish Boundaries: The Catholic Encounter with Race in the Twentieth Century Urban North* (Chicago, IL: University of Chicago Press, 1996), 19.

40. Ibid., 24–25.

41. McGreevy, *Parish Boundaries,* 14–15.

42. Bryk et al., *Catholic Schools and the Common Good,* 337.

43. Marie Aikenhead, "Board Refuses School Funding: Votes Against Diocese Inner City Aid," *The Youngstown Vindicator,* 1, November 17, 1976.

44. Bryk et al., *Catholic Schools and the Common Good,* 52.

45. "Diocese OKs New Enrollment Rules," *The Youngstown Vindicator,* 10, May 22, 1974.

46. James Youniss and John T. Convey, eds., *Catholic Schools at the Crossroads: Survival and Transformation* (New York, NY: Teachers College Press, 2000), 2–3.

47. Ibid., 2.

48. Scott Cech, "Catholic Closures Linked to Growth of City Charters," *Education Week,* February 13, 2008, 1–2.

49. Ron Cole, "Finances Close St. Dominic School," *The Vindicator,* B-1, April 10, 1999.

50. Bryk et al., *Catholic Schools and the Common Good*, 46.

51. John W. O'Malley, *What Happened at Vatican II* (Cambridge, MA: The Belknap Press of Harvard University Press, 2007), 5.

52. Glen Gabert, Jr., *In Hoc Signo? A Brief History of Catholic Parochial Education in America* (Port Washington, NY: Kennikat Press, 1972), 108.

53. Bryk et al., *Catholic Schools and the Common Good,* 51–52.

54. Kenneth Briggs, *Double Crossed: Uncovering the Catholic Church's Betrayal of American Nuns* (New York, NY: Doubleday, 2006), 9.

55. Bryk et al., *Catholic Schools and the Common Good,* 34.

56. John T. McGreevy, "Racial Justice and the People of God: The Second Vatican Council, the Civil Rights Movement, and American Catholics," *Religion and American Culture* 4, No. 2 (Summer 1994): 221–24.

57. Leon Stennis, "Leadership's View on Diocese's Approach Toward Blacks Differ," *The Youngstown Vindicator,* 7, September 6, 1975.

58. Morris, *American Catholic,* 257.

Chapter 2

Rise of a Parochial School System

On October 30, 1923, 1,500 women gathered in Youngstown's Epworth Methodist Episcopal Church to listen as Dorothy Nickols, a former Roman Catholic, described abuses she allegedly suffered at the hands of nuns at Chicago's House of the Good Shepherd. Nickols's characterization of American Catholicism as a cruel, authoritarian, and anachronistic institution prompted bursts of enthusiastic applause from attendees, who apparently needed little convincing on this point. As historian William D. Jenkins observed, the young speaker's narrative was "a variant of the escaped-nun tales that arose during previous anti-Catholic crusades." Jenkins added, "Rumors also abounded: classic tales of Catholic fathers who purchased a gun to be placed in St. Columba's basement whenever a child was born and of Catholic efforts to build a palace in Washington for the pope."[1] The women who packed the church that autumn day were members of the Kamelias, a women's auxiliary of the Ku Klux Klan, which flourished on a local wave of anti-immigrant sentiment. As the large number of attendees at the event suggests, the Klan, along with its auxiliary organizations, was hardly a fringe movement in 1920s Youngstown. The organization enjoyed the public support of respected Protestant leaders, and a pro-Klan candidate would soon emerge as the victor in a hotly contested mayoral race.[2] To understand the organization's (relative) respectability, it is important to grasp that the northern Klan, unlike its violently racist southern counterpart, directed its tactics of intimidation at new immigrants, especially Catholics.[3] In Youngstown, the Klan, in its haste to define a common enemy, blamed local Catholics for a sharp increase in the area's crime rate. In addition, the nativist organization criticized the potential insulating effects of Catholic schools and called for legislation that would render attendance at public schools mandatory.[4]

The growth of nativist organizations in the Youngstown area coincided with a demographic shift that occurred in the community between 1900 and 1920. As Jenkins noted, the city's population was predominantly Welsh and German at the outset of the twentieth century. Both of these groups began to arrive in the Mahoning Valley in the mid-nineteenth century, and by 1900, they "had outstripped the older Scotch Irish and English settlers." The arrival of significant numbers of Irish immigrants during the same period apparently fueled the rise of local Catholic institutions. As Jenkins observed, "the area remained a missionary outpost of the Catholic church until after the Irish migrations of the 1840s and 1850s." This influx of Irish Catholics inspired the development of some anti-Catholic organizations, including a local chapter of the American Protective Association. These earlier nativist movements, however, failed to attract the level of local support that the Klan enjoyed decades later. The rise of the Klan came in the aftermath of a more dramatic change in the area's ethnic and religious composition, which occurred toward the end of the nineteenth century. Jenkins noted that, between 1880 and 1900, "the arrival of immigrants from southern and eastern Europe dramatically altered the composition of Youngstown's population and of the entire valley." Most of these new arrivals were drawn by the community's expanding steel industry. In 1920, two of Youngstown's largest steel manufacturers, Republic and Sheet and Tube, "hired between 23,000 and 24,000 workers." That same year, according to census reports, "two-thirds of the population was foreign-born or the children of foreign-born."[5]

While circumstances in the Youngstown area were exceptionally conducive to the rise of ethnic and religious tension, the local Klan's opposition to Catholic influence, in general, and Catholic parochial schools, in particular, was consistent with trends that swept the country in the wake of World War I. In 1922, for example, the state of Oregon passed legislation that made attendance at public elementary and secondary schools compulsory. As Joseph Moreau observed, the Oregon law originated with a referendum sponsored by "a coalition of organizations that included the Ku Klux Klan."[6] In 1925, this legislation was overturned by the Supreme Court, in *Pierce v. Society of Sisters,* which determined that "the Oregon law was in violation of the Fourteenth Amendment, for its effect would be to destroy all private and religious schools and thus deprive the owners of their property 'without due process of the law.'"[7] While the Court's ruling dashed "hopes among militant anti-Catholics that the struggle to close parochial schools could succeed anywhere in the United States," the intolerant attitudes that inspired such legislation remained prevalent.[8]

Youngstown-area nativists, like those elsewhere in the country, viewed parochial schools as insidious obstacles to the "Americanization" of immigrants.[9] Therefore, they were alarmed at the Catholic community's achievements in the realm of institution building. Anxious Protestant leaders pointed out that, in the course of a few decades, a handful of rustic churches and schools had blossomed into an intricate network of agencies, providing Catholics with replicated services ranging from health care to education. This pattern of institution building reached its climax in the late nineteenth and early twentieth centuries, but the roots of Catholicism in Youngstown can be traced back to the days of the Connecticut Western Reserve, a 120-mile stretch of land in modern-day northeastern Ohio that the state of Connecticut claimed as its share of the Northwest Territory.[10] For much of the nineteenth century, Catholics represented a small fraction of the population in the region, which was dominated by transplanted New Englanders and Scotch-Irish migrants from neighboring Pennsylvania. As the number of primarily Catholic immigrants increased, so did native resistance to their influence—and to their parallel institutions.[11]

ORIGINS OF A CATHOLIC COMMUNITY

Most historical accounts of the rise of Catholic institutions in Youngstown refer to pioneer Daniel Sheehy, an Irish Catholic immigrant who accompanied the community's founder, John Young, on a 1796 surveying expedition of the surrounding Mahoning Valley.[12] While Sheehy was supposedly devoted to his religion, he had few opportunities to participate in religious services during the early years of the "Young's Town" settlement. Few priests were active in America at the time, and large stretches of the Connecticut Western Reserve were bereft of the handful of missionary priests who helped sustain Catholic religious practices in other remote regions of the country. Reliable pastoral ministry was evidently unavailable to Catholics in the Youngstown area until 1817, when Father Edward Fenwick, a Dominican priest, encountered the German-Irish settlement of Dungannon, which was located in neighboring Columbiana County.[13] It was not until 1831 that a log chapel was built in the community. Father Fenwick and other missionary priests reportedly paid subsequent visits to Dungannon to administer the sacraments, celebrate mass, and provide limited religious instruction.[14]

The first mass to be celebrated in what later became the Diocese of Youngstown was held in the home of Daniel Sheehy's daughter and son-in-law, a Mr. and Mrs. McAllister.[15] Sparse historical accounts have suggested that the small number of Catholic families then living in Youngstown faithfully made the journey to Dungannon on those occasions when a priest was available to say mass. Decades later, observers of the city's thriving Catholic

community contrasted the "prosperity" of the present with the "scarcities" of
the past. As a late nineteenth-century historical text stated: "The mustard seed
of religion, planted by the Dominican Father, Rev. E. Fenwick, near Dungannon in 1817, has grown to a large and vigorous tree under whose shadow rest
two hundred and twenty-five churches and many institutions, spreading their
benign influence on behalf of religion, education and charity."[16] In 1821,
Father Fenwick, the scion of a distinguished Anglo-American family from
Maryland, was appointed as the first bishop of the new Diocese of Cincinnati, which included much of northeastern Ohio. In the years preceding his
appointment, Fenwick founded three parishes that were later incorporated into
the Diocese of Youngstown. These included St. Paul and St. Philip Neri, in
Dungannon, and St. John, in Canton.[17] It was not until 1826, however, that a
mass was celebrated within the present-day boundaries of Youngstown itself.
The service took place at the home of another Sheehy in-law, one William
Woods. Nine years later, Dungannon assumed the status of a permanent parish, with Father James Conlon as pastor. Although, at this point, Youngstown
still lacked a parish of its own, Father Conlon reportedly served the religious
outpost as a missionary priest who visited several times a month.[18]

    In 1847, the nucleus of Youngstown's first parish was formed during
a meeting at the home of William Woods. Plans to establish the parish
developed under the guidance of an unnamed missionary priest. Ten years
later, a permanent parish was organized on Youngstown's north side, with
Father William O'Connor as pastor.[19] According to some accounts, land for
the project was donated by local industrialist David Tod, who later served
as governor of Ohio in the first years of the Civil War.[20] Even before the
parish's official establishment, however, a simple frame chapel was raised
and placed under the patronage of St. Columba, a medieval Irish monk who
was revered for his missionary work in western Scotland. One newspaper
account observed that the chapel that became St. Columba's Church was
built of "rough boards" by the parish's charter members. As the article stated:
"Parishioners felled the trees, hewed the logs, and using oxen and chain,
logs were dragged to the church site."[21] This frame church, completed about
1853, was replaced in 1868 by a brick structure in the Gothic style.[22] The
construction of a massive granite church building, which began in 1893, was
delayed until 1900 because of a severe economic turndown. This impressive
neo-Gothic structure was finally dedicated in 1903.[23] Four decades later, with
the establishment of the Diocese of Youngstown, it was designated as the
city's cathedral parish.

    As Youngstown expanded, other Catholic parishes grew up around the
city. Naturally, many of these churches were connected to the community's
premier parish, St. Columba's Church. As an article in *The Youngstown*

Telegram noted, "While all the 20 or more Catholic churches in Youngstown are virtually the outgrowth of the original St. Columba's parish, there are six parishes that have been organized directly from this parent Catholic church of the city." In 1869, St. Ann's Parish, "the eldest of the children of St. Columba's," was established (under the authorization of Cleveland Bishop Amadeus Rappe) for Catholics in the working-class Brier Hill district, an unincorporated village that was annexed by Youngstown in 1900. During this period, the growing diversity of the city's Catholic community introduced new challenges arising from cultural and linguistic differences. In response to an expanding German-speaking population, the national parish of St. Joseph was established on Youngstown's north side in 1870.[24] The church, which served mainly German immigrants, also attracted parishioners who had emigrated from Austria, Hungary, France, and Lithuania.[25] A commemorative history described the circumstances leading up to the parish's foundation. "In March of 1869, the Vicar General of the [Cleveland] diocese, Father Wester-holt, came to Youngstown to meet with the German Catholics," the document stated. "This memorable meeting took place in the basement of St. Columba's Church . . . where with great enthusiasm, they voted to separate from St. Columba's Parish and to organize a parish of their own."[26] Significantly, St. Joseph's congregation was not restricted to German speakers living within clearly defined parish boundaries, and during its many decades of operation, the church drew parishioners from around the Youngstown area. This characteristic later became a source of controversy. As national parishes developed in the community, they sometimes found themselves in conflict with church leaders who favored a universal model of territorial parishes (those with well-defined boundaries), while warning against the potentially insulating effects of those parishes designed to preserve Old World languages and traditions. These conflicts often pitted a heavily Irish American clergy against representatives of other ethnic groups within the Catholic community.

For the most part, however, the city's earliest Catholic parishes were territorial and English-speaking. The territorial parish of Immaculate Conception was established on the city's east side in 1882, and a neighboring parish known as Sacred Heart of Jesus appeared six years later. St. Patrick's Church was organized on the city's rapidly expanding south side in 1911,[27] and three more English-speaking (and quasi-suburban) parishes—St. Edward's (north side), St. Brendan's (west side), and St. Dominic's (south side)—appeared within the first quarter of the twentieth century. Yet, a growing number of national parishes also emerged in the late nineteenth and early twentieth centuries. In 1896, Slovak immigrants organized Sts. Cyril and Methodius Parish; and four years later, the congregation completed the brick structure that now overlooks the onetime working-class neighborhood of Smoky Hollow, on the city's north side.[28] Two more Slovak American parishes appeared in quick succession: St. Matthias (south side) and Holy Name (west side). Then, in 1898, St. Anthony's Parish was organized by Italian Americans living in the northwestern district of Brier Hill.[29] This community of Italian-speaking families had previously attended services at St. Ann's and St. Columba's churches.[30] Ten years later, St. Anthony's was joined by another Italian American national parish, Our Lady of Mt. Carmel, which was built less than a block to the east of Sts. Cyril and Methodius Parish.[31] During the same period, Croatian Americans built the brick complex of Sts. Peter and Paul Parish and School, which stood scarcely a mile from St. Anthony's Church.[32]

The early 1900s, a period of tremendous demographic change in the Mahoning Valley, saw a veritable explosion of national parishes. Among the earliest of these new ethnic parishes was St. Stanislaus's Church, which was established by Polish immigrants on the south side in 1902. The parish's approximately 80 families had earlier attended services in the basement of St. Columba's Church.[33] Five years later, in 1907, St. Casimir's, another Polish American parish, was organized in the vicinity of Brier Hill.[34] Interestingly, the Brier Hill district alone boasted three Catholic parishes—St. Anthony's, St. Casimir's, and St. Ann's. A fourth neighborhood church, St. Rocco's, represented a faction within St. Anthony's parish that broke off, formed a national parish, and became part of the Episcopal community in the 1920s.[35] In 1907, Youngstown's first Hungarian American parish, St. Stephen's, was established on the east side; and about 12 years later, the parish of Our Lady of Hungary was organized in a Hungarian enclave on the west side.[36] Churches of other national groups also appeared, including St. Maron's Syro-Maronite parish (1903), St. Mary's Romanian parish (1910), and St. Francis's parish for Lithuanian Catholics (1917). The city's sole African American parish, St. Augustine's Church, did not appear on the city's east side until 1944, one year after the establishment of the Diocese of Youngstown.[37]

EMERGENCE OF A PATTERN OF PAROCHIAL EDUCATION

Many of Youngstown's Catholic parishes, though not all, eventually established elementary schools that were maintained primarily through parishioner donations. Catholic parochial schools began to appear in the city after 1860. The earliest of these modest institutions was connected to the premier parish of St. Columba, and it was based in a small frame building staffed by two lay teachers. Four years later, a more developed school was established in the basement of St. Columba's Church, again with lay teachers in charge. By

1868, teaching nuns had taken charge of the elementary school; and with the arrival of Ursuline nuns from Cleveland, who founded a community in 1874, Catholic education at the elementary level became firmly established.[38] The Ursulines not only started a private school for girls and boys, but also trained their sisters to teach in other parochial schools that appeared in the city later on.[39] Among the most celebrated of these teaching nuns was a Scottish immigrant named Mother Columba Gettins, who admonished her students as follows: "Be minding your lessons today, I tell you, for tomorrow you will have to help make the living."[40] The Ursulines were soon joined by other religious communities, including the Sisters of the Holy Humility of Mary, the Sisters of St. Joseph, the Notre Dame nuns, the Franciscan Sisters of Charity, the Vincentian Sisters of Charity, and the Sisters of St. Dominic. The Ursuline Sisters, however, were the only order to establish a mother house (a convent led by a mother superior) in the Youngstown metropolitan area.[41]

Conditions in Youngstown's earliest schools tended toward the rustic. In 1919, Monsignor John T. O'Connell, a Youngstown native who went on to become vicar general of the Diocese of Toledo, described early Catholic education in his hometown as follows: "It is true that in the earlier days, educational facilities were lacking; systems of heating, ventilation and devices for school room hygienics [sic] were not dreamed of in our philosophy; the ologies [sic] had not yet found a place in the curriculum of studies; and there is a lingering impression in the minds of older pupils that some of the instructors were none too familiar with pedagogy; but it is disparaging no one to say that difficulties and interruptions that would have destroyed other institutions only stimulated priests and people to more generous efforts." These "generous efforts" were reflected in the steady growth of Catholic education throughout the Youngstown area. In 1874, the Ursuline Academy was established as a coeducational institution that offered classes for both girls (to the eighth grade) and boys (to the fourth grade). Around 1905, two rooms of the Ursulines' north side convent were set aside for a high school department for girls. This program continued to grow until the need for a larger building required the purchase of the former Chauncey Andrews estate, a vacant mansion located on the city's north side. The Andrews homestead was used for several years as a school and, upon completion of the current high school facility, became a novitiate for nuns.[42]

Local Catholic efforts in the realm of education, however, were most conspicuous at the elementary level. St. Ann's, which operated in the working-class district of Brier Hill, opened its doors in 1869. St. Joseph's parish school, which was designed to benefit the children of German-speaking immigrants, was established on the north side one year later. Finally, Immaculate Conception parish school opened on the east side in 1883.[43] Scores of others followed, and for some observers, the growth of the city's Catholic schools in ensuing decades was nothing less than spectacular. By 1871, a handful of Catholic pupils had swelled to 500; and less than 60 years later, the local media observed that 700 students were scheduled to graduate from local Catholic schools that year alone, a figure suggesting that students then numbered in the thousands. In 1937, *The Youngstown Vindicator* announced, "Nineteen parochial schools and one Catholic high school are making last-minute preparations for the opening of school here Tuesday, when nearly 7,200 children will resume their studies under 158 nuns, eight lay teachers and several priests."[44]

Another explosion of growth among Catholic institutions occurred in the two decades that led up to the establishment of the Diocese of Youngstown. In 1923, Youngstown's Catholic community benefited from a trend toward expansion and modernization that was overseen by Cleveland Archbishop Joseph Schrembs, a gifted administrator and fund-raiser. As historian Michael J. Hynes observed, Schrembs's gift for organizational design facilitated a period of impressive growth in the Cleveland Diocese, which then included Youngstown. Hynes noted that, "[o]f the 271 churches (in the Cleveland Diocese), and of the 180 elementary schools, fifty-eight per cent were built" during the nearly two-decade tenure of Archbishop Schrembs. He added: "In the area now comprised in the Diocese of Youngstown seventeen parishes were started, eleven of them territorial; in the older parishes thirty-three new churches, nineteen new schools, eight new church-school combinations were put up and six buildings were refitted for Catholic worship." Much of the building within Youngstown's city limits occurred in the rapidly expanding working- and middle-class neighborhoods that emerged on the west and south sides of the city. Hynes offered a detailed overview of church and school construction within the municipal limits:

In the city of Youngstown, at its western end, the parish of St. Brendan was organized by Father Andrew A. Crehan who completed a brick combination church and school in 1925 . . . The Dominican Fathers returned to northern Ohio when Father Charles A. Haverty was appointed to organize the parish of St. Dominic in the southern section of the city: he put up a frame church in 1923 and completed a brick combination church-school in 1929. The Magyar parish of Our Lady of Hungary, a division of St. Stephen's, was inaugurated by Father Stephen Nyiri who directed the building of a brick basement church in 1929 and of a frame schoolhouse and hall shortly afterwards . . . In the older parishes in the same city much progress was to be recognized. In the Slovak parish of the Holy Name of Jesus a modern twelve-room school and auditorium put up under the supervision of Father Stephen Kocis was dedicated in 1927. In the parish of the Sacred Heart of Jesus a modern stone schoolhouse was completed by Father John I. Moran in 1923. St. Casimir's brick combination church and school put up by Father Ignatius L. Dembowski was dedicated by Bishop Schrembs in 1927. The frame Church of St. Francis of Assisi was completed in 1925 under the direction of Father Dominic Alinskas. The fine brick Romanesque Church of St. Matthias was finished by Father Francis Kozelek in 1926; the old frame church was converted into classrooms. The imposing stone Church of St. Patrick, in the Spanish Gothic style, put up under the direction of Father William A. Kane, was dedicated by the Bishop in 1926; in the same year six class rooms and a gymnasium were added to the school. In the parish of Sts. Peter and Paul a modern two-story brick schoolhouse was completed by Father John A. Stipanovic in 1927. In the parish of St. Stanislaus Kostka a brick combination church and school put up by Father John M. Zeglen was dedicated by the Bishop in 1925.[45]

Before the end of World War II, Youngstown's vitality and growth made it a natural candidate as the seat of a newly created diocese. In 1943, St. Columba's Church was designated as a cathedral (a church that contains the seat of a bishop), and six counties in northeastern Ohio were placed under the jurisdiction of the bishop of Youngstown.[46] The optimism that accompanied the creation of the Diocese of Youngstown was generally reflected in the developments of the next two decades. As late as the mid-1960s, parochial elementary schools and diocesan high schools posted unexpectedly high enrollments.[47]

FACTORS IN A SCHOOL SYSTEM'S DECLINE

As the 1960s drew to their discordant close, however, diocesan schools entered a period of gradual decline—a pattern that was especially acute among Youngstown's parochial elementary schools. The extent of this system's deterioration seems all the more dramatic when one considers that its vigorous expansion in the early twentieth century inspired fearful jeremiads from some of the city's most respected Protestant leaders. As local parochial schools began to disappear, their image (ironically enough) began to improve, a trend that was evident across the country. Beginning in the 1970s and early 1980s, a period when urban parochial schools lost many of their traditional constituents, their administrators began to focus increasingly on nonwhite, non-Catholic student populations—often with impressive results. "Catholic schools most closely resemble the ideal of the common school model; that is, they educate children from different backgrounds and achieve promising academic outcomes," Vernon C. Polite contended in the early 1990s. In addition, he pointed to research indicating that most of the African American students enrolled at these schools hailed from working-class rather than privileged backgrounds.[48] The growing diversity seen in the classrooms of urban Catholic schools dovetailed with a very different trend in urban public schools, which appear to be "rapidly resegregating." As Jonathan Kozol wrote in 2005, urban public schools in major metropolitan areas have become, if anything, more segregated than they were at the outset of the civil rights movement. "One of the most disheartening experiences for those who grew up in the years when Martin Luther King Jr. and Thurgood Marshall were alive is to visit public schools today that bear their names . . . and to find out how many of these schools are bastions of contemporary segregation," Kozol lamented.[49] Some urban parochial schools in Youngstown, though not all, followed the pattern that Polite praised in his article on the contributions of urban Catholic schools. Yet, despite the fact that a number of these schools contributed to the educational development of disadvantaged students, all but five of them had closed by the opening of the twenty-first century.[50] This book closely examines factors that contributed to this outcome.

NOTES

1. William D. Jenkins, *Steel Valley Klan: The Ku Klux Klan in Ohio's Mahoning Valley* (Kent, OH: Kent State University, 1990), 48.

2. Ibid., 51–54.

3. Ibid., 1–3.

4. Ibid., 47–48.

5. Ibid., 19.

6. Joseph Moreau, *Schoolbook Nation: Conflicts over American History Textbooks from the Civil War to the Present* (Ann Arbor, MI: The University of Michigan Press, 2006), 132.

7. Edwin S. Gaustaud, *Proclaim Liberty Throughout the Land: A History of Church and State in America* (New York, NY: Oxford University Press, 1999/2003), 93–94.

8. Moreau, *Schoolbook Nation,* 133.

9. Jenkins, *Steel Valley Klan,* 47–48.

10. Sara Varley, "Catholic Churches and Schools Take Big Part in Life of Youngstown: Had Beginning in One of First Log Cabins Built in Forest of Mahoning Valley—First Mass at Dungannon," *The Youngstown Telegram,* A-37, June 29, 1931.

11. Jenkins, *Steel Valley Klan,* 19–20.

12. Varley, *The Youngstown Telegram,* June 29, 1931.

13. James A. McFadden, *The March of the Eucharist from Dungannon* (Youngstown, OH: Diocese of Youngstown, 1951), 11.

14. Grace Goulder, "Youngstown's Catholic Cathedral Has European Air," *The Cleveland Plain Dealer Picture Magazine,* April 20, 1947.

15. Varley, *The Youngstown Telegram,* June 29, 1931.

16. George Francis Houck, *The Church in Northern Ohio and in the Diocese of Cleveland, from 1749 to September, 1887* (Cleveland, OH: Short & Forman, Printers, 1889, c1887), 219.

17. McFadden, *The March of the Eucharist from Dungannon,* 11.

18. Varley, *The Youngstown Telegram,* June 29, 1931.

19. Ibid.

20. Marie Claire Davis, "St. Columba's Climaxes 90-Year History Here," *The Youngstown Vindicator,* 14, July 21, 1943.

21. "St. Columba's Contributes Much to Catholicity's Growth: St. Columba's Parent Church of the City," *The Youngstown Telegram,* 5, May 3, 1919.

22. Albert Hamilton, *The Catholic Journey Through Ohio* (Columbus, OH: Catholic Conference of Ohio, 1976), 65.

23. Varley, *The Youngstown Telegram,* June 29, 1931.

24. "St. Columba's Contributes Much to Catholicity's Growth," *The Youngstown Telegram,* May 3, 1919.

25. Varley, *The Youngstown Telegram,* June 29, 1931.

26. "St. Joseph's Church, 1869–1967" (commemorative history printed in 1967, reproduction, Hogan-Cullinan Family Collection, #314, Mahoning Valley Historical Society, Youngstown, OH).

27. "St. Columba's Contributes Much to Catholicity's Growth," *The Youngstown Telegram,* May 3, 1919.

28. Varley, *The Youngstown Telegram,* June 29, 1931.

29. St. Anthony's Church, "St Anthony's Church 100 Year Commemoration Program" (commemorative program printed in 1998, Reuben-McMillan Public Library, Youngstown, OH), 1.

30. McFadden, *The March of the Eucharist from Dungannon,* 125.

31. Ibid., 145.

32. Ibid., 161.

33. St. Stanislaus Church, "St. Stanislaus Kostka Church—Youngstown, 1902–1977" (commemorative booklet printed in 1977, Reuben McMillan Public Library, Youngstown, OH), 15.

34. "Bishop to Dedicate St. Casimir's Parish Church and School," *The Youngstown Telegram,* 3, September 17, 1927.

35. Tony Trolio, *Brier Hill USA* (Poland, OH: Ciao Promotions, 2001), 48–53.

36. Varley, *The Youngstown Telegram,* June 29, 1931.

37. McFadden, *The March of the Eucharist from Dungannon,* 235.

38. "Parochial Teachers Have Hands Full," *The Youngstown Vindicator,* J-4, March 27, 1938.

39. Varley, *The Youngstown Telegram,* June 29, 1931.

40. "Parochial Teachers Have Hands Full," *The Youngstown Vindicator,* March 27, 1938.

41. Varley, *The Youngstown Telegram,* June 29, 1931.

42. Ibid.

43. "Parochial Teachers Have Hands Full," *The Youngstown Vindicator,* March 27, 1938.

44. "Expect 7,200 Enrollment: Twenty Catholic Schools Prepare to Open with Bigger Rosters," *The Youngstown Vindicator,* 13, September 4, 1937.

45. Michael J. Hynes, *History of the Diocese of Cleveland: Origin and Growth (1847–1952)* (Cleveland, OH: Diocese of Cleveland, 1953), 310–12.

46. Hamilton, *The Catholic Journey Through Ohio,* 65.

47. "Six-County Parochial Enrollment Is 44,274," *The Youngstown Vindicator,* August 29, 1965.

48. Vernon C. Polite, "Getting the Job Well Done: African American Students and Catholic Schools," *The Journal of Negro Education* 61, no. 2 (1992): 213.

49. Jonathan Kozol, "Still Separate, Still Unequal: America's Educational Apartheid," *Harpers,* September 2005, 41–42.

50. Ron Cole, "Finances Close St. Dominic's School," *The Vindicator,* B-1, April 19, 1999.

Chapter 3

"The Immaculate": One School's Experience

On the afternoon of June 7, 2006, Sister Charlotte Italiano, OSU, described her "mixed feelings" as she watched 12 eighth-grade students participate in the final graduation ceremony of Immaculate Conception Elementary School. The ceremony marked the imminent closure of an educational institution that had prevailed for more than 120 years. Immaculate Conception's physical plant, built 22 years after the school's establishment, had been an east side landmark for more than a century, a legacy of the parish's second pastor, Father Michael P. Kinkead.[1] Since 1905, the elegant and spacious brick building had towered above the same working-class neighborhood, as it changed hands from Irish to Italian immigrants and then, more recently, to African Americans. "We have to close because of the lack of enrollment," Sister Charlotte told a reporter employed by the *Vindicator*, Youngstown's daily newspaper. "This is bittersweet," she added. "We are very, very sad."[2] Given the enormity of her responsibilities, however, the energetic principal of Immaculate Conception had little time to dwell on the poignant events unfolding before her. Sister Charlotte was, after all, responsible for closing down an institution that had been in operation since the late nineteenth century. Among others, she was charged with disposing of the detritus of Immaculate Conception's lengthy mission. Significant historical artifacts were transferred to the parish archives, and a faded volume of handwritten records was reserved for the recently established archives of the local Ursuline religious community, whose members had staffed the school from its inception and retained a presence until the end. Meanwhile, representatives of the Youngstown City Schools claimed materials and equipment they had provided to the school over the years.

I had a chance to speak with the principal on Friday, June 9, 2006, one day after the school's official closing. Security measures at Immaculate Conception's school building remained tight, and it was necessary for me to confirm my appointment with an administrator via intercom before the main entrance was unlocked electronically. As I walked in, Sister Charlotte was hurriedly giving instructions to a half-dozen workers who carried crates, furniture, and other items marked for transport through the wide corridors of the school building. After a brief greeting, she gestured in the direction of a nearby classroom filled with overflowing cardboard boxes, jumbled cleaning supplies, and a bevy of pre–Vatican II religious images. "That's most of what's left, and it's nothing compared to the load we moved out of here over the past few weeks," she said. Sister Charlotte then ushered me into the only area of the building that remained partially furnished: a small office, where she, along with another administrator, organized what was left of the school's voluminous files. Sister Charlotte rifled through a few items on top of a desk that sat in the middle of the office. She quickly located a worn scrapbook filled with newspaper clippings and handed it to me. "These may be of interest," she said. As I paged through the album, I scanned articles that ranged from a 1957 feature story on the parish's seventy-fifth anniversary to more recent accounts of the school's long struggle to survive.

For many, the closing of this urban institution was an occasion for sadness. Given the decades of news reports predicting such an outcome, however, it probably came as no surprise. An article marking the school's closing notes that Immaculate Conception's enrollment, which approached 700 pupils in the 1960s, fell to a record low of 63 students during the 2005–2006 academic year.[3] Amid the school's precipitous decline, many administrators showed patience and understanding, the principal explained. Sister Charlotte noted that Monsignor John Zuraw, administrator of Immaculate Conception Parish and diocesan chancellor, "tried very hard to work with us," even offering to keep the school open if 70 students were enrolled.[4] She added that the institution's closure was no isolated incident. On the morning that Sister Charlotte announced her school would suspend operations, another local Catholic institution held its final graduation ceremony. The *Vindicator* reported that the south side parish school of St. Matthias, which had served a traditionally Slovak American neighborhood since 1917, would not reopen for the 2006–2007 academic year.[5] Media reports on the two school closings probably saddened many Youngstown-area residents, some of whom had come to view parochial schools as a permanent (and desirable) fixture of the urban landscape. Others may have been shocked to learn that, as of June 2006, only one parish school continued to operate within the city limits. The surviving school was (and is) connected to St. Christine's Church, a quasi-suburban parish that straddled the borders of nearby Austintown and Boardman townships.[6]

Of all the parochial schools that once operated in Youngstown, Immaculate Conception has one of the longest, and most representative, stories to tell. Like many other urban "territorial" parishes (those with clearly defined geographical boundaries), Immaculate Conception maintained its school long after the bulk of the neighborhood's Catholic residents had moved elsewhere. In addition, the parish school's development intersects with all of the major urban trends explored in this study. While subsequent chapters will examine a number of these trends in greater detail, this chapter will illustrate the successive impact of developments such as ethnic enclaving, anti-Catholic discrimination, urban depopulation, demographic change, urban economic decline, and sweeping internal religious reforms on the history of one institution.

ORIGINS OF A PARISH SCHOOL

When Immaculate Conception Parish was organized on Youngstown's near east side, the district still retained a distinctly bucolic flavor. In 1882, neighborhoods were just beginning to take shape in an area ringed with woodlands and family-operated farms. The majority of the east side's earliest Roman Catholics were Irish Americans, and few were far removed from the mud hamlets and rock-strewn fields of western Ireland. This period was revisited in a 1934 newspaper interview with a 97-year-old east side resident, who emphasized the Irish character of the neighborhood in the late nineteenth century, when it was "scarce built up at all."[7] The district was not only undeveloped; it was also curiously isolated. During periods of heavy rain, residents were cut off from the rest of the city by the Crab Creek Valley, a steep gulley with a creek that overflowed habitually. As another elderly east side resident recalled in a later interview, the nearest parish was St. Joseph's Church, which had been "established . . . for German-speaking peoples."[8] Thus, before the construction of Immaculate Conception Church, the east side's Irish Catholic residents were compelled to make the arduous trek across the Crab Creek Valley to St. Columba's Church, the community's oldest parish, which was located on the north side, a few blocks to the southwest of St. Joseph's Church.

As the city's industrial base expanded, the Diocese of Cleveland (which then encompassed Youngstown) came under pressure to establish more English-speaking parishes in the community, and in 1881, Father Edward Mears, the pastor of St. Columba's Church, donated $5,000 toward the establishment of Immaculate Conception Church.[9] Local Irish Americans quickly dubbed the new parish as "the Immaculate." Unlike St. Joseph's Church, a national parish whose German-speaking members were dispersed throughout the area, Immaculate Conception was established as a territorial parish, one technically designed to meet the needs of all Catholics who lived in the surrounding neighborhood. The distinction between territorial and national parishes was crucial for many American Catholics, and controversies surrounding these competing models exacerbated tensions between a heavily Irish American hierarchy and those German immigrants who envisioned their churches as repositories of Old World culture.[10]

American bishops' general preference for territorial parishes drew criticism from German Americans, who claimed that this policy tended to favor the Irish. Although German immigrants were as likely as their Irish counterparts to cluster in tight-knit enclaves, many of those who lived in smaller communities like Youngstown established a centrally located national parish that was designed to serve German Americans living throughout the community. Critics of the territorial model also noted that the overwhelming majority of Irish Americans spoke English exclusively. This circumstance practically ensured that Irish American attempts to maintain a sense of ethnic identity would emphasize religious and political commitments, as opposed to concentrated efforts to preserve language and culture.[11] Irish American pastors, on the one hand, promoted the cultural assimilation of immigrants and strongly emphasized American patriotic values. On the other, they instilled within Irish American parishioners a strong sense of loyalty to their ancestral homeland, an emotion that found expression in political activities aimed at Ireland's independence from Great Britain. As Kerby A. Miller noted, in his landmark study of the Irish Diaspora in North America, Irish American nationalists of the late nineteenth century "made sincere but tortuous efforts to reconcile competing allegiances and identify Irish freedom with native American traditions and interests."[12] Perceiving a double standard, German American Catholics were offended by Irish American allegations that "these Germans were more interested in preserving their subculture than in protecting the faith."[13] The debate over nationality and religion reached a climax in 1891, when German Catholic layman Peter Paul Cahensly delivered to Pope Leo XIII a letter drafted by representatives of a German emigrant aid society. The letter, among others, called for separate parishes and parochial schools for each nationality in the United States.[14] While the pope declined to support the proposals outlined in the society's letter, the nationality debate continued, with Polish Americans mounting "the most aggressive and significant campaign against Americanization."[15] Meanwhile, proponents of national parishes throughout the northern United States remained keenly aware that "territorial" parishes often functioned as de facto Irish American parishes.[16]

One year after the establishment of Immaculate Conception Parish, an elementary school was set up in a section of the wooden church. Seating at the institution was extremely tight, and a newspaper article later reported that "there were about 175 boys and girls enrolled" at a school that took up the church's first floor and a segment of the chapel. Eight years later, a new church was built, and the rooms of the older frame building were used exclusively as classrooms. A steady increase in enrollment, however, guaranteed that overcrowding would remain a problem, and the parish school was forced to lease (or borrow) space in nearby buildings, including the church itself.[17] By modern standards, of course, the small frame school on Youngstown's east side was severely overcrowded, and grossly understaffed. One alumnus observed, "We were a hundred strong in the old classroom—50 to a side of the old-time pot-bellied stove."[18] Yet, the school, for all its physical limitations, served as a locus of community activity and a source of neighborhood pride. The school's teaching staff—including Mother Columba Gettins (the principal), three teaching nuns, and two lay teachers—encouraged high levels of student involvement in local, regional, and national events.[19]

In 1893, the students assembled a prize-winning exhibit of their schoolwork for the Chicago World's Fair. During the previous October, they helped to mark the four hundredth anniversary of America's "discovery" by assembling a float for a local Columbus Day parade. A retrospective newspaper article reported that the float represented "a small schoolhouse" that featured a "group of Ursuline Sisters instructing the Indians." The "Indians" who waved and smiled atop the "Columbus Day" float, as it trundled through the streets of Youngstown on that October in 1893, bore names that were unmistakably Irish—Cregan, Lyden, and Murtha.[20] Notably, the newspaper article that commemorated the event 40 years later suggested that Immaculate Conception's ethnic orientation had changed little in all that time. Perhaps the parish's location in the middle of a traditional Irish American enclave enabled it to preserve an essentially Celtic atmosphere. Another likely factor, however, was the degree of hegemonic control wielded by Irish Americans within the U.S. church. Writing in the mid-1980s, Jay P. Dolan observed, "This Irish hegemony has remained consistent throughout the twentieth century, so that by 1972, 37 percent of the American clergy and 48 percent of the hierarchy still identified themselves as Irish."[21] Bolstering the essentially Irish American character of "mainstream" Catholicism during the early twentieth century were images of the church presented by the film industry. "When Hollywood produced a film about Catholics, it often chose an Irish priest as the hero," Dolan wrote. "There were Italian, Polish, and German Catholics, but the Irish were Hollywood's Catholics."[22]

Significantly, the ethnically based segregation of many of Youngstown's Catholics was reflective of a national trend. John T. McGreevy noted that urban parishes with well-defined ethnic identities were commonplace in neighborhoods throughout the northern United States. Hence, McGreevy's characterization of early twentieth-century Catholic parishes in Chicago's

"Back of the Yards" district resembles the situation in Youngstown during the same period. "Each parish was a small planet whirling through its orbit, oblivious to the rest of the ecclesiastical solar system," he wrote. "The two Irish churches were the 'territorial' parishes—theoretically responsible for all Catholics in the area." He added, however, that "all churches—formally territorial or not—tended to attract parishioners of the same national background." Indeed, many parishioners were inclined to purchase homes in the vicinity of churches and parish schools, thereby "helping to create Polish, Bohemian, Irish, and Lithuanian enclaves within the larger neighborhood."[23] This dynamic was evident at the Immaculate, where St. Patrick's Day was treated as a major religious holiday, and the details of Ireland's long struggle against religious persecution were part of every student's reservoir of knowledge.

IRISH AMERICAN HEGEMONY AT THE IMMACULATE

At no time was the parish's ethnic character more clearly defined than during the eventful 15-year tenure of Father John R. Kenny, an Irish immigrant who assumed the pastorate in 1910. Outspoken and charismatic, the burly, 6-foot-tall pastor successfully pressured the municipal government to move forward on the long-delayed Oak Street Bridge, a project whose completion connected the east side to the rest of the city. Father Kenny's obituary noted that he was an advocate of Catholic education who lobbied tirelessly for the establishment of Ursuline High School, the city's first Catholic secondary school, which was located on the north side. Whether he directed his efforts toward improving education, infrastructure, or public morality, Father Kenny took a decidedly assertive approach. His obituary observed that, when children on the east side "were being forced to walk to Rayen School if they wanted a high school education, it was Father Kenny who led the campaign to get secondary facilities for his people." Unlike some of his more faint-hearted contemporaries, the pastor of Immaculate Conception often took sides on potentially controversial issues.[24]

Father Kenny was particularly outspoken on matters related to the political fate of his beleaguered homeland. A native of County Leitrim, Ireland, the pastor offered warmhearted tributes to Irish patriots, even in cases where their actions were criticized by large segments of the American public. Such was the case with the Easter Rising of 1916, a rebellion led by Irish nationalists at a time when the United Kingdom was embroiled in military conflict with Europe's Central Powers. Ignoring the American public's growing sympathy for Great Britain and its European allies, Father Kenny used the occasion of an Irish writer's upcoming visit to laud the insurgents. "Folks may differ on the wisdom of the recent insurrection in Dublin, but who can shut his eyes to the fact that the men who died there and everyone who gave his life for Ireland lives in the heart of that nation and inspires the young men of every generation with hope and courage," Father Kenny stated. "This means that from all these abortive uprisings the conscience of the Gael selects the central fact that the cause of the rebels—like Washington's cause—was essentially just and noble, and therefore the men who made the supreme sacrifice should never be forgotten." Father Kenny concluded by stating that, so long as the story of the insurgents was preserved in memory, "the hearts of the scattered children of the sea-divided Gael will throb with pride and a hope of some day being able to avenge them."[25]

The pastor once again voiced support for Irish political independence at the height of the Anglo-Irish conflict, whose escalating violence dominated local and national headlines throughout 1921 and 1922. Among others, Father Kenny sharply criticized the policies of the British government in a series of local newspaper articles that ran under the heading, "Ireland at Valley Forge." The series opened as follows: "The fact that nationhood is not denied to Ireland, except by those that have an obvious special interest in the denial, makes it unnecessary to labor any proof." From there, the priest devoted two densely packed columns to an inventory of such "unnecessary" proof, tapping sources as diverse as the essays of English writer G. K. Chesterton and entries from the now obscure "Cyclopedia of American Government."[26] The pastor's activities on behalf of his homeland went beyond editorial writing, however. Earlier that year, Father Kenny initiated at the parish level an Irish relief fund that raised $6,500. The priest stated in a newspaper announcement that the funds were distributed to leading Irish bishops as well as to several convents whose operations were "disrupted" by British auxiliaries known as "Black and Tans."[27] Perhaps not coincidentally, the pastor's initiation of the relief fund came on the heels of a speaking engagement by Donal O'Callaghan, the newly elected lord mayor of Cork, who had arrived in the United States as a stowaway some time earlier. On the evening of March 2, 1921, the young mayor delivered an emotional address to a capacity crowd at Youngstown's Moose Temple, where he condemned the excesses of British auxiliaries in Ireland.[28]

Unsurprisingly, the same pastor who celebrated the Immaculate's "Irish" identity also staunchly defended its territorial mission. Anecdotal evidence suggests that Father Kenny was angered over the tendency of non-Irish neighborhood Catholics to register at churches (and schools) located outside the parish boundaries. Among those who frequently ignored the pastor's territorial recommendations were the district's German Americans, scores of whom journeyed westward—often passing directly before the Immaculate—to attend services at St. Joseph's Church on the north side. In an interview, a close relative, Joan (Donnelly) Welsh, described her German American mother's oral account of reprimands that she had received from the pastor of Immaculate Conception in the early 1900s. She recalled that her mother, the late Mary Wilma (Fitch) Donnelly, often recounted how the pastor "yelled" at children and adults as they made their weekly sojourn to "the German church." In Mrs. Donnelly's account, the priest stood on the front steps of Immaculate Conception Church, jabbing his finger in the air, and bellowing, "You belong here, not there."[29]

There is no evidence that Father Kenny, or his predecessors, made similar appeals to the east side's Italian American Catholics. As a product of his times, the pastor may even have discouraged them from joining the parish. Anecdotal accounts suggest that Immaculate Conception, like most Irish American parishes, offered a cool reception to Italian immigrants—a response that reflected the prejudices of the era. Whatever the case, Father Kenny was undoubtedly aware of the rapidly expanding presence of Italian immigrants in the Youngstown area. A 1930 census report issued by The International Institute, a service bureau for immigrants connected to the local Young Women's Christian Association (YWCA), observed that by 1920, there were 5,538 foreign-born Italian Americans living in Youngstown—a substantial 16.3 percent of the immigrant population. By contrast, the report indicated that the number of foreign-born Irish Americans living in Youngstown in 1920 was 1,578, a mere 5 percent of the city's immigrant population.[30] Moreover, the Italian American population in the Mahoning Valley—which included Youngstown, Warren, and smaller communities like Struthers and Campbell—reached 30,000 in 1932, a development that led the Italian government to establish a vice-consulate in the area.[31] In 1937, the *Vindicator* reported that more Italians "than members of any other nationality have become naturalized American citizens in Mahoning County since 1896." The article noted that, between 1880 and 1937, 4,634 Italian-born residents of the county were naturalized.[32]

As the number of Italian Americans residing in the community continued to rise, the newcomers found themselves in periodic conflict with more established immigrant groups, especially Irish Americans. Beyond commonplace ethnocentricity, the widely documented conflict between the Irish and the Italians appears to have stemmed from the two groups' divergent approaches to religious observance. Irish Americans, for their part, evidently feared that Italian Catholics, with their pre-migration experience of state-subsidized churches, would offer little in the way of material contributions to the parish, while at the same time, reaping the benefits of membership. Italian immigrants, on the other hand, were mystified over the central role that Catholicism apparently played in the lives of many Irish Americans. "With both the Irish and the Polish—as well as most other Slavic immigrants—the Catholic Church moved from center stage in Europe to center stage in America with little difficulty," observed historian Paul W. McBride. "The Church belonged in their communities and they belonged in their Church." The situation could scarcely have been more different in the Italian American community. "So tenuous was the role of the village priest in Italy that only rarely did he venture to follow his parishioners to America," McBride noted. "Even more rare was an Italian priest who spoke with any authority for his people. The Church which he represented was a wealthy, distant landlord and feared authority figure to the adults and contadini who emigrated to America." The vast majority of adult Italian males attended church "on only three occasions—baptisms, weddings, and funerals," and Italian families saw little sense in giving "precious money to the Church which was so rich and state supported." Hence, when Italians immigrated to America, "they did not rush to found their own parishes, they did not support the Catholic Church they found there, and they did not send their children to Catholic school." Consequently, Italian Americans became known as "the Italian Problem" among members of an Irish-dominated hierarchy, clergy, and religious communities. "That problem was far-reaching and complex," McBride concluded. "It encompassed the meeting of Italians and Irish who understood little of each other, the efforts of Protestants to capitalize upon Italian disaffection with their Church and the very essence of the Italian concept of religion."[33]

Those Italian Catholics who were exposed to mainstream American Catholicism invariably experienced culture shock. As Rudolph J. Vecoli observed, most Italian immigrants were alienated by the unfamiliar brand of Catholicism they encountered in the United States. "Those Italians who ventured into Irish or German churches found them as alien as Protestant chapels," Vecoli noted. "The coldly rational atmosphere, the discipline, the attentive congregation, were foreign to the Italians who were used to behaving in church as they would in their own house."[34] Many recoiled from this less than congenial environment, and a distinctive brand of Italian American religiosity prevailed for decades. Herbert J. Gans, in his classic study of Italian Americans residing on Boston's West End, outlined the profound differences that separated Italian and Irish Catholics as recently as the early 1960s. "Irish Catholicism stresses, among other things, the Trinity, which is male, and its source of authority is patriarchal," Gans wrote. "But as Italians are notably resistant to patriarchal authority, those who did give any thought to this matter had little sympathy for the stern and less permissive Irish Catholicism being taught to their children at church and in the parochial school."[35]

Significantly, this level of engagement with Irish Catholic values was often difficult to achieve for many Italian immigrants who arrived in the United States in the late nineteenth and early twentieth centuries. During this period, "poorly dressed, sometimes unwashed" Italian immigrants were often "turned away" from churches established by other nationalities "or seated in the rear with Negroes." On occasion, Italian Americans "heard themselves denounced as 'Dagos' from the pulpit and told that they were not wanted."[36] Vecoli noted that, as a general rule, "American Protestants *and* Catholics agreed that the Italian immigrants were characterized by ignorance of Christian doctrine, image worship, and superstitious emotionalism."[37] Ultimately, the disdain many Irish Americans directed toward Italian immigrants produced a bitter legacy, and relations between the two groups were characterized by tension and distrust. One alumnus of Immaculate Conception Elementary School, Attorney Robert E. Casey, recalled that Italian American classmates often shared stories about the icy reception their ancestors had received at the "Irish church," where they were often "told that they might be better served at Our Lady of Mount Carmel [Church], which was predominantly Italian."[38]

Unsurprisingly, lingering resentment over the erstwhile insensitivity of many Irish Americans has found expression in literature by local Italian American authors. An exceptional example is Carmen J. Leone's work of creative nonfiction, *Rose Street: A Family Story,* which is based on stories passed down by his mother, the late Josephine Vitullo, and other close relatives. Leone's narrative indicates that the Vitullos, like most Italian American families of the era, preferred to send their children to public schools rather than parochial ones. This decision, he suggested, was rooted in the parents' fears that their children would be ridiculed and marginalized at the nearby "Irish" school. "The Irish had come to Youngstown long before the Italians and the other Southern and Eastern Europeans," Leone observed. "Though they were mostly Catholic themselves, many resented these 'foreigners,' who came to take work in this city that they had built up from a coal and iron town to the thriving steel town it had become." Leone noted that his grandmother, Gesilda, "did not hesitate to worship at [Immaculate Conception Church], for she and her family could keep to themselves and did not have to deal with the parishioners, but she would not even consider sending [her daughter] Jo to that Irish school."[39]

Later in the narrative, the Vitullos' concerns about the potentially hostile atmosphere at Immaculate Conception Elementary School are seemingly validated when their six-year-old daughter, Jo, is harassed by a group of Irish American teenagers as she walks home from the nearby public school, a journey that leads her past the steps of the "Irish church." The adolescents, who are gathered on the steps, descend upon the girl and bait her with ethnic slurs and other insults. "They completely surrounded her, shouting strange words and giggling and snorting," Leone wrote. "Cigarette smoke encircled her. They were giants in dirty white shirts, tails hanging, and blue trousers."[40] Leone's dramatic retelling of family lore sheds light on the mutual antipathies that divided Irish and Italian Catholics in the early twentieth century and reverberate even today. At certain junctures, the rift between the two ethnic groups threatened to contribute to a schism within the U.S. Catholic Church. Italian American resentment toward an Irish-dominated hierarchy was endemic, and tensions mounted whenever national parishes insisted upon a degree of local control that bishops found unacceptable. As noted, one local Italian Catholic parish took the momentous step of breaking ties with the Diocese of Cleveland, only to be embraced by the Episcopal community.[41] Predictably, Protestant missionaries throughout the country sought to capitalize on Italian Americans' alienation from the U.S. Catholic hierarchy as they looked for potential converts.[42]

Tensions between Irish and Italian Americans were overshadowed, if only temporarily, by pressures exerted on the city's Roman Catholic community by the local Ku Klux Klan, an organization that viewed "papists" in largely monolithic terms. Like most northern chapters of the organization, Youngstown's Klan targeted local Catholics and Jews,[43] while largely ignoring the community's relatively small black community. Although the local Klan publicly supported a state bill that would ban interracial marriage, its representatives made no attempt "to bring southern racial mores to Youngstown."[44] Shaping their platform to conform to local conditions, Youngstown's Klan leaders promoted the maintenance of "a Protestant culture that was essential to the preservation of a moral society."[45] In line with this project, they criticized parochial schools as obstacles to assimilation. One local Klan leader, in a newspaper interview, expressed views that seemed specifically designed to offend local Catholics. "[The Klan leader] expressed grave concern that parochial schools taught children the principle of church rule, thus violating the constitutional principle of separation of church and state," the article reports. "The best solution in his mind was the required attendance of every child (age 6 to 16) in a public school, where the values of Americanism and patriotism could be taught."[46]

The Klan's characterization of parish schools as "un-American" infuriated many of the community's Catholics, especially the substantial percentage who patronized these schools. Yet, the Klan's capacity to offend didn't end there. The group's sympathizers condemned the purportedly corrupting influence of recent immigrants, many of whom were Catholic.[47] Thus, within a short period of time, the organization succeeded in alienating even those Catholics who generally avoided parochial schools, especially Italian Americans, some of whom viewed the Klan's moral crusade "as an unwarranted and disrespectful attack on the Italian way of life."[48] Unsurprisingly, the Klan's wholesale condemnation of a deeply divided religious minority worked to its disadvantage, as Catholics of different backgrounds brushed aside their differences to confront the vigilante organization directly. The conflict between local Klan members and Catholics reached a climax on November 1, 1924, when regional chapters of the Klan planned a massive march through neighboring Niles, Ohio, a town that hosted a large number of Irish and Italian American residents. In their often violent campaign to prevent the march, anti-Klan activists in Niles benefited from the support of Catholics in Youngstown and Warren, who helped establish checkpoints along roads leading into Niles. When the motorists halted at these checkpoints were found to be in possession of Klan robes, they were beaten—sometimes severely—and turned away.[49]

Cooperation across ethnic lines was not restricted to the area's Catholic laity. Significantly, when the vigilante organization attempted to secretly transport hundreds of reinforcements into Niles, the Mahoning Valley's heavily Irish American clergy played a crucial role in routing the Klan. On the morning of the heaviest fighting between Klansmen and (mostly Italian American) anti-Klan rioters, a young Irish woman "happened to be at the Erie Depot [in Niles], where she overheard the railroad agents discussing the scheduled arrival in the afternoon of a special train with carloads of Klan members." The young woman promptly informed her local pastor, who, in turn, contacted Monsignor Joseph Trainor, the pastor of St. Columba's Church in Youngstown. "No one knows how the information filtered down," Jenkins observed, but the next afternoon, about 50 heavily armed anti-Klan activists gathered at the depot. When the train pulled into the depot at Niles, "its iron carriages full of 1,200 unsuspecting and untested Klansmen," the Klan leader aboard quickly sized up the situation and shouted: "It's no place for us. We go right back." Finally, the Klan suffered a humiliating blow when, in response to the violence in Niles, Ohio Governor Victor Donahey imposed martial law, a move that ensured cancellation of the planned march. As Jenkins concluded, the Niles riot was a rare, but compelling, instance of cooperation between Italian and Irish Catholics. "The public image of the Klan as an organ of prejudice, rather than of law enforcement, had drawn together the Italian community," he wrote. "Assisted by the Irish, it had successfully defied the Klan."[50]

GROWING ETHNIC DIVERSITY AT THE "IRISH CHURCH"

Although it is difficult to gauge the long-term effects of Klan-era cooperation involving Irish and Italian Americans, there is evidence that the late 1920s and early 1930s witnessed a gradual opening up of Irish-dominated territorial parishes to less-established ethnic groups. This process did not always go smoothly. "Lines between 'race' and what is now considered 'ethnicity' were unclear," McGreevy observed. "The assumption that Celtic, Polish, and German races existed was common; as was the belief that differences between these races and the 'Anglo-Saxon' race were deep and enduring."[51] Therefore, boundaries between various ethnic groups were carefully maintained, even in neighborhoods that appeared, on the surface, to be relatively diverse. As Dolan noted, "The major importance of such ethnic colonies was cultural, rather than residential."[52] In other words, members of different ethnic groups often ignored one another, even when they lived in close proximity to each other. JoEllen McNergney Vinyard, in her study of Catholic education in Detroit, stressed that this pattern was well established by the late nineteenth century. "Irish and German families might live on the same block yet have little cause for serious interaction, because their private lives centered around the separate parishes they built," she wrote. "The right to ethnic rather than territorial parishes was an accepted reality in the American Catholic Church."[53]

In Youngstown, as elsewhere in the northeastern United States, conservative Irish American parishioners often resisted the efforts of liberal pastors to make parish schools available to "new arrivals." This was especially true when these newcomers were associated with national parishes that did not maintain schools of their own. Former north side resident Paula McKinney recalled her mother's description of tensions that were unleashed during the "integration" of St. Columba's Parish in the 1920s:

> . . . St. Columba's [Church] basically was an Irish parish, or had been. And of course, over the years, the neighborhood was changing. And the people were moving in. And quite a few of them were foreign born. We had Italian people, and Lebanese people, and Black people. And Monsignor [Joseph] Trainor, who was our pastor, said, "The school is open to all"—meaning all of our children. . . . He said: "The facilities have been paid for by those who came before you. The place was built where it was, which is in the neighborhood. And the children are welcome." Now, some of the Irishmen didn't want that. . . . [M]y mother said it was pretty bad for awhile, I guess. But [the pastor] stuck to his guns, and . . . we all went to school together.

Tellingly, she added: "Of course, all these Italian people, and Lebanese people, and Black people sang, 'All Praise to St. Patrick,' with the rest of us. . . . We always had a real nice St. Patrick's Day show and all that kind of thing."[54] Evidently, the acceptance of non-Irish students at St. Columba's Elementary School did not result in an immediate weakening of Irish American cultural hegemony.

Once the city's oldest "Irish" parish opened its doors to newer immigrant groups, it was a matter of time before Immaculate Conception followed suit. The parish's diversification came about only gradually, however. As late as the 1930s, the bulk of the near east side's Italian Americans continued to worship at the national parish of Our Lady of Mount Carmel and pointedly ignored the Immaculate's school. Yet, a small but growing number of them became involved in what many local Italian Americans still regarded as the "Irish church." In a 2007 interview with a *Vindicator* reporter, Immaculate Conception parishioner Kelly Stilson noted that her family's affiliation with the parish traced back to the 1920s, when her great-grandmother, the late Catherine Carano, began attending religious services at the church. "My grandmother was 5 years old when [she] started walking to church here . . . on her own," Mrs. Stilson said. "And then she brought her siblings along."[55]

Perhaps the growing ethnic diversity of territorial parishes like Immaculate Conception owed something to the economic depression that followed the stock market "crash" of 1929. While the subsequent muting of economic differences between Italian and Irish Americans most likely heightened mutual tensions in some ways—as members of the two ethnic groups competed for a shrinking pool of resources—it may also have simultaneously weakened divisions that were rooted in perceived class differences. In addition, the Great Depression pressured many U.S. Catholics to abandon their insularity and "to become more concerned about the welfare of American society."[56] The emergence of a broader social perspective may well have contributed to a weakening of ethnic barriers within the Catholic community. No less significant, however, was the fact that immigration legislation enacted in the 1920s, which reflected prevalent eugenic values, bolstered restrictions on immigration from southeastern Europe.[57] This development deprived Italian enclaves, among others, of large numbers of newcomers, who might have shored up the community's collective sense of identity, while stiffening resistance to cooperation with "outsiders." As many observers have noted, declining levels of ethnic identity among communities of "new" immigrants had a profound effect on race relations throughout the northern United States. Matthew Frye Jacobson noted that the Immigration Act of 1924 minimized the perceived threat to U.S. democracy that some Americans had associated with "inferior" white groups, and therefore "decreased the political and social stakes that had kept such distinctions alive."[58] A weakening of traditional barriers between ethnic whites was duly reflected in the growing number of Italian Americans who joined Immaculate Conception Church during the late 1920s and 1930s. Both parish and school emerged from the Great Depression as more diverse—and less affluent.

A PARISH SCHOOL'S STRUGGLE WITH ECONOMIC ADVERSITY

Former parishioners and staff members who lived through the lean years of the Depression and World War II have continued to share anecdotes about Immaculate Conception's financial difficulties. Many of these stories focus on the cost-cutting measures employed by the church's long-suffering pastor. While most of the parish's earliest debts (accrued mainly through building projects) were paid off during the long tenure of Father Kenny, a fire that devastated the school building in 1929 left the Immaculate about $89,000 in arrears.[59] The parish's financial predicament, while unusual in its severity, reflected the kinds of challenges many parishes faced as they struggled to maintain schools amid shrinking contributions. During the Depression, declining levels of giving were often a by-product of mass unemployment. Evidence that the problem was widespread among local parishes is found in news reports suggesting that some parish schools were unable to cover even the modest salaries of religious instructors. In a 1935 *Vindicator* article, Monsignor William A. Kane, the dean of Mahoning Valley clergy, stated: "State aid will be absolutely necessary to continue the work of the parochial schools in Youngstown. . . . The situation is very bad at the present time, although the parishes are doing their best to keep them going." The article emphasized that parochial schools were "unique in that [their] only source of revenue is through the contributions of parishioners." The newspaper's description of conditions at one particularly hard-hit local parish may refer to the situation at Immaculate Conception. "In one parish, where approximately 50 percent of the parishioners are now out of work, the contributions are 70 per cent less than they were four years ago," the article stated. "It has been impossible for the parish to pay the sisters, although the salary of each is but $50 a month."[60]

While Youngstown's steel-centered economy picked up dramatically after America's entry into World War II, Immaculate Conception remained, in many ways, a struggling parish community. In 1941, the parish recorded about 800 families, most of whom were dependent on the modest wages of blue-collar workers.[61] Former instructor Sister Virginia McDermott, OSU, recalled that close to 600 students were enrolled at the parish school in the early 1940s. She noted that their fathers were "[m]ostly working in the mills, and rather poor." The school's mainly Irish and Italian American families were so inured to material deprivation, she added, that few of them even bothered to conceal their plight. "I always loved Immaculate Conception, and I loved the simplicity of it, and the openness of the people to you," Sister

Virginia recalled. "They would say: 'We don't have enough to eat. We don't have this. We don't have that.' They were poor. And they were a wonderful example of how to live simply, because they all did." By this time, she noted, the percentage of Italian American students enrolled at the parish school had risen substantially.[62]

Demographic changes, however, did not discourage those elements within Immaculate Conception's leadership who were committed to reinforcing the school's residual Irish American identity. Anecdotal accounts suggest that students of Irish ancestry continued to receive preferential treatment at the hands of some of the school's teachers and administrators. Alumnus Robert Casey recalled that, as late as the 1950s, Italian American students complained of ethnically based discrimination. He described one incident involving a close friend named Don Greco, who, despite his mixed Irish and Italian heritage, was widely perceived as an Italian American and treated accordingly. Some weeks before an important religious service at which the bishop was expected to officiate, Greco competed for the position of head altar boy at the event. When he arrived at the church for the competition, Greco reportedly discovered that his main rival was an Irish American classmate named Danny Lyons. Attorney Casey described Greco's account of what happened next. "[H]e said, when he got over there, Danny Lyons had the assistant altar boys [who] looked like a well-practiced precision drill team," Casey said. "[A]nd they brought over the 'ne'er-do-well' fellows, and they put them with my buddy, Don Greco." Predictably, the inexperienced altar boys made a poor showing, and Casey's friend "didn't get that honor." Casey concluded that, at Immaculate Conception Elementary School, "there seemed to be a bias . . . in favor of the Irish—and certainly not in favor of the Italians."[63] Cases of ethnocentric bias were bound to decline, however, as the student body became more diverse; and this process was well under way in the 1950s. Within a decade of the incident Casey described, Italian Americans had emerged as the largest single ethnic group at Immaculate Conception Elementary School. Italian American students were gradually joined by representatives of other groups who were traditionally underrepresented at the school, including African Americans.[64]

SIGNS OF URBAN CHANGE IN THE POSTWAR ERA

Although Immaculate Conception emerged intact from the Depression and World War II, it was hardly a thriving enterprise. The parish's postwar challenges included massive debt and a decaying physical plant. Furthermore, the parish's financial tribulations had been alleviated only mildly by the frugal policies of Father Joseph McCann, who had assumed the pastorate in 1941.[65] Anecdotal accounts suggest Father McCann dispensed with the services of a custodian in order to save money. Sister Virginia noted, in an interview, that the Immaculate had no salaried maintenance workers in the 1940s. "Father McCann was a very hard worker himself," she recalled. "He was also aware of the huge debt that the parish had, and he was trying to take care of that debt his way." Sister Virginia added that, during her tenure as a classroom instructor, the pastor personally handled most maintenance issues, including plumbing. "He did any kind of work that had to be done—except the scrubbing," she said. "The kids did that." The retired instructor recalled that Father McCann "disapproved" of students participating in the school's maintenance. "But you can't stand a dirty classroom," she added.[66] Sister Virginia's recollections were corroborated by those of Robert Casey, who attended the school in the early 1950s. "I remember [that] we cleaned the blackboards after school; certain students were designated," he said. "We swept the classroom floors." Casey recalled that students threw cornmeal on the hardwood floors and polished the planks with their feet, which were usually wrapped in strips of cloth. "But the good part of this is that we felt it was our school," he added.[67]

While this sort of "communal" maintenance was commonplace among local parochial schools during the 1930s and 1940s, the tradition was maintained at Immaculate Conception well into the 1950s. Yet, despite such cost-cutting measures, the parish was unable to pay off debts that originated during the period of the Great Depression. When Father McCann died in 1954, Bishop Emmett Walsh replaced him with a younger priest, Father Arthur B. DeCrane, the popular chaplain of Youngstown College's Newman Club, a campus organization for Catholic students.[68] In a move that might well have scandalized his predecessor, Father DeCrane's first decision was to seek forgiveness for the years of back wages the parish owed to the Ursuline religious order. Decades later, Sister Virginia described this episode, which had been a topic of discussion within her religious community. "I remember Father McCann speaking . . . to Sister Alice and me," she said. "He said that he owed a debt to the Ursulines that . . . was a huge debt from years back." Sister Virginia indicated the pastor seemed determined to settle the debt. "And Father McCann said, 'I will not go to my grave without paying that debt to those sisters,'" she added.[69] Ultimately, the aging pastor was unable to keep this promise. When his successor, Father DeCrane, persuaded the Ursuline community to "write off" the parish's longstanding debt, he wasted no time in launching a fund-raising campaign to secure money for the repair of the school and church facilities, which had endured decades of haphazard maintenance. The new pastor showed a rare aptitude for fund-raising, and it soon became apparent that Immaculate Conception's physical plant would be presentable for the parish's seventy-fifth anniversary in September 1957. As the *Vindicator* reported, "rejuvenation" of the Immaculate's physical plant had been Father DeCrane's "principal occupation" in the three years since his appointment. By the time of the anniversary celebration, the young pastor had "succeeded in painting and decorating the church, modernizing the rectory, remodeling the school to add classrooms and kitchen facilities in the original building as well as constructing an addition."[70]

Despite such material improvements, however, Father DeCrane probably recognized that his parish faced long-term challenges. The Immaculate was gradually losing its most precious resource—its parishioners. This trend may have escaped the notice of less involved observers, given that the neighborhood's declining Catholic population was not reflected immediately in the parish school's enrollment levels. In 1955, Immaculate Conception Elementary School was holding its own with 535 students enrolled, thereby retaining its place as the city's third-largest parish school in terms of enrollment. Yet, this figure, while only slightly lower than enrollment figures described in the 1940s, appears sobering when one considers that the postwar "baby boom" fueled explosive growth elsewhere in the city. During the mid-1950s, enrollment at St. Patrick's Elementary School, another urban parochial school, rose by one-third, as student numbers soared from 800 to 1,204.[71] The relatively high numbers recorded at St. Patrick's, however, were no less deceptive. As historian Glen Gabert, Jr., observed, the percentage of Catholics who were sending their children to parochial schools declined sharply, even as enrollment figures were pushed upward by the population increase of the baby boom.[72] For those who looked closely, Immaculate Conception revealed signs of a parish in transition. A 1957 newspaper article intended to highlight the Immaculate's seventy-fifth anniversary festivities inadvertently called attention to the fact that the east side was losing many of its long-time residents. "Informality will prevail during the day-long event which is expected to bring together many former parishioners who have moved to different portions of the Youngstown district or away from the area altogether," the *Vindicator* reported. "Reminiscing will substitute for a program of speakers. No formal addresses will be made at either the dinner or the dance."[73] As the 1950s progressed, a growing number of former east side residents settled in the relatively affluent neighborhoods of the south side as well as neighboring suburban communities like Boardman, Poland, and Canfield townships. This mobility was fueled, in part, by a government-subsidized building boom, which enabled white working-class families across the country to purchase affordable housing in outlying areas.[74]

It appears likely that the depopulation of the east side was driven, in part, by the concerns of white urban dwellers about demographic changes taking place in the area. By the 1950s, the district had a growing African American population, and oral accounts suggest that blacks and whites living there interacted only sparingly. Notably, there is little evidence that community leaders took steps to bridge the social gulf that separated blacks and whites who were living together on the east side. Robert Casey, who spent most of his childhood and adolescence on the east side, could not recall a "single effort" on the part of Immaculate Conception's leadership to reach out to the neighborhood's growing African American population. "Now, in the forties and the fifties, I believe a large number of African Americans had come up from the South and had settled in the streets between Immaculate Conception and the Oak Street Bridge," Casey said. "And yet, I remember there [were] no African Americans in my class, the class before me, or the class after me, or most classes, almost all classes." During the same period, Casey observed, scores of visiting priests entered classrooms "to talk about their missions in Africa and other places, and asking for donations from the parishioners to spread Catholicism around the world." It seemed "ironic," he added, that Catholic missionaries would "go halfway around the world to spread Catholicism," while the parish took no pains "to make Catholicism known to the African American families" in the vicinity of the Immaculate.[75] The reticence toward blacks that Casey described was common within urban Catholic enclaves throughout the northeastern United States. As recently as the late 1950s, when their neighborhoods were threatened with extinction by urban renewal projects, white Catholics who remained in the city continued to view demographic change as the single greatest threat to their way of life.[76]

Although racial prejudice was a factor in the cool reception awaiting some blacks as they moved into traditionally white neighborhoods such as those located on the east side, material considerations also came into play. The district's white residents, like their counterparts in larger northern cities, were probably concerned about the economic implications of demographic change. During the postwar era, whites throughout the urban North perceived a strong relationship between racial diversity and the depreciation of residential property values.[77] Most of them found it hard to grasp that the isolation of poor blacks in undesirable residential areas owed much to the policies and practices of the white establishment. Nevertheless, amid unparalleled levels of black migration from the South, institutionalized racial discrimination in housing markets played a crucial role in the postwar transformation of northern cities, as federal agencies like the Home Owners Loan Corporation issued low ratings to neighborhoods featuring racial diversity.[78] Meanwhile, urban whites were not alone in their concerns about the implications of demographic change. In an ironic twist, many established black urban dwellers became alarmed when scores of southern migrants arrived in their neighborhoods. Ronald P. Formisano, in his

analysis of Boston's "busing wars," noted that the postwar migration of southern blacks proved especially destabilizing for those African Americans who
had settled in northern cities decades earlier and, in many cases, were poised to
move into the middle classes. Formisano argued that the migration of thousands
of impoverished southern blacks to northern cities "caused the black population
as a whole to lose status and the quality of schools in black neighborhoods to
plummet."[79]

The plight of urban blacks, who found themselves in increasingly overcrowded neighborhoods, was compounded by a network of legally sanctioned
obstacles that consigned them to older housing stock in declining areas. In his
magisterial study of postwar Detroit, Thomas J. Sugrue described challenges
that urban blacks faced in any number of northern communities. "Although
Detroit had a stock of well-built if modest homes that blue-collar workers
could afford, blacks were systematically shut out of the private real estate
market," Sugrue wrote. "White real estate brokers shunned black clients and
encouraged restrictive covenants and other discriminatory practices that kept
blacks out of most of the city's single-family houses." Meanwhile, financial
institutions "seldom lent to black home buyers, abetted by federal housing
appraisal practices that ruled black neighborhoods to be dangerous risks for
mortgage subsidies and home loans." As a result, many black urban dwellers found themselves "trapped in the city's worst housing, in strictly segregated sections of the city." Such discriminatory policies "set into motion a
chain reaction that reinforced racial inequality," while appearing to confirm
northern whites' longstanding prejudices against blacks. At the outset of this
"vicious cycle," disadvantaged blacks "had to pay more for housing, thus
deepening their relative impoverishment." To make matters worse, these
home buyers were consigned to urban properties "in most need of ongoing
maintenance, repair, and rehabilitation," but they "could not get loans to
improve their properties." The inevitable deterioration of black neighborhoods, in turn, "offered seemingly convincing evidence to white homeowners
that blacks were feckless and irresponsible and fueled white fears that blacks
would ruin any white neighborhood that they moved into." In the final stage
of this vicious cycle, the poor condition of these neighborhoods "seemed
definitive proof to bankers that blacks were indeed a poor credit risk, and
justified disinvestment in predominantly minority neighborhoods."[80]

Black residential patterns in Youngstown generally conformed to patterns that Sugrue identified in postwar Detroit. As Thomas G. Fuechtmann
observed, Youngstown's neighborhoods became increasingly homogeneous
in the decades that followed World War II. He noted that, while the growth
of suburbs "tended to scatter steelworkers' places of residence over a wider
geographical area around the urban rim," the center city "became increas-

ingly occupied by black residents." The relatively limited housing options available to African Americans belied the fact that blacks had begun to settle in Youngstown in the early stages of its industrial development. Indeed, black residents were well established in the community by the mid-nineteenth century, decades before the arrival of large numbers of immigrants from southern and eastern Europe. Moreover, the African American community expanded dramatically in the early twentieth century, when thousands of black workers were drawn by opportunities in the steel industry. Fuechtmann noted that the steel industry brought several thousand southern blacks into Youngstown as strikebreakers during the 1919 steel strike. "Steel employment did provide an avenue for upward economic mobility," he added, "but, except for company housing, their residential location had been limited largely to the old ethnic neighborhoods of inner-city Youngstown, the largest concentration of blacks in the Youngstown-Warren area."[81] Unsurprisingly, the fact that 5,000 black laborers had arrived in Youngstown at the height of the national steel strike of 1919 became indelibly etched upon the collective memory of the area's white working classes. During the strike, white steelworkers were often demoralized at "the sight of smoke rising from the mills and the sound of whistles announcing the change of a shift" at the peak of the conflict.[82] Many of these local workers were immigrants from predominantly Catholic European countries.[83] The interracial tension fueled by such labor strife may have compounded the so-called shortage of housing available to African American workers.

That said, it was perhaps inevitable that white Catholic urban dwellers would come to fear the prospect of demographic change, given that northern whites, on the whole, linked black migration to urban decay. McGreevy noted that, for urban Catholics in the 1950s, "the stakes remained high," and the timing of changes that undermined the viability of their neighborhoods could not have been worse. "Exactly at the point of triumph, having weathered the Depression, built the school, and finished the church," McGreevy wrote, "Catholic parishes in the northern cities confronted the possibility that generations of painstaking work might be rendered obsolete in a few years."[84]

Nevertheless, Youngstown's center-city neighborhoods were spared the jarring racial tension and violence that accompanied demographic change in many other northern communities during the 1950s. Some local observers attribute the city's relatively calm racial climate to its modest size. Father Joseph Rudjak, an urban pastor who grew up in the multiracial north side neighborhoods of "Monkey's Nest" (also known as "Riverbend") and Brier Hill, aptly expressed this view. "What . . . made Youngstown great is that [we were] too small to isolate ourselves," Father Rudjak said. He went on to describe harmonious relationships among residents of the diverse, working-class neighborhoods in which he spent his youth. "We got along well," the pastor recalled. "Our attitude as a family was just enjoying . . . the people. . . . The D'Nunzio family yielded to the Futkos family—the Hungarian family. The Futkos family yielded to the Puerto Rican family." He referred to close and enduring friendships with African American and Latino neighbors.[85] As Sherry Lee Linkon and John Russo pointed out, however, "some of that community harmony was facilitated by careful maintenance of ethnic identities through churches, civic groups, and informal networks."[86] Even so, diverse neighborhoods like Brier Hill were bound to experience a degree of conflict, especially among adolescents. Youngstown native Tony Trolio recalled high levels of competition among members of the various ethnic and racial groups who made their home on the city's north side. In his popular history, *Brier Hill, USA,* Trolio noted that rivalries among Italian, Jewish, Irish, and black teenagers occasionally degenerated into "fisticuffs." The author treated these incidents lightly, however, attributing them to adolescent high spirits. He adopted a humorous tone when admitting to countless fights with the *medigones* (non-Italians). Trolio recalled that he often returned home "all bloodied and banged up," much to the consternation of his mother, who smacked him with a broom.[87]

Some observers, on the other hand, have seriously challenged the claim that postwar Youngstown was characterized by high levels of tolerance, especially where issues of race were concerned. African American author Mel Watkins, a onetime resident of the city, suggested that racism in Youngstown, while subtle, was practically ubiquitous. In spite of "the well-publicized gangland flare-ups, a pervading sense of tranquility cloaked Youngstown's quietly restrictive social arrangements," Watkins wrote. "Conformity reigned among both blacks and whites. It was as if everyone had determined to grasp and tenaciously hold on to a brief moment of calm and apparent order." This code of conformity was reinforced, Watkins suggested, by widespread fear over the likely alternative. "Peace, security, prosperity, and a superficial equanimity held sway," the author continued. "Somehow, at least unconsciously, everyone seemed to understand that the illusion or fabrication, like an inexpensive knit sweater, would completely unravel if even one loose strand were pulled too forcefully or examined with any real intensity."[88] In other words, the surface amicability which existed between blacks and whites in postwar Youngstown depended upon the maintenance of well-defined social boundaries.

Watkins illustrated the fragile nature of local race relations when he described an incident that occurred when he was enrolled at a neighborhood high school. As a student athlete (popularly known as "Pepper"), Watkins was on good terms with most of his white neighbors and classmates. One afternoon, a normally friendly Italian American shoemaker happened to be watching as the teenager strolled home with a white female classmate. When Watkins entered the shoemaker's shop a few days later, the proprietor "took time to share a bit of his Sicilian folk wisdom." Watkins "listened impatiently" as the shoemaker "wound through a seemingly friendly harangue, which ended with, 'You know, Pepper, I love you people. Give you the shirt off my back. You can have my clothes, my liquor, my money—but don't ever mess with *my* women!'" When Watkins responded with a comment the older man considered sarcastic, the shoemaker coldly turned his back on him. According to Watkins's memoir, the man never spoke to him again.[89] Watkins concluded that acceptance for blacks in 1950s Youngstown came at the price of smiling acquiescence to the vigorously maintained conventions of the white majority. In postwar Youngstown, such conventions included the segregation of various public spaces, including swimming pools.[90]

THE TRANSFORMATION OF THE EAST SIDE

By the 1960s, the neighborhood surrounding Immaculate Conception Parish was "changing" in a multitude of ways. Judith Magielski, who grew up on the east side during the 1950s, nostalgically described a tight-knit, mostly Italian American neighborhood that was studded with small, family-owned businesses, including the grocery store operated by her grandfather, Stephen Montella, a leading member of the parish. "We lived directly across from the grocery store," she recalled. "So, everything was really [within] walking distance. I walked to the church. I walked to school. And we always went home for lunch, because we were in the neighborhood."[91] Little more than a decade later, however, the construction of an interstate highway virtually bisected the neighborhood, wiping out blocks of housing and accelerating an ongoing decline in the parish's congregation.[92] Between the late 1960s and 1970s, the parish's membership fell from 1,500 people to 700 people.[93] At the same time, the district, which had become known as an Italian American enclave, seemed to be evolving into an African American neighborhood. Most of the area's newer residents were poorer than their predecessors had been; and with the advent of rising poverty, the east side seemed destined to resume its former status as a neglected outpost of the city.

These changes were apparent to many contemporary observers. In 1969, when Sister Teresa Winsen, OSU, was transferred from the south side parish school of St. Patrick's to Immaculate Conception Elementary School, she was startled by the differences she observed between the two institutions.[94] At the Immaculate, endemic poverty, combined with demographic changes that reduced the number of Catholic residents, fueled a trend toward declining enrollment. As the decade came to a close, it became difficult to imagine that, as recently as the fall of 1960, Immaculate Conception had opened with a peak enrollment of 693 students. By the time Sister Teresa arrived in 1969, enrollment had slipped to a paltry 411 students. Possibly, more optimistic observers perceived the decline in Immaculate Conception's enrollment as a temporary development. Over the years, the school's sagging enrollment showed occasional signs of turning around, and administrators may have been encouraged by modest spikes that were recorded in the early 1960s. Between 1963 and 1964, for instance, student numbers rose from 645 to 665. Such short-lived boosts in enrollment, however, did little to offset a rather insistent downward trend.[95]

As she assumed her duties at Immaculate Conception, Sister Teresa also took note of the school's growing diversity. Although statistical data on the ethnic and racial composition of the institution's student body are incomplete, an informal survey of parents who had children enrolled in the school was conducted by the institution's administrators in the late 1960s. The results of the survey suggested that most of the Catholic students enrolled at the school were Italian Americans, while those of Irish ancestry comprised the second-largest ethnic group. Only 14 percent of the 266 sets of parents who responded to the survey indicated they were African Americans; but this result may be misleading, given that about 35 percent of survey participants failed to respond to this question. Another (admittedly crude) indicator of the school's diversity might be the shrinking number of parents who indicated they were Catholic. Only 162 (or 61 percent) of the male parents who responded to the survey described themselves as Catholic, while 187 (or 70 percent) of the female parents did so.[96] (The reasons behind this apparent disparity in religious affiliation between male and female parents are unclear. Perhaps such disparity reflected a sharp rise in interreligious marriages.) The apparent drop in the percentage (and absolute number) of Catholic families with children enrolled in the school underscored another challenge facing the Immaculate—a decline in the number of parishioners, which, of course, translated into fewer donations at the parish level.

The challenges facing Immaculate Conception School did not stop there. These trends coincided with another development: rising operational costs among diocesan schools. At this stage, teachers' salaries were probably a minor factor in the institution's escalating expenses, given that most lay instructors were parishioners who received modest remuneration for their services. Salary agreements were often worked out between teachers and the pastor, and lay teachers at schools like Immaculate Conception were paid little more than their religious counterparts, whose salaries were virtually stipends. Still, the growing percentage of lay teachers ensured that expenses required to meet instructors' salaries would continue to rise. Furthermore, salary increases at diocesan secondary schools intensified pressures on parish schools to boost their teachers' salaries. As the *Vindicator* reported in 1969, diocesan high schools were paying lay teachers "95 percent of the public high school salary schedule." The same article noted that the modest salaries of teaching nuns would be supplemented over time: "Salaries for nuns are to be increased from $1,400 to $1,800 as of Sept. 1, 1969, to $2,200 in September, 1970, and to $2,500 in September, 1971."[97]

The astonishingly low rate of pay afforded religious instructors highlights the significance of a growing trend among Catholic elementary and secondary schools—a substantial increase in the number, and percentage, of lay instructors.[98] As Sister Charlotte Italiano noted, "the success of the Catholic school system in the United States . . . was on the backs of the nuns."[99] This is scarcely an exaggeration. According to a 1952 survey conducted by the National Catholic Education Association (NCEA), 45 percent of the participating religious communities reported "that the cost of supporting a sister at a basic level exceeded the amount of her teaching stipend." A close examination of this figure reveals that many religious communities "were subsidizing Catholic school systems rather than the other way around."[100] Thus, it should come as no surprise that the arrival into the classroom of large numbers of lay teachers, who required greater remuneration, placed a considerable strain on parish schools.

In 1970, Sister Mary Conroy, OSU, a faculty member at Youngstown State University, drew a strong correlation between declining religious instructors in the classroom and the upward trend of parochial school operational expenses. She noted that diocesan school salaries, which totaled $917,000 in 1965, had risen to $1,882,000 in 1970. In an interview with the *Vindicator,* Sister Mary attributed this rise largely to the fact that a growing number of lay teachers received "95 per cent of the scale paid public school teachers in the district where the Catholic high schools are located."[101] Notably, this trend was hardly restricted to the Youngstown area. Its impact was felt throughout the United States. "There is a pathetic shortage of religious teachers caused by lack of vocations, those leaving the sisterhood, and religious sisters going into other fields of work," observed historian Harold A. Buetow, writing in 1970. "Catholic schools must face daily the need to make savings brought about by the increased faculty salaries, of lay teachers in particular." Buetow added that, by 1960, "the number of lay teachers increased by 537% over the 7,422 lay teachers in the Catholic schools of 1948."[102]

A trend toward laicization of the teaching staff was clearly reflected at the Immaculate. Traditionally, the parish school's staff had been dominated by members of religious teaching orders, who accepted what would be considered today as subsistence wages. By 1969, however, two-thirds of Immaculate Conception Elementary School's teachers were members of the laity. Apart from longtime instructor Marion Steadman, a fixture at the Immaculate since 1929, the lay teachers were relatively recent hires. Only one of them had been teaching at the school for more than five years, and two of the lay teachers had been hired for that academic year.[103] Perhaps the economic impact of such personnel changes was softened at the earliest stages, given that local parish schools were relieved of the responsibility of providing transportation to students. The provision of public transportation to students of nonpublic schools in the mid-1960s was an outcome of the 1947 Supreme Court decision *Everson v. Board of Education,* which ruled in favor of the constitutionality of a New Jersey law that made such services available.[104] Financial pressures on Catholic schools were also mitigated by the Ohio State Board of Education's decision in 1969 to provide salary assistance to instructors at nonpublic schools. This law, overturned by the U.S. Supreme Court in 1975, stipulated that supplemental salaries would "not exceed $600 per classroom hour, $3,000 a year, or 85 per cent of the total nonpublic school aid from the state."[105] Nevertheless, growing operational expenses were taking a toll on many urban parochial schools, even those that provided modest salaries to lay teachers.

Given that the Diocese of Youngstown was unprepared to provide much in the way of additional funding to ailing urban parish schools, the principals of these institutions were eventually forced to resort to unorthodox strategies (including citywide fund-raising efforts and grant-writing campaigns) to maintain operations. A growing number of these institutions were also taking steps to ensure that educational services were available to underprivileged children in the neighborhood, many of whom had no connection to the parish. Sister Teresa apparently had few rivals in the areas of fund-raising and community outreach. Apart from raising money to establish a school scholarship fund, she visited homes to get a clearer picture of challenges facing the district's poor families. "As an administrator, I found it necessary to provide donations and services to the poorer families in the area," Sister Teresa recalled. "To get an idea of the poverty that existed among those families, I really needed to visit the homes." She was startled at the level of material deprivation she encountered in some households. "I remember visiting one home, and the children said to me, 'We have no food,'" she recalled. "Well, I couldn't believe that, so I said, 'Let's look in the cupboard,' and there was nothing—absolutely nothing. I returned to the school and collected extra lunches for these children."[106]

During this period, Sister Teresa's administration took an active interest in the surrounding neighborhood—a development that echoed Father Kenny's tireless lobbying for the construction of the Oak Street Bridge in the early twentieth century. At the beginning of 1970, the parish school became a force in municipal politics, when Sister Teresa helped to call attention to the district's substandard infrastructure. Visits to students' homes had brought her face-to-face with problems that demanded the city's intervention. The principal recalled entering one home in which "there were no water lines and no lavatories." When she inquired about a restroom, a resident "showed me a room with several buckets."[107] With a sense of urgency, Sister Teresa alerted Youngstown Mayor Jack C. Hunter and the local city council about the need to install sewer lines in some of the poorer neighborhoods surrounding Immaculate Conception Parish.[108] The *Vindicator* reported that "she made a personal investigation of conditions in the area and found them appalling." Sister Teresa said she found "some occupied homes without toilet facilities of any type, others with defective septic tanks, and some without water, sewers, or toilet facilities." The same article noted that Dr. William Greissenger, Youngstown's health commissioner, presented a map to the Youngstown City Council that revealed that "about a dozen streets" in the environs of Immaculate Conception Parish were "without sewers or water lines or . . . both." Greissenger described the situation as "a health hazard."[109]

Looking back on this episode, Sister Teresa praised municipal leaders for their response, in language that reflected her commitment to the neighborhood. She recalled that her first opportunity to alert the city to conditions on the east side arose when Second Ward Councilman "Pete" Starks, a leader in Youngstown's black community, invited her to speak before a caucus of the City Council. "When I begged for sewer lines and water lines on the east side, the municipal government listened," she said. "We had to be the advocates and voice for the poor."[110] Paradoxically, most of the homes in question had been built only a few years beforehand. For reasons that remain unclear, these newer homes were erected in areas that lacked access to existing water lines, and no attempt had been made to extend water lines to these neighborhoods. The east side residents who lived in these dwellings were overwhelmingly poor, and most of them were black.

In some respects, the social commitments reflected in Sister Teresa's actions underscored a shift in the mission of American Catholic education. U.S. Catholic schools had already witnessed sweeping structural changes, which went into effect in the late 1950s and early 1960s. Monsignor O'Neill C. D'Amour, then assistant secretary of the NCEA, proposed that "altered political and social realities called for separating the pastoral from the professional in Catholic schools and for establishing lay boards with policy-making powers." In 1972, following the social and political upheavals that precipitated a reevaluation of the traditional model of Catholic education, U.S. bishops issued a pastoral letter titled,

"To Teach As Jesus Did," which outlined the "threefold purpose of Catholic education among children and young people" in the following terms: "1) to teach doctrine, the message of hope contained in the gospel; 2) to build community, 'not simply as a concept to be taught but as a reality to be lived'; and 3) [to provide] service to all mankind, which emanated from the sense of Christian community."[111] This concept of Catholic education, with its emphasis on service to the larger community, was, to some extent, presaged by the activities of urban educators like Sister Teresa.

As the decade progressed, both the Immaculate and its south side neighbor, St. Patrick's, were categorized as "inner-city" parochial schools, a term that revealed less about the institutions' respective locations than it did about the demographic characteristics of their surrounding neighborhoods. Over time, the term "inner city" was applied to more urban parish schools, as they showed qualities that were plainly evident at institutions like Immaculate Conception School. Such characteristics included declining parish contributions, growing numbers of low-income neighbors, and a larger percentage of non-Catholic students with minority backgrounds. Surprisingly, even as the Immaculate struggled with the material challenges that faced other urban institutions, the school gained positive attention for its innovative educational programs. In 1970, the year Sister Teresa had lobbied the municipal government for sewage and water lines on the city's east side, she conferred with Dr. James Steele, a professor at Youngstown State University's Department of Education, on a plan to implement a pilot program called Individually Guided Education (IGE).[112] Youngstown State University had received a grant through the Kettering Foundation of Dayton, Ohio, to train educators in urban schools. When the program was implemented two years later, Immaculate Conception was the only parochial institution out of six schools selected to participate in the program.[113] Within a year, Sister Teresa became one of the community's most visible proponents of the IGE program, an approach to curricula designed to help students learn at their own pace. In 1973, she secured a foundational grant to attend the third annual international seminar on individualized curriculum in Amsterdam, Holland. The following year, in 1974, the principal shared her experiences with local educators at a teachers' workshop.[114] Significantly, by the mid-1970s, Immaculate Conception Elementary School had gained regional recognition for its implementation of the IGE program. "Immaculate Conception became the model school for the city of Youngstown—and beyond," Sister Teresa recalled. "People came from all parts of the state to see what we were doing at Immaculate."[115]

Overall, the IGE program was in sync with student-centered approaches to education that swept public schools during the late 1960s and early 1970s. Five years earlier, in 1969, Herbert R. Kohl's groundbreaking handbook, *The Open*

Classroom, questioned "authoritarian" approaches to teaching and student evaluation. "Tests are made to measure one student against another student or to measure a student's performance against some standard which is to be expected of him," Kohl's text advised. "When a teacher abandons the notion that all students must live up to some given standards, or have their worth measured against the worth of other students, new means of evaluating a student's work must be developed."[116] As she hastened to point out, Sister Teresa did not wholeheartedly embrace the trends that were then sweeping public education. "Now bear in mind, I didn't apply every aspect of the [IGE] program," Sister Teresa said. "I didn't believe in tearing down walls; but I applied other aspects of the program, and the whole city knew about what we were doing."[117]

Given that Sister Teresa often worked closely with public school counterparts in local workshops, the parish school's participation in the IGE program opened new avenues of cooperation between public and private schools. She later evaluated the rapport among representatives of public and private schools as "excellent." Sister Teresa stated that, in her view, Youngstown Schools Superintendent Robert Pegues "was concerned about the children, showing no bias against private religious schools."[118] When viewed in the context of the period, the principal's willingness to work closely with public educators highlights the extent to which parochial schools were influenced by their public counterparts in the wake of Vatican II. This is not to suggest that cooperation between public and private schools was nonexistent beforehand. Sister Mary Jerome Leavy, OSB, in her unpublished dissertation, observed that U.S. public and parochial schools had enjoyed a symbiotic relationship since the late nineteenth century. The U.S. hierarchy, Sister Mary Jerome argued, "created a school system which is parallel to the one created by legislators; they did not establish an alternative form of schooling in America."[119] Nevertheless, the interrelationship between public and private schools became more pronounced in the 1970s, as Catholic parochial schools—despite their image as bastions of traditional education—served as "laboratories" for innovative teaching strategies. The IGE program that Sister Teresa implemented at Immaculate Conception was introduced at other local parochial schools, beginning with St. Brendan's Elementary School on the city's west side.[120]

Ultimately, Immaculate Conception's much-deserved recognition for academic excellence served as a bright spot in an increasingly gloomy landscape for local parish schools. Schools operating in Youngstown's oldest neighborhoods were especially vulnerable, and some battled for their very survival. In spring 1972, the city's premier parish school, St. Columba's, was forced to close its doors when the surrounding neighborhood was practically eradicated by a combination of urban renewal projects. During the late 1960s and early 1970s, large swaths of the residential district north of Youngstown State University were razed to accommodate projects that included the construction of Interstate 680, an urban beltway built as part of the national interstate highway development program. As Linkon and Russo noted, "The promised residential and commercial development resulting from the construction of I-680 never occurred in the city, but the suburbs boomed." Indeed, the highway project virtually isolated the city's traditional center, "directing drivers, and more important, shoppers to the new strip malls being built by two rising local families, the DeBartolos and the Cafaros."[121] Unsurprisingly, influential support for urban renewal and public works projects frequently trumped the concerns of neighborhood residents, nearby shopkeepers, and members of the clergy. In May 1971, when a public hearing was scheduled regarding a proposed ordinance that would close a large section of Elm Street (a main artery on the city's north side) to facilitate an $11 million university expansion project, a *Vindicator* article highlighted statements of support from the chancellor of the Ohio Board of Regents and the president of the Youngstown Area Board of Realtors. The same article made brief mention of the fact that the proposal was "vigorously opposed" by north side residents.[122] North side native Paula McKinney recalled that, in the 1960s, her own mother was approached by university representatives, who pressured her to relocate. "It was like she was a two-year-old," Mrs. McKinney said. When her mother sought the advice of an attorney, he supposedly offered this blunt advice: "I think, if you're smart, you'll take the money and run. They'll pull eminent domain on you, either way."[123]

Local Catholic leaders, who were apparently hesitant to criticize popular public works projects, downplayed the impact of urban renewal on Catholic institutions. Diocesan officials assured local Catholics that the needs of students affected by the school's closure would be addressed, and they announced that St. Columba's would be consolidated with Immaculate Conception and St. Edward's schools. These officials most likely grasped that the problem of declining enrollment was not limited to Youngstown's center city. A newspaper article on the consolidation of St. Columba's with two other parish schools noted that enrollment among all schools of the six-county diocese was dropping "because of a declining birth rate and tuition costs."[124] For center-city parishes, such trends intersected with sweeping demographic changes (and the unintended consequences of urban renewal) to produce overwhelming economic challenges.

THE PAROCHIAL SCHOOL FUNDING CRISIS

Economic difficulties recorded at center-city parishes like Immaculate Conception were reflective of a larger trend. In an atmosphere informed by deepening economic strain, Monsignor Benedict Franzetta, the diocesan treasurer, released a financial report indicating that the Diocese of Youngstown was barely solvent. In February 1972, Monsignor Franzetta reported that the diocese had an income of $22,160,000 for the fiscal year ending on June 30, 1971, while it incurred expenses totaling $21,900,000. He emphasized that more than 50 percent of these expenses were related to the maintenance of the 73 elementary schools and 6 high schools then operating within the 6-county diocese.[125] In truth, pressures related to the rising cost of Catholic schools had arisen much earlier. Throughout the 1960s, diocesan officials actively pursued state funding and sought to strengthen their case by publicizing the extent to which Catholic schools alleviated the public's tax burden. If Catholic schools were to suddenly close their doors, the officials argued, former students of these institutions would automatically enroll in neighboring public schools, a development that would drive up the cost of maintaining public education. In a 1969 fact sheet titled, " . . . On Catholic Schools," the diocese reported that Mahoning County's 30 Catholic schools (which served 17,090 students in the 1968–1969 school year) saved taxpayers $9,672,940.00. According to the fact sheet, the 6-county diocese's 84 Catholic schools, with 41,909 students, saved taxpayers $23,720,494.00.[126]

Initially, the diocese appeared to have a good chance of securing state aid. In August 1969, the *Vindicator* reported that a bill passed by the Ohio General Assembly would deliver more than $2 million to Catholic schools in the Diocese of Youngstown over the 1969–1970 and 1970–1971 school years. "On the basis of an anticipated enrollment of 41,909 pupils in the six-county diocese," the *Vindicator* reported, "the diocese will get $2,095,450 or $50 a pupil." Monsignor William A. Hughes, then diocesan superintendent of schools, lauded the bill's passage, commenting that the Ohio Senate and House's bipartisan support for the legislation "showed a keen understanding on the part of our elected officials of the great contribution that parochial schools make in each community."[127] As a growing number of U.S. private schools received state and federal assistance, however, some observers began to question the constitutionality of this aid. In fall 1970, for instance, a front-page story in *The Wall Street Journal* cited Cardinal Mooney High School, on Youngstown's south side, "as an example of a nonpublic school operating under state and federal aid." The story warned that the wall between church and state appeared to be "crumbling," while highlighting the fact that the U.S. Supreme Court was poised to hear "a landmark case in which the constitutionality of Pennsylvania's $20-million-a-year aid program to private schools is being challenged." The article added that the "most heated opposition to public aid to nonpublic schools has arisen in states with sizable Catholic populations," given that aid packages in these states "would amount to millions of dollars."[128]

Within six months of the story's publication, the diocese's efforts to shore up Catholic schools were dealt a severe blow. In May 1971, a U.S. Supreme Court ruling that state aid to nonpublic schools was unconstitutional raised questions about the continued viability of parochial and diocesan schools in the Diocese of Youngstown. Nevertheless, Youngstown Bishop James W. Malone stated that no schools in the diocese would be closed down "as a retaliatory measure to the U.S. Supreme Court decision," and he vowed to honor teacher contracts. The bishop did, however, emphasize the need for extreme measures to preserve Catholic education. In July 1971, Bishop Malone informed parents that a $100 tuition fee would be introduced at all diocesan schools to help them "meet the challenges of the immediate future." In a meeting with almost 1,000 parents at Ursuline High School, on the city's north side, Bishop Malone, Monsignor Hughes, and Assistant Superintendent John J. Augenstein "stressed the importance of maintaining levels of enrollment and expressed optimism over the chances of state reimbursement."[129]

Predictably, plans to introduce tuition at all diocesan parish schools met resistance from parents, some of whom warned that such a policy would drive down enrollment even further. Among these parents was Martin "Jack" O'Connell, who attended a meeting led by diocesan officials at John F. Kennedy High School, located in nearby Warren, Ohio, during the summer of 1971. "I had five children at St. Rose [Elementary School in Girard, Ohio], at the time," O'Connell said, "and tuition was quite a burden to me, and to many, many other people." At one point, O'Connell stood up, addressed the bishop, and described what he considered a viable alternative to the introduction of tuition. O'Connell recommended that the diocese require parents of parochial school students to make a direct (and tax-deductible) donation to the church. "Well . . . some other priest said [he] didn't think that was right," O'Connell recalled. "That [plan] was a 'charade.' . . . And, well, I don't remember the whole conversation, but it was, shall I say . . . a spirited dialogue."[130] This response is not surprising, given that O'Connell's plan, while ingenious, might have created legal problems for parishes across the diocese. Furthermore, his recommendation conflicted with the diocese's plans to promote legislation designed to alleviate the financial burden of parents with children attending parochial schools.

In August 1971, diocesan officials publicly endorsed a bill to establish state grants that would reimburse parents who made "bona fide payments for their children attending parochial schools."[131] As the *Vindicator* later reported, the legislation was expected to provide "reimbursements of $90 per pupil for parents of nonpublic school children."[132] The legal counsel of the Catholic Conference of Ohio (CCO), in an effort to facilitate the process, issued guidelines to guarantee the "constitutionality" of the proposed legislation. The CCO's guidelines to safeguard "the principle of bona fide tuition payment by . . . parents" included the following: (1) parishes should "not lend money to the parents for tuition payment"; (2) parishes should "not take a special collection with the intent of giving the proceeds of the parents for their tuition payment"; (3) parishes should "not accept notes of promise to pay tuition in lieu of tuition payment"; (4) parishes should "not guarantee to return tuition paid by parents if the expected new state aid-to-parents legislation fails"; (5) parishes should "not arrange for the endorsement of parental grant checks from state funds"; (6) parishes should "not form a credit union with church money to parents for tuition payment."[133]

Despite pockets of resistance to such legislation, particularly from the American Civil Liberties Union (ACLU), diocesan officials expressed confidence that the "present type of aid-educational grants to parents will meet the test of constitutionality both in Ohio and with the U.S. Supreme Court."[134] In the wake of an ACLU lawsuit challenging the reimbursement plan, diocesan officials gained the influential support of Ohio Governor John J. Gilligan. Governor Gilligan argued that, in the absence of additional public aid to "financially troubled" private schools, taxpayers in Ohio might be compelled to pay an additional $200 million a year, that is, "if they had to finance schooling for children currently in private schools." The governor's vote of confidence, however, was not enough to guarantee the plan's implementation—especially if serious questions arose about its constitutionality. In a decision rendered on April 17, 1972, the U.S. District Court in Columbus "ruled out reimbursements of $90 per pupil for parents of nonpublic school children." On the same day, the U.S. Supreme Court upheld a federal court ruling in St. Louis, Missouri, that "a state is constitutionally entitled to forbid use of any public funds to support a school controlled by a religious denomination."[135]

Diocesan officials responded to the rulings with expressions of shock and dismay. In a press conference, Monsignor Hughes stated that the federal court's decision "was difficult to understand," given that "the Supreme Court has in the past recognized the right of a parent to choose the school he wishes his child to attend and set standards which the nonpublic system must meet." Monsignor Hughes added that he was especially concerned "for those with large families and the poor who will suffer most from the court's denial of tuition reimbursement." The diocesan superintendent affirmed, however, that the fight for public assistance would continue. He noted that "a federal income tax credit plan" had won the support of Arkansas Senator Wilbur Mills and then Michigan Senator Gerald R. Ford, the Senate majority leader. In addition, the Ohio governor's administration, along with a number of Ohio legislators, was "considering a system of state income tax credits for parents of nonpublic school students."[136]

Conspicuously absent from the debate over public aid to private schools were traditional accusations that Catholic schools, in particular, posed a threat to a pluralistic democratic society. "The struggle over public funding for parochial schools in the postwar decades was calm and orderly compared with the previous three decades," noted Catholic historian Timothy Walch. "Gone were the accusations that parish schooling was un-American and therefore unworthy of community support."[137] In Ohio, the ACLU's legal battle focused squarely on potential violations of the First Amendment. Likewise, federal judges who reviewed the case restricted their comments to this issue. All parties in the legal struggle refrained from making allegations that parochial schools were a divisive influence. Indeed, federal judges John W. Peck, Joseph P. Kinneary, and Carl B. Rubin, who determined that the reimbursement plan was unconstitutional, took pains to express their appreciation of the potential benefits of private schooling. In their 34-page decision, the judges made clear that their ruling was based strictly on their understanding of the Constitution's requirements: "However much we may approve, however much we may respect, however much we may admire the role of nonpublic education, we cannot substitute such approval, respect and admiration for the plain language of the First Amendment of the United States Constitution." Although the three judges acknowledged that "parochial schools offer only one hour a day in religious instruction, while providing five hours daily in nonreligious courses," they reiterated their view that Ohio's private sectarian schools "retain a substantial religious purpose and denominational character."[138]

The Ohio judges—citing a 1971 U.S. Supreme Court ruling on public aid for private schools in Pennsylvania and Rhode Island—revealed that they were "guided by three elements" the Court considered essential to justify assistance for nonpublic schools. These elements were as follows: (1) "The aid and its method of distribution must have a secular legislative purpose"; (2) "Aid must, as its primary effect, neither advance nor inhibit religion"; (3) "Assistance must not foster 'an excessive government entanglement with religion.'" The Court took issue with the main argument presented by the plan's defenders, which asserted "that parents of nonpublic school students contribute to [the] overall economic benefit of the state." The federal judges responded that, if economic benefit were regarded as "the sole and controlling factor of a statute's constitutionality, any direct aid to church-related enterprises could be justified." Under such conditions, the First Amendment's "separation requirement" would become "a hollow shell," they concluded.[139]

While these legal battles over public aid to parochial schools were less acrimonious than those of the past, the effects of the court rulings proved deeply problematic for many of Youngstown's parish schools. The institution of tuition at all diocesan schools had the detrimental effect on enrollment that many observers had predicted; and in September 1972, the *Vindicator* reported that parish schools in the six-county diocese expected 2,249 fewer students than were enrolled in the previous school year. The article noted that diocesan elementary school enrollment, which was recorded at 23,473 in fall 1971, was expected to drop to 21,224 in fall 1972. In Youngstown alone, elementary and secondary schools predicted a loss of 695 students, given that enrollment was expected to fall from 5,937 in 1971 to 5,242 in 1972. The declining birth rate was evidently a substantial factor in this development, and the *Vindicator* reported that this decline was "indicated by figures showing that 2,993 eighth graders graduated last June and only 2,225 first graders are entering parochial schools in this area of Ohio this week, a drop of 768 students." The article added, however, that the drop in enrollment owed much to the introduction of tuition at all parish schools in the diocese.[140]

The adverse effects of falling enrollment were most apparent among the diocese's center-city parochial schools. Despite rising economic challenges, however, the diocese appeared reluctant to close these institutions. In February 1973, the diocesan school board announced its refusal to act on a tentative plan to shut down Sacred Heart of Jesus Elementary School, located in a declining neighborhood on the city's east side. The board instead determined that it would develop "provisional resolutions to eliminate grades one through five of Sacred Heart." The *Vindicator* reported that Sacred Heart was not the only ailing parish school operating in Youngstown. On the city's rapidly deteriorating south side, once-vibrant St. Patrick's Elementary School also faced financial difficulties.[141] Within four days of the meeting on the fate of Sacred Heart, the board gathered to discuss the future of St. Patrick's, one of two urban institutions in the diocese that stood on the brink of insolvency. (The other was St. Benedict's Elementary School, in Canton, Ohio.) Bishop Malone, in an apparent effort to influence the board's decision, stressed the church's responsibility to the poor. Among others, Bishop Malone stated that there was an urgent need for Catholics to move beyond a concept of responsibility that focused exclusively on delivering services "where we live." "Geographical boundaries do not divide us ideologically," the bishop said. In line with the bishop's recommendations, the board voted unanimously in favor of a resolution to keep St. Patrick's operational for at least three years, "subject to an annual review of the financial situation and enrollment."[142]

During the same meeting, the board indicated a stronger commitment to urban parish schools that were likely to serve the poor. Board members approved a resolution stating that the diocese would "have a commitment to continue to provide Catholic education in those schools of the diocese that serve poverty areas and provide this education as a missionary service of the church." In addition, the board agreed to set up a 15-member committee "to determine which schools are in poverty areas, what type of aid might be given and what students are to be served." The committee was charged with recommending policy decisions "regarding schools with increasing proportions of non-Catholics; regarding schools in parishes no longer able to meet all of their financial obligations, and schools serving the poor in increasing numbers."[143]

As the diocese struggled to balance its economic concerns with its expressed commitment to support troubled urban parish schools, the new school superintendent, John J. Augenstein, continued his predecessor's legislative battle for a share of Ohio's educational funding. During Augenstein's tenure, the diocese experienced greater success in this effort. Shortly after the state's tuition reimbursement plan was ruled unconstitutional, Ohio lawmakers developed a funding plan to subsidize "auxiliary services" in the state's nonpublic schools, and by fall 1974, diocesan schools were beginning to enjoy the benefits of the new plan. In September of that year, the Youngstown Board of Education accepted a check for $681,888 from the Ohio Board of Education, which was earmarked to support auxiliary services for the city's Catholic schools. The *Vindicator* reported that the amount represented "just half the total $1,363,776 that will come to diocesan schools in the 1974–75 school year."[144]

As anticipated, the ACLU challenged the funding plan, claiming that it violated the First Amendment "by promoting an advancement of religion and by fostering an excessive entanglement between church and state."[145] This time, however, the ACLU's efforts to block state assistance to private religious schools proved less successful. In 1975, the *Vindicator* reported that "the amount of money given for auxiliary services continued to grow throughout the year." The *Vindicator* article observed that, for the first time in years, "state funds may be used to purchase physical education equipment for non-public students as long as this equipment is for general use and not permanently attached to non-public buildings."[146] Notably, the efforts of Ohio's Catholic educators to secure meaningful public assistance reflected a nationwide trend. "The unwillingness of the Catholic community to abandon its cause was evident in the number of church-state-school cases filed with the [U.S. Supreme] Court during the rest of the decade," Walch noted. "Legislatures in Pennsylvania, New York, and Ohio persisted in passing legislation that granted goods and services to parochial school students; and in many cases, the Court passed judgment on the constitutionality of these services."[147] Finally, in 1977, the Supreme Court ruled in *Wolman v. Walter* that the State of Ohio could legally "provide standardized testing, diagnostic services, therapeutic work, and remedial instruction to parochial school students if these services were provided away from school grounds."[148]

In the interim, the Diocese of Youngstown benefited from limited public assistance that targeted students from low-income backgrounds. In the mid-

1970s, the diocese received educational assistance under the Title I provisions of the Elementary and Secondary Education Act of 1965, which provided "special services to economically and educationally deprived children." In June 1975, Nicholas Wolsonovich, then director of government programs and resource development for diocesan schools, noted that the diocese reported 3,148 students from low-income families in its 72 elementary and secondary schools. Nearly half of these students, he added, "reside within Mahoning County, especially Youngstown City School District." Wolsonovich pointed out that "inner-city" Catholic school enrollments were "almost 100 per cent low income and in some cases, half of them are non-Catholic and from various ethnic backgrounds." These figures, he concluded, reflected "the church's strong commitment to serve the poor and the many different races and ethnic backgrounds which make up the community."[149] While supplementary aid alleviated the economic problems of some urban parish schools, the fate of others remained uncertain. In time, the future of beleaguered center-city parish schools like Immaculate Conception would be debated by members of the increasingly divided diocesan school board.

THE FIGHT TO PRESERVE CENTER-CITY PARISH SCHOOLS

The question of how the diocese should respond to economically strapped urban parochial schools was complicated by a trend that overlapped with those of rising costs and declining parish contributions. In 1977, the *Vindicator* reported that 8.2 percent of the 10,408 students enrolled in Mahoning County's Catholic schools were members of minority groups, and 8.2 percent were also non-Catholics. Again, most of the schools with large numbers of nonwhite and non-Catholic students were based in Youngstown's center city. The article stated:

> Having the highest per cent of minority students are: St. Patrick [on the city's south side] with 68.2 per cent or 165 children, representing 145 blacks and 20 with Spanish surnames; Immaculate Conception [on the east side] with 43.0 per cent or 141,124 of whom are black and 17 have Spanish surnames; St. Stanislaus [on the south side], 37.7 per cent or 78 children, of whom 65 are black and 17 have Spanish surnames; and Sacred Heart [on the south side] with 32.4 per cent or 66 children, 43 of whom are black, 18, Spanish surnamed, four, oriental, and one, American Indian.

According to the *Vindicator,* non-Catholic enrollment at Immaculate Conception was 43 percent, or 142 students. This compared to 52 percent (or 126 students) at St. Patrick's, 40 percent (or 83 students) at St. Stanislaus, and 21 percent (or 44 students) at Sacred Heart.[150] Immaculate Conception's inclusion on a list of the diocese's most diverse parish schools would have serious implications for its future. The fact that the school served a large percentage of non-Catholic students apparently influenced the diocesan school board's decision in autumn 1976 to reject an appeal by the Immaculate's pastor, Father John Summers, to secure additional funding.

Earlier in 1976, Father Summers proposed a modest increase of taxes for parishes throughout the Diocese of Youngstown to benefit struggling center-city schools like the Immaculate, which served large numbers of underprivileged children. According to the plan, the heaviest tax burden would fall upon those parishes that did not maintain their own schools. Advocates of Father Summers's proposal included former diocesan school superintendent and then Auxiliary Bishop William Hughes, who urged the board to adopt the plan immediately. "The church has an obligation to be interested in the minority and underprivileged peoples," Bishop Hughes said. "How better to provide them help than to educate them rather than through other social programs?" Opponents of Father Summers's proposal outnumbered its supporters, however. Furthermore, the opposition was led by none other than the chair of the diocesan finance committee, Raymond Pelanda, a resident of nearby Canton, Ohio. Pelanda's argument to reject the plan seemingly boiled down to the following admonition: diocesan funding proposals should be designed to meet the needs of all parish schools, not specific ones. In this vein, he urged board members to weigh the idealism behind the Immaculate's mission against the sobering economic realities then pressing down on other diocesan parish schools. In the course of the meeting, Pelanda stressed that economic pressures had intensified amid increased salary demands by parochial school teachers and administrators. The diocese, he stated, should not lose sight of its obligation to "provide education for our children in all our churches, not only for those who are poor." While he acknowledged a need to "be sensitive to the needs of all private schools," Pelanda quickly added, "our backs are against the wall." The finance chair's position enjoyed the prestigious support of the board's former president, Father Robert Brentgartner, who cautioned, "Priests are all for helping the poor and non-Catholics, but we would like to see the people voluntarily do this, rather than have added tax imposed upon them." While Pelanda himself refrained from citing the large number of non-Catholic students at the parish school as a factor in his opposition to the funding plan, an ally on the board drew attention to this detail, observing that "of the 327 children enrolled at Immaculate Conception, 186 are Catholic and 144, non-Catholic." The finance chair presumably represented the position of other opponents of the proposal when he stressed that members of disadvantaged minority groups had access to public education. "If there were no public schools in Youngstown, I would think differently," Pelanda said. "The poor and minorities can get an education in the public schools. We are backed up to the wall." The finance chair concluded his comments dramatically. "If the Lord has not provided for everyone, how can we?" he said. "I hear much rebelling."[151] The undercurrent of frustration in Pelanda's statement reflected his evident conviction that it would be unreasonable for the diocese to ask parishioners to subsidize the education of non-Catholics when the future of the parochial school system itself seemed uncertain.

The finance chair and his allies were swiftly challenged, however. Arguing in favor of Father Summers's proposal was board member Ronald Garmey, who emphasized the diocese's "responsibility" to reach out to the poor. A parish council president and father of four, Garmey fit the profile of local Catholics who would be most affected by a diocesan tax increase. If his suburban parish were made responsible for additional taxes to the diocese, this would leave fewer funds for the operation of the parish school his own children attended. Nevertheless, Garmey insisted that this was a small price to pay to further the cause of "social justice." As the recently elected chair of the North Mahoning Deanery, a diocesan district comprising Youngstown and the adjacent suburb of Austintown, Garmey argued that the Immaculate required more assistance than the deanery alone could provide. He added that the center-city parish had taken all available steps to support its school, channeling 77 percent of its budget toward the school's operation while charging "the maximum tuition of $250 to its pupils." Still, the parish could not "continue to operate the school without going into debt." A diocesan-wide prorated tax was therefore essential to keep the school open. Garmey concluded that spreading the tax thinly across the diocese would guarantee that individual parishes experienced modest increases of 0.5 to 3 percent. These rates would depend on whether a parish maintained a school or provided support to diocesan high schools. The *Vindicator* summarized the taxation plan as follows: "Parishes with their own schools and also high school assessments, would pay .5 per cent increase, while those with schools, but no high school assessment, would pay one per cent; parishes without schools, but with high school assessment, would pay 2.5 per cent and those with neither schools nor high school assessments would pay 3 per cent." Despite the support of Auxiliary Bishop Hughes, and Garmey's emotional argument that additional taxes were the only way "to pay for our missionary commitments," the board rejected Father Summers's proposal in a six-to-five vote.[152]

The issues that divided the diocesan school board were evidently reflective of deepening discord among American Catholics over the purposes of parochial education. As noted, a growing number of urban Catholic schools in the post–Vatican II era showed a commitment to a brand of "social justice" that appeared compatible with liberal conceptions of civic virtue.

Significantly, political theorist Stephen Macedo has attributed the emergence of what he called "civic-happy" Catholic schools to reforms taken within the church after 1964. "After centuries of often quite effective opposition to liberal democracy, the Catholic Church reversed its position and became a positive force for democracy around the world," Macedo wrote. "Those changes within Catholicism were, in important respects, concessions to liberal democratic political values, and were also in part a consequence of the Catholic experience in America."[153] Hence, the efforts of certain urban Catholic educators to reach out to nonwhite and non-Catholic students were consistent with the postconciliar church's emphasis on serving the needs of the larger community. Unsurprisingly, this model of Catholic education drew fire from traditionalists. "In the Roman Catholic Church, the reverberations of the revolution begun with the election of Pope John XXIII in 1958 remain deeply felt," observed Buetow, writing in 1970. "A wave of questioning of all traditional structures, such as the parish church, is taking place. Those Catholics committed to the sacral aim of 'saving souls' have grave problems with a Catholic schooling which they see as providing an intellectual atmosphere in which the traditional faith does not seem to flourish sufficiently."[154] Apparently, the board, in its decision to reject Father Summers's bid for additional aid to Immaculate Conception, tacitly supported a more traditional model of parochial education, one that focused mainly on the interests of the Catholic community.

UNEXPECTED AID FOR THE IMMACULATE

In the wake of the board's decision, Immaculate Conception School's future appeared more uncertain than ever. Yet, the ground shifted in early 1977, when the school was granted a last-minute reprieve because of "conflicting recommendations from the Diocesan School Board and the Senate of Priests." The senate, composed of local pastors and other diocesan clergy, strongly supported Father Summers's proposal and pressured the board to explore alternative means to keep Immaculate Conception's school operating for at least another year. According to the *Vindicator*, Bishop Malone met with "pastors of parishes sending pupils to the schools," and secured their agreement to increase funding for the Immaculate. The article reported that Immaculate Conception's school was to "remain open one year more," while its anticipated operating deficit of $30,000 for the 1977–1978 academic year was "met by increased payments from St. Columba and St. Casimir parishes of $8,000 and $16,000, respectively, and by a $6,000 payment from the home mission fund of the Youngstown Society for the Propagation of the Faith." The same article highlighted the extent of the Immaculate's economic difficulties when it reported that a $20,000 gift from the estate of late Youngstown-area industrialist Charles B. Cushwa enabled the school to remain open during the 1976–1977 academic year.[155]

Beginning in the late 1970s, the Immaculate's proponents scrambled to organize annual public appeals and fund-raising events, while soliciting the aid of individual philanthropists. Nevertheless, the institution teetered on the edge of economic collapse. By the end of 1977, the parish school once again faced the threat of closure, this time in the form of a diocesan consolidation plan. Immaculate Conception's pastor took the lead in organizing yet another appeal, and encouraged pupils at the school to engage in a letter-writing campaign that targeted the diocesan school board as well as the city's daily newspaper. As a member of a committee set up by the diocese to explore alternatives to consolidation, Father Summers advocated that the parish be treated "as a mission, as a stabilizing force in an older part of town basically made up of middle- and lower-income families." Father Summers observed that the school had raised $7,000 through "bake sales, raffles, carnivals and other special events," but added that it would need a total of $40,000 to maintain the school's operations. To secure the remainder of the funds required, Father Summers visited other parishes throughout the diocese to "collect money and other forms of aid they can supply," an approach that won the approval of Bishop Malone. In line with his "mission concept," the pastor stressed that the school served a large number of students of other religious denominations. "To prove the school is a strong positive influence on the East Side, Father Summers points to the fact that 40 percent of the school's 394 students are non-Catholic," the *Vindicator* reported. "Non-Catholic parents send their children to school there because they believe the children will receive a better education and better values, he said." This overview of the school's religious diversity was followed by a reference to the fact that "non-Catholic students get the same religious training the Catholic students receive." The article's conclusion included quotes from an interview with Bob Jenkins, a white instructor at Youngstown's Ursuline High School whose child was enrolled at Immaculate Conception's school. Jenkins stated that, in choosing to entrust his child's education to the Immaculate, he was "setting an example to the rest of the diocese and the community."[156]

In the end, the parish's well-orchestrated appeal to the community's collective conscience paid off. When the *Vindicator* reported in early 1978 that Father Summers's "mission concept" was working well, this proved to be an understatement.[157] By November of that year, the school's fund-raising campaign had exceeded its goal of $40,000 by a comfortable margin. The fact that this outcome coincided with the failure of public school levies throughout the Youngstown metropolitan area ensured that Immaculate Conception's success would become the subject of a newspaper editorial. "It was somewhat ironic that last Wednesday's Vindicator should report both the defeat of many important school levies and the fact that more than enough money had been raised to avert the closing of Immaculate Conception school," the editorial stated. "The Rev. John Summers, pastor, who led his parishioners in their own effort to raise money and who went out to appeal for help from more prosperous parishes, said the effort had yielded $52,000 when only $40,000 in additional funds was needed to meet the budget." The editorial went on to comment that diocesan finance chair Raymond Pelanda, the most vocal opponent of the plan to fund Immaculate Conception's school through a modest tax hike, "said the parish's action was vastly better as a 'labor of love.'" The editorial concluded by musing that public school officials, in the wake of failing levies, might learn something from Father Summers's successful appeal: "If school boards and officials could arouse that kind of devotion among parents and voters, fewer systems would be in danger of closing."[158] Father Summers later recalled that, during this period, three younger priests—Father Robert Bonnot, Father Daniel Venglarik, and Father Philip P. Conley—resided at the parish rectory and often conducted weekly religious services. "So, it was because they were there, taking care of Immaculate Conception, that I was able to go out to the area's churches and publicize the mission of the church," he added.[159]

The Immaculate's high-profile success in the area of fund-raising masked an array of other challenges facing the school, however. Like many parish schools operating in neighborhoods where few families could afford even minimal tuition rates, Immaculate Conception struggled to maintain adequate enrollment. The Youngstown area was beginning to feel the impact of the collapse of its steel-manufacturing sector, a crisis that began with the 1977 closure of Youngstown Sheet and Tube's massive plants in nearby Campbell, Ohio, and was exacerbated by the shutting down of U.S. Steel and Republic Steel's facilities over the next three years. The loss of more than 10,000 jobs between 1977 and 1980 significantly accelerated the depopulation of urban neighborhoods like those on the east side, while pushing up levels of poverty throughout the city.[160] Flagging enrollment figures were consistent with census records that showed a sharp decrease in the Youngstown area's population. In 1980, Mahoning County experienced an overall 7.1 percent drop in population, compared to a decade earlier. While 304,545 people lived in the county in 1970, only 282,813 remained in 1980. Still more dramatic was the 20.4 percent drop in Youngstown's population, which plummeted from 140,909 people in 1970 to 112,146 in 1980.[161] This trend continued unabated into the 1980s. A 1984 study released by the New York-based research firm of Dun and Bradstreet Corporation showed that Youngstown ranked twenty-third on a list of the nation's fastest-shrinking urban areas. According to the report, Youngstown's population had experienced another 1.8 percent drop between 1980 and 1984.[162]

By fall 1979, the diocesan school board's already substantial concerns about falling enrollment deepened considerably. The board reported a decline of 511 students in Youngstown's Catholic elementary and secondary schools, "a 2.2 percent drop from the official 1978–79 enrollment of 22,869." Predictably, the most severe losses occurred among schools based in urban neighborhoods with shrinking Catholic populations. Along with St. Patrick's and St. Dominic's schools on the south side, and St. Edward's on the north side, the Immaculate experienced among the worst drops in enrollment seen among Youngstown's parish schools, recording 53 fewer students than during the 1977–1978 academic year. Heavy losses at Immaculate Conception and St. Patrick's (which had 41 fewer pupils) prompted Father Philip Conley, then diocesan vicar of religious education, to comment, "That's saying something about our outreach to the poor."[163] As the Immaculate's enrollment figures continued to fall into the early 1980s, the school once again faced the prospect of closure through consolidation.

CONTROVERSIES OVER SCHOOL CONSOLIDATION

When the Immaculate opened for the 1981–1982 academic year, it welcomed a meager 235 students into its classrooms. Enrollment figures were still lower at Sacred Heart of Jesus Elementary School, the only other parish school serving the city's east side. At Sacred Heart of Jesus (popularly known as "Sacred Heart"), enrollment fell to 155 students. Although the diocesan school board recognized a need for immediate action, it chose to move with caution. Board members probably understood that the two schools were beloved institutions in their respective neighborhoods. Furthermore, both schools were connected to parishes with long, rich histories. The more recently established of the parishes, Sacred Heart, had been organized in 1888, just a few years after the founding of the Immaculate, and its school had served east side Catholics since 1924. Therefore, emotions at both parishes were bound to run high when the diocesan school board announced that the two schools were being considered for consolidation. It was clear to most observers that one of the two schools would cease operations. As the *Vindicator* reported, the "reorganization" of Immaculate Conception and Sacred Heart schools "would entail closing one school and possibly laying off teachers."[164]

Veteran diocesan officials, in particular, were probably inclined to move cautiously. Amid postwar urban changes, the diocese had become acquainted with some of the challenges involved in merging parish schools with established identities. In 1960, after highway construction forced the closure (and eventual razing) of St. Ann's Church and School in the north side's Brier Hill district, diocesan officials responded by merging St. Ann's with nearby St. Casimir's Parish. To accommodate the merger, St. Casimir's Elementary School opened two additional classrooms.[165] As practical as this decision might have seemed on paper, it puzzled observers on the ground, given that St. Ann's remained an Irish-dominated territorial parish, while St. Casimir's had been established by Polish immigrants. Father Joseph Rudjak, then a young parishioner at St. Casimir's Church, recalled that, before the merger, Father William P. Dunn, the pastor of St. Ann's, expressed confidence that his parish would be "resurrected." Ultimately, Father Dunn's optimism was misplaced. In quick succession, St. Casimir's was stripped of its status as a national parish, plans for a consolidation between the two churches were announced, "and the bishop said: 'No Polish traditions. No Irish traditions. We're all Americans now.'" Father Rudjak went on to describe a widely reported incident in which St. Casimir's choir began to sing a traditional Polish hymn, only to be confronted by the pastor, Father Aloysius Rzendarski, and school principal, Sister Regina, who "[stormed] the choir loft" and screamed "that this is not to be sung any longer."[166]

Clearly, a consolidation involving the parish schools of Sacred Heart and Immaculate Conception posed fewer challenges than those that arose during the difficult merger of St. Ann's and St. Casimir's parishes on the north side in 1960. The two east side schools, after all, were attached to territorial parishes that had become ethnically diverse over time. More importantly, the parishes themselves would be preserved. Still, the diocesan school board chose to move surreptitiously, in what some critics later interpreted as an effort to outflank opponents of a consolidation.[167] In spring 1982, Superintendent John Augenstein issued a press release stating that both Immaculate Conception and Sacred Heart of Jesus schools were "plagued with declining enrollments and inflationary costs." The press release added that the schools "were expected to run up a combined deficit of $100,000 by June 30, 1983." An article covering the statement explained that, while parish schools were generally supported through parish collections and tuition, those of Immaculate Conception and Sacred Heart had received "additional voluntary support from other parishes in the diocese." The article also noted that both schools had been exempted from "a diocesan tax that supports the services provided by the central office and from a quota payment that supports the diocesan high schools."[168] The gist of the press release was clear: the diocese had done everything in its power to accommodate the two parish schools, and it was time for the diocesan school board to make tough decisions regarding the schools' respective futures.

News of a possible consolidation involving the two schools was especially upsetting to parishioners and staff members at Sacred Heart, who had waged a decade-long "uphill battle" to keep the parish school open. Onetime parishioner Paula McKinney recalled that former pastor Father Edward Stanton had threatened to close Sacred Heart's school in the early 1970s but reconsidered the move in the face of stiff opposition. "[Father Stanton] went through all kinds of exciting programs . . . and remodeled the rectory and remodeled the basement of the rectory," she said. "Well, then, the next thing you know, we didn't have enough money to have the school. Well, the nuns and the parents fought it tooth and nail. And we won. Ten years we staved it off."[169] By spring 1982, however, the school's situation was more precarious than it had been in the early 1970s. Moreover, the institution's fate was in the hands of the diocesan school board, not the parish council. While some observers at Sacred Heart might have been encouraged by the noncommittal tone of the diocesan press release, others recognized that the board's upcoming decision was practically a foregone conclusion. It was clear to many of them that, in the eyes of the diocese, Immaculate Conception had decisive advantages over its sister school on the east side. Apart from the fact that Sacred Heart served a smaller student population, its one-story school building also offered less space than Immaculate's two-story facility. In addition, Sacred Heart's staff was less than half that of the Immaculate's. While Sacred Heart employed four lay teachers, including its principal, Catherine Daley, the Immaculate retained eight lay teachers, along with one teaching nun, Sister Darla Jean Vogelsang, who served as principal.[170] Sensing the weakness of their school's position, Sacred Heart's parish council adopted a defensive tone early on, and the consolidation controversy soon took on the atmosphere of a "turf war."

Alert to the possibility of resistance from disgruntled parishioners, the diocesan school board struggled to find a way to prevent eclipsing the identity of the school that would be closed in the course of the consolidation. Hence, on April 28, the board announced that the "new" institution would be called "Bishop McFadden Elementary School," an ostensible tribute to the diocese's first bishop that was hoped to "avoid the perception that the action was merely the closing of one of the schools."[171] In the end, this awkward recommendation pleased no one, given that it effectively terminated the identity of *both* schools. The question of what to call the reorganized school barely came up at a meeting on the consolidation that involved diocesan representatives and parishioners and parents of both parishes. During this meeting, held at Youngstown's Ursuline High School, the worst fears of Sacred Heart's supporters were confirmed. Although media accounts of the three-hour meeting failed to describe its atmosphere, statements by several participants suggest that it was a contentious affair. Apparently, at least some of the parents and parishioners who attended had earnestly looked forward to a dialogue on the consolidation. They encountered something rather different. In the course of the meeting, diocesan representatives announced that the school board had already determined, in a vote of 9 to 3, that Immaculate Conception's building would be the site of the consolidated school. Diocesan officials reported that Catherine Daley, the lay principal at Sacred Heart, would serve as the new school's top administrator, while the Immaculate's principal, Sister Darla Jean Vogelsang, would act as director of religious education. Participants then learned that the school's combined staff would be reduced from 12 to 8 teachers, with appointments rendered on the basis of seniority. In addition, James Boyle, director of marketing and development for diocesan schools, revealed that a finance and development committee comprising representatives of both schools would be set up "to make sure there is no instability in the system as a result of consolidation."[172]

In public comments on the consolidation, Superintendent Augenstein described the move as unavoidable and argued that immediate steps needed to be taken "if Catholic education were to continue on the East Side."[173] Members of Sacred Heart's parish council were apparently unconvinced, and many complained of negligible input on a decision that would have a profound effect on their parish. Brian Cahill, president of Sacred Heart's parish council, expressed the frustration of others when he said: "We really felt we were shafted and we weren't consulted." Cahill went on to imply that the school board's approach had been undemocratic. "If I could draw, I would have drawn a sickle and hammer" to represent what happened at the meeting, he said.[174] The parish council president's comments boded ill for the kind of smooth consolidation the board evidently preferred. On May 7, the Sacred Heart Parish Council expressed its dissatisfaction officially when it passed a resolution criticizing the diocesan school board's decision to use Immaculate Conception's physical plant for the consolidated school. In a nine-to-three vote, the council also resolved that it would "refuse to cooperate" with the diocese in the consolidation. Although Sacred Heart's pastor, Father John Tully, stressed that the resolution would have "no practical effect," the council protest underscored the challenges the diocese would face when seeking to consolidate schools with established identities.[175]

Yet, more was at stake in the consolidation of Sacred Heart and Immaculate Conception schools than issues such as "turf" and identity. Many east siders, including the district's shrinking pool of white residents, viewed parochial schools as vital alternatives to troubled urban public schools. Given that public schools in Youngstown's center city served large numbers of African American students, interpreting the motives of white parents can be a complicated task. It is difficult to determine where racial prejudice ends and legitimate dissatisfaction with the quality of urban public education begins. It would be simplistic to suggest that schools like Sacred Heart and Immaculate Conception functioned solely as "havens" for white parents seeking to insulate their children from integrated public schools. Both of these institutions, after all, served racially diverse student populations. In 1977, six years before Sacred Heart Elementary School closed in the consolidation, the *Vindicator* reported that 22 percent of the school's 204 students were African American, while 40 percent of Immaculate Conception's students were African American.[176]

At the same time, there appears to be a relationship between the closure of urban private schools and the accelerated flight of white residents from Youngstown's center city. Paula McKinney recalled making this observation in the early 1970s, in the course of a public forum on the future of Sacred Heart's school. "At an open meeting, I said, 'Father, this will be the end,'" Mrs. McKinney recalled. "I said, 'Close that school and . . . the 'for sale' signs will go up, and people will move out. Why shouldn't they, if there is no school for their children? Well, that's exactly what happened."[177] McKinney was hardly alone in her opinion. Her statement reflected the views of many Catholic observers in the 1970s, who stressed the role of parochial schools in "anchoring a portion of the white population" in urban areas. McGreevy outlined this position in his discussion of Catholic responses to critics who contended that urban parish schools "prevented public school integration." "Catholic schools clearly pulled substantial numbers of white students out of the public school system," McGreevy wrote. "Given that white families tended to abandon a neighborhood when the number of minority students in the public schools increased dramatically, however, the schools also enabled white Catholic families (at least in the short run) to remain in the city longer than their non-Catholic counterparts." McGreevy concluded by pointing to studies suggesting that "Catholic schools fostered neighborhood integration even as they limited potential integration within the public schools."[178]

Given that Sacred Heart's student population was relatively diverse, the dynamics at this institution differed from those McGreevy identified in overwhelmingly white urban parochial schools. Nevertheless, the percentage of students from minority backgrounds at Sacred Heart was low when compared to Youngstown's center-city public elementary schools. (For that matter, the percentage of minority students at Sacred Heart was lower than at Immaculate Conception Elementary School.) It is also significant that the mostly white parishioners who fought to retain the parish school apparently regarded the institution as essential, if they were to raise children in the neighborhood. Hence, developments at Sacred Heart conformed, in some respects, to patterns found in other northeastern urban neighborhoods. A vicious cycle soon became apparent: earlier waves of white migration to the suburbs severely hampered urban parish schools, and the closure of these beleaguered institutions ensured the departure of most of those whites who remained behind.

An explosive intersection of issues—including territorial claims, efforts to maintain parish identity, and fears arising over demographic change—prompted Sacred Heart's parish council to defy diocesan administrators. While the diocesan school board's efforts to consolidate the two schools were ultimately successful, board members could not ignore that the move inspired bitter recriminations from parishioners. In the wake of the controversy that swirled around the closure of Sacred Heart, the school board proved reluctant to promote further consolidations among Youngstown's parish schools. Even the board's effort to make conciliatory gestures provoked criticism. The board's attempt to placate all parties in the merger by naming the consolidated institution "Bishop McFadden Elementary School" drew fire from all sides, including representatives of Sacred Heart Parish. Brian Cahill and other council members repudiated the proposal, contending that the name "would have nothing about it with which the East Side could identify."[179] Thus, while Sacred Heart assumed a portion of financial responsibility for the consolidated school, most area residents identified the institution exclusively with Immaculate Conception Parish.

Not long after the consolidation, Immaculate Conception marked its centennial, an event that received extensive media coverage. A photo spread in the *Vindicator*'s rotogravure section referred briefly to the consolidation, noting that the Immaculate and Sacred Heart "were reorganized as one school to keep Catholic education on the East Side." On the whole, however, the feature downplayed the school's recent challenges and focused instead on its lengthy history. Throughout, the consolidated institution was implicitly described as the descendant of the Immaculate's earliest parish school.[180] Few, if any, would have contended that the "spirit" of Sacred Heart somehow lived on within the consolidated school.

Strangely enough, news coverage of the school consolidation included no references to the small number of African American families who evidently came to depend on Sacred Heart of Jesus Elementary School. Media reports also failed to indicate the number of former Sacred Heart students who made their way to the combined school at Immaculate Conception. The large percentage of nonwhite and non-Catholic students enrolled at Sacred Heart suggests that urban parish schools held a strong appeal for neighborhood residents of minority backgrounds. Many non-Catholic parents were apparently impressed with the orderly environment Catholic schools provided, especially at a time when a growing number of urban public schools seemed to be experiencing a breakdown in discipline. Ida Carter, an African American public school teacher who sent each of her four children to an urban parochial school, described a classroom environment that featured a pleasing combination of discipline and warmth. "Everybody knew each other, and it seemed like everybody cared about each other," she recalled. "There was . . . total respect. . . . For whatever reason . . . when a sister walked into that room, the children stopped, stood up, and [said], 'Good morning, Sister Mary.' . . . The kids all seemed to gel. So, the closest thing I can say is, it was really like a family."[181]

The growing perception that urban Catholic schools bolstered achievement levels among minority students owed much to controversial research that appeared in the early 1980s. In 1982, James Coleman, Thomas Hoffer, and Sally Kilgore's landmark study, *High School Achievement: Public and Private Schools,* reported that Catholic secondary schools provided relatively high levels of academic achievement, were less racially segregated, and created an academic atmosphere in which academic achievement was less dependent on family background. The study drew on data from the 1980 national survey, *High School and Beyond,* which served as the database for Father Andrew Greeley's 1982 study, *Catholic Schools and Minority Students.* In his more specialized interpretation of the data, Father Greeley, a sociologist, concluded that achievement levels of minority students enrolled in Catholic schools were significantly higher than those observed among minority students in public schools. He also contended that the most dramatic differences in the effectiveness of private and public schools were found among the most disadvantaged students.[182] These findings led some researchers to conclude that urban Catholic schools were more in line with the "common school ideal" than their public counterparts.[183] It was against the background of this contested research that urban parochial schools garnered increasing attention among non-Catholic observers, including urban Protestant leaders.

A NEW SUPERINTENDENT STRUGGLES TO SAVE THE SYSTEM

Although the Immaculate had managed to survive the threat of closure through consolidation, questions about the school's long-term viability surfaced with renewed vigor in spring 1985, when it was announced that retiring diocesan school superintendent John Augenstein would be replaced by a more assertive administrator, Dr. Nicholas M. Wolsonovich. The new superintendent, appointed by Bishop Malone on the recommendation of the diocesan school board, came with credentials that included a bachelor's degree from Catholic University, a master's degree from Westminster College, and a doctorate in education administration from Kent State University. Dr. Wolsonovich pledged to emphasize the "religious identity" of the diocese's parish schools, an agenda with questionable implications for urban schools that had moved beyond their traditional mission by serving large numbers of non-Catholic students. Speaking on the *raison d'être* of Catholic education, the incoming superintendent contended that parochial schools "were not created to duplicate public school education."[184] Given that urban parochial schools in this period were widely praised for their work with at-risk, minority students, the superintendent's restatement of a more traditional ethos may have inspired some to question his commitment to schools like Immaculate Conception and St. Patrick's, which were based in neighborhoods with shrinking Catholic populations.

In the end, however, Dr. Wolsonovich proved generally supportive of the mission of schools like the Immaculate. In 1990, five years into his tenure as superintendent, he addressed the issue of non-Catholics who attended urban parish schools. Dr. Wolsonovich observed that, among diocesan elementary schools, 11 percent of the students were non-Catholics. The percentage of such students, he added, was far higher among center-city schools. The superintendent specifically mentioned Immaculate Conception and St. Patrick schools. He pointed out that both institutions "have almost 90-percent non-Catholic" students, and speculated that urban parents, regardless of religious background, were "looking for a strong, faith-filled, value-filled education."[185] Dr. Wolsonovich neglected to add that, while the percentage of non-Catholic students in these schools was rising, overall enrollment had continued to drop.

By 1990, Immaculate Conception Elementary School recorded a mere 122 students, while its budget deficit soared to tens of thousands of dollars. Instructor Lianna Scarazzo later recalled, "There were a lot of months that we weren't sure what the situation would be for the next year—would we be here or not?"[186] The following year, enrollment crept up slightly to 129 students, and the school once more faced the prospect of closure. In March 1991, the Diocese of Youngstown announced that two special collections would be taken up at churches throughout Mahoning and Trumbull counties to benefit two urban parish schools, Immaculate Conception and St. Patrick's. The diocese's efforts were synchronized with those of a group that called itself the Mahoning County Center City Catholic Schools Task Force. Significantly, the task force included representatives of urban Protestant Christian churches who supported the two schools' efforts to provide educational opportunities to center-city youth. One task force member, the Reverend Lonnie Simon, the black pastor of New Bethel Baptist Church on the south side of Youngstown, sent a letter of appeal to Protestant churches throughout the area, noting that students from 59 Christian churches attended the two schools.[187] Reverend Simon's public comments on the benefits of urban Catholic parochial schools distinguished him from the majority of local black ministers, who were more guarded in their statements regarding these institutions. There is little doubt, however, that a growing number of local Protestant clergy came to appreciate the quality of urban Catholic education, a development that paved the way for the eventual establishment of an ecumenical private academy on the city's south side in the mid-1990s.

The task force's stated goal was to raise $115,000 annually for the two schools over a five-year period. Group representatives predicted that about $78,000 would be generated in the two special collections held at local Catholic churches. Fund-raisers also noted that similar campaigns would be held at local parochial schools, where students were encouraged to participate in a fund-raising effort called "Kids Helping Kids," whose stated goal was to raise the equivalent of $3 per student. The task force indicated that, with the monies generated through the fund-raising campaigns, it would establish an endowment fund "that will take over funding assistance at the end of five years of collections." Diocesan school superintendent Dr. Wolsonovich also issued a letter to diocesan school principals that praised the two schools in the following terms: "Immaculate Conception and St. Patrick Schools are a significant outreach to the community at large by educating with Christian values those students who are predominantly minority and non-Catholic." At the time Wolsonovich issued the letter, 83 percent of the Immaculate's students were African American, with the same percentage recorded as non-Catholic.[188] Less than a month later, news accounts reported that the fund-raising campaign had reached its $115,000 goal, thus securing reprieves for the two schools. Youngstown Bishop James Malone announced that both Immaculate Conception and St. Patrick's schools would remain open for the 1991–1992 school year. "We are encouraged in this mission by the support of the entire community, including individual donors, foundations, churches, and young students of other schools," Bishop Malone said. The *Vindicator* reported that Mahoning County parishes raised a total of $56,763, while the "Kids Helping Kids" campaign yielded $6,602. In addition, four urban Protestant churches—New Bethel Baptist, Elizabeth Baptist, Gospel Baptist, and First Presbyterian—donated a total of $660. Bishop Malone stressed, however, that the drive was only the first of a five-year program. As a newspaper article reported, "the financial situation of the schools will be evaluated for each of the following four years."[189] As it turned out, the results of subsequent fund-raising drives for the two schools were disappointing.

At the outset of 1992, the diocese again announced that special collections would be taken up at local churches to support the two "financially strapped" schools. Bishop Malone issued a written statement to churches throughout Mahoning County, which read, "We have a mission to bring the good news and gospel values to everyone, especially to the poorer members of the community."[190] This time, the campaign goal was $125,000, and once again, advocates of the schools reached out to private donors, parochial school students, and urban Protestant churches. Despite these efforts, however, the campaign fell short of its goal by $60,000. Judging from a breakdown of the contributions, the shortfall owed mainly to flagging contributions from local Catholics. Donations raised among parishes in Mahoning County fell from the previous year's $56,763 to $42,104 in 1992. Even donations among parochial school students witnessed a substantial decline, falling from $6,602 to $4,804. Meanwhile, the relatively sparse contributions of urban Protestant congregations rose from $660 to $1,025.[191]

In the wake of the shortfall, diocesan school superintendent Dr. Wolsonovich issued an appeal for broader support, stating, "Only with the entire community's help can we make these schools a viable solution to help young people rise out of the poverty they were born into." Although the diocese was able to keep the schools open through contributions from anonymous donors, questions arose about the continued support of local Catholics for center-city schools like Immaculate Conception and St. Patrick's.[192] How long would Youngstown's Catholic community fund endangered schools whose students were mostly non-Catholic, especially when traditional parochial schools were showing signs of financial strain? In the face of this uncertainty, Immaculate Conception not only maintained its operation, but to the surprise of many observers, experienced an unexpected rise in enrollment. Within two years, the school's student body grew from 179 to 246.[193] This jump was consistent with a rise in enrollment among all diocesan schools, which was recorded at 15,482—an increase of 249 over the previous year's figure. According to a newspaper report, parochial elementary schools saw their figures rise by 108 students, while high schools recorded an increase of 141.[194] Another news article indicated that Immaculate Conception Elementary School enrolled "a mostly black or Hispanic, non-Catholic student body from low-income households." The article noted that almost half of the students enrolled at Immaculate Conception came from "single-mother homes."[195]

While this temporary boost in enrollment may have been encouraging, it didn't resolve the Immaculate's longstanding financial difficulties. The school's tuition—kept low to accommodate poorer families—failed to cover the cost of educating individual students. As the media noted, the school's 246 kindergarten-through-eighth-grade students paid a yearly average of $750 in tuition, while the annual cost of educating each student ranged from $1,700 to $1,800.[196] The remainder needed to be made up through fund-raising efforts. Worse yet, the scope of diocesan fund-raising campaigns had widened considerably as more and more of Youngstown's urban parochial schools experienced financial difficulty. In early 1995, the diocese launched an 18-month, $451,000 fund-raising campaign designed to create "long-term financial stability" to five struggling parish schools—Immaculate Conception; St. Patrick's, on the south side; St. Anthony's, on the lower north side; St. Edward's, on the upper north side; and St. Dominic, on the south side. Sister Brendon Zajac, the diocese's new assistant school superintendent, explained, "'We're trying to build an ongoing base of support so that we don't have to keep going back again and again asking for money in a crisis situation to deal with our deficit." A subtext of the fund-raising campaign was the diocese's threat that, if contributions fell short, one of the urban parish schools—most likely St. Patrick's—would close. In its coverage of the campaign kickoff, the *Vindicator* observed that Immaculate Conception and St. Patrick's "have teetered on the brink of closure for several years."[197]

The next month, the diocese announced that the fund-raising campaign had fallen substantially short of its goal of $451,000, raising a total of only $100,000. In spite of this shortfall, Dr. Wolsonovich announced that St. Patrick's Elementary School would remain open, though in a truncated form. To save up to $60,000 in operating costs, grades five through eight at St. Patrick's would be eliminated, the superintendent said. The diocese announced that the change would force 75 students to seek education elsewhere, and also estimated that at least four teaching positions would be cut. "We just didn't raise the money we needed to sustain everything as it is," Wolsonovich said. The diocese's efforts to attract an additional $150,000 from 70 individual donors also proved disappointing. As a newspaper article reported, a mere 35 donors pledged $25,165. Wolsonovich explained that the diocese's decision to "make changes at St. Patrick's" rested on the fact that "Immaculate is the only Catholic school on the East Side."[198] These "changes," as things turned out, would serve as the prelude to St. Patrick Elementary School's closure at the conclusion of the 1995–1996 academic year.

Looking back on the situation, Father Edward P. Noga, pastor of St. Patrick's Church, suggested that the closing down of most of the city's parish schools was partly the result of resistance to strong diocesan recommendations that surviving schools consolidate. In the early 1990s, Father Noga recalled, a consultant had advised the diocese to cluster the city's surviving elementary schools into three groups, as a step toward future consolidations. "Turf issues" among local pastors and parishioners, however, worked against any substantial effort to "downsize" the school system. Father Noga described the response of many local Catholics to the issue of consolidation. "I think the essence of Catholic parishes and parish schools [is] their personal identities," he said. "And I think the church promoted, and rightly so, that the parish become all-encompassing—social service, school, liturgy, social life, etc." At the same time, Father Noga indicated that, in the wake of "skyrocketing" costs, "the places that looked more regionally at schools met with . . . a little bit more success." Still, the strategy of consolidation, which looked good "on paper," was difficult to implement because parishioners could not accept the loss of a beloved school's identity.[199]

In what became a common practice, the building that housed St. Patrick's Elementary School was put to use after the closing of the parish school. Father Noga explained that, in the late 1990s, the Diocese of Youngstown cooperated closely with the Lutheran bishop of Akron to establish at St. Patrick's former site an "ecumenical school that would be Christian-based, but not denominationally based."[200] The enterprise, which became known as New Hope Academy, operated on the south side for five years and drew national publicity for its inclusive approach to Christian education. In 1998, Oprah Winfrey's Better Life Foundation donated $25,000 to the school.[201] Today, the former parish school building serves as the site of a charter school managed by Summit Academy, Inc., an enterprise that operates three charter schools in Youngstown—all of which are housed in former parochial school buildings.

The closing of St. Patrick's Elementary School in 1996 raised questions about the long-term viability of other urban parochial schools, especially Immaculate Conception. Indeed, the Immaculate's enrollment dropped to a mere 195 students in 1998. Yet, in the face of this trend, Immaculate Conception once again made headlines for its implementation of innovative educational practices. This time, however, the innovations came at the urging of the diocesan superintendent. Dr. Wolsonovich had, since 1996, actively promoted a year-round school calendar that increased mandatory school days from 178 to 181. The calendar also added 15 voluntary "enrichment" days and pared down summer vacation from 11 to 6 weeks.[202] Dr. Wolsonovich's recommendation that the diocese's 48 elementary schools and 5 high schools adopt the year-round program was couched in a diocesan report, "Cornerstone of Excellence." With the superintendent's approval, the Immaculate became the second school in northeastern Ohio to adopt a year-round calendar in late summer 1998. Immaculate principal Patricia Yacucci's decision to "take the plunge" and adopt the schedule echoed Sister Teresa Winsen's openness to the IGE program in 1970. The new schedule did not elicit praise from all staff members, however. One disgruntled teacher called into question the practicality of holding additional summer classes in an older building that lacked air conditioning. The same teacher complained that hard-pressed parochial school instructors like herself were being asked to give up extended summer breaks with their children. Dr. Wolsonovich, on the other hand, expressed confidence that the year-round schedule was "the basis of what the future of education will be."[203]

THE DEMISE OF URBAN CATHOLIC SCHOOLS
IN YOUNGSTOWN

In spring 2002, Dr. Wolsonovich announced that he would step down as diocesan school superintendent to accept a comparable post with the Archdiocese of Chicago.[204] His successor, Dr. Michael Skube, did not share Wolsonovich's enthusiasm for innovations like the year-round school schedule.[205] Yet, the new superintendent's concern about the viability of Youngstown's center-city parish schools became immediately apparent. In August 2002, Dr. Skube met with pastors of four parish schools in Youngstown, including Immaculate Conception, St. Brendan's, St. Edward's, and St. Matthias's. Given that the diocese had already closed three city schools in the previous decade—St. Patrick's and St. Anthony's in 1996, and St. Dominic's in 1999—the Immaculate's future, once again, hung in the balance. The *Vindicator* reported that the Immaculate, "where the majority of pupils are black, non-Catholic and from low-income families," was "the most vulnerable."[206]

Such characterizations of the school were dismissed by the Immaculate's new principal, Amy Ricci Ellis, who stated that "rumors of the school's demise have become routine." In the face of pessimistic speculation, she expressed confidence in the school's continued longevity. "You can have two attitudes," she said. "I'm here for a year or I'm here for 10 years. The attitude I have is that the school is going to be here."[207] Amid such optimistic forecasts by the school's supporters, the Immaculate's enrollment remained at a dangerously low level, never rising about 120 for the remainder of its operation. Nevertheless, the school remained a focal point of fund-raising campaigns; and in 2004, Father Edward Glynn, SJ, president of John Carroll University, served as keynote speaker at a local benefit that raised $23,000 for the institution.[208] Ultimately, however, these additional funds failed to compensate for a precipitous decline in enrollment, and during its final years, student numbers at Immaculate plunged to an all-time low. Within four years of Dr. Skube's initial meeting with the pastors of Youngstown's endangered public schools, all four of these institutions would be closed. Astonishingly, Immaculate Conception Elementary School, whose closure seemed imminent as early as the 1970s, was among the last of these endangered schools to cease operation.[209]

About two months after Immaculate Conception closed its doors, the Diocese of Youngstown announced a plan to "save" local Catholic education. In a news story that appeared in August 2006, Dr. Skube attributed the recent closings of Immaculate Conception and St. Matthias elementary schools to factors including the decline in urban population, growing economic hardship, and rising tuition levels. "The trend is down," Skube said, acknowledging that the rate of attrition was highest among parish schools in Youngstown itself. Observing that each parochial school was free to set its own tuition, Skube pointed out that tuition costs for parishioners ranged from between $1,300 and $2,300 per year for elementary pupils in the Youngstown area, while non-parishioners paid between $800 and $1,800 more for elementary pupils. Skube indicated that the Youngstown Diocese might play some role in easing parents' economic burden. In a bid to preserve the 20 diocesan schools that were still operating in the metropolitan area—which includes Mahoning, Trumbull, and Columbiana counties—the diocese would increase financial aid programs to assist parents who wanted to send their children to Catholic schools, he added.[210]

For Youngstown residents, the diocese's promise to "save" local parochial schools most likely had a hollow ring to it. The city's "system" of parish schools officially came to an end two months earlier, with the closing of all but one of the schools within the municipal limits. As the *Vindicator* reported, six parish schools in Youngstown had closed since 1994. In Skube's view, the shutting down of these schools could be attributed to one fundamental circumstance: "The bottom line is that there are just fewer pupils available as a parish population declines."[211] If the situation Skube described was bleak, the decline of parish schools (particularly those based in urban areas) was a nationwide phenomenon. Despite a slight national increase in the late 1990s, enrollment at Catholic parochial schools across the country dropped noticeably in the early twenty-first century. In 2005, the NCEA reported that 1,992,183 children were attending Catholic elementary schools in the 1993–1994 school year, and in 1998–1999 that number rose to 2,013,102. In the 2003–2004 academic year, however, enrollment fell dramatically to 1,842,918. In 2004, 123 Catholic elementary schools across the country were forced to either close or consolidate.[212]

LEGACY OF AN URBAN PARISH SCHOOL

In May 2007, almost a year after the Immaculate's closing, I spoke once again to the school's last principal, Sister Charlotte Italiano, who was then serving as director of the Ursuline Preschool and Kindergarten in neighboring

Canfield, Ohio. The walls of her brightly decorated office were covered with plaques and certificates that attested to her decades of community service, and it occurred to me that her brief tenure as principal of Immaculate Conception Elementary School was a footnote in a long, varied career. During our conversation, however, it became clear that Sister Charlotte's connections to the Immaculate reached beyond her experiences as the school's "closing" principal. She had spent a portion of her childhood in an Italian American enclave located a few blocks from the parish. It was a neighborhood of "first-time landowners" who took "extreme pride in their property," maintained well-cultivated gardens, and worked "together in canning the vegetables and fruits of the summer." In the 1940s, Sister Charlotte attended Immaculate Conception for the first few years of her elementary education. Therefore, when she took on her duties at Immaculate Conception Elementary School in late summer 2005, the assignment struck her as something of a homecoming, although it turned out to be unexpectedly bittersweet.

Her mood became reflective as she recalled the moment she first learned of the parish council's decision to close the school. "Oh, I was very upset," she said. "In fact, when I went to the parish council meeting . . . I didn't think they were going to end up closing the school." The news left her feeling "overwhelmed," but also angry. "I think I was angry because the diocese did not do anything, in my opinion, to keep the school going." Although Sister Charlotte did not specifically mention Thomas J. Tobin, the former bishop of the Youngstown Diocese, she did say, "I think with the new bishop [George V. Murry, SJ] . . . being an educator himself, as a Jesuit, he sees the importance of Catholic education and urban education." She also affirmed that diocesan leadership could—and often did—play a decisive role in determining the success, or failure, of an urban parochial school. She added that Bishop Tobin's predecessor, Bishop James Malone, treated Catholic schools as a personal priority during his long tenure. "He was an educator," she said. "He saw to it that good things happened in the schools."

Although Sister Charlotte suggested that diocesan intervention might have altered the fate of Immaculate Conception Elementary School, she was not inclined to minimize the challenges arrayed against the city's parochial schools. Among the destabilizing trends she described was the rise of charter schools, which featured smaller class sizes, greater numbers of credentialed staff, specialized programs, and (not least of all) free admission. Sister Charlotte explained that charter schools could afford to keep two certified teachers in each classroom. "And then, all of the extra programs came in, the Title programs that [provided] extra help for the youngsters in the public schools, that originally were not part of the opportunities that Catholic schools had," she added. "So, if you had a child with special needs and local Catholic schools didn't have anything, where do you go?" In addition, many of the neighbor-hood parents who depended on Immaculate Conception Elementary School evidently failed to heed warnings about the school's likely shutdown in the event of low enrollment. Sister Charlotte noted that late student registration was a perennial problem. In spring 2006, however, prompt registration was nothing less than essential for the school's continued operation. Sister Char-lotte recalled that the school had only 43 students enrolled for the upcoming school year. "No way could you keep a school open that way," she said. Sister Charlotte added that parents had been warned repeatedly about the seriousness of the situation. "[Immaculate Conception Parish administrator] Monsignor Zuraw told people, all along, that these were critical times," she said. "If they were going to sign their children up, they had to do it so that we would know what to do, because teachers had to be on board. And we had to look at how we would get the money to keep the place open."

Sister Charlotte suggested that the factors contributing to the Immaculate's closure were complicated, and deeply enmeshed with the challenges that faced Youngstown in general. She could not seem to decide whether the school's closing was the inevitable outcome of larger trends or the result of diocesan administrators' flagging commitment to urban Catholic education. On the issue of Immaculate Conception's legacy, however, Sister Charlotte spoke with clarity and conviction. "[W]e have provided a very firm, solid, working class of people to go on to further the ideals—not just Catholic or Christian, but human ideals," she said. "We . . . have had the privilege of hav-ing an impact . . . on these youngsters. And I think that's going to be one our legacies, that we have spent the time and energy to make difficult situations easier for many people. . . . And the influence isn't going to be felt right away. It's going to take time to move out into different circles."

Our discussion on the school's long-term impact eventually turned to the fate of the 12 students who participated in the Immaculate's final gradua-tion ceremony. Sister Charlotte noted that four of these students had become "standout" athletes at Ursuline High School, one of Youngstown's two Cath-olic high schools. She went on to share her memories of the ceremony itself. The students' graduation ceremony, she recalled, was held in the neo-Gothic interior of Immaculate Conception Church, which despite postconciliar reno-vations, looked much as it had when the structure opened in 1890. A banner designed by the children stretched across the church's old main altar, reading, "Thank You for All the Good Times!" Sister Charlotte described the mass as "inspiring," but added that only one of the graduating students was a Roman Catholic. The service was followed by a graduation party that reflected "the influence of other people on the less fortunate." Friends and acquaintances of the principal who were active members of Holy Family Church, a parish located in the affluent suburb of Poland Township, donated time and material for the graduation party. "They came down and they provided the food, the table arrangements, the whole party for the graduation," she recalled. "They not only bought everything and set it up, but they also stayed to serve it. They brought their children with them. So, those children saw how our children were at that time. Now, you're talking [about children who are] very affluent [compared] to the marginalized, and those who are struggling to make it." For Sister Charlotte, such opportunities for interaction between rich and poor, black and white, Catholic and non-Catholic, were among the enriching benefits of urban parish schools like the Immaculate. "So, that was a good thing," she said, her mind apparently drifting back to the post-graduation festivities. "And that's a good memory to keep."[213]

NOTES

1. "Parish Profile: Immaculate Conception, Youngstown," *The Catholic Exponent,* 7, August 13, 1993.

2. Harold Gwin, "Final Bell Tolls for Two Schools," *The Vindicator,* B-1, June 7, 2006.

3. Ibid.

4. Sister Charlotte Italiano, OSU, interview by the author, May 31, 2007, transcript, Hogan-Cullinan Family Collection, #314, Mahoning Valley Historical Society, Youngstown, OH.

5. Gwin, *The Vindicator,* June 7, 2007.

6. Harold Gwin, "Plan to Save Schools: The Diocese Had 10,868 Pupils Last Year," *The Vindicator,* A-1, August 20, 2006.

7. Joseph L. Heffernan, "City's Oldest Irishman Is Interviewed by Former Mayor on St. Patrick's Day: John Slavin, 97, Says He Was Born during the Year of 'the Big Wind,'" *The Youngstown Telegram,* 1, March 17, 1934.

8. William Wirtz, "East Side Church Marks 75th Year," *The Youngstown Vindicator,* A-15, September 29, 1957.

9. James A. McFadden, *The March of the Eucharist from Dungannon* (Youngstown, OH: Diocese of Youngstown, 1951), 115.

10. Glen Gabert, Jr., *In Hoc Signo? A Brief History of Catholic Parochial Education in America* (Port Washington, NY: Kennikat Press, 1972), 46–47.

11. Ibid.

12. Kerby A. Miller, *Emigrants and Exiles: Ireland and the Irish Exodus to North America* (Oxford, UK: Oxford University Press, 1985), 495.

13. Gabert, *In Hoc Signo?* 46.

14. Jay P. Dolan, *In Search of an American Catholicism: A History of Religion and Culture in Tension* (New York, NY: Oxford University Press, 2002), 97.

15. Jay P. Dolan, *The American Catholic Experience: A History from Colonial Times to the Present* (Garden City, NY: Image Books, 1985), 299.

16. David R. Roediger, *Working toward Whiteness: How America's Immigrants Became White—the Strange Journey from Ellis Island to the Suburbs* (New York, NY: Basic Books, 2005), 168.

17. Grace Tracy, "Old Immaculate Conception Pupils Recall '93 Honors: Work from Little Frame School Won World's Fair Awards—to Mark 50 Years," *The Youngstown Vindicator,* A-7, January 22, 1933.

18. Wirtz, *The Youngstown Vindicator,* September 29, 1957.

19. Tracy, *The Youngstown Vindicator,* January 22, 1933.

20. Ibid.

21. Dolan, *The American Catholic Experience,* 144.

22. Jay P. Dolan, *The Irish Americans: A History* (New York, NY: Bloomsbury Press, 2008), 231.

23. John T. McGreevy, *Parish Boundaries: The Catholic Encounter with Race in the Twentieth Century Urban North* (Chicago, IL: University of Chicago Press, 1996), 10.

24. Esther Hamilton, "Death Takes Msgr. Kenny: Was Pastor of Immaculate Conception Here from 1910 to 1925," *The Youngstown Vindicator,* A-1, March 31, 1943.

25. "Irish Poet and Scholar—Seumas M'Manus Here on Dec. 3: Will Present Two Entertainments Under Auspices of Immaculate Conception," *The Youngstown Vindicator,* 4, November 24, 1916.

26. Rev. J. R. Kenny, L.L.D., "Ireland at Valley Forge: A Series Specially Compiled for Information of Students and Respectfully Submitted to the Thinking, Scholarly Readers of This Paper," *The Youngstown Vindicator,* 5, March 24, 1921.

27. "Irish Relief Fund: The Immaculate Conception Parish," *The Youngstown Vindicator,* 15, March 5, 1921.

28. "'Only Desire Recognition'—O'Callaghan: Lord Mayor of Cork Pleads for Ireland to Vast Crowd at Moose Hall," *The Youngstown Vindicator,* 16, March 3, 1921.

29. Joan (Donnelly) Welsh, interview by the author, September 15, 2006, transcript, Hogan-Cullinan Family Collection, #314, Mahoning Valley Historical Society, Youngstown, OH.

30. The International Institute, "1930 Census Statistics Foreign-Born Stock: Youngstown-Campbell-Struthers" (undated report, Reuben-McMillan Library, Youngstown, OH), 2–4.

31. H. J. Scarnecchia, "First Italians Settled in Coalburg," *The Youngstown Vindicator,* 3, February 7, 1932 (magazine supplement).

32. "Italians Lead Nationalities in Naturalization in County: Record of 91 Years Shows 4,634 Became Citizens—Hungarians Second with 2,213, *The Youngstown Vindicator,* C-8, April 18, 1937.

33. Paul W. McBride, "The Solitary Christians: Italian Americans and Their Church," *Ethnic Groups* 3, no. 4 (December 1981): 334.

34. Rudolf J. Vecoli, "Prelates and Peasants: Italian Immigrants and the Catholic Church," *Journal of Social History* 2, no. 3 (Spring 1969): 230.

35. Herbert J. Gans, *The Urban Villagers: Group and Class in the Life of Italian-Americans* (New York, NY: The Free Press, 1962), 113.

36. Vecoli, "Prelates and Peasants," 230.

37. Rudolph J. Vecoli, "Cult and Occult in Italian-American Culture: The Persistence of a Religious Heritage," in *Immigrants and Religion in Urban America*, eds. Randall M. Miller and Thomas D. Marzik (Philadelphia, PA: Temple University Press, 1977), 25.

38. Attorney Robert E. Casey, interview by the author, February 13, 2007, transcript, #314, Mahoning Valley Historical Society, Youngstown, OH.

39. Carmen J. Leone, *Rose Street: A Family Story* (Youngstown, OH: Carmen John Leone, 1996/1998), 10.

40. Ibid., 12–13.

41. Tony Trolio, *Brier Hill USA* (Poland, OH: Ciao Promotions, 2001), 47–53.

42. McBride, "The Solitary Christians," 346–50.

43. William D. Jenkins, *Steel Valley Klan: The Ku Klux Klan in Ohio's Mahoning Valley* (Kent, OH: Kent State University Press, 1990), 33.

44. Ibid., 159–60.

45. Ibid., 53–54.

46. Ibid., 47–48.

47. Ibid., 31–32.

48. Ibid., 119–20.

49. Ibid., 130.

50. Ibid., 136–38.

51. McGreevy, *Parish Boundaries,* 30.

52. Dolan, *The American Catholic Experience,* 201.

53. JoEllen McNergney Vinyard, *For Faith and Fortune: The Education of Catholic Immigrants in Detroit, 1803–1925* (Chicago, IL: University of Illinois Press, 1998), 55.

54. Paula (Lehnerd) McKinney, interview by the author, June 14, 2007, transcript, Hogan-Cullinan Family Collection, #314, Mahoning Valley Historical Society, Youngstown, OH.

55. Linda M. Linonis, "Diversity and Friendliness Make Immaculate Conception Special: The Church, Which Is Marking Its 125th Anniversary Dec. 9, Remains Committed to the City," *The Vindicator,* A-10, November 24, 2007.

56. Dolan, *In Search of an American Catholicism,* 152.

57. Matthew Frye Jacobson, *Whiteness of a Different Color: European Immigrants and the Alchemy of Race* (Cambridge, MA: Harvard University Press, 1998), 82–85.

58. Ibid., 95.

59. "Parish Profile," *The Catholic Exponent,* August 13, 1993.

60. "Nuns in One School Here Unpaid 4 Yrs.: Many Parishes Face Desperate Problem in Education," *The Youngstown Vindicator,* B-1, April 14, 1935.

61. "Parish Profile," *The Catholic Exponent,* August 13, 1993.

62. Sister Virginia McDermott, interview by the author, May 31, 2007, transcript, Hogan-Cullinan Family Collection, #314, Mahoning Valley Historical Society, Youngstown, OH.

63. Casey, interview.

64. Internal Records for Immaculate Conception, 1969–1970, reproduction, Hogan-Cullinan Family Collection, #314, Mahoning Valley Historical Society, Youngstown, OH.

65. "Parish Profile," *The Catholic Exponent,* August 13, 1993.

66. McDermott, interview.

67. Casey, interview.

68. Wirtz, *The Youngstown Vindicator,* September 29, 1957.

69. McDermott, interview.

70. Wirtz, *The Youngstown Vindicator,* September 29, 1957.

71. "Catholic School Enrollment Is Record 11,364," *The Youngstown Vindicator,* 20, September 16, 1955.

72. Gabert, *In Hoc Signo?* 93–94.

73. Wirtz, *The Youngstown Vindicator,* September 29, 1957.

74. Kenneth T. Jackson, *Crabgrass Frontier: The Suburbanization of the United States* (New York, NY: Oxford University Press, 1985), 232–38.

75. Casey, interview.

76. Dolan, *The American Catholic Experience,* 365.

77. Thomas J. Sugrue, *The Origins of the Urban Crisis: Race and Inequality in Postwar Detroit* (Princeton, NJ: Princeton University Press, 1996), 34–36.

78. Jackson, *Crabgrass Frontier,* 197–200.

79. Robert P. Formisano, *Boston against Bussing: Race, Class, and Ethnicity in the 1960s and 1970s* (Chapel Hill, NC: The University of North Carolina Press, 1991), 25–26.

80. Sugrue, *The Origins of the Urban Crisis,* 34–36.

81. Thomas G. Fuechtmann, *Steeples and Stacks: Religion and Steel Crisis in Youngstown* (Cambridge, UK: Cambridge University Press, 1989), 23–24.

82. David Brody, *Steelworkers in America: The Nonunion Era* (Cambridge, MA: Harvard University Press, 1960), 254–55.

83. Fuechtmann, *Steeples and Stacks,* 17.

84. McGreevy, *Parish Boundaries,* 84–85.

85. Father Joseph S. Rudjak, interview by the author, June 22, 2008, transcript, Hogan-Cullinan Family Collection, #314, Mahoning Valley Historical Society, Youngstown, OH.

86. Sherry Linkon and John Russo, *Steeltown U.S.A.: Work & Memory in Youngstown* (Lawrence, KS: University Press of Kansas, 2002), 33.

87. Trolio, *Brier Hill USA,* 74–76.

88. Mel Watkins, *Dancing with Strangers: A Memoir* (New York: Simon & Schuster, 1998), 141–42.

89. Ibid, 149–50.

90. "The Swimming Pool Problem," *The Youngstown Vindicator,* 20, July 7, 1949, editorial.

91. Judith Falconi and Joseph Magielski, interview by the author, June 22, 2009, transcript, Hogan-Cullinan Family Collection, #314, Mahoning Valley Historical Society, Youngstown, OH.

92. "Parish Profile," *The Catholic Exponent,* August 13, 1993.

93. Marie Aikenhead, "Board Refuses School Funding: Votes against Diocese Inner City Aid," *The Youngstown Vindicator,* A-1, November 17, 1976.

94. Sister Teresa Winsen, OSU, interview by the author, January 30, 2007, Hogan-Cullinan Family Collection, #314, Mahoning Valley Historical Society, Youngstown, OH.

95. Internal Records for Immaculate Conception School, 1969–1970.

96. Ibid.

97. "Diocese Schools in Bind," *The Youngstown Vindicator,* June 13, 1969, 25.

98. Internal Records for Immaculate Conception School, 1969–1970.

99. Italiano, interview.

100. Kenneth Briggs, *Double Crossed: Uncovering the Catholic Church's Betrayal of American Nuns* (New York: Doubleday, 2006), 52–53.

101. "1,800 Hear of Catholic School Crisis," *The Youngstown Vindicator,* 8, November 16, 1970.

102. Harold A. Buetow, *Of Singular Benefit: The Story of Catholic Education in the United States* (New York, NY: The Macmillan Company, 1970), 347.

103. Internal Records for Immaculate Conception School, 1969–1970.

104. Buetow, *Of Singular Benefit,* 269.

105. "State to Add Up to $3,000 for Nonpublic Teacher," *The Youngstown Vindicator,* 1, September 9, 1969.

106. Winsen, interview.

107. Ibid.

108. Ibid.

109. "School Principal Urges Northeast Sewer Action," *The Youngstown Vindicator,* 5, February 12, 1970.

110. Ibid.

111. Thomas C. Hunt and Norlene M. Kunkel, "Catholic Schools: That Nation's Largest Alternative School System," in *Religious Schooling in America*, eds. James C. Carper and Thomas C. Hunt (Birmingham, AL: Religious Education Press, 1984), 1–34.

112. Winsen, interview.

113. Marie Aikenhead, "Family of 4 Teachers Gets Involved: Winsens Tackle Inner City Problems," *The Youngstown Vindicator,* A-3, January 16, 1972.

114. "100 Area Teachers Here for Workshop on I.G.E.," *Liberty News,* 2, January 16, 1974.

115. Winsen, interview.

116. Herbert R. Kohl, *The Open Classroom: A Practical Guide to a New Way of Teaching* (New York, NY: The New York Review, 1969), 106.

117. Winsen, interview.

118. Ibid.

119. Mary Jerome Leavy, "The Catholic Incarnation of America's One Best System: The Relationship of the Catholic and Public School Systems in the United States" (dissertation, University of South Florida, Tampa, 1989), 1.

120. "Parochial Rolls Dropping: Down to 27,690 Students," *The Youngstown Vindicator,* A-12, September 3, 1972.

121. Linkon and Russo, *Steeltown U.S.A.,* 43–44.

122. "Set Elm Street Hearing June 9: Council Gets Millet Endorsement," *The Youngstown Vindicator,* 37, May 27, 1971.

123. McKinney, interview.

124. "Parochial Rolls Dropping," *The Youngstown Vindicator,* September 3, 1972.

125. "Diocese Is Barely Solvent: First Fiscal Report Shows Balance," *The Youngstown Vindicator,* 1, February 25, 1972.

126. " . . . On Catholic Education," factsheet, reproduction, Reuben-McMillan Public Library, Youngstown, OH.

127. "Catholic Schools to Get $2 Million from New Law," 1, *The Youngstown Vindicator,* August 15, 1969.

128. Ralph E. Winter, "Crumbling Wall: Public Aid to Schools Operated by Churches Increases Despite Foes," *The Wall Street Journal,* 1, November 10, 1970.

129. "Bishop Asks Catholics to Stick by Schools," 2, *The Youngstown Vindicator,* July 23, 1971.

130. Martin John "Jack" O'Connell, interview by the author, transcript, Hogan-Cullinan Family Collection, #314, Mahoning Valley Historical Society, Youngstown, OH.

131. "All Catholic Students to Re-Register," *The Youngstown Vindicator,* 1, August 13, 1971.

132. "Diocese Eyes Aid Solution," *The Youngstown Vindicator,* 1, April 18, 1972.

133. "All Catholic Students to Re-register," *The Youngstown Vindicator,* August 13, 1971.

134. "DiSalvatore Confident on Catholic Pupil Aid," *The Youngstown Vindicator,* December 24, 1971, 4.

135. "Diocese Eyes Aid Solution," *The Youngstown Vindicator,* April 18, 1972.

136. Ibid.

137. Timothy Walch, *Parish Schools: American Catholic Education from Colonial Times to the Present* (Washington, DC: The National Catholic Educational Association, 2003), 207.

138. "Diocese Eyes Aid Solution," *The Youngstown Vindicator,* April 18, 1972.

139. Ibid.

140. "Parochial Rolls Dropping," *The Youngstown Vindicator,* September 3, 1972.

141. "Keep Diocese Schools Open: Okay St. Luke and Sacred Heart Classes," *The Youngstown Vindicator,* 26, February 28, 1973.

142. "Says Diocese Owes Poor Schools Aid," *The Youngstown Vindicator,* A-1, February 28, 1973.

143. Ibid.

144. "Diocesan Schools to Get $681,888," *The Youngstown Vindicator,* A-6, September 6, 1974.

145. Associated Press, "ACLU Continues Parochial Fight," *The Youngstown Vindicator,* 29, September 2, 1974, 29.

146. Marie Aikenhead, "Catholic School Enrollment Dips," *The Youngstown Vindicator,* A-13, January 12, 1975.

147. Walch, *Parish School,* 219.

148. Ibid., 220.

149. "Diocese Lists 3,148 Low-Income Students," *The Youngstown Vindicator,* 11, June 5, 1975.

150. Marie Aikenhead, "Diocesan Schools Reveal Ethnic Makeup; 8.2% of 10,408 Students Are from Minorities," *The Youngstown Vindicator,* B-7, April 3, 1977.

151. Marie Aikenhead, "Board Refuses School Funding: Votes against Diocese Inner City Aid," *The Youngstown Vindicator,* 1, November 17, 1976.

152. Ibid.

153. Stephen Macedo, *Diversity and Distrust: Civic Education in a Multicultural Society* (Cambridge, MA: Harvard University Press, 2000), 133.

154. Harold A. Buetow, "The United States Catholic School Phenomenon," in *Perspectives on the American Catholic Church,* eds. Stephen J. Vecchio and Sister Virginia Geiger, (Westminster, MD: Christian Classics, 1989), 212.

155. "School to Remain Open 1 More Yr.," *The Youngstown Vindicator,* January 19, 1977, 40.

156. Chris Amatos, "Immaculate Conception Pupils Love Their School: Join with Pastor, Parents in Effort to Save Facility," *The Youngstown Vindicator,* A-24, December 11, 1977.

157. Chris Amatos, "A Look at the Past and Future of Catholic School," *The Youngstown Vindicator,* B-3, January 29, 1978.

158. "Taxes and Love," *The Youngstown Vindicator,* 14, November 14, 1978, editorial.

159. Father John R. Summers, interview by the author, August 9, 2009, transcript, Hogan-Cullinan Family Collection, #314, Mahoning Valley Historical Society, Youngstown, OH.

160. Terry F. Buss and Stearns Redburn, *Shutdown in Youngstown: Public Policy for Mass Unemployment* (Albany, NY: State University of New York Press, 1983), 1.

161. "Mahoning Co.'s Census Shows 7.1 Percent Drop," *The Youngstown Vindicator,* 1, July 8, 1980.

162. "Youngstown and Steubenville among Top 25 in Population Drop," *The Youngstown Vindicator,* 1, May 28, 1984.

163. "Enrollment Declines 511 Students in Youngstown Diocesan Schools," *The Youngstown Vindicator,* 17, September 19, 1979.

164. "Diocese May Close 1 School," *The Youngstown Vindicator,* 1, April 15, 1982.

165. "County Catholic Rolls Grow 6 Pct. to 16,550," *The Youngstown Vindicator,* A-14, August 28, 1960.

166. Rudjak, interview.

167. Timothy Fitzpatrick, "Parents Protest Diocesan Move," *The Youngstown Vindicator,* 19, April 30, 1982.

168. "Diocese May Close 1 School," *The Youngstown Vindicator,* 1, April 15, 1982.

169. McKinney, interview.

170. "Diocese May Close 1 School," *The Youngstown Vindicator,* April 15, 1982.

171. "Diocesan Schools Merger Is Set," *The Youngstown Vindicator,* 12, April 28, 1982.

172. "Will Use Immaculate Conception School," *The Youngstown Vindicator,* 13, April 29, 1982.

173. Ibid.

174. Fitzpatrick, *The Youngstown Vindicator,* April 30, 1982.

175. Timothy Fitzpatrick, Council at Sacred Heart Hits Merger of Schools," *The Youngstown Vindicator,* 1, May 7, 1982.

176. Aikenhead, *The Youngstown Vindicator,* April 3, 1977.

177. McKinney, interview.

178. McGreevy, *Parish Boundaries,* 240–41.

179. Fitzpatrick, *The Youngstown Vindicator,* May 7, 1982.

180. "Centennial for East Side Church," *The Youngstown Vindicator,* 4, December 5, 1982, photo spread with captions.

181. Ida Carter, interview by the author, May 4, 2007, transcript, Hogan-Cullinan Family Collection, #314, Mahoning Valley Historical Society, Youngstown, OH.

182. Anthony S. Bryk, Valerie E. Lee, and Peter B. Holland, *Catholic Schools and the Common Good* (Cambridge, MA: Harvard University Press, 1993), 57–58.

183. Ibid., 11.

184. Thomas Ott, "Dr. Wolsonovich promises direct involvement in schools," *The Youngstown Vindicator,* 53, April 25, 1985.

185. "One on One with Nicholas Wolsonovich: We Need to Rethink Financing, Catholic Schools Chief Says," *The Vindicator,* 1, August 20, 1990.

186. "Immaculate Redemption: Urban School Rebounds," *The Vindicator,* A-1, October 2, 1994.

187. Marie Shellock, "Fund-Raiser Begins for Two Catholic Schools," *The Vindicator,* A-8, March 16, 1991.

188. Ibid.

189. John Goodall, "Fund Drive Spares 2 Catholic Schools," *The Vindicator,* A-1, April 9, 1991.

190. Ron Cole, "Diocese to Launch Drive to Keep 2 Schools Open: The Survival of Two Youngstown Catholic Schools Could Turn on a Special Collection Next Weekend," *The Vindicator,* A-1, January 2, 1992.

191. "Bishop: Catholic Schools Stay Open: The Fundraising Efforts Didn't Bring In Enough Money, but Three Diocesan Schools Will Still Be Open," *The Vindicator,* B-2, April 7, 1992.

192. Ibid.

193. Ron Cole, "Immaculate Redemption: Urban School Rebounds," *The Vindicator,* A-1, October 2, 1994.

194. "Diocese's Schooling Cost Less than U.S. Average—Other Good News: School Enrollment in the Diocese Showed a Healthy Increase This Year," *The Vindicator,* B-3, November 30, 1994.

195. "Immaculate Redemption," *The Vindicator,* October 2, 1994.

196. Ibid.

197. Ron Cole, "Catholic Schools Launch Fund Drive: Diocese Officials Hope to Know by March 15 If They Can Raise the Money. If Not, a School Could Close," *The Vindicator,* B-1, February 12, 1995.

198. Ron Cole, "Fund-Raiser Falls Thousands Short of Goal, *The Vindicator,* A-1, March 16, 1995.

199. Father Edward P. Noga, interview by the author, June 18, 2007, transcript, Hogan-Cullinan Family Collection, #314, Mahoning Valley Historical Society, Youngstown, OH.

200. Ibid.

201. "Oprah Raises New Hope at School: Oprah Winfrey's For a Better Life Foundation Has Donated $25,000 to New Hope Academy," *The Vindicator,* B-15, September 17, 1998.

202. Ron Cole, "In a Class by Itself: Parochial School 1st with Year-round Plan," *The Vindicator,* A-1, April 5, 1998.

203. Ibid.

204. Ron Cole, "Catholic Schools Superintendent Takes Same Position in Chicago: Youngstown's Bishop Said a Search for a New Superintendent Will Begin Soon," *The Vindicator,* 1, May 4, 2001.

205. Ron Cole, "Immaculate Conception: Does Bell for Pupils Also Toll for School: The School Has Opened Early; the New Principal's Attitude Is That It Won't Be Closed," *The Vindicator,* B-1, August 14, 2002.

206. Ibid.

207. Ibid.

208. Lou Jacquet, "IC Dinner Speaker: Laity Have Responsibility to Serve Those in Need—John Carroll University President Praises Work of Those Who Teach at, Support the School," *The Catholic Exponent,* 9, March 12, 2004.

209. Gwin, *The Vindicator,* June 7, 2006.

210. Harold Gwin, "Plan to Save Schools: The Diocese Had 10,868 Pupils Last Year," *The Vindicator,* A-1, August 20, 2006.

211. Ibid.

212. Joseph O'Keefe, "How to Save Catholic Schools: Let the Revitalization Begin," *Commonweal,* March 25, 2005, 15–18.

213. Italiano, interview.

Chapter 4

Urban Exodus: Depopulation and Urban Parish Schools

Father Edward P. Noga said he could still remember the morning that he first became aware of profound changes in Youngstown's center city. In the early 1960s, as a seventh-grader in the suburban parochial school of Immaculate Heart of Mary, the future priest (along with his classmates) was introduced to a couple of new students who had just relocated to Austintown Township from Youngstown's south side. The newcomers, who had previously attended St. Patrick's Elementary School, "lived in the path of the highway." They were among scores of urban residents who were forced to retreat from the city when their neighborhoods were leveled "in the name of progress." Years later, circumstances led Father Noga to reflect on this incident. In the 1980s, he was appointed pastor of St. Patrick's Church, the same parish his "uprooted" classmates at Immaculate Heart of Mary Elementary School had been compelled to leave almost two decades earlier. By this time, the urban parish's Spanish Gothic–style church and adjacent brick school building appeared out of place on the city's near south side, with its long stretches of dilapidated housing punctuated by vacant lots. Then, over the next decade, the pastor watched as the beleaguered neighborhoods surrounding St. Patrick's Church became so thinly populated that bus service to the district was virtually discontinued.[1] In 1996, St. Patrick's Elementary School, which had served more than 1,000 students in the early 1960s, enrolled just 107 children.[2] That same year, the diocese announced that the school would close, only to be reopened as New Hope Academy, an ecumenical school operated by the Diocese of Youngstown, the Lutheran Church, and the Ursuline Sisters of Youngstown.[3]

Father Noga interpreted the retreat of residents from Youngstown's center-city neighborhoods as a response to a host of destabilizing trends that rendered urban neighborhoods less viable. "I think what happened was, things were changing socially," he said. "People were looking outside the city as a way of restabilizing."[4] The "social changes" to which Father Noga referred were the by-products of urban developments that included demographic change, deindustrialization, and suburbanization. The cumulative effect of these trends was exacerbated by massive urban construction projects that transformed the city. In Youngstown, as elsewhere in the country, entire neighborhoods were swept away to accommodate building projects that included interstate highway construction.[5] Most of these projects placed a disproportionate burden on blacks and ethnic whites, who tended to live in targeted neighborhoods—a situation that prompted some observers to argue that highway construction was a contributing factor to the "brutal and deadly race riots of the 1960s." Highway construction "made living in the walled-off downtown communities much more difficult," and the challenges posed by noise pollution, air pollution, and urban blight "were exacerbated by the difficulty of passing over or under the huge superstructures" built to accommodate the interstates.[6] Moreover, few urban dwellers experienced the benefits of highway building projects, which facilitated the flow of suburban commuters to and from the center city, even as they "sliced through urban neighborhoods, thereby eliminating housing and disrupting communities."[7] "It destabilized the whole town," recalled longtime Youngstown resident Paula McKinney. "This was a real nice town till the freeway came through. I mean, at least you had regular blocks, and you knew where you were. . . . But now, it's a disaster."[8]

The construction of interstate highways also encouraged the flow of capital out of the city and into outlying areas. Robert A. Beauregard noted that interstate highways "gave impetus to the trucking industry and improved its competitiveness relative to railroads and international shipping." As ports and railway yards declined in importance, the highway "enabled businesses . . . that relied on trucking to relocate outside the city, where they would have better access to the metropolitan market via the new regional highway network." In addition, the construction of limited-access highways "created high-value intersections throughout the suburban periphery," thereby fueling the creation of shopping malls that "diverted retail expenditures from central business districts."[9] As Kenneth T. Jackson observed, in his classic study of suburbanization, the apotheosis of the automobile during the postwar era "so vastly changed the equation that cities began to 'come apart' economically and functionally even as they had earlier begun to come apart legally with the breakdown of annexation."[10] All of these trends were well-represented in northeastern Ohio. As Linkon and Russo noted in their study of post-industrial Youngstown, the city's Interstate 680 beltway "effectively cut downtown Youngstown off from much day-to-day traffic, directing drivers and, more importantly, shoppers" to newly built suburban shopping plazas and malls.[11] By the early 1980s, the long-term effects of these developments had transformed Youngstown's once-bustling downtown district into a bleak vista of decaying buildings.

Yet, interstate highway construction was just one of many factors that fueled the decline of urban neighborhoods in places like Youngstown. Across the country, thousands of cities were undermined by a phenomenon later termed as "parasitic urbanization," in which suburban communities grew at the expense of neighboring cities. As Beauregard noted, the growth of suburbs in the post–World War II era was "inseparable" from the contraction of industrial urban areas. Declining cities "provided residents for the burgeoning, peripheral housing developments" and "spun off the businesses that anchored shopping malls and industrial parks." As traditional urban centers lost residents, jobs, consumer expenditures, and tax revenues, "decline struck these cities with a vengeance."[12] The growth of suburbs was facilitated by a host of factors that included population growth, the federal government's housing and economic policies, postwar industrial patterns, white responses to demographic change, urban renewal projects, the rise of the automobile as a chief mode of transportation, the wider availability of affordable housing, and (not least of all) the U.S. population's "national distrust of urban life and communal living."[13] Interestingly, these developments were not entirely specific to the United States.

Trends that affected Midwestern cities like Youngstown were evident in urban communities among most of the "developed" nations of the postwar era. The decline of U.S. cites was, in many ways, reflective of "the deindustrialization of the global North and the rise of manufacturing in the global South."[14] By the end of the twentieth century, major Western cities such as New York, London, and Paris "had been eclipsed by cities outside North America and Europe."[15] At the same time, developments within the continental United States intensified domestic patterns of urban depopulation. These developments included the migration of tens of thousands of African Americans from the rural South to the industrial North during the first half of the twentieth century. The sudden arrival of large numbers of onetime rural dwellers in largely unprepared cities would have placed a burden on urban institutions under the best of conditions. Difficulties attending the "Great Migration," however, were compounded by factors including institutionalized racism and tragically poor timing. In the 1950s, thousands of blacks—who were eventually joined by Latinos—flooded into northern industrial cities "just as manufacturing jobs were leaving."[16] By that time, the trends that contributed to urban deindustrialization were already beginning to unfold, as "capitalism left behind huge sections of the United States, mainly older industrial cities in the North and East and rural areas in the South and Midwest."[17]

URBAN PARISHES AS SACRED GROUND

The forces that devastated urban economies also undermined entrenched models of U.S. Catholic identity that had evolved in a largely urban context since the mid-nineteenth century. Catholic historian John T. McGreevy noted that European Catholic immigrant groups "invested an inordinate amount of their savings in property" when compared to other urban dwellers. Some analysts have described the tendency of white Catholics to cluster in enclaves as part of "a conscious attempt to recreate old patterns of community in a new environment." McGreevy, on the other hand, stressed the influence of group loyalties that centered on neighborhood parishes.[18] For Catholics, he argued, "neighborhood, parish, and religion were constantly intertwined."[19] McGreevy further contended that Catholic desires for "a more ordered community" were implicitly supported by Catholic doctrine, as articulated in Pope Leo XIII's 1891 encyclical, *Rerem Novarum* ("Of New Things"), which advocated a corporate society "with the various classes linked by mutual obligations."[20] This essentially organic view of society informed Pope Pius XII's 1939 encyclical on the "Mystical Body of Christ," which compared participants in a community to the organs of the divine corpus.[21] McGreevy noted that, for many American Catholics, an individual who was alienated from the community "was a tragic figure since proper habits could be learned only in the context of specific moral traditions." In a formal sense, "church-sanctioned institutions—notably marriage and the family—were crucial to inculcating virtue, but so too were local groups ranging from church societies to trade unions and political parties." McGreevy pointed out that "[s]uch structures were essential to creating a civil society, one capable of resisting either an overreaching state or an unchecked market economy."[22]

Given the role that urban enclaves played in the transmission of traditional religious values, it is difficult to ignore that many of the factors driving suburbanization in the postwar era also undermined the integrity of established Catholic neighborhoods. A tendency to abandon long-held conceptions of American Catholic identity was accelerated in the early 1960s, when developments in the public sphere inspired a growing number of Catholics to question whether their religious community was as marginalized as they once believed it to be. In 1961, John Fitzgerald Kennedy became the first Roman Catholic president of the United States, undercutting the widely held perception that a "papist" presidential candidate was "unelectable," while signaling to American Catholics "that they were accepted by a wider culture once disposed toward suspicion of them."[23] The following year, the initiation of the Second Vatican Council opened an unprecedented era of ecumenism. So-called Vatican II Catholics moved "beyond the religious world of their parents and grandparents" and, in many cases, "drew an analogy to growing up."[24] This new official openness to non-Catholics, which flew in the face of the Catholic Church's traditional insularity, "provided a basis for Catholics to begin reaching across" traditional religious boundaries.[25] Patterns of suburbanization facilitated this process. As McGreevy noted, most Catholics of the preconciliar era resided in a neighborhood that he described as a "cultural ghetto constructed by the parish." Notably, the "parish boundaries" that defined many urban neighborhoods helped American Catholics to establish cohesive communities, even as they limited opportunities for meaningful interaction with urban dwellers who subscribed to other religions.[26] The religiously integrated neighborhoods of the early 1960s "confirmed how fully [Catholics] had blended into the rest of society."[27]

In Youngstown, as elsewhere in the northeastern United States, traditional Catholic neighborhoods were drained of their vitality as younger people retreated from the central city. When large numbers of ethnic white families moved to the suburbs, they left behind churches and schools that were once cherished social, cultural, and religious centers. Hundreds of Croatian Americans relocated from the lower north side neighborhoods that encircled Sts. Peter and Paul Church and Elementary School, prompting the school's closure in 1973.[28] Likewise, Italian Americans gradually retreated from the traditional ethnic strongholds that had sprung up around the parishes of St. Anthony and Our Lady of Mt. Carmel, both based on the city's north side. While a significant number of Slovak Americans remained loyal to the modest, but meticulously maintained, neighborhoods abutting the south side parish of St. Matthias, most of their children moved elsewhere. This exodus of white, middle-class Catholics from the city imperiled the institutions they left behind, and parochial schools were especially vulnerable, given that they faced the double threat of declining enrollment and shrinking donations. Some Catholic observers, including diocesan officials, responded to these developments by emphasizing the church's "responsibility" to maintain a presence in the city by, among others, preserving urban parish schools.[29] Around the country, liberal Catholic educators, motivated by their awareness of racial and economic inequality in American society, supported religion programs that placed "greater emphasis on personal and social responsibility," while reimagining urban parish schools as training grounds for community leaders.[30] Other leaders in the Catholic community, however, clung to more traditional concepts of religious education and raised questions about continued diocesan support for parish schools that no longer served a majority of white, middle-class Catholic students.[31]

Debates over the future of urban parish schools unfolded against a backdrop of deepening internal discord. The nation's Catholics were evidently unable to agree on many of the fundamental ingredients of their collective religious identity. Liberal Catholics, inspired by the inclusive language of Vatican II, advocated engagement with the larger society. The council, they noted, had shown that the church was "*in* the modern world—not above it, not below it, not for it, not against it." Hence, the church was obliged to "assume its share of responsibility for the well-being of the world, not simply denounce what it finds wrong."[32] Conservatives, on the other hand, remained focused primarily on the interests (spiritual and material) of a traditionally defined Catholic community. Such internal discord left some U.S. Catholics rather disoriented, especially those who were at ease with the uniformity of the past. Crucially, this uniformity was not simply a matter of perception. McGreevy has noted that, despite "intra-Catholic disputes," preconciliar American Catholics held many values in common, and all of them "placed enormous financial, social, and cultural weight on the parish church as an organizer of local life."[33] Surprisingly, the diversity of the post–Vatican II era was more consistent with the church's premodern past. "There are various ways of being Catholic, and people are choosing the style that best suits them," Dolan observed, in his 1985 overview of U.S. Catholic history. "Though this is something new for modern Catholicism, it is not new in the history of the church. For centuries, there were always differing schools of theology, differing liturgical traditions, and differing ways of being Catholic."[34] Those Catholics who continued to view the church as a "perfect" and "unchanging" society, however, could not have been expected to share this perspective.

The weakening of a group solidarity that many U.S. Catholics had taken for granted coincided with—and was, to some extent, exacerbated by—the arrival of more Catholics into suburban communities. As these transplanted urbanites encountered large numbers of Protestants and Jews (often for the first time), they began to lose touch with the traditional identities that had shaped their values and general outlook in an earlier era. "American suburbs were one of the great experiments in social mixing," Charles R. Morris observed. "America's racial lens obscures how radically suburbs scrambled traditional ethnic and social categories."[35] The question of how urban depopulation influenced U.S. Catholic identity is complicated and difficult to track, however. Therefore, it would be a daunting challenge to weave into this chapter a meaningful discussion of Catholic disunity, given its primary focus on the trends that facilitated Youngstown's deterioration—a development that, in turn, weakened the position of local urban parish schools. A detailed examination of U.S. Catholic disunity that highlights its relationship to the decline of urban parish schools appears in a later chapter. For now, the reader is encouraged to take note of the many ways in which urban trends dampened the vitality of Catholic enclaves that once fostered the maintenance of traditional institutions and values. The loss of these neighborhoods (along with major events like World War II and the implementation of the G.I. Bill) smoothed the path for the integration of Catholics into the American mainstream; and by the early 1960s, many Catholics, separated from their traditional urban settings, began to question the long-term efficacy of religious elementary schools. Within a decade, the Catholic exodus from the city inspired a new (equally contentious) debate concerning the viability and overall purpose of urban Catholic schools, a growing number of which served nonwhite, non-Catholic students.[36]

THE ROLE OF DEINDUSTRIALIZATON

To understand how these trends played out in Youngstown, one must take into account the city's dramatic economic decline, which fueled a level of depopulation beyond that witnessed in most other northeastern cities. As a 2005 Youngstown city planning brochure noted, few communities have made the journey from "third largest steel producing city in the U.S." to "poster child" for deindustrialization. In the late 1970s, Youngstown gained national attention for "losing 40,000 manufacturing jobs overnight" and secured a reputation for "crime and corruption."[37] Worse yet, the disappearance of traditional industrial elites left behind a yawning "power vacuum." Some observers contend this vacuum was eventually filled by interest groups who set out to develop "their own plan of action in the wake of the city's decline and competed with each other to achieve their own narrow goals." As Sean Safford observed, in his comparative study of Youngstown and Allentown, Pennsylvania (two communities deeply affected by deindustrialization), "The result has been nothing short of catastrophic decline and hollowing out."[38] As Youngstown's leaders struggled with challenges arising from suburbanization, the city's position as a major manufacturing center was eroded by factors that included the unchecked deterioration of its industrial infrastructure. Thus, it is proper to consider the role extreme patterns of deindustrialization may have played in the deterioration of the city's parochial school system. These patterns clearly accelerated the "out-migration" of potential consumers of urban parochial education.[39]

Youngstown's longstanding reputation as an industrial center was dealt a mortal blow in September 1977, when the New Orleans-based Lykes Corporation announced that the firm's Youngstown Sheet and Tube Division was "pulling out of town." In 1978, one journalist described the steel shutdown in Youngstown as "simply the largest and most dramatic industrial debacle in recent memory."[40] The rapid decline of the local steel industry deprived the community of its most enduring icon, all but ensuring that it would become divorced from its own past. Those Youngstown residents who experienced the dynamic "boom" years of the early twentieth century could hardly have predicted that the city would gain a national reputation as a worst-case scenario for the phenomenon of deindustrialization. Although urban trends in Youngstown were broadly consistent with developments in other northeastern industrial centers, the community has not "[recovered] as well as some other deindustrialized cities."[41] In stark contrast to cities like Allentown, a former steel-manufacturing center that experienced economic resurgence in the wake of industrial collapse, Youngstown has seen "the continuing exodus of 'good' factory jobs and the succession of scandal-ridden attempts at bringing prosperity back to a once-proud community." Moreover, as Safford noted, Youngstown's recent and widely publicized efforts to scale down its "footprint" to match a shrinking population could be interpreted as "an acknowledgment that its best days are past and that its future lies with making do with diminished circumstances."[42]

It would be difficult to exaggerate the role that deindustrialization played in the decline of Youngstown, a community that once took pride in its position as a regional center of iron and steel production. Significantly, the industrial sector's collapse in the late 1970s and early 1980s occurred against a backdrop of perceived economic stability—a circumstance that probably amplified its impact. As local labor attorney and activist Staughton Lynd observed, residents of Youngstown, in the years leading up to the industrial shutdowns, viewed the community's steel plants as "permanent fixtures." Most found it hard to envision a collective economic future that did not revolve around steel production. In the early 1980s, Lynd, who witnessed the dislocations brought on by steel plant closures, described the far-ranging effects of deindustrialization. "A plant closing affects more than the workers at the plant," Lynd wrote. "City income from industrial property taxes goes down, schools start to deteriorate and public services of all kinds are affected. Layoffs occur in businesses which supplied raw materials for the shut-down plant and in businesses which processed the product, retail sales fall off. All the signs of family strain—alcoholism, divorce, child and spouse abuse, suicide—increase."[43]

Notably, the long-term impact of deindustrialization in Youngstown was more pronounced than in many other communities of the industrial northeast. Youngstown—unlike neighboring manufacturing centers like Cleveland, Akron, and Canton—was an economic monoculture, heavily dependent on steel production for its economic vitality as well as its identity. While some observers have blamed the community's postindustrial difficulties on a (widely publicized) prevalence of political corruption and organized crime, others have emphasized the long-term impact of local industrial leaders' continual efforts to limit economic competition. Linkon and Russo observed that, "throughout the 1950s and 1960s, the steel industry fought to exclude the growth of the aluminum industry in Youngstown by making land acquisition difficult and creating a hostile climate for business." As a result, the city "stagnated economically" during the 1950s, even as "other regions with similar infestations of organized crime saw increases in production, construction, and economic diversification."[44] In the wake of subsequent steel-plant closures, the community was stripped not only of a viable future, but also of a meaningful past. Linkon and Russo noted that the community's loss of industry precipitated "the fragmentation of Youngstown's constitutive narrative as locals began to argue about how to think about their shared history."[45] The question that seemed to be on everyone's mind was articulated in a *Vindicator* article published five years after the initial plant closures: "How could an industry so much a part of the history of the community, and so vital to its economic life, simply cease to be or move away?"[46]

THE RISE OF AN INDUSTRIAL "BOOMTOWN"

Local observers in the early twentieth century held a radically different view of the community and its problems. In the 1920s, Youngstown's more established residents feared that their city had grown too quickly, drawing too many people of diverse backgrounds—people who often disagreed on fundamental values. As Safford noted, the city's "elite actors formulated responses that drew on their cohesiveness, time and again, to circle the wagons in the face of uncertainty." Anglo-American elites "banded together" to protect the community from the external threat of industrial consolidation, while at the same time, taking steps to contain the influence of "eastern European immigrants and workers," who were "perceived as threatening the established social order."[47] The city's self-described "pioneers" looked back wistfully on an era when Youngstown's residents were seemingly on familiar terms with most of their neighbors. It appeared those days were gone forever by the 1920s. The city's population more than tripled between 1900 and 1920, soaring from 44,885 to 132,358.[48] In 1925, a *Vindicator* survey showed that the population had risen to 161,477,[49] and engineers with the Ohio Bell Telephone Company predicted that Youngstown's population would reach 470,000 by 1950 if growth continued at the same pace.[50] Despite the tensions that arose in the wake of ethnic and religious diversity, immigrant communities were quickly established. Furthermore, in a climate of exponential growth, urban institutions of all kinds thrived, including Youngstown's parochial elementary schools, which numbered 15 by the close of the 1920s. Within a decade, the city hosted a total of 19 parochial elementary schools, staffed by 7 orders of nuns and enrolling about 6,750 children.[51]

Youngstown's early-20th-century population boom closely paralleled the growth of the local steel industry, which had evolved from the burgeoning iron industry of the previous century. The area's first blast furnace had been established in 1803 in Poland Township, a community to the immediate southeast of Youngstown.[52] By the mid-nineteenth century, Youngstown itself was the site of several iron industrial firms, notably David Tod's Brier Hill Iron and Coal Company.[53] The continued expansion of the community's iron industry depended heavily on a vast network of railroad connections that ensured a consistent supply of coal and iron ore from other parts of the country.[54] Despite this dependence on transported raw materials, "growth in the steel industry was generating a boom-town expansion" by the opening of the twentieth century.[55] In 1900, local industrialists George D. Wick and James A. Campbell, in response to the perceived threat of nationwide industrial consolidation, organized the Youngstown Iron, Sheet and Tube Company (later known as Youngstown Sheet and Tube Company), which became one of the country's most important regional steel producers.[56] In 1923, the firm expanded its operations by acquiring steel plants in the Chicago metropolitan area.[57] Between the 1920s and 1970s, the Youngstown metropolitan area also hosted the furnaces and foundries of Republic Steel and U.S. Steel. Although Youngstown's industrial sector remained relatively stable until the post–World War II era, the population projections of the 1920s proved wildly optimistic. The city's population approached its peak in 1930, when it was recorded at 170,002, rendering it the third largest city in Ohio—and the forty-fifth largest city in the United States.[58] Less dramatic growth was tracked over the next few years. In 1936, a census bureau estimate placed the population at 182,550,[59] while a WPA property survey arrived at the more modest figure of 175,000.[60] Significantly, by 1940, the urban population had dipped below 170,000, and for the next couple of decades, the municipality's numbers rose only incrementally, even as the metropolitan area experienced dramatic gains in population.

THE GROWING IMPACT OF SUBURBANIZATION

A pattern of suburbanization became more pronounced as the decade of the 1940s came to a close. In 1950, Youngstown's population was estimated at 168,000, a slight increase from the 1940 census record of 167,200.[61] As the 1950s progressed, the city continued to experience only limited growth, despite the postwar population boom. In 1954, for instance, a *Vindicator* estimate showed that Youngstown's population rose modestly to 168,330, a gain of merely 610 residents. The newspaper reported that these meager gains were indicative of "one of the biggest population shifts in Youngstown's history," a massive movement of people to the suburbs. The newspaper also noted that, according to its survey, "nearly all the major cities in a five-county area around Youngstown have failed to record much population growth in the last fourteen years but that astounding increases have been noted in areas bordering on the municipalities." In addition, the survey revealed that the adjoining suburbs of Austintown and Boardman townships saw their respective populations practically double during the same period.[62]

While Youngstown's population trends were eventually reflected in the progress of its parochial elementary schools, some local Catholics initially failed to grasp the long-term implications of suburbanization. The post–World War II baby boom, which brought about a temporary rise in the city's population, bolstered enrollment in Youngstown parish schools. This development most likely encouraged false hopes among urban Catholic educators, as declining neighborhoods were temporarily infused with new life. Media accounts suggest that diocesan representatives were generally optimistic about the future of parochial schools. In the mid-1950s, for example, the *Vindicator* reported that, based upon "the annual number of infant baptisms, the Youngstown Catholic Diocese must be ready to meet more than a 50 per cent increase in elementary school enrollment by 1960."[63] Such optimism about the future seemed well founded at the time. In 1959, parish school enrollment for Youngstown and surrounding Mahoning County reached an all-time high, with 16,914 enrolled.[64]

To meet the demands of rising enrollment, two new parochial school facilities were established within the city limits. In 1955, St. Christine's Church, a new parish located on the quasi-suburban west side, opened an elementary school. That same year, St. Patrick's Church, on the south side, established a junior high school annex called St. Patrick's Glenmary.[65] As the decade proceeded, other parish schools were forced to expand their facilities to meet the needs of an expanding student population. In 1957, administrators of the south-side parish of St. Dominic's announced the construction of a 14-room annex. The building, which was designed to relieve overcrowding in the parish's original 16-room structure, featured state-of-the-art teaching facilities and an audiovisual classroom.[66] In 1958, St. Anthony's Parish, forced to relocate because of highway construction, erected a $500,000 church and school complex on the fringes of the north side's Brier Hill district.[67] The school's administrators were compelled to build additional classrooms when St. Anthony's enrollment jumped from 201, in 1959, to 436, in 1963.[68]

This expansion was consistent with developments elsewhere in the city. A 1961 Youngstown school board estimate indicated that 13,318 students were enrolled in Catholic schools—elementary and secondary—while 27,324 attended public schools. In short, about one-third of the city's school-age population was enrolled in Catholic schools.[69] While the *Vindicator* article outlining the estimate failed to specify how many of these pupils were enrolled in parochial elementary schools (as opposed to high schools), these students certainly accounted for the largest share of this figure.

By the early 1960s, however, signs of dwindling enrollment were becoming apparent, and some urban parishes were unable to maintain annexes that had been built little more than a decade earlier. In 1967, St. Patrick's Church closed its elementary school annex in response to a dramatic decrease in enrollment. Between 1960 and 1967, the parish school's student population fell from 1,057 to 615, reflecting a loss of about 40 percent of the student body.[70] Scarcely an isolated incident, the contraction of St. Patrick Elementary School's enrollment reflected a substantial shift in the community's population during the early 1960s. Indeed, the Ohio Department of Development (ODD) reported that Youngstown's population had fallen from 166,689, in 1960, to 164, 242, in 1965—a decline of 2,447.[71] The population estimate reflected, once again, a movement of urban residents to suburban areas. The ODD reported, in 1966, that the Youngstown metropolitan area, on the whole, enjoyed a population increase of almost 8 percent, jumping from 509,006, in 1960, to 548,303, in 1965.[72] The trend continued into the next decade, as Youngstown's final census count for 1970 was set at 139,788, reflecting a 16.1 percent drop since 1960, when the population was recorded at 166,689. At the same time, however, the Youngstown metropolitan area swelled to 536,003 (compared to 509,606 in 1960), a development that supported widespread perceptions that suburbanization was a major factor in the city's depopulation.[73]

Ironically, some projects that were framed as efforts to "revitalize" the city accelerated the flow of people into the suburbs. During the 1960s, Youngstown, like many other U.S. cities, launched highway construction and urban renewal programs that targeted older residential areas. In some cases, the disappearance of aging neighborhoods adversely affected established institutions and businesses, including parochial schools. One of the earliest casualties of interstate highway construction was St. Ann's Church and Elementary School, a landmark of the Brier Hill district on the city's north side. For more than 90 years, the red brick church and school had overlooked the steel mills that snaked along the basin of the Mahoning River. In 1960, however, the large, Norman-style parish complex was closed and pulled down to make way for the extension of a nearby expressway.[74] Significantly, St. Ann's

Parish was not alone in its fate. The first edifice of St. Anthony's Church, an Italian national parish located in the same district, was also razed.[75] Several years later, the growth of Youngstown State University imperiled longstanding neighborhoods on the city's lower and upper north side; and in 1967, the expansion of the university contributed to the closing of St. Joseph's Elementary School, a north side institution since 1874. The former church building was converted into a facility for the Newman Center, a campus organization for Catholic students, while the university leased the vacant school building until it was destroyed by fire in 1969.[76] Around the same time, highway construction resulted in the removal of the traditional Irish American and Italian American enclaves that surrounded Immaculate Conception Church and Elementary School on the city's east side.[77] The combined effect of highway construction and urban renewal projects continued to affect heavily Catholic center-city neighborhoods over the next decade.

The human cost of urban construction projects was often overlooked by city planners. Paula McKinney, a graduate of St. Columba's Elementary School, recalled in a 2007 interview that the clearing of aging homes to accommodate Youngstown State University's northward expansion hastened the demise of her alma mater. The north side boundaries of St. Columba Parish, which covered an area of approximately 20 blocks, extended from the downtown area to the lower reaches of the upper north side, she explained. "Now, all that's gone," McKinney said. "And . . . those houses had kids in them that went to school. Well, of course the enrollment dropped."[78] McKinney's interpretation of events echoed statements that were issued by local Catholic leaders more than 30 years earlier. When St. Columba's Elementary School closed in 1972, the diocesan superintendent of schools, Monsignor William A. Hughes, stated that the city's urban renewal program, "which removed many homes from the area and provides the opportunity for the beautiful campus of Youngstown State University," meant the removal of many parishioners from the near North Side." Monsignor Hughes concluded that the university's expansion project had a critical impact on the parish school's enrollment and helped to make closure inevitable.[79] Notably, the developments Monsignor Hughes described were hardly limited to communities like Youngstown; they were reflective of trends in many northern cities that adversely affected urban parishes.[80]

PUBLIC HOUSING AND THE "RACIALIZATION" OF THE CITY

Urban renewal projects often coincided with the building of public housing, given that renewal efforts frequently involved the razing of older housing stock. Significantly, decaying neighborhoods "targeted by the public housing program were often adjacent to the main commercial district, and their condemnation and demolition were central to the vision of a renewed downtown." In the period stretching from the late 1940s to the mid-1970s, about 500,000 housing units were razed in urban renewal efforts, and more than 900,000 public housing units were constructed. As Beauregard observed, "Most notably, and further racializing the image of the city, the percentage of minority tenants in public housing rose from approximately 2.5 percent to over 60 percent."[81] The concentration of low-income housing projects in urban areas often reflected the vested interests of civic leaders. Jackson noted that legislation "tended to concentrate public housing in the center rather than in the suburbs" because "housing authorities were typically made up of prominent citizens who were more anxious to clear slums and to protect real-estate values than they were to rehouse the poor."[82]

Beyond the impact of construction projects that isolated or destroyed center-city neighborhoods, urban depopulation was driven by the growing allure of the suburbs themselves. As early as 1954, the *Vindicator* reported that "country life" offered all of the "comforts and conveniences of the city . . . plus some room to move around in."[83] Furthermore, a growing number of white urban dwellers looked to the suburbs as a "safe zone" that would insulate them from demographic changes that were occurring throughout much of the center city. Former Youngstown resident Mel Watkins, in his memoir *Dancing with Strangers*, described racist residential restrictions that were prevalent on the city's south side in the 1950s. One evening, upset over a violent argument between his parents, Watkins left the family home and strayed into the all-white enclaves that bordered suburban Boardman Township. Watkins recalled this nocturnal journey as a risky violation of the community's informal—but vigorously maintained—policies of racial segregation. "I walked down Woodland to Hillman Street, then, in a daze, started up Hillman, past the Falls Avenue playground, where on many occasions I'd joined kids and adults from that Italian neighborhood in nightly softball games," he wrote. "Kept moving, aimlessly, past Princeton Junior High School, into the all-white, middle-class neighborhood above Indianola Avenue; then farther south to Midlothian Boulevard and the restricted enclave of the well-to-do whites, where a Negro's mere appearance was cause for alarm, and arrest was likely should one be caught loitering on foot after nightfall."[84]

The construction of low-income housing projects in the central city ultimately increased the isolation of African American urban dwellers, given that such projects became closely associated with disadvantaged minority groups. Westlake Terrace, the first of these local projects, made its appearance in the late 1930s.[85] Within two decades, other public housing projects were completed, including the Kimmel Brooks Homes [86] and McGuffey Terrace,[87] both located on the racially diverse east side. The presence of such low-income housing in cities like Youngstown probably drove suburbanization. As Jackson noted, public housing was "confined to existing slums," and the prevalence of center-city projects "reinforced the image of suburbs as a place of refuge from the social pathologies of the disadvantaged."[88] Tellingly, efforts in the late 1970s to build low-income housing on Youngstown's heavily white, working-class west side met fierce resistance that threatened to derail the project.[89] The retreat of whites into restricted suburban communities contributed significantly to Youngstown's depopulation, but this trend was one factor among many. Whatever motives led individual middle-class whites to relocate to the suburbs, the result was much the same for urban neighborhoods. As the city's wealth declined, vital urban institutions—including public and private schools—suffered the consequences.

URBAN DEPOPULATION AND DECLINING ENROLLMENT

In the 1960s, the media gradually began to draw a connection between the city's waning population and the decline of urban parochial schools. In 1967, the *Vindicator* reported that the planned closing of St. Patrick's junior high school annex was the result of "declining enrollment due to the changing character of the parish."[90] Interestingly, this ambiguous statement not only calls attention to the impact of urban depopulation; it also implies that the surrounding neighborhood was experiencing demographic change. More than two years later, in December 1969, the *Vindicator*'s coverage of a parent-teacher meeting at St. Edward's Elementary School, located on the city's upper north side, refers more explicitly to the impact of demographic change. In an interview, Attorney Richard P. McLaughlin, a parishioner who had two children enrolled at the school, described the challenges of raising a family in a "changing inner-city." Although the attorney did not specifically mention the movement of African Americans into north side neighborhoods, the tenor of his comments suggested that growing racial diversity was among the "changes" discussed at the meeting. "It is vital that we, as parents, take a firm role in helping our children to understand the changes in our neighborhoods," McLaughlin said, "and accept them in the spirit of charity and brotherhood so perfectly exemplified by the Man whose birthday we will celebrate this month."[91]

Curiously, the media sometimes underplayed the fact that declining enrollment among urban parish schools was driven, in large part, by the steady movement of people from the city into outlying areas. Local media often placed more emphasis on developments such as rising tuition. This tendency is surprising, given that reports of "horizontal growth" in the Mahoning Valley filled the columns of local newspapers a decade earlier. Furthermore, by the late 1960s and early 1970s, newspaper coverage of census reports and estimates highlighted the fact that the county's once pastoral suburbs were showing consistent growth, even as the city contracted. Although the 1970 census count for Youngstown was recorded at 139,788, reflecting a 16.1 percent drop from the 1960 figure of 166,689, a newspaper article noted that suburban growth had "offset the loss," ensuring that Mahoning County's final census count would be "1 per cent higher than a decade earlier."[92] In other words, the suburbs continued to grow, albeit modestly, even as the city's population steadily contracted. Youngstown's declining census figures were invariably reflected in falling enrollment levels at urban parochial schools, which fueled a situation that the media began to describe as a "Catholic school crisis."[93] In 1971, the *Vindicator* reported that Youngstown's parochial elementary schools would open in September with 951 fewer students than the previous academic year—a 14 percent decline in enrollment.[94]

Initially, these dramatic losses were attributed almost exclusively to the introduction of tuition fees among local parochial schools. In August 1971, for instance, the *Vindicator* reported that 2,000 students were expected to depart from Catholic elementary and high schools throughout Mahoning County "as the result of parochial tuition fees."[95] While the advent of tuition was most likely a major contributing factor to the drop in enrollment that occurred in the early 1970s, this development does not fully explain the continuation of this trend in subsequent years, when parents became increasingly dissatisfied with urban public schools. A more consistent factor in declining enrollment among urban parochial schools was the city's shrinking pool of potential subscribers. During the early 1970s, falling parish school enrollment was especially pronounced in the aging neighborhoods of Youngstown's central city. In the north side's Brier Hill district, St. Casimir's Elementary School, an institution connected to a Polish national parish established in 1906, closed its doors in the spring of 1971. A similar development occurred at Westlake's Crossing, a working-class district located to the west of the city's downtown, and about a half-mile from the southern edge of Brier Hill. In 1973, the diocese announced the imminent closure of Sts. Peter and Paul Elementary School, an institution sponsored by a Croatian national parish that was founded in 1911.[96] Given the district's tumultuous recent history, this development probably struck many local observers as inevitable.

The area's metropolitan housing authority had repeatedly targeted the area's neighborhoods for "redevelopment" between the 1930s and 1950s.

In 1939, Westlake's Crossing became the site of Youngstown's first low-income housing development, which was christened Westlake Terrace.[97] The district's transformation was completed in 1958, when the majority of its white ethnic and black neighborhoods were razed in the course of slum-clearance projects. Then, in the early 1960s, the "Monkey's Nest," a predominantly black neighborhood that stood to the south of Westlake's Crossing, was demolished to make way for the building of the city's Mahoning Avenue–West Federal Street Expressway as well as an industrial park.[98] Throughout the 1960s and 1970s, older housing stock along the western edge of the district's Croatian American enclave was pulled down to accommodate public housing. Hence, by 1973, the elegant brick bell tower of Sts. Peter and Paul Church stood over a gritty neighborhood composed of dilapidated homes, crumbling nineteenth-century commercial buildings, low-income housing units, and industrial warehouses. Enrollment at the parochial elementary school, which was recorded at 204 in 1967, had fallen to 73 by 1972.[99] These developments were most likely ignored by the majority of the Youngstown area's white Catholics. At this point in the community's history, the most glaring symptoms of urban decline were restricted to the decaying central city, which had been largely abandoned by white, middle-class urban dwellers. In time, however, negative trends within the city's industrial sector affected the metropolitan area as a whole, including outlying suburban townships. The city's position as an important center of steel manufacturing was about to come to an end.

THE END OF YOUNGSTOWN STEEL

Many observers regard the collapse of Youngstown's steel-manufacturing plants as a product of corporate greed and mismanagement, and there is evidence to suggest that the absentee owners of the area's industrial facilities viewed these properties as dubious long-term investments. The community's manufacturing plants, unlike those of many other northeastern industrial cities, were never transferred to outlying areas. While Youngstown Sheet and Tube relocated its headquarters to Boardman Township in the early 1960s, actual steel production was largely restricted to the aging industrial facilities of Youngstown and nearby Struthers and Campbell, Ohio. These facilities, for the most part, required drastic refurbishment to remain competitive. As Fuechtmann observed, in his study of religious responses to the community's deindustrialization, the mechanisms in some of Youngstown's plants "could probably qualify as industrial antiques." He pointed out that a "1908 vintage steam engine with a 22-foot flywheel" continued to serve as the primary power source of one U.S. Steel facility until its closure in 1979.[100] Likewise, a 1983 study noted that, at the time of the plant closures, the community's "newest blast furnace, an essential component in most steel-making activities, was constructed in 1921."[101] The deplorable condition of Youngstown's industrial infrastructure may have owed something to the departure of the community's traditional industrial class, whose members had virtually abandoned the city by the early 1950s. As John Ingham wrote, the exodus of Youngstown's industrial leaders "was so complete that by 1968, only 16 percent of the original thirty-seven iron and steel families remained in the area."[102] In short, the city's industry was no longer in the hands of individuals that were invested in the community. Worse yet, this development coincided with a period of unprecedented international competition. In 1959, during a protracted 116-day strike, "steel consumers relied on the newly built steel mills of Japan and Europe to maintain their inventories." For the first time in the twentieth century, the United States was importing more steel than it was producing, and steel imports increased over time "as hedge buying against a strike."[103]

While the collapse of Youngstown's steel industry had unusually severe consequences for the surrounding community, it was by no means an isolated incident. Developments in the city's industrial sector were broadly consistent with trends seen elsewhere in the nation. In his analysis of Detroit's postwar economic decline, Sugrue observed that America's once formidable industries were overwhelmed by developments "in communication and transportation, the transformation of industrial technology, the acceleration of regional and international economic competition, and the expansion of industry in low-wage regions, especially the South." A regional shift in U.S. industry was discernible as early as the 1930s, when the government "channeled a disproportionate amount of resources to the South, culminating in the Sunbelt-dominated military-industrial complex of the Cold War era." This trend was pushed forward by advances in transportation. Federally subsidized highway construction, for instance, "made central industrial location less necessary by facilitating the distribution of goods over larger distances."[104] Ultimately, this radical shift in the transportation sector rendered Youngstown's massive urban steel-production plants (all "strategically" located along major rail lines) as artifacts of the past. Local industrial leaders were warned repeatedly about the looming crisis. As Safford noted, a series of consultants' reports requested by local industrialists during the 1940s and 1950s predicted that the local steel industry would face challenges related to rising costs and decreased competitiveness. Among others, the reports urged local steel manufacturers to consider "industrial diversification."[105] Fuechtmann observed that, by the 1950s, "the city of Youngstown and to a varying extent its manufacturing suburbs were moving into a period of no growth, and eventually of population decline."[106] Despite mounting questions about the continued viability of Youngstown's steel industry, however, local industrial and political leaders "sought federal funding to build a canal linking Lake Erie to the Ohio River Valley through Youngstown"—a last-ditch effort to salvage local steel concerns that ultimately met with failure.[107]

An ominous turning point in the community's industrial history came in 1969, when Youngstown Sheet and Tube Company, the area's primary steel producer, fell victim to a hostile takeover by New Orleans-based Lykes Corporation, a family-owned business that focused on shipbuilding and ocean transportation. With the escalation of the Vietnam War, the small firm dramatically grew its assets by transporting war matériel across the Pacific, and by the late 1960s, Lykes "was looking around for a way to [further] expand and diversify its assets through the corporate takeover route." Youngstown Sheet and Tube, with assets of $806 million, lost no time in rejecting Lykes's proposal for a merger. The company's representatives noted that the New Orleans firm lacked experience in the steel sector, while its assets amounted to a mere $137 million—a fraction of Sheet and Tube's assets. Lykes's owners persisted, however, attracted by Sheet and Tube's annual cash flow of $100 million and the relatively low selling price of its stock, which offered a chance to complete "a billion-dollar merger for something like 30 cents on the dollar." In January 1969, to the shock of many local observers, Lykes Corporation completed the corporate takeover of Sheet and Tube, borrowing $150 million in bank loans and issuing about $191 million in debentures to finance the move.[108] Consequently, the newly merged company "assumed a debt liability of nearly $350 million."[109] Given the disparity in assets between the two companies, few observers predicted that the merger would benefit Sheet and Tube. Indeed, a report prepared by the Anti-Trust Division of the Department of Justice went so far as to question the legality of the merger. The report also accurately predicted that Lykes Corporation would abandon the previous management's long-term strategy to upgrade Sheet and Tube's facilities and plunder the firm's resources. In the absence of existing legislation to prevent the merger, however, U.S. Attorney General John Mitchell lacked firm legal grounds to oppose it. Before long, the steel company found itself on a treacherous downward spiral. Denied adequate investment, Sheet and Tube managed to lose money even during the short-lived domestic steel boom of 1973 and 1974, despite the fact that it was operating at 100-percent capacity. These losses were the result of continual breakdowns that arose from the company's dependence on outmoded equipment. Sheet and Tube's failure to modernize also ensured a more expensive product, because "[labor costs for running the small blast furnaces, as well as for the slow open hearth furnaces, made Youngstown steel comparatively expensive in a highly competitive market period." Meanwhile, U.S. banks became more reluctant to extend loans to the beleaguered steel company, at a time when "they were significantly expanding their loans to Japanese steel companies."[110] Within eight years of the ill-fated merger with Lykes Corporation, Sheet and Tube began the painful process of closing down its Youngstown-area operations.

Unsurprisingly, Youngstown's most dramatic population losses occurred in the 1980s, following the collapse of its core steel industry. This grim chapter in the community's history opened on September 19, 1977, when representatives of Lykes Corporation announced the closing of the company's huge facility in nearby Campbell, along with smaller plants in neighboring Struthers. The Campbell shutdown itself resulted in the loss of 5,000 jobs in the Youngstown area, and it proved to be the first in a series of crippling economic developments.[111] The layoffs in Campbell sent ripples of uncertainty across the community. Father Edward Noga, then an assistant pastor at St. Christine's Church, recalled that his parish lost 50 families in the months immediately following Lykes's announcement. "Today, we see people moving for jobs all the time," the priest recalled. "But that was . . . unprecedented [at the time], especially as we look back . . . and [recognize] all the federal legislation that has come out of our experience of companies just pulling up stakes and not telling anybody and not giving governments notice."[112] The shutdown of Youngstown Sheet and Tube's operations in Campbell and Struthers was followed by the staged withdrawal of U.S. Steel in 1979 and 1980, which resulted in the closing of massive steel plants in Youngstown and neighboring McDonald, Ohio.[113] Another string of closings came with the bankruptcy of Republic Steel in the 1980s. Thus, in the course of several years, "the Steel Valley"—a onetime industrial zone comprising Mahoning and Trumbull counties as well as portions of western Pennsylvania—"had lost forty thousand manufacturing jobs, four hundred satellite businesses, $414 million in personal income, from 33 to 75 percent of the school tax revenues, and some very good neighbors."[114]

This situation was compounded by the fact that local responses to the crisis were "characterized by extreme fragmentation, infighting, and ultimately inaction."[115] Those efforts taken were frequently informed by a desire to revitalize the Youngstown area's crippled steel sector. The community's ongoing attachment to steel was reflected in the high-profile activities of the Ecumenical Coalition of the Mahoning Valley, a local activist group comprising church leaders and steelworkers. Between 1977 and 1979, the coalition raised funds in a courageous attempt to reopen the Campbell Works of the defunct Youngstown Sheet and Tube Company.[116] Many observers questioned the wisdom of this grassroots effort, and some, like former labor leader Jack O'Connell, contended that "it was one of those things that hurt this valley more than anything else." For O'Connell, the coalition's "Save Our Valley" campaign prevented local residents from coming to terms with the fact that the steel industry was gone forever. "We had the old-timers in this valley still sitting in their kitchen, waiting for a call back to the mill, when we reopened the mill," he said. "The mills stayed there, and they became a monument to extinction."[117]

The impact of these events on the city's population proved devastating. Although population estimates for the late 1970s were unavailable for this study, preliminary census figures released in 1980 revealed that Youngstown's population fell from 140,509 to 112,146 between 1970 and 1980—a decline of 20.4 percent. Meanwhile, the population of Mahoning County, which includes several large suburban townships, fell by a less dramatic 7.1 percent, slipping from 304,545 in 1970 to 282,813 in 1980.[118] Within a couple of years, local researchers suggested that urban depopulation had outstripped—by a wide margin—figures recorded in the 1980 census. In 1982, Dr. Terry Buss, director of Youngstown State University's urban studies program, speculated that the city's population was already 10,000 lower than the 1980 census indicated. Buss pointed out that it "usually takes up to three years for the effects of a mill shutdown to develop fully." His statements were supported by Dr. John Russo, director of Youngstown State University's labor studies department, who agreed that the community had experienced a "substantial drop" in population since 1980.[119]

These predictions of a continuous and steep decline in the city's population were prescient. Within several years, the cumulative effects of years of population decline—coupled with the disastrous plant closures of the 1970s and early 1980s—were reflected in Youngstown's diminished ranking among American cities. In 1984, the *Vindicator* reported that Youngstown, which had been the country's forty-fifth largest city in 1931, ranked one hundred and forty-fifth nationally. Similarly, the former "boomtown," once the third-largest city in Ohio, dropped to the position of seventh-largest.[120] At the same time, the city gained unwanted exposure for its postindustrial difficulties. A 1984 study conducted by the New York-based research firm, Dun & Bradstreet Corporation, ranked Youngstown as twenty-third among the country's twenty-fifth fastest-shrinking metropolitan areas in the period stretching from 1980 to 1983. The study estimated that the Youngstown area experienced a 1.8 percent drop in population between 1980 and 1983.[121] Then, in 1985, Youngstown's surrounding Mahoning County was ranked fourteenth in population loss in the country.[122] To the alarm of civic leaders, researchers anticipated that the situation would worsen over time. A preliminary report issued by the Ohio Data User's Center, a research institute connected to the ODD, forecasted that depopulation would continue into the next century. The report projected that Mahoning County, which recorded 289,487 people in 1980, would have just 248,530 people in 1995, and only 229,687 by the year 2010.[123] These population projections, based on available census data from the period between 1970 and 1980, were supported by studies released near the end of the decade. In 1987, a Dun & Bradstreet survey of 414 counties with populations exceeding 100,000 ranked Youngstown seventeenth nationally in percentage of population decrease. The survey suggested that in 1986, Mahoning County's population stood at 276,230, compared with 289,487 in 1980.[124]

As municipal leaders scrambled to respond to chronic depopulation, they were hampered by decades of city planning based on the assumption of continued growth. A citywide plan proposed by the municipal government in 2005 observed that two previous city plans—issued in 1951 and 1974, respectively—"were for a different era that anticipated a population between 200,000 and 250,000."[125] Youngstown's oversized infrastructure contributed to mass vacancies in residential, institutional, commercial, and industrial zones. Over the years, deterioration of structures in these zones powerfully underscored Youngstown's image as a city in decline, thereby encouraging the out-migration of residents. Excess housing units, in particular, had a "devastating" effect on urban neighborhoods, as structures without economic value were "abandoned and looted of anything that [had] scrap value." Meanwhile, the shells of vacant homes became "convenient places for criminal activity." In the absence of appropriate planning, the decline of the city's population quickly outstripped the scaling down of its oversized infrastructure. As a 2005 city planning proposal indicated, Youngstown's population fell from 115,423 to 82,026 between 1980 and 2000, while the number of the city's housing units declined more modestly during the same period, falling from 45,105 to 37,158.[126]

In the wake of rampant deindustrialization, Youngstown's shrinking population found its parallel—predictably enough—in the flagging rolls of the city's parish schools. Diocesan records show that, between 1979 and 1980, total enrollment for Youngstown's parochial elementary schools fell from 4,034 to 3,922—a loss of 112 students. Records also show that, by 1984, parochial school enrollment had slipped to 3,102, reflecting a staggering loss of 820 students since 1980. Then, in 1985, the city's parochial school rolls showed 2,838 students, a reduction of 264 students from the previous year. The initial effects of urban depopulation, once again, were most pronounced in those schools based in aging center-city neighborhoods. Between 1979 and 1980, for instance, schools that showed the most severe enrollment losses included St. Dominic's (–31), on the south side; St. Edward's (–32), on the north side; and Sacred Heart (–40), on the east side. A handful of center-city parish schools saw a modest boost in enrollment—notably St. Patrick's Elementary School, which gained 24 students—while a few others maintained status-quo enrollment.[127] On the whole, however, schools located in neighborhoods that experienced depopulation before the collapse of Youngstown's steel sector were among those seriously affected by the accelerated depopulation characteristic of the 1980s.

Naturally, center-city ethnic parish schools were among the most vulnerable of Youngstown's urban institutions. Heavily dependent on the sponsorship of white ethnic groups who had mostly retreated to suburban areas, these schools were struggling even before the advent of the 1980s. Therefore, few local observers could have been surprised in 1983, when the diocese announced that Sts. Cyril and Methodius Elementary School, a fixture on the north side since 1907, would close at the end of the school year. The parish and school, which were established primarily for Slovak Americans, also served hundreds of Lithuanian, Polish, Hungarian, and Greek Uniate Catholics. At its peak, Sts. Cyril and Methodius enrolled 250 students, the vast majority of whom belonged to the parish. Yet, by the end of the 1977–1978 academic year, the school enrolled only 95 students. While enrollment fell only modestly over the next few years, the composition of the student body changed significantly. The *Vindicator* reported that, at the time of Sts. Cyril and Methodius's closure, only 48 of the school's 90 students were "from the parish," a circumstance that could be interpreted to suggest that some of the remaining students were non-Catholic and nonwhite.[128] The decision to close the school came on the heels of a diocesan projection that only 78 students would be enrolled for the upcoming academic year.[129]

As the effects of deindustrialization and unemployment bore down on the community, urban parochial schools continued to grapple with plummeting enrollment. In 1986, the diocesan school board announced the closure of St. Stanislaus Elementary School, a south side institution affiliated with a Polish national parish. While the school had served 333 students in 1965, it enrolled just 71 in 1985. Tellingly, just 28 of these students were members of the parish—further evidence of demographic changes that resulted in a smaller percentage of Catholics in urban neighborhoods.[130] In time, even those ethnic parish schools that operated in majority-white, working- to middle-class neighborhoods were showing the effects of depopulation. This became evident in 1990, when Holy Name Elementary School, which was established on the west side in 1920, announced it would close its doors permanently. Although it was based in a relatively stable neighborhood, the school's fate had hung in the balance for nearly a decade. Holy Name faced the prospect of closure in 1982 and, once again, in 1987, when the diocese demanded that the school enroll at least 70 students in order to remain open. On the second of these occasions, Dr. Nicholas Wolsonovich, the diocesan school superintendent, granted Holy Name a reprieve when a recruitment drive boosted enrollment to almost 60 students. It was clear to most people involved, however, that the parish school's days were numbered. Between 1975 and 1989, Holy Name's enrollment plummeted from 212 to 43, while the school's cost-per-pupil average rose from $500 to $2,500.[131] In the face of such discouraging data, parishioners continued to support the school. For many, the institution held a significance that outweighed its utilitarian value. Holy Name Elementary School was the centerpiece of a Slovak American neighborhood that, despite highway construction, retained a measure of its central European charm. Over the years, the school's alumni had included Brooklyn Dodgers legend George "Shotgun" Shuba, whose career was immortalized in Roger Kahn's 1972 sports classic, *The Boys of Summer.* As Kahn observed, Shuba developed his early baseball skills on the streets and vacant lots of this apparently stable and unchanging west-side ethnic enclave.[132] Parishioners of Holy Name, conscious of the school's rich history, successfully fought its closure on two occasions. By 1990, however, Holy Name's enrollment had been reduced to a paltry 43 students, and the school was forced to cease operation.[133]

Meanwhile, in the face of popular predictions that the community had "hit rock bottom" and was likely to rebound, Youngstown's population continued its inexorable slide, falling to 95,732 residents in 1990. Indeed, the opening of the new decade marked an unsettling milestone in the community's demographic history. With its population recorded at just below 100,000, Youngstown lost its official status as a major American city.[134] More troubling developments were on the horizon. The following year, in 1991, statistics showed that surrounding Mahoning County was losing younger workers at a rate many observers considered alarming. The *Vindicator* reported that, between 1980 and 1990, the number of county residents aged 18 to 24 fell from 35,509 to 23,569.[135] Although occasional media reports suggested that the urban population was stabilizing, less optimistic forecasts consistently proved more accurate. Nevertheless, some municipal leaders persisted in characterizing realistic demographic projections as by-products of "negativity." In 1996, when the *Vindicator* predicted that Youngstown's population would fall to 90,109 in 2000, the director of the Mahoning County Planning Commission dismissed the projection as "pessimistic."[136] The *Vindicator*'s forecast, as it turned out, was unduly optimistic. In 2000, the U.S. Census Bureau recorded the city's population at 82,026, a figure that fell considerably below the *Vindicator*'s 1996 forecast.[137]

In sync with the city's declining population, parochial school enrollment continued its precipitous slide. Urban parish school administrators, faced with flagging rolls and shrinking resources, were compelled to be resourceful to keep their schools operating. As early as the 1970s, Immaculate Conception Elementary School, located on the city's east side, developed a "mission concept" that enabled it to engage in diocesan-wide fund-raising efforts.[138] This surprisingly effective strategy proved crucial to the survival of several center-city parish schools; and by 1991, both Immaculate Conception and St. Patrick's elementary schools depended heavily on donation drives that targeted diocesan parishioners and parochial school students. In April, the two schools narrowly averted closure when they met their joint goal of $115,000.[139] Both of these institutions survived to enroll students the following academic year; and to the surprise of many, Immaculate Conception remained in operation for another decade. Schools with less visibility, however, were poorly equipped to weather urban trends that chipped away at their economic viability.

The 1990s shaped up as a decade of serial parochial school closings. In 1996, diocesan superintendent Dr. Wolsonovich announced that another urban icon, St. Anthony's Elementary School, would cease operation. The relatively modern school building was the pride of a working-class, Italian American neighborhood on the city's lower north side. Until the 1990s, St. Anthony's Parish had weathered many of the urban trends that conspired against its existence. In the late 1950s, as noted, the parish's original church building was pulled down to make way for interstate highway construction, a project that eventually claimed the large complex of St. Ann's Parish, which had served the neighborhood's Irish American Catholics. By the time the buildings were demolished, few of St. Ann's parishioners remained in Brier Hill, and the old parish was relegated to history. The story of St. Anthony's Church was different, however. Not only did the parishioners pool their resources to rebuild the church (along more elaborate lines than the original), but they also established a parish school. St. Anthony's Elementary School opened in 1959 with 201 students and saw its enrollment expand dramatically over the next several years. The school's enrollment peaked at 436 students in 1963.[140] Yet, by fall 1996, St. Anthony's rolls had slipped to 122, making closure all but unavoidable.[141]

St. Anthony's fate was shared by one of the city's most widely admired urban parish schools. That same year, in 1996, St. Patrick's Elementary School abandoned its long struggle to remain in operation. The parish school had been a landmark on the city's south side since 1914, when it opened with 500 students, and enrollment grew dramatically over the next several decades. By the 1950s, St. Patrick's served more than 1,000 pupils and was required to build a new junior high school building. Yet, within a decade, the school's rolls began to fall; and by spring 1996, the parish school served just 107 students, a figure that represented a decline of 126 pupils from the previous academic year.[142] Significantly, however, the institution's story did not end with its closing as a parish school. In May 1996, Thomas J. Tobin, bishop of the Diocese of Youngstown, announced that the school would be "transformed" into a joint Lutheran-Catholic ecumenical school known as New Hope Academy.[143] The new school was to be cosponsored by the Diocese of Youngstown and the Northern Ohio Synod of the Evangelical Lutheran Church. Within a decade, the building—like several other former parish school facilities in Youngstown—was leased to a charter school franchise.

In certain respects, the challenges facing St. Patrick's Church were emblematic of those confronting many other urban parishes that sponsored elementary schools. Burdened with aging and oversized physical plants, these parishes were barely able to pay the utility bills that kept their facilities heated and properly lit. Under such circumstances, the difficulties involved in maintaining a parish school often seemed overwhelming. The challenges facing Father Edward Noga, pastor of St. Patrick's Church, were particularly daunting. Upon assuming the pastorate in 1985, Father Noga struggled to maintain a sprawling physical plant that included a neo-Gothic church that towered more than 100 feet above street level. The church building featured a 92-foot ceiling, 140-foot nave, and 72 stained-glass windows, most of which were in need of restoration work by the 1990s. Father Noga noted that, in recent years, the parish had spent $200,000 to repair the church's leaking roof, while devoting hundreds of thousands of additional funds to the remodeling of the parish social hall and the restoration of its stained glass windows. These projects have generated some debate within the parish community. The pastor recalled that, during parish council meetings, some members objected to the planned restoration of the church's stained-glass windows, contending that the $300,000 needed for the project could be used to develop outreach programs. "And they're right," Father Noga acknowledged. "But, at the same time, [the church building is] like our home." Gesturing to the neo-Gothic church that stands just north of the parish rectory, he added, "Over twenty-one years, the amount of money put into the maintenance and upkeep of that building that's forty feet from us is no less than staggering."[144] St. Patrick's parishioners are uncomfortably aware of the amount of money the parish has devoted to the preservation of its physical plant, and one member of St. Patrick's Parish Council agreed with Father Noga that the costs involved in maintaining parish facilities contributed substantially to the school's closing. At the same time, he described the shutting down of the parish school as unavoidable. "I think it's terribly sad," said parishioner T. Gordon Welsh. "I also think, however, that it's . . . realistic to recognize that our little parish of St. Pat's could no more afford to keep that school than fly in the air."[145]

GROWING COMPETITION FOR A SHRINKING
POOL OF STUDENTS

The decade of the 1990s brought with it new challenges, including the rise of competitive charter schools that drew from a shrinking pool of urban pupils. These state-funded schools were not the first institutions to compete directly with Youngstown's parish schools, but their impact was unprecedented. The local media reported on the growth of private religious schools in center-city neighborhoods during the late 1970s and early 1980s. In 1981, the *Vindicator* noted that the city's Protestant schools had doubled their enrollment, even as public school rolls fell by 23.1 percent (from 133,145 students to 102,123) and Catholic schools enrollment slipped by 9.5 percent (from 15,093 students to 13,560). One of the first Christian private schools to appear in Youngstown was Watkins Christian Academy, which opened on the city's east side. Given its location, the academy most likely competed for students with Immaculate Conception and Sacred Heart elementary schools. In short order, Watkins Christian Academy was joined by Youngstown Christian School and Calvary Christian Academy. Both schools opened on the south side, where they probably appealed to non-Catholic clients of St. Patrick's Elementary School. Despite the steady growth of these schools, however, they posed a relatively modest threat to urban parish schools. The reason was simple and straightforward. Many private Christian schools charged exorbitant tuition fees. Youngstown Christian School, for example, charged $750 a pupil, compared with the $250 tuition fee charged at most local Catholic elementary schools.[146]

A more serious threat to urban parish schools emerged in the next decade, with the rise of nondenominational, state-funded charter schools that offered amenities that were traditionally associated with parish schools. Adding to their appeal was the fact that these schools did not charge tuition. Eagle Heights Academy, Youngstown's premier charter school, opened on the city's south side in 1998. Located in a massive Beaux Arts building that once housed a large public school, Eagle Heights emerged in the wake of state legislation authorizing the establishment of charter schools within Ohio's eight major urban school districts. The academy was one of 15 charter schools that opened across the state in 1998 alone. While nonsectarian schools like Eagle Heights Academy received state funding, they operated independently of any school district. Furthermore, despite their nondenominational status, some of these schools were supported and managed by local religious leaders, who deplored the record of urban public schools. Eagle Heights Academy, for instance, was established and managed by a group of local Protestant ministers that included the late

Reverend Jay Alford, a conservative activist who was then pastor of Highway Tabernacle Church, an evangelical Christian community in Austintown Township.[147] Within less than a decade, Reverend Alford emerged as cochairman of an organization calling itself Citizens for Public Service, whose stated goal was to elect local political leaders "who will recognize their responsibility to God and to the citizens who elect them."[148] Reverend Alford participated in the school's five-member board of trustees, which was led by the Reverend Gary L. Frost, an African American civic leader who served as pastor of Rising Star Baptist Church in Youngstown.[149]

Reverend Frost, who developed the concept behind Eagle Heights, was the chief organizer of Warriors, Inc., a group of Protestant ministers that purchased the former South High School building when the public school ceased operation in 1993. By summer 1998, Warriors, Inc., raised $400,000 to renovate the 87-year-old school building, which had been vacant for five years. Faced with the task of securing the $1 million needed to restore the structure, Reverend Frost expressed confidence that the group would achieve its goals. He predicted that 450 students would participate in the school's kindergarten-through-sixth-grade program in the coming fall, and he was not disappointed. Reverend Frost appeared equally optimistic about the group's fund-raising campaign to refurbish the school building. "God has really come through," he said, "in allowing people and business people to come forward" to assist in the building's renovation.[150] Reverend Frost's confidence was evidently well placed. In October 1998, Eagle Heights Academy received a powerful economic boost when the banking firm National City Corporation contributed more than $1 million to the charter school. A ceremony marking the contribution featured an appearance by Ohio's then Governor George Voinovich. Reverend Jay Alford, who spoke at the ceremony, praised the Republican governor for his support of charter schools and described him as "the greatest governor in the history of Ohio and the greatest governor in the United States."[151] Reverend Alford had reason to be pleased with the state's Republican leadership. At this point, developments at the state level were working to the advantage of those supporting the charter school movement. In July 1998, for instance, the Ohio State Board of Education approved legislation that authorized the opening of more charter schools around the state, including a second one in Youngstown.[152] This legislation eventually paved the way for Youngstown Community School, which was scheduled to enroll 36 at-risk kindergarten students on the city's impoverished south side.[153]

Significantly, the state government continued to enact policies that facilitated the expansion of charter schools. In spring 1999, the Ohio legislature allowed for the creation of 37 new charter schools statewide, and in April, 2 more prepared to open in Youngstown. Hope Academy (Youngstown Campus), the largest of the 2 schools, was authorized to enroll up to 390 students in classes ranging from kindergarten to eighth grade. The new school operated as a franchise of the Akron-based firm Hope Academy Limited Liability Corporation, an educational enterprise that served as a consultant for Eagle Heights Academy. Hope Academy's local campus was joined by the Life Skills Center of Youngstown, which was prepared to serve up to 120 at-risk students in grades 9–12. The *Vindicator* reported that the city's 4 charter schools were expected to enroll a combined 1,200 students "who otherwise would be in the city's public or parochial schools." A disproportionate percentage of these students would attend Eagle Heights Academy, which experienced considerable growth since its establishment in 1998. Within a year, the charter school enrolled 624 students and had a waiting list of 1,000.[154]

The impact of the city's charter schools upon parish schools was almost instantaneous. In 1999, administrators at St. Dominic's Elementary School—described in the local media as "a stronghold of the city's South Side for 75 years"—announced that the institution would close at the end of the school year. St. Dominic's enrollment, which peaked in 1964 at 1,297 students, fell to 150 in 1999. Father Joseph Allen, pastor of St. Dominic's Church, attributed the closure to factors such as "the school's increasing dependence on parish subsidies, uncollected tuition, and chronic enrollment declines." Tellingly, the pastor added that the most recent drop in St. Dominic's enrollment coincided with the opening of Eagle Heights Academy on the city's south side.[155] In what emerged as a "perfect storm" scenario, Youngstown's urban parochial schools—long deprived of adequate enrollment, tuition dollars, and parishioner donations—were now in competition with free, publicly funded schools that offered many of the benefits of private schools.

With the rise of competitive charter schools, the trend toward declining enrollment among urban parish schools escalated in the early twenty-first century. In June 2003, Wallace Dunne, a diocesan school board member and former parochial school principal, addressed a crowd gathered for the final baccalaureate mass of St. Edward's Elementary School. The speaker's connection to the school was strong—he had served as principal of St. Edward's between 1971 and 1989—and his words were poignant. "I'm very sad about the closing, but this school has made a tremendous contribution to the community over the years," Dunne said to the crowd. "If you go to city hall or the hospitals or the legal profession . . . you'll find St. Edward's graduates have done well."[156] Indeed, the parish school had been one of the most successful institutions of its kind in Youngstown. St. Edward's Elementary School had opened on the city's affluent upper north side in 1917, and it quickly emerged as one of the city's major parochial schools. In the 1960s, the parish's boundaries were extended into adjoining Liberty Township, a move that mitigated the effects of suburbanization; and as recently as the mid-1990s, the parish seemed relatively stable. Moreover, St. Edward's leadership appeared committed to the development of both parish and school. In 1994, the parish raised $750,000 to refurbish the church interior, a project that involved the construction of a new marble altar, the installation of new pews, and the placement of several arched windows where a side entrance had been located.[157] By the turn of the twenty-first century, however, St. Edward's Church was forced to confront the realities connected to an aging parish population, as more and more young families moved elsewhere. To make matters worse, neighboring Liberty Township, the home of a large percentage of St. Edward's parishioners, was struggling with challenges once associated with Youngstown's north side, as more low-income families moved into the suburban community.

The end came swiftly. In February 2003, Father Frank Lehnerd, pastor of St. Edward's Church, announced that the parish's elementary school would not reopen for the upcoming academic year. In a prepared statement, Father Lehnerd attributed the school's terminal difficulties to an exodus of Catholics from the city. "St. Edward School has had a long history of serving the Catholic families on the North Side of Youngstown and Liberty Township," the pastor stated. "As the Catholic population has moved further from the parish, the need for a Catholic school has declined."[158] Absent from the pastor's comments was any reference to the parish school's increased reliance on the patronage of the mainly nonwhite, non-Catholic families residing in surrounding neighborhoods. Many of these families had apparently chosen alternatives to Catholic education. Interestingly, the school's dependence on the patronage of non-Catholic students could hardly have been predicted 30 years earlier. In 1977, only 5.4 percent of St. Edward's 614 pupils were African American, and just 5.2 percent of the student body was non-Catholic.[159] By 2002, however, the *Vindicator* reported that St. Edward's was among the city's endangered parish schools. Like Immaculate Conception Elementary School, St. Edward's served students who were mainly from low-income, non-Catholic, and minority backgrounds.[160]

Local residents who were surprised to learn about the closing of St. Edward's Elementary School, an institution sponsored by a traditionally affluent parish, were probably shocked two years later, when the media reported the imminent closure of St. Brendan's Preschool and Elementary School. Since 1925, the parish school had been a landmark on the city's working- and middle-class west side. Moreover, the parish appeared to be vibrant. Although the effects of deindustrialization were painfully evident throughout much of Youngstown, the city's west side had weathered the economic storm surprisingly well. Neighborhoods surrounding St. Brendan's

Church were generally well-maintained, even as homes elsewhere in the city fell into disrepair. In addition, with 119 students enrolled in its kindergarten through eighth-grade classes, St. Brendan's appeared healthier than some of its center-city counterparts. However, when compared to St. Christine's Elementary School, another west side institution, St. Brendan's enrollment seemed extraordinarily low. In 2005, St. Christine's Elementary School enrolled 444 students, more than three times the number of students recorded at St. Brendan's.[161] Therefore, in February 2005, St. Brendan's pastor, Father James Daprile, visited classrooms and confirmed widespread rumors that the school would close in June of that year—a move that angered parents who believed that they should have been the first to be informed.[162] The local media placed the school's scheduled closing in the context of the city's declining population; and Bishop Thomas J. Tobin underscored this theme, noting that Youngstown had lost 41 percent of its population since 1970, "bringing with it a 56 percent decrease in Catholic population." Bishop Tobin indicated that the final decision to close the school, though "difficult," was practically unavoidable.[163] Nevertheless, news of the decision inspired angry protests from the small number of families who depended on the school, and some observers went so far as to predict the rapid deterioration of the west side. Paula McKinney, whose grandson attended the parish school at the time, recalled warning the pastor that the move would have devastating consequences for the neighborhood. Among others, she predicted that "for sale" signs would appear on lots throughout the district. "[The pastor] closed the doors, and you see what's happening," she said, referring to the accelerated departure of white, middle-class families from the west side. "And I told him it was going to happen, too."[164]

Despite detailed news coverage of these developments, the serial closure of the city's parochial schools went virtually unnoticed by a surprising number of local residents. Many of the community's Catholics took the schools for granted, assuming they would always be part of the urban landscape. This stubborn illusion was dispelled on June 6, 2006, when Youngstown's pattern of parochial schools came to an official end. On that date, administrators of two of the city's three remaining parish schools—Immaculate Conception, on the east side, and St. Matthias, on the south side—announced that these institutions would cease operation. Sister Charlotte Italiano, OSU, principal of Immaculate Conception, observed in an interview with a local journalist that the school's final graduating class of 12 students was the smallest in its entire history. Meanwhile, Cheryl Jablonski, the principal of St. Matthias Elementary School, told reporters that the school's 61 students (from pre-kindergarten to eighth grade) would make a bittersweet journey to a regional amusement park "to mark the end of the school year and the permanent closure."[165] As local media pointed out, the simultaneous closings of St. Matthias and Immaculate Conception elementary schools left only one parish school operating within the city limits, and few could ignore that St. Christine's Elementary School (based in a neighborhood that straddled Austintown and Boardman townships) was "urban" only in the most technical sense.

Overall, developments seen in Youngstown during the 1990s and early twenty-first century were consistent with trends seen elsewhere in the United States. In cities across the country, private religious schools—especially Catholic parochial schools—were fighting what appeared to be a losing battle for survival. In neighboring Cleveland, for instance, Catholic parochial schools continue to face strong pressure to consolidate.[166] In January 2008, then President George W. Bush acknowledged in his State of the Union address that faith-based schools were "disappearing at an alarming rate in many of America's inner cities." Advocates of Catholic education were acutely aware of this trend, and many attributed this development to the adverse effects of urban charter schools. Father Ronald J. Nuzzi, director of the Alliance for Catholic Education leadership program at the University of Notre Dame, referred to charter schools as "one of the biggest threats to Catholic schools in the inner city, hands down." Ironically, the most influential advocates of charter schools have turned out to be the same conservative political leaders who now express concern about the decline of center-city private religious schools. Supporters of charter schools respond to the concerns of Catholic educators by pointing out that Catholic schools remain a vital force in America's educational landscape, with "more than 2.3 million K-12 students in about 7,500 U.S. Catholic schools." This is about twice the number of students enrolled in the nation's charter schools. In response, critics of charter schools have called such figures misleading. They note that, since the passage of the first state charter school law in 1991, charter schools have grown consistently, while urban Catholic schools have continued to decline. *Education Week* reported that since 2000, "urban Catholic schools in the United States have lost 20 percent of their enrollment, or 187,283 students." Meanwhile, a 2006 study of enrollment patterns in private and charter schools in Michigan showed that between 1994 and 1999, charter schools drew nearly the same rate of students from public and private schools. However, given that only 8 percent of Michigan's students attended private schools, these schools were disproportionately affected.[167]

Catholic leaders in Youngstown have cited the growth of charter schools as an important contributing factor in the decline of urban parish schools, which were already dealing with the effects of urban depopulation. Sister Charlotte Italiano, OSU, who served as principal of both St. Patrick's and Immaculate Conception elementary schools, called the impact of the charter schools decisive, noting that they "pulled people away from the [parochial] schools" because of the huge financial incentive. "If parents could save money at the elementary school level to advance their kids into high school or college, that's what they would choose to do," she added. Sister Charlotte noted that charter schools often provided amenities that were not offered at Catholic elementary schools. Furthermore, parochial school class sizes were, on average, larger than those at charter schools, making the student-teacher ratio considerably higher. In addition, while charter schools "could afford to have two certified teachers in every classroom," urban parish schools "struggled to keep one full-time teacher in the classroom." Finally, parish schools were far less equipped to serve "special needs" children, given that government funds dispensed for this purpose could not "compare with what the public schools get."[168] Father Noga, pastor of St. Patrick's Church, concurred with Sister Charlotte's assessment. "The charter schools were perceived as private schools that were free," he said.[169] For urban parishes that were already struggling to maintain elementary schools, the challenge posed by charter schools may have been the last straw.

SIGNS OF RESURGENCE IN A BELEAGUERED CITY?

The closing of most of the city's parish schools had its parallel in the consolidation of Youngstown's public schools. Scores of public elementary schools have merged or closed down, while Youngstown's six original public high schools have reconfigured and consolidated; only two operate within the city limits today. Meanwhile, Youngstown's population continues to fall, and linear population predictions developed by the ODD a decade ago suggested it would slip from over 82,000 to 54,000 by 2030.[170] In March 2011, this dire prediction was lent considerable weight by the findings of the 2010 U.S. census, which revealed that Youngstown's population had dropped 18.4 percent since 2000, falling from 82, 026 to 66,982—a staggering loss of 15,044 residents.[171] Under such conditions, perennial forecasts of Youngstown's imminent revitalization have often fallen on deaf ears. Residents, after all, have been bombarded with proposed economic panaceas since the collapse of the community's industrial sector in the late 1970s. Moreover, as Safford noted, responses to the city's ongoing crisis have too often "balkanized along the narrow interests of powerful elites" rather than reflecting "a relatively unified set of community-oriented actions."[172] Yet, there have been hopeful signs, some of which earned the community's positive attention.

In recent years, Youngstown's leadership has moved in the direction of comprehensive planning. In 2002, municipal leaders unveiled "Youngstown

2010," a citywide plan that was developed in partnership with Youngstown State University and community leaders, many of whom participated in workshops and public discussions that helped shape the plan's agenda. Crucially, "Youngstown 2010" was designed to address the community's postindustrial realities, while developing strategies for the development of new businesses. By 2008, the *Vindicator* reported that economic development incentives put in place three years earlier had "helped secure $9.5 million in new investments in the city."[173] Meanwhile, residents of the metropolitan area were heartened by General Motors Corporation's announced plan to invest $350 million in its production plant in Lordstown, Ohio—a development that gained regional and national media attention.[174]

Tangible results of the renewal effort are most evident in the downtown area, where aging buildings have been razed or restored. The downtown has seen modest construction, and in recent years, it has attracted small businesses, including restaurants, nightclubs, and art galleries. In 2005, a high-tech convocation center known as the Chevrolet Centre (now called the Covelli Centre) opened on the site of a closed steel mill.[175] During this time, the Youngstown Business Incubator (YBI), which began supporting business-to-business software companies five years earlier, redeveloped a once decaying block of the downtown area. The YBI currently occupies three state-of-the-art facilities, where it fosters the growth of software companies "by offering them free rent, Internet bandwidth and services such as mentoring." The rapid growth of the YBI's most celebrated business, Turning Technologies, was a factor in *Entrepreneur* magazine's decision, in July 2009, to cite Youngstown as one of the nation's top 10 cities in which to start a business. During an interview with the magazine, Turning Technologies' cofounder, Mike Broderick, observed that his company "was able to grow faster in Youngstown than it would have in Silicon Valley because affordable rents and taxes have freed up more money for expansion."[176] Meanwhile, the city is expected to benefit from a $650 million expansion project at Youngstown's V&M Star Steel, a company owned by the French firm Vallourec.[177]

Those who hope to lay the groundwork for Youngstown's revitalization cannot afford to ignore the ravaged state of many of the city's neighborhoods, however. The once prosperous north side, for instance, remains trapped in a vicious cycle of poverty and crime, despite efforts to transform the area into a thriving historical district; and crack houses operate within blocks of the Tudor- and Spanish Colonial Revival–style homes that were built by Youngstown's industrial barons in the early twentieth century. The situation is even worse on the south side, a once solidly middle-class residential district whose vacant homes serve as way stations for drug addicts, dealers, and the indigent. In 2004, a study conducted by Youngstown State University revealed that almost 20 percent of respondents "rated their neighborhood quality of life as 'poor.'" In the same study, 50 percent of respondents indicated that they felt "unsafe in their neighborhood." Although community organizers have established neighborhood block watches throughout the city, while working to remove businesses and vacant structures that serve as centers of illicit activity, crime has remained one of the city's most intractable problems. In February 2008, one east side resident complained to a newspaper reporter, "We're tired of being held hostage in our backyards."[178] More recently, in February 2011, the city gained unwanted national attention when 1 young adult was killed and 11 others were wounded in a shooting at a fraternity house located in the vicinity of Youngstown State University.[179]

Nevertheless, a number of civic leaders insist that the community can be turned around. Father Noga, the pastor of St. Patrick's Church, is among those who see hope for the future. Pointing to the depopulated neighborhoods that surround his parish, the pastor argued that they could serve as the ground for future revitalization. The disappearance of older residential areas might well pave the way for new development, given that such vacant tracts of land "have become the new neighborhoods" in other cities. When Father Noga came to St. Patrick's in 1985, the main artery of Hillman Street, which runs a block west of the parish, was "peppered with substandard and abandoned homes." Today, most of those dilapidated structures are gone—a circumstance that could appeal to developers, who tend to prefer vacant land. Father Noga pointed out that most developers prefer to avoid the responsibility of removing older structures from property slated for redevelopment, especially in view of Environmental Protection Agency regulations that frequently add to the cost of demolition. "We've had to change the bus route on the south side, because there's nobody [who] lives on Hillman Street," the pastor said. "So, that [area] could become some of the new neighborhoods, because there's land."[180] While Father Noga's vision for the rebirth of the south side may seem fanciful, such redevelopment is not unprecedented in Youngstown. The pastor's observations must be understood in the context of an ongoing revitalization project focused on Smoky Hollow, a former ethnic enclave on the city's north side that was destroyed by developments that included the eastward expansion of Youngstown State University.

Nestled in a serpentine, half-mile ravine that stretches along the main artery of Wick Avenue, the neighborhood once produced luminaries such as Hollywood mogul Jack Warner, who grew up in "the Hollow," and shopping mall developer Edward J. DeBartolo, Sr., who was born there. By the 1930s, Smoky Hollow was the home of a thriving Italian American neighborhood that featured one of Youngstown's signature institutions, the Mahoning Valley Restaurant, better known to locals as "the MVR Club." Six decades later, however, all that remained of the Hollow was the resilient MVR Club; a small, well-tended World War II monument; and a handful of wooden frame homes that survived the university's persistent efforts to create additional parking space for students. Like many other ethnic neighborhoods, Smoky Hollow had fallen victim to slum-clearance and urban renewal projects that exacerbated ongoing depopulation. In 2001, however, the district was redeveloped as a site of upscale apartments and townhouses, in the hope that a revitalized Smoky Hollow would attract university students, faculty members, and younger professionals. Over the years, the project has secured more than $4 million in grants and municipal assistance, which has been earmarked for the development of infrastructure required for its realization.[181] Yet, if the city does manage to rebound, as many hope, the turnaround is unlikely to bring with it a resurgence of urban Catholic schools. The disappearance of a once-vibrant pattern of urban parish schools may be a permanent legacy of the city's dramatic decline.

NOTES

1. Father Edward P. Noga, interview by the author, June 18, 2007, transcript, Hogan-Cullinan Family Collection, #314, Mahoning Valley Historical Society, Youngstown, OH.

2. Shirley Ann Giura, "Youngstown St. Patrick Parish Marks 85th Anniversary," *The Catholic Exponent,* 12, March 8, 1996.

3. Ron Cole, "Finances Close St. Dominic School," *The Vindicator,* B-1, April 10, 1999.

4. Noga, interview.

5. Sherry Linkon and John Russo, *Steeltown U.S.A.: Work & Memory in Youngstown* (Lawrence, KS: University Press of Kansas, 2002), 43.

6. Bill McNichol, *The Roads That Built America: The Incredible Story of the U.S. Interstate System* (New York: Barnes & Noble, 2003), 154.

7. Robert A. Beauregard, *When America Became Suburban* (Minneapolis, MN: University of Minnesota Press, 2006), 85.

8. Paula (Lehnerd) McKinney, interview by the author, June 14, 2007, transcript, Hogan-Cullinan Family Collection, #314, Mahoning Valley Historical Society, Youngstown, OH.

9. Beauregard, *When America Became Suburban,* 85.

10. Kenneth Jackson, *Crabgrass Frontier: The Suburbanization of the United States* (New York, NY: Oxford University Press, 1985), 188.

11. Linkon and Russo, *Steeltown U.S.A.,* 44.

12. Beauregard, *When America Became Suburban,* 37.

13. Jackson, *Crabgrass Frontier,* 287–96.

14. Beauregard, *When America Became Suburban,* 67.

15. Ibid., 66.

16. Ibid., 21.

17. Thomas J. Sugrue, *The Origins of the Urban Crisis: Race and Inequality in Postwar Detroit* (Princeton, NJ: Princeton University Press, 1996), 6.

18. John T. McGreevy, *Parish Boundaries: The Catholic Encounter with Race in the Twentieth-Century Urban North* (Chicago, IL: University of Chicago Press, 1996), 18–19.

19. Ibid., 22.

20. Ibid., 43.

21. Ibid., 52.

22. Ibid., 24.

23. James M. O'Toole, *The Faithful: A History of Catholics in America* (Cambridge, MA: The Belknap Press of Harvard University Press, 2008), 197–98.

24. Ibid., 201.

25. Ibid., 255.

26. McGreevy, *Parish Boundaries,* 20.

27. O'Toole, *The Faithful,* 252–53.

28. "Will Close Sts. Peter-Paul: School Board to Keep 9th Grade at St. Ed's," *The Youngstown Vindicator,* 1, January 17, 1973.

29. "Says Diocese Owes Poor Schools Aid," *The Youngstown Vindicator,* 1, February 28, 1973.

30. Anthony S. Bryk, Valerie E. Lee, and Peter B. Holland, *Catholic Schools and the Common Good* (Cambridge, MA: Harvard University Press, 1993), 9–10.

31. Marie Aikenhead, "Board Refuses School Funding: Votes against Diocese Inner City Aid," *The Youngstown Vindicator,* 1, November 17, 1976.

32. John W. O'Malley, *What Happened at Vatican II* (Cambridge, MA: The Belknap Press of Harvard University Press, 2008), 297.

33. McGreevy, *Parish Boundaries,* 13.

34. Jay P. Dolan, *The American Catholic Experience: A History from Colonial Times to the Present* (Garden City, NY: Image Books, 1985), 453.

35. Charles R. Morris, *American Catholic: The Saints and Sinners Who Built America's Most Powerful Church* (New York, NY: Vintage, 1997), 275.

36. Aikenhead, *The Youngstown Vindicator,* November 17, 1976.

37. *Youngstown 2010 Citywide Plan* (Youngstown, OH: The City of Youngstown, 2005), 15.

38. Sean Safford, *Why the Garden Club Couldn't Save Youngstown: The Transformation of the Rust Belt* (Cambridge, MA: Harvard University Press, 2009), 146.

39. Peter H. Milliken, "Many Bid Farewell As St. Edward School Closes," *The Vindicator,* 1, June 6, 2003.

40. Paula L. Cizmar, Steelyard Blues, *Mother Jones,* April 1978, 36–52.

41. Linkon and Russo, *Steeltown U.S.A.,* 3.

42. Safford, *Why the Garden Club Couldn't Save Youngstown,* 2.

43. Staughton Lynd, *The Fight against Shutdowns: Youngstown's Steel Mill Closings* (San Pedro, CA: Singlejack Books, 1983), 3–4.

44. Linkon and Russo, *Steeltown U.S.A.,* 47.

45. Ibid., 3.

46. "District Mills Remain Dark," *The Youngstown Vindicator,* 1, September 19, 1982.

47. Safford, *Why the Garden Club Couldn't Save Youngstown,* 140.

48. John R. Rowland, "Youngstown's Purse: Growth of Population in Youngstown Pictured from U.S. Census Records," *The Youngstown Telegram,* 9, March 7, 1930.

49. "Survey Shows 161,477 Here," *The Youngstown Vindicator,* 3, December 7, 1925.

50. "Sees 470,000 Here in 25 Years: Ohio Bell Man Tells Club of City's Prospects," *The Youngstown Telegram,* 7, October 23, 1925.

51. "Expect 7,200 Enrollment: Twenty Catholic Schools Prepare to Open with Bigger Rosters," *The Youngstown Vindicator,* 13, September 4, 1937.

52. Frederick J. Blue, William D. Jenkins, H. William Lawson, and Joan M. Reedy, *Mahoning Memories: A History of Youngstown and Mahoning County* (Virginia Beach, VA: The Donning Company, 1995), 19.

53. Ibid., 37.

54. Ibid., 66–67.

55. Thomas G. Fuechtmann, *Steeples and Stacks: Religion and Steel Crisis in Youngstown* (Cambridge, MA: Cambridge University Press, 1989), 11.

56. Blue et al., *Mahoning Memories,* 94.

57. Fuechtmann, *Steeples and Stacks,* 94.

58. "Youngstown Is 45th Among American Cities: City, However, Ranks Fifth in Home Ownership among Nation's Communities," *The Youngstown Telegram,* A-45, June 29, 1931.

59. "Population Gains 12,548: Youngstown Now Estimated to Have 182,550—Increase Since 1930," *The Youngstown Vindicator,* 1, September 9, 1936.

60. "City's Population 175,000 WPA Property Survey Shows: Check Reveals 41,000 Work in Mills—Data Gathered on Housing, Home Conditions," *The Youngstown Vindicator,* 12, October 14, 1936.

61. "Population Up 16,000 in County: Youngstown Is Expected to Hold Its Own in Census Report," *The Youngstown Vindicator,* A-1, June 11, 1950.

62. "Shift to Suburbs Shown in Population Figures," *The Youngstown Vindicator,* A-6, August 1, 1954.

63. "Diocese Schools Prepare for 50 Pct. Gain by 1960," *The Youngstown Vindicator,* 2, June 7, 1955.

64. Ann Jean Schuler, "Parochial Schools Found 1959 Big Year; Enrollment at Record," *The Youngstown Vindicator,* E-10, January 10, 1960.

65. "Parochial Schools Will Open with Record Enrollment," *The Youngstown Vindicator,* A-5, September 4, 1955.

66. "Huge Elementary Building to Include 14 Classrooms," *The Youngstown Vindicator,* 10, January 22, 1957.

67. "Work to Begin Soon on New St. Anthony Church, School: Structure to Cost $500,000; Includes Rectory, Social Hall," *The Youngstown Vindicator,* 3, January 24, 1958.

68. "Bishop Gives His OK to Recommendation to Close St. Anthony: In the Past 11 years, the School's Enrollment Has Dropped by 40 percent While Tuition Has Risen by 71 percent," *The Vindicator,* B-1, March 4, 1996.

69. "Catholic Schools to Have Third of City's Students," *The Youngstown Vindicator,* 7, July 14, 1961.

70. "St. Patrick's Parish Will Close School," *The Youngstown Vindicator,* 2, January 13, 1967.

71. "City Population Drops 2,447 in 4-Year Period," *The Steel Valley News,* 1, February 28, 1965.

72. "Area Metro Population Shows 7.7 Pct. Gain," *The Youngstown Vindicator,* 1, April 7, 1966.

73. "Metropolitan Area Is 536,003: City Census Drops to 139,788," *The Youngstown Vindicator,* 1, January 13, 1971.

74. Leon Stennis, "St. Ann Reunion Planned in July," *The Youngstown Vindicator,* A-16, November 29, 1981.

75. "Work to Begin on New St. Anthony Church, School," *The Youngstown Vindicator,* 3, January 24, 1958.

76. "St. Joseph School to Be Razed," *The Youngstown Vindicator,* 4, August 5, 1969.

77. "Parish Profile: Immaculate Conception, Youngstown," *The Catholic Exponent,* 7, August 13, 1993.

78. McKinney, interview.

79. Mary Claire Sheehan, "St. Columba School Ends 112 Years of Education," *The Youngstown Vindicator,* B-1, June 4, 1972.

80. McGreevy, *Parish Boundaries,* 126–27.

81. Beauregard, *When America Became Suburban,* 81.

82. Jackson, *Crabgrass Frontier,* 225.

83. "Shift to Suburbs Shown in Population Figures," *The Youngstown Vindicator,* August 1, 1954.

84. Watkins, *Dancing with Strangers,* 114.

85. "Rents Fixed for Westlake: Will Range from $19 to $22.25 a Month, Including Utilities," *The Youngstown Vindicator,* 1, October 11, 1939.

86. "Open House Beginning at Kimmel Brook," *The Youngstown Vindicator,* A-6, August 15, 1951.

87. Jerry Knight, "Dedication of 154-Unit Project Will Be Held by City Wednesday," *The Youngstown Vindicator,* B-1, October 11, 1959.

88. Jackson, *Crabgrass Frontier,* 227.

89. Tim Yovich, "West Siders Hit Housing Project," *The Youngstown Vindicator,* 1, October 26, 1978.

90. "St. Patrick Parish Will Close School," *The Youngstown Vindicator,* 2, January 13, 1967.

91. "Air North Side Problems at St. Edward's Meeting," *The Youngstown Vindicator,* 3, December 3, 1969.

92. "Metropolitan Area Is 536,003," *The Youngstown Vindicator,* 8, January 13, 1971.

93. "1,800 Hear of Catholic School Crisis," *The Youngstown Vindicator,* 8, November 16, 1970.

94. "2,000 to Leave Catholic Schools," *The Youngstown Vindicator,* 1, August 30, 1971.

95. Ibid.

96. "Will Close Sts. Peter-Paul," *The Youngstown Vindicator,* January 17, 1973.

97. "Housing Cost Near Average: $3,154 Figure Is Set for Each Apartment on Westlake Site," *The Youngstown Vindicator,* B-1, July 2, 1939.

98. Ernest Brown, Jr., "Chic It Wasn't, but Monkey's Nest Was Home, and More, to Its People," *The Youngstown Vindicator,* B-3, August 14, 1977.

99. "Will Close Sts. Peter-Paul," *The Youngstown Vindicator,* January 17, 1973.

100. Fuechtmann, *Steeples and Stacks,* 18–19.

101. Terry F. Buss and F. Stevens Redburn, *Shutdown in Youngstown: Public Policy for Mass Unemployment* (Albany, NY: State University of New York Press, 1983), 16.

102. John Ingham, *The Iron Barons: A Social Analysis of an American Elite, 1974–1965* (Westport, CN: Greenwood Press, 1978), 203.

103. Fuechtmann, *Steeples and Stacks,* 34.

104. Sugrue, *The Origins of the Urban Crisis,* 127.

105. Safford, *Why the Garden Club Couldn't Save Youngstown,* 70.

106. Fuechtmann, *Steeples and Stacks,* 18.

107. Safford, *Why the Garden Club Couldn't Save Youngstown,* 71.

108. Fuechtmann, *Steeples and Stacks,* 42–43.

109. Richard Bruno, *Steelworker Alley: How Class Works in Youngstown* (Ithaca, NY: Cornell University Press, 1999), 113.

110. Fuechtmann, *Steeples and Stacks,* 44–51.

111. Ibid., 1–2.

112. Noga, interview.

113. Douglas R. Sease, "Closing of a Steel Mill Hits Workers in U.S. with Little Warning: Though They Keep Getting Incomes, Retraining Aid, Creation of New Jobs Lag," *The Wall Street Journal,* 1, September 23, 1980.

114. Bruno, *Steelworker Alley,* 149.

115. Safford, *Why the Garden Club Couldn't Save Youngstown,* 72.

116. Fuechtmann, *Steeples and Stacks,* 4–5.

117. Martin John "Jack" O'Connell, interview by the author, April 13, 2007, transcript, Hogan-Cullinan Family Collection, #314, Mahoning Valley Historical Society, Youngstown, OH.

118. "Mahoning Co.'s Census Shows 7.1 Percent Drop," *The Youngstown Vindicator,* 6, July 8, 1980.

119. "Data Fail to Reflect Full Slump," *The Youngstown Vindicator,* A-1, December 19, 1982.

120. "Youngstown Is 145th Most Populous U.S. City," *The Youngstown Vindicator,* 4, May 1, 1984.

121. "Youngstown and Steubenville among Top 25 in Population Drop," *The Youngstown Vindicator,* 2, May 28, 1984.

122. "Mahoning Co. Ranks 14th in Population Loss in U.S.," *The Youngstown Vindicator,* 26, May 6, 1985.

123. Ernest Brown, Jr., "Continued Area Population Drop Likely," *The Youngstown Vindicator,* 1, September 12, 1985.

124. Tim Roberts, "Population Drops in District Counties: Mahoning Is Hardest Hit with Exodus of 13,257 Residents," *The Youngstown Vindicator,* 19, March 31, 1987.

125. *Youngstown 2010,* 7.

126. Ibid., 31.

127. Statistics on School Enrollment from Youngstown Diocese (1979–1997), reproduction, Hogan-Cullinan Family Collection, #314, Mahoning Valley Historical Society, Youngstown, OH.

128. Marie Aikenhead, "Diocesan Schools Reveal Ethnic Makeup: 8.2% of 10,408 Students Are from Minorities," *The Youngstown Vindicator,* B-7, April 3, 1977.

129. William Owen, "Board Votes to Close Sts. Cyril and Methodius School," *The Youngstown Vindicator,* 13, March 30, 1983.

130. "St. Stanislaus School to Close as Pupil Enrollment Declines," *The Youngstown Vindicator,* 4, February 25, 1986.

131. "Diocesan School to Stay Open," *The Youngstown Vindicator,* 4, June 22, 1987.

132. Roger Kahn, *The Boys of Summer* (New York, NY: Harper and Row, 1972), 231–33.

133. "Catholic Diocese Plans Closing of West Side Elementary School," *The Youngstown Vindicator,* 1, March 8, 1990.

134. "Valley Population" (pictorial graph), *The Vindicator,* B-6, January 22, 1995.

135. John Goodall, "3 Counties Lose Young Workers: The Drain of 18-to-24-Year-Olds Will Spell Problems for the Valley's Job Market, Said a Labor Analyst," *The Vindicator,* A-1, June 3, 1991.

136. Andrew Welsh-Huggins, "Despite Spotty Growth, Population Will Drop: The Mahoning County Planning Commission Director Disputes This Picture of a Slowly Deflating Population," *The Vindicator,* A-1, May 26, 1996.

137. Roger Smith, David Skolnick, and Peter H. Milliken, "Despite City's Loss, Valley Sees Growth: Several Communities—Including Canfield, Cortland, Columbiana and Calcutta—Grew Significantly in the '90s," *The Vindicator,* 1, March 17, 2001.

138. "Diocese School May Not Close," *The Youngstown Vindicator,* 8, December 16, 1977.

139. John Goodall, "Fund Drive Spares 2 Catholic Schools: The Community Has Responded to the Financial Plight of Two Catholic Schools," *The Vindicator,* A-1, April 9, 1991.

140. "Bishop Gives His OK to Recommendation to Close St. Anthony," *The Vindicator,* B-1, March 4, 1996.

141. Lou Jacquet, "Youngstown St. Anthony to Close in June," *The Catholic Exponent,* 3, March 8, 1996.

142. Giura, *The Catholic Exponent,* March 8, 1996.

143. Peter H. Milliken, "Parish the Thought: Can St. Pat's Be 85?" *The Vindicator,* B-2, May 19, 1996.

144. Noga, interview.

145. T. Gordon Welsh, interview by the author, May 1, 2007, transcript, Hogan-Cullinan Family Collection, #314, Mahoning Valley Historical Society, Youngstown, OH.

146. B. David Wolf, "Enrollment Doubles at Area's 'Christian Schools': 18 Here Teaching 2,000," *The Youngstown Vindicator,* A-10, August 30, 1981.

147. Ron Cole, "Charter School Gets Set to Open: Private Donors Have Given $400,000 to Renovate the Old High School, the Board President Said," *The Vindicator,* A-1, June 30, 1998.

148. Linda M. Linonis, "Politically Active Pastor Dies at 75: The Pastor's 'Love and Mentorship Will Be Missed,'" *The Vindicator,* B-1, May 28, 2008.

149. Cole, *The Vindicator,* June 30, 1998.

150. Ibid.

151. Dennis LaRue, "National City Commits $1 Million to Charter School: Bank CEO on Hand to Greet Voinovich As Governor Defends His Education Initiatives," *The Youngstown-Warren Business Journal,* 3, October 1998.

152. "Youngstown: State OKs Plan for Second Charter," *The Vindicator,* A-1, July 15, 1998.

153. Ibid.

154. Dan Trevas, "2 Charter Schools OK'd for the City: The New Schools, Along with Eagle Heights Academy and Youngstown Community School, Have a Total Enrollment of about 1,200 Pupils," *The Vindicator,* A-1, April 14, 1999.

155. Ron Cole, "Finances Close St. Dominic School," *The Vindicator,* April 10, 1999, B-1.

156. Peter H. Milliken, "Many Bid Farewell As St. Edward School Closes," *The Vindicator,* 1, June 6, 2003.

157. Marie Shellock, "Parishioners at St. Edward's Have Good Reason to Celebrate: Refurbishment Is Part of a $750,000 Project," *The Vindicator,* B-4, January 8, 1994.

158. "St. Edward to Close at School Year's End: The Declining Enrollment Is Due in Part to the Movement of Catholics to the Suburbs, the Diocese Said," *The Vindicator,* 1, February 25, 2003.

159. Marie Aikenhead, "Diocesan Schools Reveal Ethnic Makeup: 8.2% of 10,408 Students Are from Minorities," *The Youngstown Vindicator,* B-7, April 3, 1977.

160. Ron Cole, "Immaculate Conception: Does Bell for Student Also Toll for School? The School Has Opened Early; the New Principal's Attitude Is That It Won't Be Closed," *The Vindicator,* B-1, August 14, 2002.

161. "St. Brendan's Elementary: Declining Numbers Led to School Closing," *The Vindicator,* 1, March 1, 2005.

162. "St. Brendan's in Final Year: The Diocese Says an Official Announcement Will Be Released Monday," *The Vindicator,* 1, February 26, 2005.

163. "St. Brendan's Elementary: Declining Numbers Led to School Closing," *The Vindicator,* 1, March 1, 2005.

164. McKinney, interview.

165. Harold Gwin, "Final Bell Tolls for Two Schools: There Were Some Long Faces As Children Left St. Matthias on Tuesday," *The Vindicator,* B-1, June 7, 2006.

166. Edith Starzyk, "Catholic Schools Facing Pressure to Consolidate: Parish Classrooms' Conversion, However, Not Strictly Paired with Church Closings," *The Plain Dealer,* 1, March 30, 2009.

167. Scott Cech, "Catholic Closures Linked to Growth of City Charters," *Education Week,* February 13, 2008, 1–2.

168. Sister Charlotte Italiano, OSU, interview by the author, May 31, 2007, transcript, Hogan-Cullinan Family Collection, #314, Mahoning Valley Historical Society, Youngstown, OH.

169. Noga, interview.

170. *Youngstown 2010,* 7.

171. "Census: Youngstown Population Drops 18.3 Percent," *The Vindicator,* March 9, 2011, www.vindy.com/news/2011/mar/09/census-youngstown8217s-population-drops-/ (accessed April 18, 2011).

172. Safford, *Why the Garden Club Couldn't Save Youngstown,* 92.

173. Angie Schmitt, "Hope and Gloom: Some 24,000 Jobs Have Been Lost in the Mahoning Valley Since 2000. What Does the Contracting Economy Mean for the Youngstown Revitalization Plan?" *The Vindicator,* 1, February 13, 2008.

174. "V&M Star Steel the Latest in Positive News for Valley," *The Vindicator,* February 21, 2010, www.vindy.com/news/2010/feb/21/vampm-star-steel-the-latest-in-positive-/ (accessed April 27, 2011).

175. David Skolnick, "Sealing the Deal on the Chevrolet Centre," *The Vindicator,* A-1, November 18, 2005.

176. Don Shilling, "Dare to Dream? City's Potential Noted," *The Vindicator,* July 18, 2009, www.vindy.com/news/2009/jul/18/dare-to-dream-city8217s-potential-noted/ (accessed April 27, 2011).

177. "V&M Star Steel the Latest in Positive News for Valley," *The Vindicator,* February 21, 2010.

178. Angie Schmitt, "Taking Back Our Neighborhoods: Fifty Percent of Youngstown Residents Feel Unsafe in Their Neighborhoods at Night, a 2004 Study Said," *The Vindicator,* 1, February 11, 2008.

179. Thomas J. Sheeran, "YSU Student Fatally Shot at Ohio Frat House," Associated Press, February 7, 2011, www.usatoday.com/news/nation/2011–02–07-ysu-student_N.htm (accessed April 28, 2011).

180. Noga, interview.

181. Denise Dick, "Smoky Hollow Revitalization Plan Taking Shape," *The Vindicator,* October 8, 2010, www.vindy.com/news/2010/oct/08/8216it8217s-a-beginning8217/ (accessed April 29, 2011).

Chapter 5

Demographic Change and Urban Parish Schools

On January 30, 2007, Bishop George Vance Murry, SJ, the first African American to lead the Diocese of Youngstown, held a press conference to discuss issues affecting local Catholics. The newly appointed religious leader—whose physical resemblance to actor James Earl Jones was widely noted—had emerged as something of a local celebrity. The bishop's image appeared regularly on the front page of news publications, and representatives of the local media seemed impressed with his eloquence, warmth, and facile wit. During the press conference, a reporter opened a question-and-answer period with a lighthearted query on the speaker's impressions of northeastern Ohio's climate, a teasing reference to the fact that Bishop Murry's previous post was in the balmy Diocese of St. Thomas, in the Virgin Islands. It didn't take long for the reporters' questions to take a more serious turn, however. Weeks earlier, four young people had perished in an execution-style slaying on the city's crime-ridden south side. All four of the victims had been black, and police suggested the incident was related to gang activity.[1] The bishop was pressed for a response to the tragedy.

Bishop Murry, a native of Camden, New Jersey, was no stranger to the kinds of social problems that confronted a city like Youngstown. In addition, he was alert to the realities of institutional discrimination. Within months of his installment, he spoke out publicly against local policies and practices that reflected the persistence of racial inequality.[2] In response to a reporter's question on the church's role in quelling urban crime, the bishop said, "There is definitely a place for the Church, not only in calming violence, but [also] in interacting with the city." He went on to point out that urban ministries could play a significant role in curbing gang activity, given that young people attracted to such organizations "are without a sense of belonging."[3]

143

Bishop Murry's overview of the Catholic community's outreach to local urban youth featured references to several social welfare agencies and highlighted the efforts of individual pastors. He made no mention, however, of parochial schools, which had disappeared from impoverished urban neighborhoods during the decade-long tenure of his predecessor, Bishop Thomas J. Tobin, and the subsequent yearlong period when the diocese lacked episcopal leadership. Indeed, Bishop Murry mentioned none of the rich and relevant history of the African American history in his new diocese. Much of this history was informed by conflict with ethnic whites, a large number of whom were Catholic. Although "free-born" blacks who arrived in the nineteenth century tended to reside throughout the community, those who came during the period of the Great Migration generally moved into aging urban neighborhoods with large white Catholic populations. A deeper understanding of the role that demographic change played in the decline of Youngstown's urban parish schools requires an examination of the complex relationship that developed between African Americans and white Catholics during the period stretching from the late nineteenth century to the opening of the twenty-first century.

ORIGINS OF A BLACK COMMUNITY

African Americans formed a small but well-organized community in Youngstown by the mid-nineteenth century, decades before the arrival of the thousands of southern and eastern European immigrants who eventually comprised a large percentage of the community's Catholic population. The first African American known to reside within the city limits was Malinda Knight, who arrived in the community in 1831.[4] One source suggested that Knight was "born in freedom in Columbus."[5] She was later joined by members of a family that played a prominent role in the local African American community and, for some, symbolized the prospect of black mobility in a white-dominated society. In the mid-1800s, Pennsylvania-based bricklayer Lemuel Stewart arrived with two of his brothers and established a niche in the local building industry.[6] The Stewarts eventually participated in the construction of several of the city's landmarks, including the second edifice of St. Columba's Church, a massive granite structure that was consecrated as a cathedral in 1943. Like many black families who settled in Youngstown during this period, the Stewarts benefited from some degree of formal education. As local African American journalist Leon Stennis observed, Youngstown (unlike neighboring Warren and Salem, Ohio) was never a stop in the Underground Railroad, and therefore most blacks who arrived in the community during the nineteenth century were freeborn and skilled.[7] This sophisticated population wasted little time in establishing the foundations of a vibrant community.

In 1871, the city's relative handful of black residents organized an African Methodist Episcopal church, whose descendant, St. Andrewes AME, stands on the north side's West Rayen Avenue, just blocks from an industrial zone that once encompassed the retail area of Westlake's Crossing and a traditional black enclave known (perhaps pejoratively) as the "Monkey's Nest." Several years later, in 1876, the community's oldest African American Baptist congregation, Third Baptist Church, was organized on the sparsely developed south side; and by 1910, there were four churches serving a population that had grown to almost 2,000 people.[8] Although a large percentage of blacks continued to attend Protestant churches where white congregants predominated, a trend toward segregation became more pronounced in later years, as the African American population expanded. At this point, however, the city's residential districts witnessed relatively few instances of racial segregation. As George D. Beelen observed, "there seemed to be no more pressure on [African Americans] as to where they could live than on the recent white immigrants from southern and central Europe."[9] Moreover, by the 1920s, the black community boasted a small class of professionals, and a half-dozen churches served as vital centers of social, cultural, and political activity.[10]

Perhaps the African American community's most visible representative was onetime lawmaker William R. Stewart, the most accomplished of Lemuel Stewart's children. William Stewart eventually settled in the North Heights district, an upscale residential area that stretched along the city's northeastern border. This leafy neighborhood was the preserve of local industrialists, bankers, professionals, and business leaders.[11] An anomalous figure, in terms of both prestige and material wealth, Stewart paid for his studies at the Cincinnati Law School with earnings derived from a part-time practice helping Civil War veterans secure their pensions. In 1888, he had been elected as a Republican to the first of two terms in the state legislature, where he sponsored anti-lynching legislation and bills that provided pensions to civil servants. Then, between 1907 and 1914, Stewart served as local attorney for the Austro-Hungarian monarchy, representing the Washington, D.C., embassy through the consulate in neighboring Cleveland.[12] His remarkable career inspired ambitious young African Americans who believed they, too, could achieve success in a white-dominated world. In the late 1950s, when Stewart passed away at the age of 93, local blacks were proud—and perhaps astonished—to learn that the attorney had left behind an estate of $425,833.[13]

Youngstown's black population began to grow steadily in the late nineteenth century. Between 1880 and 1890, the total number of African Americans residing in the city rose from 320 to 648. A more dramatic expansion occurred over the following two decades. Between 1900 and 1910, the city's African American population rose from 1,015 people to 1,936, while the percentage of blacks in the community moved up slightly, from 2.0 to 2.4 percent.[14] An accelerated period of growth occurred between 1910 and 1920, when the black population tripled, jumping from 1,936 people to 6,662. As Stennis observed, the expansion of the black population between the outbreak of World War I and the early 1920s was encouraged, even facilitated, by local steel interests. Agents of steel plants, he wrote, "went through the South and induced large numbers of blacks to come north, assuring them higher wages." Among others, potential recruits were shown pictures "of large homes in which prominent blacks lived," an approach that evidently proved effective. In any event, steel agents had little difficulty persuading blacks to leave behind the poverty and brutally enforced discrimination they faced in the South. As Stennis wrote, "Carloads of blacks were shuttled into plants. Often the majority of a black congregation—pastor and all—would come."[15] Northern industrial recruitment peaked in 1919, when African American workers became unwitting tools of industrialists seeking to "break" widespread labor strikes—a strategy that exacerbated the antipathy of ethnic whites toward blacks. Labor historian David Brody noted that the widespread practice of employing black strikebreakers "was especially damaging in the Youngstown district."[16]

Although black migration to northeastern Ohio leveled off temporarily in the mid-1920s, largely due to a slump in industry and chronic discrimination in employment, the African American population in Youngstown remained large in comparison with other northern communities. A 1925 *Vindicator* editorial noted that Youngstown and Cleveland were among the "big ten" black centers in the northern United States. The same editorial acknowledged that black migrants from the South faced discrimination in employment, housing, and education. The editorial advised, "If [African American migrants] are to come here and stay, they must have better means of livelihood than they have in the South, better housing, better schooling for their children, and equal protection of the law."[17] Indeed, discrimination in the workplace was endemic, and those blacks who secured steady employment in the area's steel mills found themselves limited to the "grimy jobs in the coke plants and blast furnaces."[18] Despite such hardships, black workers often remained aloof from the labor movement in the first half of the twentieth century. As Brody noted, blacks were wary of labor unionists during this period; and union leaders, for their part, failed to encourage the participation of African American workers. Brody pointed out that black steelworkers who entered the industry in the early 1900s "had been rebuffed or badly used by unions."[19] Many unions excluded blacks from membership, and African American workers frequently discovered (to their dismay) that unionization was followed by the replacement of black workers with white ones. Meanwhile, black critics of labor unions questioned what they viewed as discriminatory practices, including apprenticeship examinations "that did not test knowledge or expertise relative to the particular skill but extraneous academic material."[20]

Not until the 1930s did local unions draw substantial support from African American steelworkers. By this time, the Steelworkers Organizing Committee (SWOC)—forerunner of the United Steelworkers of America (USW)—had benefited from the guidance and financial assistance of another union, the United Mine Workers (UMW). In what turned out to be a successful campaign to establish an independent union in the local steel industry, the UMW "threw their money, organizing skills and non-discriminatory clause into the union effort to attract the black worker."[21] As local black historian E. Wayne Robinson observed, however, most skilled African American steelworkers felt a need to work as "jack-legged craftsmen" (skilled laborers who worked without union approval) well into the 1940s.[22] Hence, in a community that was rife with ethnic and religious tension, blacks were forced to conclude that whites, whatever their abiding differences, operated in ways that tended to limit the social and economic mobility of African Americans. Restrictions on black mobility became even more apparent between 1920 and 1930, when the city's black population more than doubled, jumping from 6,662 people to 14,352.[23]

RACIAL TENSION ON YOUNGSTOWN'S WEST END

Tension between blacks and whites occasionally spilled over into violence on Youngstown's "West End," a residential and retail district to the northwest of the downtown area that was a major destination for black migrants. Throughout the first half of the twentieth century, instances of violence on the city's West End not only called attention to the distrust and resentment that existed between blacks and whites; they exposed the extent to which the legal establishment discriminated against African Americans. One incident, in particular, stands out. The 1921 shooting of a white police officer by an unknown black assailant inspired an official response so extreme that it forced the community's normally reticent black leadership to speak out against racial intolerance. On the evening of May 3, 1921, Patrolman Alexander R. Warren was conversing with an acquaintance near the corner of Belmont and West Rayen avenues, several blocks from Westlake's Crossing, when he noticed "two suspicious characters, shabbily dressed," moving along the opposite side of the street. Those on the scene later described the unidentified men as "colored."

Officer Warren reportedly told his acquaintance that he was going to "look them over." At that point, the policeman crossed the street and confronted the two men. Witnesses later stated that one of the two men pulled out a gun, aimed it at Warren's chest, and fired. The men then fled the scene "and were lost in the darkness." Police detectives, speculating that the pair had jumped a freight train at Westlake's Crossing, telegraphed a depot at Leavittsburg and requested that the train be stopped and searched for men matching the descriptions of the two suspects. Within hours, two black men were detained at a train depot in neighboring Braceville, Ohio, although they were later released. The search for suspects didn't end there, however. The city's police captain ordered that "all police . . . arrest any and all suspects upon their respective beats." Eventually, local police arrested 200 "colored persons on the open charge of suspicion." The following day, an account of the incident appeared on the front page of the *Vindicator,* under a banner headline reading, "Officer Is Slain; 200 Are Jailed." Unsurprisingly, this indiscriminate roundup of black males on the city's West End—in spite of its breathtaking scale—yielded few practical results. On May 6, 1921, the *Vindicator* reported that 198 of the 200 black suspects picked up by police had been cleared of charges and released. Furthermore, it was unclear whether the two remaining suspects, who were held on charges of carrying concealed weapons, were involved in the shooting death of Officer Warren.[24]

Criticism of the police dragnet came from a variety of sources. An article that appeared in the *Vindicator* on May 5, 1921, outlined the concerns of local black leaders, in particular, who complained that the police had gone "too far" in their investigation of Warren's death. One black leader stated that, if the same rules had been applied to the slaying of Youngstown racketeer James "Big Jim" Falcone, which had occurred a few days earlier, police would have rounded up scores of local Italian Americans.[25] The following day, a *Vindicator* editorial sharply criticized the police investigation, noting that the roundup "serves again as a reminder that on occasions of this kind the position of a large class of our people is anything but enviable."[26] The same edition of the paper carried a written protest from the executive committee of the local chapter of the National Association for the Advancement of Colored People (NAACP). "We find that 200 or more colored citizens who have been in the city for a number of years, were arrested and embarrassed," the letter stated. "We know that 250 men did not commit the murder and we resent the insults which have been heaped upon innocent colored citizens of this city during the last two days."[27] Ironically, a close examination of the same paper that carried the editorial and letter of protest reveals the extent to which news coverage in Youngstown was racially biased. On May 6, 1921, the *Vindicator* published a front-page story that featured the following headline: "Negro

Bandits Hold Up Store on South Side."[28] The newspaper's treatment of this incident was consistent with its practice of highlighting the race of suspects when they were believed to be black.

Other responses to the police dragnet called attention to the cultural gap separating established blacks from those who arrived during the period of the Great Migration. On May 8, 1921, John H. Chase, supervisor of the Booker T. Washington Settlement in Youngstown, complained in a letter to the *Vindicator* that the dragnet had damaged "the self respect of our better colored element, which is the salvation of the masses." In the letter, Chase noted that the black males arrested on suspicion charges had included a nephew of prominent local contractor Charles R. Berry, a onetime business associate of Lemuel Stewart. He closed the letter with a dire warning about the long-term consequences of racial discrimination, stating that "the whole race if treated with too much scorn or brutality may rise like a madman." Such an outcome could be avoided, Chase added, if middle-class, Christian values were encouraged within the black community. Chase concluded: "The way to save the colored race from themselves and to save white people from their worst element is to give them a good Y.M.C.A. and similar features, let them know the best and not the worst white people, lead them into balance, economic opportunity, and justice—and away from fear and dread."[29] Taken as a whole, Chase's letter sheds light on the complicated position of middle-class African Americans. On the one hand, established blacks felt a need to condemn blatant acts of racial discrimination. On the other, they were careful to distinguish themselves from newer arrivals, who, in their view, were "burdened" with the "cultural baggage" of the South.[30]

The shooting death of Officer Warren occurred less than two months after another, less spectacular murder on the West End. This earlier incident inspired a more measured police response, but once again, it drew unwanted attention to Youngstown's black community. As in the case of Officer Warren's murder, media reports underscored the race of the suspected perpetrators. This time, however, responses to the crime called attention to fissures that existed within Youngstown's white community on the issue of race. According to news reports, on the early morning of March 28, 1921, two young black men entered Philip Lowenthal's small confectionary shop in the district of Westlake's Crossing. One of the men drew a pistol, while the other rifled the cash register and searched Lowenthal's pockets. A newspaper account that appeared two days later stated that the armed robbers were "disappointed in the amount of money obtained and deliberately shot the confectioner through the lung." The mortally wounded Lowenthal, a Russian-Jewish immigrant who had recently opened the business, was rushed to St. Elizabeth's Hospital, where he died the following afternoon.[31] The senselessness of the killing, along with the "respectable" character of the victim (a married man with children), ensured that the story would find a place on the newspaper's front page.

One day after the confectioner's death, the *Vindicator* ran a front-page story with a banner headline reading, "Murder Stirs West End."[32] The story reported that the municipal police department, in response to the incident, had doubled the number of officers "detailed" to the district. Police had evidently detained at least two neighborhood residents found to be in possession of firearms. Neither of the men was described as a suspect in Lowenthal's murder; but significantly, both of them had Anglo-Saxon names. Given that the arrests had occurred in the ethnically and racially mixed neighborhoods surrounding Westlake's Crossing, it seems quite possible that the detained men were black.[33] The newspaper article did not make clear whether local authorities were cracking down on a wave of violent crime in the district or taking steps to avert a race riot. An outbreak of racially motivated violence was, in fact, a realistic possibility, given that racial tension in Youngstown was concentrated in neighborhoods located on the West End—former ethnic enclaves that absorbed most of the city's black migrants. While the subject of race was not highlighted in the paper's coverage of "trouble" attending Lowenthal's murder, an anonymous letter that appeared days after the shooting suggested that racial friction was indeed a factor in the reported unrest at Westlake's Crossing. This letter, which decried the influence of "the lowest and dirtiest types of southerners who infest this district," was the second of two anonymous contributions published in the aftermath of Lowenthal's murder.[34] Taken together, these letters not only highlighted racial tensions that existed within the community; they also underscored differences that divided many of the city's white residents. As the letter helps to illustrate, disagreement among whites over fundamental values was reflected in divergent attitudes about law and order, public morality, and race relations.

The first of the two letters appeared on the same day that Philip Lowenthal was interred at Youngstown's Children of Israel Cemetery. This letter, signed "A Republican," excoriated the city's safety director, David J. Scott, for his failure to curb the rising crime rate. The letter went on to condemn unrestricted illicit activity, claiming that "[w]hiskey and beer are being sold at a dozen places in the heart of the business district, and no arrests." "Gambling in which thousands of dollars figure, is in full bloom every night, and no raids," the letter stated. "Holdups and robberies, and what percentage are apprehended? Within the radius of Commerce and Federal and Wick and Chestnut streets ninety per cent of the automobile thefts occur. What steps have been taken to break up this practice?"[35] "A Republican" then attacked an unnamed local mobster whose bootlegging and gambling operations were the subject of an earlier newspaper editorial. Finally, the letter criticized

Youngstown's chief of police, contending that neither he "nor a number of the men of his department are giving the city that honest, efficient, and impartial service for which they are being paid."[36]

A biting response to the first letter appeared two days later. The second letter, which was signed "A Resident of the West End," also took aim at the safety director's performance. This time, however, the writer adopted a more personal line of attack, calling into question the safety director's intelligence as well as his masculinity. Although "A Resident" appeared as concerned as "A Republican" about the city's rising crime rate, he defined "crime" differently and apparently resented the previous writer's emphasis on local bootlegging activities. "A Resident" complained that, if anything, "Our Lady 'Safe-tea' Director" had devoted too much time to the enforcement of Prohibition legislation, a preoccupation that had caused him to neglect more serious crimes. The writer appeared to target reform-oriented Protestants, the most visible supporters of Prohibition, when he wrote that the safety director "was apparently placed into that office for no other purpose than to chase up raisin-jack makers." The letter went on in a similar vein: "As other citizens have already written through the columns of your valued paper, if [the safety director] would apply just one-fourth of his time to give the good people of Youngstown some semblance of police protection instead of running around all hours of the night and wee hours of the morning breaking into other people's business in search of liquor, and then deliver [sic] addresses from pulpits in order to draw attention to his prowess, he would be doing something like his duty." "A Resident" insisted that the safety director was "prejudiced on certain subjects to the point of persecution," and added tartly, "A dollar to a nickel that if [he] gets a robbery or holdup call and a bootleg call at the same time, he'll make the bootleg call first."[37]

Although both letters are anonymous, they contain powerful clues to the writers' respective backgrounds. The first letter, which is signed "A Republican," leaves little doubt about the author's political orientation. The writer's ethnic and religious background is somewhat uncertain, but the views the writer expressed are broadly consistent with those held by many of the city's native-born white Protestants in the early twentieth century. Although temperance advocates were found among the local Roman Catholic clergy, the most influential supporters of Prohibition legislation were Protestants.[38] Catholics, on the whole, resented all efforts to legislate what they perceived as "Protestant" morality, and this reaction was seen throughout the northeastern United States. Irish writer Breandon Delap, a biographer of the 1920s New York gangster Vincent "Mad Dog" Coll, mirrored this interpretation when he described Prohibition as "the rearguard action of New England WASPs, who were concerned about the massive influx of immigrants from

poor European countries, where drink was a part of the culture."[39] This
view of Prohibition is echoed by Ohio historian Andrew R. L. Cayton, who
wrote that the subsequent rise of Ku Klux Klan activity throughout the state
"reflected a desire among native-born Protestants to save their world from
an onslaught of diverse immigrants."[40] It therefore seems possible, perhaps
even likely, that the author of the first letter was a native-born white Protestant. The first writer's fixation on certain types of criminal activity (bootlegging and car theft) may also provide clues to his economic background.
In 1920s Youngstown, violent crime flourished in declining neighborhoods
such as those surrounding Westlake's Crossing. This notorious stretch of
real estate, bisected by railroad tracks and studded with older housing stock,
had a reputation for vice and gang activity that traced back to the turn of the
century. In the early 1960s, Hollywood movie mogul Jack L. Warner, who
grew up on Youngstown's north side, claimed in his autobiography that he
briefly belonged to the "Westlake's Crossing Gang," a cohort of teenaged
delinquents led by one "Toughy" McElvey.[41] To the immediate south of
rough-and-tumble Westlake's Crossing stood an old neighborhood known as
the "Monkey's Nest." In the 1920s, this district was home to scores of relatively recent European immigrants, including Irish, Italian, Croatian, Polish,
Slovak, and Ukrainian Americans. It was also one of the few neighborhoods
in the city that was readily accessible to newly arrived black migrants from
the South, some of whom had been recruited by industrialists at the height of
the Steel Strike of 1919.

For reasons that included extreme poverty, the northwestern urban district
comprising Westlake's Crossing and the Monkey's Nest gained a reputation
as a locus of violent criminal activity.[42] At the same time, quasi-suburban
areas—including the city's upper north side, west side, and south side—were
relatively insulated from violent crime. In his letter, "A Republican" unwit-
tingly offered clues to his own economic status when he suggested that the
most serious threats to the community were a widespread flouting of Prohibition laws, the prevalence of illegal gambling, and a wave of automobile
thefts. (Only in passing did the writer refer to "holdups and robberies.")
When examining these claims, one must keep in mind that a large percentage of working-class ethnic whites did not regard the first two activities as
serious crimes. Indeed, many immigrants treated Prohibition as an unjust
law that Anglo-Americans had foisted upon the rest of the community, and
a sizable minority showed few qualms about exploiting its unpopularity to
their economic advantage. Gambling, too, was considered an acceptable
male pastime in many European cultures, and some immigrants interpreted
laws prohibiting such activity as biased and intrusive. Equally revealing is
the first writer's reference to car thievery. Although a significant number of

low-income Americans owned cars by the early 1920s, this tended to be less true in dense urban areas like Youngstown, where automobile ownership was often closely associated with the suburban middle classes. As David J. Goldberg noted, "the car had less of an impact on large cities, where people still lived in congested areas and relied on public transportation."[43] Hence, the writer of the first letter, given his salient concerns, apparently belonged to the middle classes. Furthermore, his almost exclusive emphasis on violations of anti-gambling and Prohibition laws suggests that "A Republican" lived in a neighborhood that was largely insulated from violent crime.

Meanwhile, the author of the second letter evidently lacked the luxury of treating violent crime as an abstraction, for he painted a picture of the West End that is almost apocalyptic. "A Resident" complained that, while official "deadheads" squandered energy "to coddle along their hobbies," residents of the West End were "at the mercy of these murdering, raping fiends such as shot down Lowenthal Monday night." According to the letter, such "fiends" were invariably black males; and the writer's avoidance of standard racial pejoratives did not prevent him from expressing his profound hostility toward the African Americans who shared his neighborhood. "A Resident" described a series of crimes allegedly committed by African Americans "within a stone's throw of Lowenthal's place." He claimed that, on the day of the murder, three "Negroes" threatened another proprietor with a razor, while an unknown black assailant struck a railroad detective on the head. The writer added that black prostitutes solicited their trade with impunity on the district's streets, while "colored" cardsharps hustled naïve customers in broad daylight. Worst of all, "A Resident" wrote, the "innocence" of the district's "white children" had been threatened daily by "that dirty undesirable southern element which the steel manufacturers are credited with having brought in here 'to keep their mills going.'"[44]

The writer's contemporaries would have recognized this last statement as an indirect reference to black steelworkers. Racist sentiment among local working-class whites had soared two years earlier, when area industrialists imported thousands of black workers from the South as strikebreakers. During the national Steel Strike of 1919, the National Committee of the American Federation of Labor (AFL) reported that more than 30,000 African Americans entered the industry. Although this number represented "roughly a tenth of the total body of strikers," industrialists accurately predicted that the tactic would demoralize the striking workers. The first to respond to pressures brought on by the recruitment of strikebreakers were skilled steelworkers, most of whom had opposed the strike from the outset. Faced with the prospect (however remote) of losing their jobs, they "led the return to work."[45] In communities like Youngstown, where 5,000 black laborers entered the steel industry between 1919 and 1920, some working-class whites attributed the strike's failure to the presence of black "strikebreakers."[46] Hence, the second writer's oblique reference to the steel strike of 1919 reflects the manner in which developments in the industrial sector deepened working-class whites' collective antagonism toward African Americans.

A NEW SOCIAL AND POLITICAL HIERARCHY

The two letters, taken together, throw into sharp relief the social and political hierarchy that had emerged in early-20th-century Youngstown. Many native-born white Protestants attributed the community's moral decline to the recent influx of southern and eastern European immigrants, who were criticized by many self-righteous congregations for their allegedly higher consumption of alcohol, their tolerance of gambling, and their disorganized lifestyles. Reservations about "foreigners" took on a political dimension as labor strife brought new immigrants into conflict with more established European groups. Anglo-American concerns about the political leanings of immigrant laborers skyrocketed in 1916, when workers striking against Youngstown Sheet and Tube burned down the retail district of East Youngstown, a village that closely bordered Youngstown's east side.[47] Local leaders' dismay over the widely reported incident proved so enduring that, in 1926, the village was renamed as "Campbell," in an apparent effort to distance the community from memories of the "unrest" of 1916.[48] Jenkins noted that immigrants had played a prominent role in the rioting. "Of the eighty-one young men arrested—their average age was twenty-seven—only seven were listed as Americans; most came from southern and eastern Europe," Jenkins wrote. "The association of the radical Industrial Workers of the World (IWW) with the strikers generated nativists' fear of the revolutionary tendencies of the foreign-born."[49]

Recent immigrants, on the other hand, were probably more inclined to attribute the rioting and vandalism in East Youngstown to a handful of "troublemakers" who had infiltrated the labor movement. Some of them resented the extent to which the industrial establishment blamed "new" immigrants (especially those from southeastern Europe) for the city's crime, corruption, and labor unrest. Indeed, recent immigrants—and Catholics, in particular—became highly defensive amid the rise of white Protestant vigi-lante organizations that presented themselves as guardians of public morality. In a passage on Ku Klux Klan activity in 1920s Ohio, Cayton described the complex network of social and political fault lines that divided heterogeneous industrial communities like Youngstown. "The Klan thrived in cities such as Youngstown," he wrote, "where the steel industry attracted immigrants from all over the world and whose population in 1920 was 59.8 percent foreign-born and 5 percent African American." The historian observed that the city's population increased by eight times between 1880 and 1920, while its black population doubled during the same period. "Tensions between native-born Protestants and Catholic and Jewish immigrants ran high, especially over the issue of alcohol," Cayton added. "In the 1920s, Klan and Klan-backed candidates won several elections in the Mahoning Valley, appealing not just to prejudice but to citizens concerned with a perceived decline in personal morality. The Klan promised to restore law and order and Protestant values over an unwieldy and assertive population of immigrants and blacks."[50]

Given that many native-born Protestants were engaged in what they regarded as a last-ditch effort to preserve their way of life, it is unsurprising that a large percentage supported a sharp reduction in European immigration. In Youngstown, as noted, many white Protestants perceived a strong causal relationship between the rise of ethnic and religious diversity and the city's soaring crime rate. This wave of criminal activity was by no means exaggerated. As Jenkins noted, the city's crime rate rose dramatically during the first two decades of the twentieth century. "Felonies, which averaged 136 per year between 1900 and 1910, increased over 73 percent by 1913," he wrote. "From 1914 through 1920 the yearly average was 537 felonies, almost a 400 percent increase over the first decade."[51] This increase owed much, of course, to the growth of the city's population during the same period. The most dramatic expansion occurred between 1910 and 1920, when Youngstown's population rose from 79,066 to 132,358.[52] Nevertheless, many white Protestants viewed "Catholic and Jewish immigrants with a . . . jaundiced eye" and actively promoted a law-and-order agenda that reflected the values of the Protestant majority.[53]

Meanwhile, African Americans readily understood that they had few, if any, allies within Youngstown's polarized white community. The hostility of recent immigrants was almost palpable; and in time, responses from native-born white Protestants were equally demoralizing. Although representatives of the local Ku Klux Klan did not "try to bring southern racial mores to Youngstown," African Americans understood that white supremacist values permeated the group's agenda.[54] It was no accident that the city's expanding south side, a bastion of pro-Klan sentiment, was overwhelmingly white, Protestant, and middle class, with only "pockets of the poor and immigrants."[55] Blacks were prevented from moving into such quasi-suburban neighborhoods through a vast array of formal and informal practices. As Kevin Boyle noted, in his study of 1920s Detroit, the maintenance of racial segregation in developing neighborhoods involved the cooperation of banks, real estate firms, and lending agencies. Boyle acknowledged that "[n]o one outside the South suggested that the flow of blacks into the cities be prohibited." Yet, urban whites gradually "carved a color line through the city," while a growing number of white business owners "banned black customers from their stores and restaurants." Ultimately, northern whites "decided that blacks couldn't live wherever they wanted," and business leaders "infused the real estate market with racist rules and regulations." In addition, white realtors "wouldn't show black tenants apartments outside the ghetto," and bankers refused to offer them mortgages.[56] Similarly, insurance agents declined to provide blacks with coverage, and real estate developers "wrote legal restrictions into their deeds, barring blacks from new housing tracts." If these manifestations of institutionalized racism were not enough, native-born white homeowners placed further restrictions on the choices of black residents by organizing "protective associations" to "keep their areas lily-white." In this way, "the glittering cities of the Jazz Age were inexorably being divided in two."[57] Notably, the pattern prevalent throughout much of the industrialized North was reproduced to a large extent in Youngstown, where most urban black neighborhoods formed an arc to the immediate northwest of the downtown area. The eroding ethnic enclaves of the city's so-called West End were among the community's least desirable residential areas. Indeed, the *Vindicator* reported in 1935 that the "dilapidated" district "was picked by federal authorities out of seven submitted by the Metropolitan Housing Authority for slum clearance."[58]

RACISM WITHIN THE WHITE PROTESTANT ESTABLISHMENT

For native-born white Protestants in Youngstown, the issue of race became a complicated, perhaps even painful, affair. Few of the community's established Anglo-American residents wished to be seen as racially intolerant. As Ohioans, they took pride in their state's role in the Underground Railroad, an intricate network of "safe houses" and secret tunnels that enabled thousands of fugitive slaves to make their way north to Canada. Indeed, the Underground Railroad became "one of the most enduring symbols in Ohio history."[59] In 1860, with the outbreak of the Civil War, Ohioans were among the Union's staunchest supporters. The wartime leadership of Governor David Tod, a Youngstown industrialist, drew praise from President Abraham Lincoln, who offered the former governor a position in his cabinet, an offer Tod was compelled to refuse because of his declining health.[60] The white establishment's reverence for the community's mythologized past was reflected in public monuments and commemorations. A stone obelisk memorializing "the

Union dead" dominated the central square, and public schools were named in honor of fallen leaders like William McKinley, the assassinated president who had fought for the Union's preservation as a young man. In 1888, only 23 years after the end of the Civil War, Youngstown's native-born white majority helped send William R. Stewart to the state legislature, making him the second African American to serve as an Ohio lawmaker.[61]

The white Protestant community's supposed commitment to racial tolerance was tested, however, as the city's population became more diverse; and the limitations of this tradition became increasingly apparent over time. Although native-born whites praised the legacy of the Thirteenth Amendment and occasionally supported leaders from the black community, they nevertheless harbored deep reservations about the impoverished southern blacks who had arrived in Youngstown during the early 1900s. As indicated, such concerns were shared by many members of the city's black middle classes, a community of skilled and educated people. These freeborn blacks had experienced neither the dehumanizing hardships of slavery nor the relentless exploitation of the postbellum sharecropping system. Too often, they showed little sympathy for the less privileged segments of the local black community. "The Negro leadership throughout [the early twentieth century] appears to have been more concerned with advancing self rather than race," observed George D. Beelen, in a 1967 academic paper. "Indeed, many of the long-time Negro residents of Youngstown were most contemptuous of the southern Negroes of the Great Migration."[62] Overall, the cultural gap separating established African American residents and migrants from the South could not have been wider. Nicholas Lemann, in his well-regarded treatment of the Great Migration, noted that the social patterns of black sharecropper society were "the equivalent of big-city ghetto society today in many ways." Lemann described this society as "the national center of illegitimate childbearing and of the female-headed family." Rural southern black society was burdened with "the worst public education system in the country, the one whose students were most likely to leave school before finishing and most likely to be illiterate even if they did finish," Lemann wrote. "It had an extremely high rate of violent crime," he added. Furthermore, chemical dependency and sexually transmitted disease "were nationally known as special problems of the black rural South; home-brew whiskey was much more physically perilous than crack cocaine is today, if less addictive."[63]

In a multitude of ways, the arrival of black migrants from the South magnified the hypocrisies and inconsistencies that had long informed the white establishment's attitude toward the African American community. Lemann indicated that, of the 6.5 million African Americans who moved from the

South to the North between 1910 and 1970, "five million of them moved after 1940, during the time of the mechanization of cotton farming."[64] The approximately 1.5 million who arrived before this period often faced a cool reception from white elites. After all, the opposition of native-born whites to the nation's more extreme racist conventions did not necessarily reflect a genuine adherence to the principle of human equality. Therefore, it did not take long for the integrated neighborhoods of the early nineteenth century to give way to the racial and ethnic enclaves of the early twentieth century. For many white Protestants, "equality" involved strict separation; and therefore, much of the philanthropy directed at the black community was informed by the white establishment's commitment to separate—and inherently unequal—social arrangements. In the early 1900s, the Reverend Abner L. Fraser, the white rector of St. John's Episcopal Parish, helped local African Americans establish the "colored" parish of St. Augustine's.[65] (This congregation should not be confused with a short-lived black Catholic parish of the same name, which was established about four decades later.) Similarly, local patrician Henry Audubon Butler, son of the well-known industrial leader Joseph G. Butler, Jr., helped organize the Butler Memorial Presbyterian Church, an institution reserved for black congregants who were denied admission to the city's fashionable First Presbyterian Church.[66] These apparently well-intentioned gestures reflect how white benevolence often served to uphold the principle of racial segregation. As William Watkins has observed, the "race philanthropy" supported by late-19th-century Anglo-American industrialists—and lauded by many northern middle-class whites—was designed, in part, to maintain social inequality along racial lines: "The possibilities of using philanthropy for social engineering were inviting. The 'Negro Problem' was among the most vexing and urgent of the time. Politics would be at the heart of using the philanthropies to guarantee . . . a compliant Black population."[67]

RACIAL, ETHNIC, AND RELIGIOUS FAULT LINES DIVIDE A COMMUNITY

The social, political, and economic tensions that rippled through the community in the early twentieth century were aggravated by demographic changes that radically altered the ethnic and racial composition of Youngstown. By the 1920s, the African American population was growing at a faster rate than the European immigrant population—a development that reflected a massive shift of rural populations to urban centers as well as the impact of sharp restrictions on immigration that were imposed in 1921 and 1924, respectively. A 1931 report issued by the International Institute, a service organization managed by the local chapter of the YWCA, showed that the city's black population had more than doubled between 1920 and 1930, jumping from 6,662 to 14,352. According to the same report, the population of "foreign-born whites" declined slightly within the same decade, falling from 33,634 to 32,938.[68] These figures were echoed by the local media. In June 1931, the *Vindicator* reported that U.S. immigration figures for the previous month "showed that the total number of aliens entering the United States was less than the number leaving."[69] This high rate of departure among immigrants undoubtedly owed something to the adversity brought on by the Great Depression, whose impact was not fully reflected in the International Institute's records on black migration.

This decline in European immigration owed much to the lobbying efforts of native-born white Protestants, who contended that many of the nation's social problems could be traced to the waves of European immigrants who had arrived during the late nineteenth and early twentieth centuries. In places like Youngstown, white elites were inclined to believe that recent immigrants had altered the social and political climate in ways that were deeply unsettling, fueling both corruption and public immorality. Thus, in the early 1920s, the local chapter of the Ku Klux Klan "did not take direct action against black residents" and focused instead on the perceived moral threat posed by recent immigrants, who were disproportionately Catholic.[70] The anti-immigrant sentiment then prevalent throughout the northern United States fueled the Warren G. Harding administration's successful bid to limit European immigration in 1921, a move that came in response to controversies involving "new" European immigrants. As a *Vindicator* correspondent observed, "the compelling motive behind . . . the immigration restriction bill . . . is hesitancy about the recent immigration which comes largely from eastern and south-eastern Europe."[71] Further restrictions on immigration were imposed as the decade progressed. As Matthew Frye Jacobson noted, "the most significant revision of the immigration policy" was the Johnson-Reed Act of 1924, which was justified through "a racial logic borrowed from biology and eugenics."[72] In the wake of this legislation, prominent eugenicist Harry Laughlin stated that, after 1924, immigrants would be viewed primarily as parents "of future-born American citizens," which "meant that the hereditary stuff out of which future immigrants were made would have to be compatible racially with American ideals."[73]

Meanwhile, a large percentage of recent immigrants—as the letter composed by "A Resident" illustrates—viewed newly arrived blacks from the South as a major source of the community's social ills. On occasion, native-born whites were moved to criticize recent immigrants for their overt intolerance toward blacks. Recent immigrants, in response, often bristled over what they regarded as the hypocrisy of white Protestants. Did local white Protestant leaders truly believe that they were in a position to condemn the racist attitudes of "new" immigrants when their own neighborhoods were racially segregated? Critics of the white middle classes noted that Protestant-dominated suburban townships such as neighboring Canfield, Ohio, were segregated along racial *and* religious lines. Indeed, the extent to which recent immigrants were excluded from suburban communities during the 1920s shocked some newcomers to the area. In 2002, the late Joseph Hill, a 101-year-old Lithuanian Jewish immigrant, recalled an incident that involved a newly appointed supervisor at his insurance firm. The supervisor, a Catholic named John Warland, encountered blatant religious bigotry when he attempted to purchase a house in a nearby suburb during the 1920s. Hill described the incident as follows: "So, [Warland] walks into the real estate office in Boardman [Ohio], and they assigned an agent to go with him to buy a house. The agent says, 'Let's go to Canfield.' And Warland asks, 'Why Canfield?' And the agent says, 'Because Canfield has very few Roman Catholics.' Warland looks at him and says: 'Well, let's keep it that way. Take me back to my hotel.' So, you see, he lost the sale."[74]

As Hill's story suggests, anti-Catholic sentiment was fairly prevalent in Youngstown during the early twentieth century. In the 1920s, *The Citizen,* a pro-Klan weekly newspaper that was distributed throughout the Youngstown area, criticized what it termed the Catholic Church's "unfriendly, hostile and unclean attitude towards American Protestants."[75] During the same period, Catholics who moved into quasi-suburban areas, especially the city's west and south sides, sometimes arose from their beds to discover that wooden crosses had been burned in their front yards during the evening hours. In a 2007 interview, former south side resident T. Gordon Welsh indicated that his own parents were targeted by the vigilante organization a few days after their marriage. "Dad had built a new house for Mother to go into when they came back from their honeymoon," Welsh said. "And the first night they were there . . . the Klan came along . . . and they set a cross in the [yard and] set fire to it."[76] It is difficult to determine whether these tactics of intimidation were widespread, but much documentation exists concerning the local Klan's ceremonial cross burnings throughout the Youngstown metropolitan area.[77] As disturbing as such incidents undoubtedly were, however, the harassment of Catholic neighbors was not necessarily in line with the Klan's overriding goal, which was to restore the dominance of native-born Protestant conceptions of morality. As Jenkins noted, there is no conclusive statistical data suggesting that the penetration of ethnic whites into "old-stock" white urban neighborhoods "served as a prime motivation for the majority of Klan members."[78]

Exclusionary policies used by white elites against blacks, on the other hand, were insistent, systematic, and enforced through quasi-legal means, including housing regulations and homeowners' agreements.[79] The subsequent participation of recent immigrants in such discriminatory policies and practices ensured that these devices would be extraordinarily effective, and their influence is felt to this day. As David R. Roediger noted, recent immigrants in large metropolitan areas like New York rushed "to draw the color line" by supporting racist property restriction organizations. In 1919, a light-skinned African American minister who had infiltrated a white "pro-restrictionist" meeting in the Hyde Park-Kenwood area commented bitterly that "Jews attended, taking time out from charitable efforts to aid pogrom victims; Irishmen came straight from Free Ireland events; Italians left the 'murder zone' in which they lived to victimize blacks; Poles, seen as having the blood of anti-Semitic massacres on their hands, showed up; Czechs and Slovaks, Russians and even 'an honorable Japanese gentleman' united against the 'coon.'"[80]

THE RISING TIDE OF SOUTHERN MIGRATION

In the decades leading up to World War II, black migration to the Youngstown area continued to grow, albeit modestly. According to a 1944 newspaper article, the city's population in 1940 was 167,720, a figure that included 10,382 residents who had migrated to the community in the previous five years. The article reported that only 334 of these new arrivals hailed from outside the continental United States, a figure that suggests many of these migrants traveled to northeastern Ohio from the nation's economically depressed regions, including the South. Records that reflect the sweeping demographic changes that occurred within Youngstown's city limits during the final years of the Depression support this interpretation. A report released by the U.S. Commerce Department in 1941, for instance, categorized more than 19,000 of Youngstown's almost 170,000 residents as "nonwhite."[81] In 1942, the first year of America's involvement in World War II, the *Vindicator* provided a more modest figure when it reported that the community had a total population of 167,720 residents, "with 126,385 native-born whites, 26,671 foreign-born whites, 14,615 Negroes, 18 Indians, and seven representatives of other races."[82]

As migration from the South escalated in the postwar era, media references to the community's expanding minority population became more frequent, and some news reports volunteered brief explanations of this unfolding demographic shift. A 1951 newspaper article, for example, quoted a U.S.

Census Bureau report that suggested that the migration of defense workers was mainly responsible for the growing percentage of "nonwhites" living in the community. The same article observed that "the nonwhite population increased from 14,664 to 21,547 between 1940 and 1950, while the white population dropped [by] almost an equivalent number, from 153,056 to 146,781, leaving the city with a net population increase of 610."[83] Naturally, the sharp rise in black migration during the postwar era contributed to chronic overcrowding in the city's traditional black neighborhoods. More established black residents, seeking relief from congested living conditions, began to migrate to the Italian American enclave of Brier Hill, a working-class district to the northwest of the city's traditional black "ghettoes." During this period, more African American residents also migrated to east-side neighborhoods, and to sections of the south side that abutted the downtown area—districts that already had small black populations. The movement of blacks into neighborhoods that were dominated by working- and middle-class ethnic whites brought African Americans into contact with large numbers of Roman Catholics.[84] White Catholics, for their part, responded warily to the presence of blacks in neighborhoods that had grown up around parishes and parochial schools. By this time, white Catholics had already begun their migration to the suburbs, although they tended to leave the city at a slower pace than their non-Catholic counterparts. Indeed, pragmatic considerations were often behind patterns that some observers interpreted as evidence of a stronger Catholic commitment to urban neighborhoods. As McGreevy observed, an unusually large percentage of working-class white Catholics were homeowners, a circumstance that limited their mobility in the wake of urban decline. Apart from such practical considerations, however, white Catholics also harbored emotional attachments to urban parishes, which made some of them reluctant to relocate to the suburbs, in spite of sweeping demographic changes.[85]

For those whites who remained in the city, urban demographic change became a matter of concern. While a variety of factors contributed to the European American exodus from the city, the growth of the urban black population weighed heavily on the minds of retreating white Catholics. "What became clear during the 1950s was that while the migration to the suburbs possessed an independent momentum, its connections to racial issues were profound," McGreevy wrote. "In fact, the most obvious distinction between suburban Catholicism and parish life within the cities was the relative importance of racial concerns." The author noted that, in the wake of "legal and economic barriers" that prevented blacks from purchasing homes in outlying areas, "racial transition was an abstraction to most suburban Catholics."[86] The growing apprehension that many urban whites felt about demographic change was reflected in their reluctance to socialize with African American neighbors. Sister Charlotte Italiano, OSU, who spent a portion of her childhood in an Italian American enclave on Youngstown's east side, recalled that in the 1940s, there was virtually no interaction between blacks and whites in what was becoming a racially diverse neighborhood. "I don't remember any fighting or friction," she said. "I do think it was just a [matter] of 'you stay on your side, and we'll stay on our side.' So, then, there wasn't confrontation."[87]

It would be a mistake, however, to assume that open racial conflict was unknown in Youngstown during this period. Tension between members of the African American community and the city's heavily white police force, for instance, surfaced in the immediate aftermath of World War II. In October 1945, the local NAACP called an emergency protest meeting on the subject of "police brutality," and the chapter's leaders went so far as to demand the resignation of Youngstown's police chief, John B. Thomas. In the course of the meeting, Fred D. Dillard, a local black union leader, claimed that Thomas had "beaten" several black youths at a local settlement house. Dillard went on to question whether "our boys had fought for a concept of democracy which permitted a police chief to beat up someone just because he didn't like the way they parted their hair, tied their shoes or wore their caps." Given the political climate of the times, which encouraged the public to regard protest meetings with a degree of suspicion, the reporter covering the event evidently felt compelled to offer the following assurances: "There were some known Communists hanging around the fringes of the protest meeting, but they were not in control. The meeting was conducted with dignity; the protest taken up in the traditional American way."[88] Other confrontations had already occurred. In September 1945, for instance, the *Vindicator* published an editorial on a series of disturbances that involved white and black youths. Describing the incidents as "an unpleasant reminder that Youngstown is constantly sitting on a racial powder keg," the editorial praised the municipal government's decision to enforce a curfew designed to prevent racially inspired gang violence in the city's downtown area. Although the editorial acknowledged that the black community "still has real grievances," it also cautioned that "leaders who inflame Negroes to demand extremes in social acceptance are only hurting their own people."[89] Such "extremes in social acceptance" evidently included black demands for the integration of local public swimming pools. In 1949, a *Vindicator* editorial described a campaign to "force the acceptance of Negroes in all of the city's swimming pools" as the handiwork of left-wing agitators. The editorial claimed that the campaign's supporters included "[political factions, the C.I.O. and now the 'Young Progressives,' a Communist front organization." It continued with this allegation: "Undesirables have been imported into Youngstown to stir up hatred and dissension among Negroes in an attempt to line them up with traitors seeking to destroy the country." The editorial concluded that local blacks "are not helped by disloyal radicals posing as young progressives, and by Communists hurrying into Youngstown from Cleveland and other places to stir up all the dissension they can."[90]

Despite such overheated rhetoric, instances of conflict between blacks and whites were still relatively uncommon during the postwar era. Amid high levels of racial segregation, local blacks and whites had few opportunities to interact at all. Catholic religious leaders, for the most part, failed to take meaningful steps to bridge this gap, an omission that appeared consistent with the U.S. church's traditionally reserved attitude toward African Americans. As noted, Robert Casey, a resident of the east side during the 1950s, could not recall any efforts on the part of clergy or religious to reach out to the growing black population in the vicinity of Immaculate Conception Church.[91] Moreover, the neighborhood's racial diversity was not reflected in the classrooms of the parish school, whose students were mainly of Irish, Italian, and Lebanese backgrounds.[92] Casey said he did not believe that a single African American student was enrolled at the institution at the time he attended Immaculate Conception Elementary School, or during the years that immediately followed his graduation.[93] The east side's small number of black Catholics apparently belonged to St. Augustine's Church, an African American parish that was established in the district during the 1940s.[94]

THE U.S. CHURCH'S RELUCTANT ENGAGEMENT WITH AFRICAN AMERICANS

The postwar Catholic engagement with African Americans in northern urban centers was probably complicated by the fact that few blacks were members of the Catholic Church. It would be misleading, of course, to suggest that the racial fears of white Catholics hinged exclusively upon the fact that most African Americans were Protestant. Generations of white Catholics, taking their cues from a racially conservative hierarchy, often expressed hostility toward African Americans, including those who shared their religion. As early as the 1850s, a black Catholic in New York City wrote an urgent letter to Pope Pius IX, in which she complained of the racism of American clerics. In her letter, Harriet Thompson noted that a proposal to establish a black school at a local parish had been rejected by Archbishop John Hughes, the charismatic leader of the Archdiocese of New York. She added that it was "well known by both white and black that the Most Reverend Archbishop Hughes . . . [hates] the black race so much that he cannot bear for them to come near him." If Hughes's racism was exceptional in its virulence, his failure to address the needs of black Catholics was sadly representative of U.S. clerical leaders during the antebellum period. Despite Pope Gregory XVI's condemnation of the slave trade in 1839, few American clerics showed much interest in the plight of African Americans in the decades leading up to the Civil War. Tragically, the bulk of the U.S. hierarchy remained indifferent to blacks in the postbellum era. In 1866, at the Second Plenary Council of Baltimore, U.S. bishops (despite the pleas of visionary leaders like Martin J. Spalding) failed to develop a plan to address the needs of recently freed slaves. Worse yet, a pastoral letter issued in the wake of the council expressed regret over the "expedient" nature of emancipation. The letter reads in part: "We could have wished, that in accordance with the action of the Catholic Church in past ages, in regard to the serfs of Europe, a more gradual system of emancipation could have been adopted, so that they might have been in some measure prepared to make better use of their freedom, than they are likely to do now."[95] Apart from the efforts of a handful of committed Catholic leaders—notably Katherine Drexel, the banking heiress who became a benefactor of both African Americans and Native Americans, and John Ireland, the radical archbishop of St. Paul, Minnesota—the U.S. church's overall efforts to reach out to blacks in the late nineteenth and early twentieth centuries were halfhearted.[96,97]

Before the late 1950s and early 1960s, the small number of U.S. Catholic leaders who took an active interest in the concerns of African Americans operated largely on the fringes of the Catholic community. Some of these leaders, in line with the conventions of their day, expressed paternalistic attitudes toward blacks. Even such towering figures as John LaFarge, SJ, and John Markoe, SJ, clerical pioneers in the realm of interracial cooperation, were guilty of such paternalism. In the 1930s, LaFarge established the Catholic Interracial Council of New York, an organization whose progressive goals inspired the opposition of influential churchmen like Chancellor James McIntyre, who "proved to be a major obstacle to interracial work in New York City."[98] Markoe was a lifelong advocate of "the cause of interracial justice"[99] who "moved comfortably in black culture" and declared "it was superior to white culture."[100] Yet, both men deeply offended the sensibilities of black Catholic leaders in 1932, when they moved against Thomas Wyatt Turner, the African American head of a national lay organization called the Federated Colored Catholics. LaFarge and Markoe's efforts to promote interracial cooperation within the Catholic community came at the expense of existing black leadership and forced a split in the organization. As a result, the group's Midwestern branch, renamed as the National Interracial Federation, fell into decline and became inactive.[101]

Whatever their shortcomings, LaFarge and Markoe were leagues ahead of their coreligionists on the issue of interracial relations, and they helped lay the groundwork for the church's belated response to the civil rights movement. David W. Southern, in his critical examination of LaFarge's ministry, observed that such pioneers "patiently bored from within the American church for almost half a century, trying to change what was essentially a racist organization."[102] As Cyprian Davis, OSB, noted, in his study of African American Catholics, only a handful of U.S. bishops addressed the issue of racial discrimination in Catholic schools, notably Joseph Cardinal Ritter, in St. Louis, and Patrick A. O'Boyle, in Washington, D.C.[103] Throughout much of the 1950s, the racial attitudes of the majority of the country's white clerical leaders ranged from indifference to outright hostility, and these kinds of attitudes were reflected within the laity. "The beliefs of the pastor and their people fed on each other," wrote Eileen McMahon, in her study of Catholic neighborhoods in postwar Chicago. "Pastors justified their positions by saying, 'My people hate the niggers,' while parishioners were given the message that it was all right to do so." Given the virulent racism that permeated American society, and the complacence (even complicity) of the U.S. Catholic hierarchy, immigrants came to view blacks as natural antagonists.[104] Roediger observed that antiblack sentiment among newer immigrants was exacerbated, albeit indirectly, by ethnic conflict within the Catholic community itself. As an Irish-dominated hierarchy took increasingly stern measures against national parishes, such institutions were relegated to the declining neighborhoods of the central city. Therefore, those recent immigrants who relocated to new developments invariably found themselves in territorial parishes that reflected an Irish American religious and cultural ethos. A significant number of newer immigrants responded by strengthening their commitment to national parishes, while seeking to "defend" traditional ethnic enclaves from the "encroachment" of outsiders, especially black migrants from the South. Ultimately, decisions to abandon aging ethnic and religious enclaves were "tense," given that "moving out of a changing neighborhood meant abandoning spectacular church buildings" and leaving behind distinctive ethnic religious traditions.[105]

The expansion of territorial parishes did little to facilitate the integration of black Catholics. "Even as hesitant Catholic initiatives for interracial harmony took shape, the Church taught by example that African Americans were different," Roediger noted. "Thus the turn to mixed territorial parishes conspicuously left out African Americans, consigning them to separate congregations."[106] This is not to suggest that all northern Roman Catholic dioceses maintained a strict policy of racial segregation. In the early twentieth century, for example, George Cardinal Mundelein reserved the parish of St. Monica's for Chicago's

The original frame structure of St. Columba Church, Youngstown's premier Catholic parish, gave way to this relatively elaborate building in the later nineteenth century.

Photograph provided by The Mahoning Valley Historical Society, The Arms Family Museum of Local History & MVHS Archival Library, 648 Wick Ave., Youngstown, OH 44502

The local Catholic community's deepening commitment to religious education was reflected in the building of St. Columba Elementary School, shown here in the early 1870s.

This 1890 portrait of an Irish American marked his First Communion ceremony at St. Columba Church. Parishioners at St. Columba were actively encouraged to enroll their children in the parish school, and they were often discouraged from utilizing local public schools, which many Catholics regarded as "Protestant schools."

The rapid growth of Youngstown's Catholic institutions was fueled by the development of the area's iron and steel industry. This early twentieth-century photograph shows the furnaces of Republic Iron & Steel Company, which formed a dense industrial zone to the immediate south of the downtown area.

Tens of thousands of Italian immigrants arrived in the Mahoning Valley in the late nineteenth and early twentieth century, including the Angelo and Cecilia Fusco family, photographed outside their home in Youngstown's Brier Hill district during the summer of 1905. Throughout the first half of the twentieth century, Italian Americans tended to avoid parish schools, and neither of the city's Italian national parishes supported a school during this period.

A 1910 photograph of the graduating class of Immaculate Conception Elementary School features the parish's second pastor, Father M. P. Kinkead. Established in 1882 to meet the needs of the east side's isolated Catholic community, Immaculate Conception opened a school the following year.

Photograph provided by Immaculate Conception - Sacred Heart of Jesus Parish, 400 Lincoln Park Drive, Youngstown, OH 44506-1798

Irish-dominated territorial parishes such as St. Columba Church co-existed (sometimes uneasily) with national parishes designed to meet the needs of non-English speaking immigrants. This 1920 photograph shows a Fourth of July celebration at St. Joseph Church, a north side parish organized to serve Youngstown's German-speaking Catholics.

Photograph provided by The Mahoning Valley Historical Society, The Arms Family Museum of Local History & MVHS Archival Library, 648 Wick Ave., Youngstown, OH 44502

The spires of St. Columba Church's third edifice (captured in this undated photograph) dominated Youngstown's skyline until 1954, when a fire ravaged the local landmark.

After the creation of the Diocese of Youngstown, in 1943, Bishop James McFadden established St. Augustine Parish, intended for members of Youngstown's fledgling Black Catholic community. The short-lived parish was practically invisible to the district's White Catholics, even though it operated within blocks of two other east side parishes.

Center city institutions like St. Casimir Parish, a Polish national parish located in the Brier Hill district, began to lose parishioners after World War II. Still relatively vibrant in 1948, when this photograph was taken, the parish fell into steep decline during the 1960s and was forced to close its school in 1972.

Photograph provided by Mrs. Mary Ann Dudzik, 3272 N. Wendover Circle, Youngstown, OH 44511

A photograph taken from the main altar of St. Columba Cathedral shows the extensive damage left behind by a fire that swept the neo-Gothic structure on September 2, 1954.

Photograph provided by Thomas Molocea, 11650 New Buffalo Road, North Lima, OH 44452

The exterior of the second incarnation of St. Columba Cathedral (shown in 2011) looks much as it did at the time of its dedication in 1958. The new cathedral's stark and modern appearance generated controversy within the local Catholic community.

Photograph provided by Thomas G. Welsh, 438 N. Osborne Avenue, Youngstown, OH 44509

By the 1960s, the neighborhood surrounding Immaculate Conception Elementary School had changed dramatically. Scores of east side residents migrated to outlying neighborhoods, and highway construction resulted in the removal of hundreds of homes. While most of the graduates shown in this 1965 photograph were parishioners, the school served mainly non-White and non-Catholic students by the late 1970s.

Photograph provided by Immaculate Conception - Sacred Heart of Jesus Parish, 400 Lincoln Park Drive, Youngstown, OH 44506-1798

Under the leadership of Immaculate Conception Church's pastor, Father John Summers, the parish school became a "mission" institution, which was supported largely by diocesan-wide fundraising campaigns. The school also benefited from the generosity of alumni, many of whom attended an annual benefit dinner. Amid dwindling enrollment, however, Immaculate Conception Elementary School was forced to close in 2006.

Photograph provided by Atty. Robert E. Casey, 8070 Paulin Drive, Boardman, OH 44514

Tenth Annual Benefit Dinner

for

Immaculate Conception School

February 21, 2001

Our Lady of Mt. Carmel Social Hall

Signage outside Summit Academy, a charter school on Youngstown's east side, continues to bear the name of the building's first occupant, Immaculate Conception Elementary School. Several of the city's former parish school buildings are leased by charter schools.

Photograph provided by Thomas G. Welsh, 438 N. Osborne Avenue, Youngstown, OH 44509

African Americans, while at the same time, emphasizing that blacks should not be "excluded from attending other parishes." As McMahon noted, however, "white territorial parishes often exercised their prerogative to exclude blacks or treat them as second-class parishioners."[107] Meanwhile, black Catholics who feared discrimination in white-dominated parishes sometimes engaged in "voluntary" segregation. McGreevy cited the example of a black family who relocated from St. Louis to the south side of Chicago in the late 1920s. One family member recalled his parents' fears "that without a 'Negro' parish African-American children would not obtain positions as altar boys and that teenagers would date members of another race."[108]

While there is no evidence that Youngstown's African American Catholics were officially excluded from local territorial parishes, a significant number of them requested permission to set up a separate parish on the city's east side in the 1940s. On the occasion of St. Augustine Church's dedication in 1944, Youngstown Bishop James A. McFadden observed, rather paternalistically, that "many of the colored people of Youngstown have asked that something special be done for them by the church." He added that the new parish "should provide an opportunity for the religious and [social] activity they desire."[109] Fourteen years later, in 1958, when the diocese determined it would close the parish, Bishop Emmet M. Walsh's announcement of the decision was hardly less paternalistic. In a letter that the pastor read aloud to the parishioners, Bishop Walsh stated, "I understand quite well that some may find the closing of St. Augustine difficult because of your affection, loyalty, and attachment to the parish." The letter added, "I ask you to take these virtues with you, exercise them in the new parish to which you will go, so that the cause of Christ among the Colored will continue to advance."[110] Unsurprisingly, the development that Bishop Walsh presented as an opportunity was perceived differently by some of St. Augustine's parishioners. Naomi Byrd, who belonged to the parish at the time, indicated she was saddened by the loss of an institution that was "just like one big family,"[111] while her sister, Beverly Blackshear, recalled thinking, "I'm going back [to the territorial parish], and these people aren't going to accept me."[112] Patronizing attitudes toward black Catholics were no less evident among clerical leaders in the neighboring Diocese of Cleveland. Dorothy Ann Blatnica, VSC, in her study of black Catholics in Cleveland, noted that Bishop Edward F. Hoban's view of African American Catholics "was still colored by a missionary perspective that did not permit him to see them as leaders in the diocesan church."[113] At the same time, the emphasis that some urban pastors placed on proselytizing had created a substantial black Catholic community where virtually none had existed.[114] These evangelizing efforts, however, were marred by the tendency of white missionaries to devalue the traditions of the black church; and the debate continues over whether "a separate rite for African

American . . . Catholics is the only useful and effective resolution of the Church's racist past."[115]

The U.S. church's policies concerning the black community began to show signs of change in the 1950s, when "a growing number of Catholic bishops and clergy, and a vocal minority of laypeople, began to speak out on civil rights issues."[116] As Buetow noted, "Many southern dioceses desegregated prior to 1954: in New Orleans, Archbishop Joseph F. Rummel started before 1949 and completed it in 1953; Bishop Vincent S. Waters in North Carolina by 1953; Archbishop (later Cardinal) Patrick A. O'Boyle in Washington, D.C., in 1948." Beginning in 1951, Archbishop Robert E. Lucey of San Antonio, Texas, "quietly but firmly integrated all institutions under his jurisdiction." During the same period, Joseph Ritter, in his consecutive posts as bishop of Indianapolis and archbishop of St. Louis, took forceful steps to eliminate segregation.[117] Sugrue noted that, in Detroit, the Catholic hierarchy's "growing racial tolerance brought it into conflict with parishioners who lived in racially changing neighborhoods and with pastors who often shared racial prejudices and looked with chagrin on white flight from their parishes."[118] By this time, northern white Catholics were increasingly (and disproportionately) affected by the unfolding trend of urban demographic change.[119]

THE WHITE CATHOLIC RESPONSE TO URBAN CHANGE

Well before the 1960s, white Catholics throughout the northeastern United States had begun their gradual migration to the suburbs. Dolan noted that the breakup of old national parishes and ethnic enclaves was partly the result of racial tension that had accompanied demographic change. As thousands of African American migrants from the South found their way into northern urban centers, many "chose to settle in neighborhoods located on the fringe of the old immigrant enclaves," and the "slow but steady trickle" of white Catholics to the suburbs that began during the postwar era "reached flood-tide levels by the 1960s."[120] Interestingly, the movement of Latinos into heavily white Catholic areas inspired relatively little anxiety among established residents. McGreevy observed that "neighborhood contacts between Euro-American and Spanish-speaking Catholics at parish activities or in the parochial school were comparatively frequent when compared to contact between Euro-Americans and African-Americans." He added that the involvement of Latinos in parish activities may have "[signified] to Euro-American Catholics that the new group was not 'black,' regardless of physical features." Perhaps the historical connection between Latinos and the Catholic Church played a decisive role in shaping white Catholic perceptions in this regard. In any event, (mostly Catholic) Latinos, unlike (overwhelmingly Protestant) African Americans, could be integrated into the parish structure that dominated most urban Catholic neighborhoods.[121]

Antiblack sentiment among white Catholics was often heightened by growing concern that the movement of blacks into Catholic neighborhoods would imperil urban parishes and parochial schools.[122] The fears of many urban Catholic laypeople were shared by a large number of clerical leaders, who watched with dismay as Catholic institutions in urban neighborhoods lost their traditional patrons. Throughout the 1940s, urban pastors around the country helped mobilize opposition to the location of housing projects in heavily Catholic neighborhoods, a move that (quite naturally) deepened some black leaders' hostility toward the Catholic Church.[123] The fears behind such drastic measures were summed up by Saul Alinsky, a community organizer who worked with residents of working-class, white Catholic neighborhoods in Chicago who were struggling to adjust to demographic change in the 1950s. "When a community changes from white to Negro, the Catholic Church is in a different position than Protestant or Jewish churches," Alinsky said. "It has a bigger real investment."[124]

Given that white Catholics were less likely than other European Americans to relocate to the suburbs, "Catholics (and their church) emerged from the decade as the single largest group (and institution) in the northern cities." While tens of thousands of white Catholics ultimately found their way into suburban communities, "the Catholic share of the [urban] 'white' population continued to climb." This trend was especially pronounced in longstanding immigrant strongholds like Boston, where some census tracts suggested that "the proportion of Catholics climbed to over 96 percent."[125] Contributing to growing racial tension in northern cities was the fact that the African American percentage of the urban population was also rising. During the 1960s, for instance, the black population of Chicago rose from 22.9 percent of the population to 32.7 percent; and the trend was similar in Cleveland, where the African American population rose from 28.6 percent to 38.3 percent. These parallel trends did not bring about integration, however. The black population became increasingly isolated as whites retreated from changing neighborhoods. As McGreevy noted, those "pockets of integration that did exist in the northern cities were usually ephemeral—areas midway through a complete turnover in population."[126] Until the late 1960s, the flight of working-class whites from some urban districts was facilitated by the policies of the Federal Housing Administration (FHA), which withheld loan guarantees from residents of urban neighborhoods that were racially and economically diverse.[127]

UNDERSTATED RACISM IN POSTWAR YOUNGSTOWN

Youngstown witnessed its share of racial tension, but the community was largely untouched by the sort of violence that attended demographic change in other cities featuring tight-knit Catholic neighborhoods. McGreevy noted that Philadelphia's Catholic leaders were widely criticized during the same period for their failure to condemn the harassment of a black family that moved into suburban Levittown. This was followed up three years later by an incident in which mostly Irish Catholic residents took to the streets of Kensington, a working-class district of Philadelphia, after hearing a rumor that a black family had moved into their neighborhood. "Rocks quickly crashed through the windows of the alleged residence of the African-American family and neither the assurances of city government officials nor police could persuade the crowd that a move-in would not take place," McGreevy wrote. "Finally, a squad car arrived on the scene with Father Charles Mallon, pastor of Ascension parish. Since 'many of the local people were members of the parish' the crowd quieted and then cheered as Mallon informed them that no move-in would occur. Only at this point, did the crowd disperse."[128]

Given the relative calm that accompanied demographic change in Youngstown during the 1950s, some contemporary observers may have concluded that the city's white residents were unusually tolerant on the issue of race. The truth, of course, was different. Most of Youngstown's public swimming pools were segregated until the late 1950s, and the local YMCA maintained a separate facility for blacks, a Tudor-style building that stood just north of the "Monkey's Nest."[129] In 1940, the establishment of one of the nation's first federally funded low-income housing projects on the city's old West End inflamed racial tension in neighborhoods to the northeast of Westlake's Crossing.[130] Moreover, there is evidence that the movement of black families into majority-white neighborhoods elsewhere in the city was followed by the abrupt departure of many European American residents. Robert Casey, who spent the later years of his adolescence on Youngstown's south side, described events that followed the arrival of the neighborhood's first black family in the 1950s. "They built a beautiful brick home . . . well kept up," Casey said. "And yet, after they purchased this home, immediately white families started to leave, because they had the view that 'Ah! There goes the neighborhood.' And I thought to myself it was almost like a self-fulfilling prophecy."[131]

Hostile responses to demographic change among local white urban dwellers were prevalent enough to draw the attention of a committee on urban affairs, which included organizations such as the Baptist Ministers Conference, B'nai B'rith, Catholic Charities, the Junior Civic League, the NAACP, and the Youngstown Civil Liberties Union. In 1958, the committee published a pamphlet on the city's "housing problem" that featured case studies of discriminatory housing practices that were common within the community. "A Negro steelworker, a veteran of World War II, entered into an agreement with [a] real estate agency to purchase a house . . . on West Dewey Avenue, a block in which at that time there were no Negro residents," one case study began. "The people who owned the house wanted to sell to him, the real estate agency wanted to sell it to him, the bank made him a loan." The sale was delayed, however, when "certain families in the block, fearful that this house was about to be sold to Negroes, protested to the bank." As a result, the bank "held up the loan, and the man never did get the house." The pamphlet also described an instance of "block busting," in which urban property owners sought to "exploit the plight of the Negro and make tremendous profits by owning slum property." The strategy was outlined as follows: "They buy a house in a deteriorating section of town, and then sell the house for two, three, or sometimes even four times what it cost on a land contract to Negroes." The pamphlet noted that a typical "block buster" encouraged "the rumor that Negroes depreciate a neighborhood and, buying from panic-stricken neighbors at very cheap prices, he reaps tremendous profits."[132]

Despite such instances of discrimination and intolerance, the overt hostility unleashed by demographic change in other northern urban areas during this period was practically unknown in Youngstown. Moreover, there is no evidence that local Catholic clergy rallied congregations to protect their neighborhoods from an "invasion" of African Americans, which was a reported occurrence in other northeastern cities.[133] At the same time, the community's racist conventions were scrupulously maintained throughout the 1950s. Mel Watkins observed that coming of age in Youngstown exposed him to "a subtle, seemingly inexplicable sense of outwardly imposed restraint and negation of self-worth." He wrote that this atmosphere left him with the sensation of "being trapped in one of Franz Kafka's nightmarish fictional allegories," where "defiance seemed imprudent unless one were himself willing to be labeled a troublemaker, deviant, or psychotic."[134] Watkins pointed out that racial discrimination within the larger community was often softened by a prevailing aura of social harmony. So long as blacks operated within certain perimeters, they could expect to be treated with a level of courtesy that existed nowhere south of the Mason-Dixon Line. In a particularly revealing passage, Watkins described the cheerful manner in which Youngstown's policies of racial segregation were enforced. At the age of 12, he arrived late for a film at a downtown movie theater and, without thinking, took a seat in the orchestra section. Watkins recalled that a white usher "calmly walked over, smiled, and said, 'I'm sorry, sir. I'm going to have to ask you to sit upstairs. It's theater policy, you know.'" The author added: "It was all done so courteously that, as I stood to leave, I felt a sudden obligation to *thank him*. Nearly asked if there was anything I could do for him. After all, it was my place—where I had intended to sit all along."[135]

When black families moved into traditional ethnic enclaves, retreating whites often observed that the neighborhood was "changing," a term that subtly conflated economic and demographic transformation. Such coded language enabled whites to express their anxieties about demographic change in a manner that, on the one hand, communicated their feelings of concern, while on the other, shielding them from the stigma of overt racism. Given that racially diverse urban neighborhoods were "redlined" by banking agencies, some white residents probably felt justified in treating economic and demographic changes as interchangeable developments. The discriminatory policies of local financial institutions, after all, were closely aligned with those of the federal government. As Jackson observed, the FHA "helped to turn the building industry against the minority and inner-city housing market, and its policies supported the income and racial segregation of suburbia." By declaring urban neighborhoods "ineligible" for loan guarantees, the FHA "exhorted segregation and enshrined it as public policy."[136]

Meanwhile, many black families who found themselves in majority-white neighborhoods were intimidated—at least initially—by their new, alien surroundings. Ida Carter, a retired public schoolteacher who continues to reside on Youngstown's south side, was a member of the first African American family to move into a home located on the district's main artery of Glenwood Avenue. She recalled in an interview that "it was strange for me, because being on the south side in 1959 was strange for Black people." She added, almost ominously, "I was living [in a home] surrounded by White people." Despite these verbal images of encirclement, Mrs. Carter went on to describe mostly harmonious relationships with white neighbors. "We moved up there, and the people embraced us," she said. "As a matter of fact the family on one side of us took my brothers and taught them how to fix washing machines." Mrs. Carter indicated these neighbors "really put in my brothers a sense of working," so that "they didn't hang out on the streets." The neighborhood impressed her as peaceful and pleasant. "No shootings," she recalled. "No loud music. It was just nice." After recounting her upbringing and schooling in positive terms, Mrs. Carter added, with a tone of finality, "I don't have any horror stories." The surrounding neighborhood, she recalled, was "gorgeous," leafy and well maintained. "I mean it was just beautiful to walk up the street and see all the beautiful grass and the trees and the flowers," she said. "And I know during the Sixties, there was a lot of trouble. But we didn't see it as kids."[137]

Without exception, Mrs. Carter compared the south side's past favorably to its almost unrelievedly bleak present. She described the current condition of her childhood neighborhood in the following terms: "The houses are torn down. . . . [I]t is like a completely different place. It feels like I'm out of town, because this is *not* the neighborhood we grew up in." While she now lives in a south-side residential district that borders the affluent suburb of Boardman Township, Mrs. Carter admitted that she no longer benefits from the feelings of safety and security that she took for granted while growing up. She wistfully recalled sleeping on the front porch of her parents' home "because we didn't have air conditioning." Then, in the same breath, she described the radically altered atmosphere of today's south side. "We could sleep out on the porch all night long—I mean on Glenwood Avenue," she said. "Windows open all night. You wouldn't dare do that now." Mrs. Carter revealed that, in her current neighborhood, she often fears for her safety. "[W]hen we bought our house up there, it was in the wintertime," she recalled. "So, it was quiet. And we thought, 'Oh, boy, this is really nice.' But that spring, all these . . . little boys [were] driving up the street, playing loud music." Today, she hears "shootings every night," and her grandchildren often "have to hit the floor" during the evening. "And we live in a decent neighborhood, we thought," she added. "So, yes, it's changed."[138]

In the grim aftermath of the 1960s, it has become easier for older black urban dwellers to downplay memories of discriminatory practices that were once ubiquitous. The past may have held its trials, but for many, these have been eclipsed by the poverty and senseless violence that plague today's center city. In the late 1970s, a *Vindicator* article on the "Monkey's Nest," a multiracial neighborhood destroyed as a consequence of local highway construction, featured comments by African Americans who described high levels of interracial cooperation. "Everybody, black and white, got along real well and we felt like we were taking care of our own little kingdom," said Deborah Williams, a former resident of the district.[139] There is no reason to doubt the sincerity of such observations, but they often fail to take into account the manner in which institutional discrimination shaped and delimited interracial relations. Significantly, a fair number of African Americans seemed unfazed by the racist conventions of the postwar era even as they experienced them. In his memoir, Watkins recalled that as a preteen, he was largely oblivious to the many instances of segregation he encountered on a daily basis. "I, for one, had no idea that in the South and, presumably, among many Youngstowners, the balcony [in movie theaters] was known as the 'buzzard's nest' or 'nigger heaven,'" he wrote. "At the same time, it didn't matter." Watkins revealed that, as a youngster, he was unconcerned that "most downtown restaurants did not serve Negroes or that blacks were not welcome at the city's hotels." He recalled that Youngstown's Idora Park Ballroom was "roped off into two sections" so that "no blacks wandered into the white section near the bandstand." He added that white patrons "regularly strayed into or hovered near the fringes of the black section to watch, loosen up, and learn how to shake their booties."[140]

Then, in the 1950s, when Watkins was in his early teens, the humiliation of a close friend forced him to acknowledge the dehumanizing effects of racial discrimination. One summer afternoon, classmate Al Bright was invited to a Little League picnic held at a municipal park, and lifeguards prevented him from entering the swimming pool area because of his race. In response to the complaints and objections of Bright's coach and teammates, the park superintendent reluctantly permitted the teenager to enter the pool, although under carefully outlined conditions. Watkins described what happened next: "When the [pool] area was cleared, Al was led to the pool and placed in a small rubber raft. One lifeguard waded in and, swimming along side the raft, took Al for one turn around the pool. 'Just don't touch the water,' he warned. 'Whatever you do, don't touch the water.'"[141] While many African Americans probably took steps to avoid situations that called attention to their subordinate status in a white-dominated society, Bright's experience suggests this was a challenging task. In a community where racism was endemic, it was difficult—if not impossible—to remain insulated from policies and practices that were destined to leave behind emotional scars.

THE "WHITENING" OF YOUNGSTOWN'S ETHNIC EUROPEANS

The unequal social arrangements that Watkins described were reinforced in the community's industrial workplaces, particularly in its steel-manufacturing plants. There, the appearance of interracial cooperation camouflaged the presence of a well-articulated racial hierarchy. As sociologist Robert Bruno noted, steelworkers of the same racial or ethnic background invariably held positions of similar status, and African American and Latino workers "were concentrated in the coke works, cinder plant, and blast furnace," those "parts of the mill [that] were traditionally thought of as outposts for unwanted jobs." Prior to the 1960s, whites were also segregated according to ethnicity, given that "work assignments tended to tribalize the working class in different departments." Bruno explained that, in the industrial workplace, "Italians were masons, Irishmen tended to be railroaders, Hungarians and Slovakians congregated around the open hearth, and foremen were usually 'Johnny Bull' English." The realities of industrial production, however, made a thoroughly segregated work force impractical. While job occupancy continued to be "associated with ethnicity," the work environment was gradually restructured in ways that tended to facilitate greater integration among various groups. "Most craft workers were not restricted to one part of the plant," Bruno wrote. "White masons, millwrights, and electricians would go anywhere a breakdown was reported." Hence, the "plant was opened up because of the need for skilled workers to work everywhere and the need for laborers to always be on site." Bruno argued that a subsequent softening of traditional boundaries contributed to "class solidarity" among steelworkers, who were more apt to collectively challenge their employers' abusive policies.[142] Linkon and Russo, however, noted that racial divisions continued to be "enforced by labor and company officials."[143]

Meanwhile, in the community at large, the gradual breakdown of traditional ethnic identities often accompanied a greater emphasis on racial differences. In a process that began with the tightening of immigration quotas in the 1920s, the United States was reconceptualized as a nation of "blacks" and "whites." Decades earlier, America had been viewed as a land of multiple races, some of whom were granted "whiteness," even as they were carefully differentiated from the dominant "Anglo-Saxon" population. "As the 'Negro Question' steadily eclipsed every other race question on the national agenda between the 1930s and the 1950s," Matthew Frye Jacobsen noted, "the interracial coalitions that formed—on the left and in labor unions, within churches, and within the Democratic Party—increasingly assumed a racially unvariegated group of whites to be precisely such a pre-existing, static, and self-evident entity."[144] Significantly, the "whitening" of ethnic European Americans often occurred in the context of struggles with African Americans. Stefano Luconi, in his descriptive analysis of growing solidarity among once hostile ethnic groups in Philadelphia, argued that the city's "Italian Americans and Irish Americans developed a common identity out of their tendency to hold African Americans responsible for the deterioration of their own standards of living." Speaking in more general terms, he pointed out that "the consolidation around whiteness among European Americans resulted primarily from their demonization of blacks for most social and economic problems of postwar United States."[145]

In the white imagination, the myriad trends that had helped to undermine cities like Youngstown were ignored in favor of a single perceived causal factor: demographic change. The influx of blacks into urban working-class neighborhoods left many whites frustrated and angry, and few were prepared to objectively examine the range of developments that had transformed the city. Such trends included the relocation of industry and retail businesses to expanding suburbs, which left urban areas with shrinking tax bases and fewer jobs, and the implementation of urban renewal and highway construction projects, which destroyed once vibrant residential and commercial districts.

Many whites who saw cherished neighborhoods fall into disrepair blamed this outcome on the perceived values of African American newcomers, who, in their view, showed no desire to improve their situation. One former south side resident described his feelings of dismay as he watched his old neighborhood decline in the late 1960s. "I almost had a feeling of abandonment, that we had abandoned it, not the people that came in," he recalled. "I still drive down Myrtle Avenue . . . just to look at . . . my [former] house," he added. "And I want so badly to go to the house where I was born and ask the people if I could come in. And I'm a little afraid to. It's a badass neighborhood. But I did sense that we left . . . you know. And then, my mother said to me . . . she said, 'Yes, sonny, but why can't they pick up the milk cartons?'"[146]

Attitudes of resentment toward blacks were particularly strong among whites of recent immigrant background, who were disproportionately affected by urban demographic change. As Sister Margaret Ellen Traxler observed, in a 1969 article, most of the four million southern blacks who migrated to northern cities between 1930 and 1968 "settled close to industrial areas where jobs and housing were available." She added: "This is where nationality groups also were located, with the subsequent 'threat' to white property owners. Social patterns of neighborhoods and parish 'life styles' changed as Negroes moved in." In the wake of demographic change, "the great migration of Catholics to suburbia left behind emptying schools and churches."[147] The perception among many whites that black migration threatened the cities deepened as urban neighborhoods became more impoverished, more dangerous, and less populated. In "Rust Belt" communities like Youngstown, these urban trends were compounded by the collapse of staple industries, which further destabilized working-class neighborhoods that had survived into the late 1970s.

DEMOGRAPHIC CHANGE DOVETAILS WITH URBAN DECLINE

Racial tension, if somewhat understated during the 1950s, was forced to the surface by the trends of the following decade. The fragile (and deceptive) stability of the immediate postwar era eroded as time moved on, and by the early 1960s, most urban dwellers were aware of unsettling developments. That said, more subtle indicators of urban change were evident to close observers by the late 1940s. As Sugrue noted in his study of Detroit, the decline of cities in the country's manufacturing belt began in the post–World War II era. Across the nation's traditional industrial belt, "major companies reduced work forces, speeded up production, and required more overtime work." Sugrue observed that the heavy industries "that formed the bedrock of the American economy, including textiles, electrical appliances, motor vehicles, and military hardware, automated production and relocated plants in suburban and rural areas, and increasingly in the low-wage labor markets of underdeveloped regions like the American South and the Caribbean." Significantly, sweeping structural changes in the economy "proceeded with the full support and encouragement of the American government."[148] In Youngstown, these larger economic trends coincided with the disappearance of the old industrial aristocracy. As Fuechtmann noted, postwar-era Youngstown "saw virtually a total exodus of the old iron and steel elite from the city."[149] The departure of the city's latter-day patricians signaled the beginning of a trend in which "Youngstown's major industries increasingly came to be controlled by out-of-town corporations."[150]

Crucially, these trends dovetailed with a significant shift of population from the city to the expanding suburbs. In 1954, the local media reported that the adjacent suburban community of Boardman Township had nearly doubled in population, jumping from 7,881 in 1940, to an estimated 18,000 14 years later. Youngstown, on the other hand, experienced negligible growth. A newspaper article reported that the county's population went from 240,251 in 1940 to 257,629 in 1950—an increase of 17,378." The article added, however, that the increase "was almost wholly in unincorporated areas, where about 17,000 people took up residence." Youngstown proper had gained only 610 people, while nearby Campbell (formerly East Youngstown) lost 921.[151] Less than a year later, Clyde E. McGranahan, executive secretary of the Home Builders Association of the Mahoning Valley, predicted that Greater Youngstown would "continue to grow as a 'horizontal' city, spilling further into the suburbs instead of growing up 'vertically' like New York and some other major cities."[152] The media attributed this population shift to the obvious advantages of suburban living. "In the past people either lived in cities or out in the country," one newspaper article stated. "Now they live their country life with all—or nearly all—the comforts and conveniences of the city." Close proximity to the cities ensured that suburban dwellers could "get the sewage and other benefits of city life plus some room to move around in."[153]

The apparent advantages of suburban living, however, were not the only draw for the tens of thousands of whites who retreated from the cities. As Linkon and Russo pointed out, "suburbanization was fueled in part by racism, which had long been reinforced by hiring practices in the mills that separated workers according to both race and ethnicity." As more Catholics fled the city for the suburbs, old ethnic enclaves such as those in Brier Hill, Smoky Hollow, and portions of the east side began to deteriorate. Linkon and Russo went on to describe the scenario that unfolded in Youngstown's increasingly beleaguered center city. "While ethnic working-class enclaves broke down, once racially integrated neighborhoods became more segregated," they wrote. "The process was supported by lending and real-estate practices, which kept black home buyers from even looking at homes in the new suburbs, much less being approved for home loans." At the same time, deepening economic disparity between black and white workers inhibited the mobility of Youngstown's African American residents. Not only were blacks traditionally relegated to the lowest-paying jobs in steel mills; they also failed to benefit proportionately from postwar-era practices such as collective bargaining, which included seniority provisions that tended to favor white workers.[154] All of these factors restricted the residential options of blacks and contributed to the transformation of traditional ethnic neighborhoods, whose churches and parish schools remained in place even as their patrons moved elsewhere.

Meanwhile, tensions that were suppressed in earlier decades became shockingly apparent in the 1960s. Physical confrontations between blacks and whites became more common, and local African American leaders were increasingly assertive in their criticism of racist policies and practices. Although Youngstown was spared the devastating violence witnessed in many other cities following the assassination of Dr. Martin Luther King, Jr., some rioting occurred in pockets of the south side. A confrontation between mostly white police officers and black youths erupted on the afternoon of April 8, 1968, just four days after Dr. King's murder. The incident served as the jarring conclusion of a day that had opened with an act of hopeful idealism. A few hours earlier, 200 black youths had participated in a peaceful march from a south side playground to the Mahoning County Courthouse, in the city's downtown. The group, under police escort, crossed over Market Street to the downtown area, where they listened to a series of speeches by local black leaders who spoke on the theme of black unity. When the event ended at 12:15 p.m., the youths, most of whom were members of a local Baptist congregation, returned to the south side.[155] Within hours of the march, police took steps to break up a larger crowd of black youths gathered at a south side intersection. According to witnesses on the scene, the police used greater force than required to disperse the crowd, and a riot ensued. The municipal government promptly requested the assistance of the National Guard, which set up headquarters at the Christy Armory, located just north of Youngstown's downtown area. Over the next few days, dozens of local businesses were looted, scores of schools and homes were vandalized, and three men were seriously injured, including two white police officers and a young black man who had been accused of firing on police.[156] Images of armed troops and a military tank moving through the streets of the south side did little to improve the area's image and may even have accelerated preexisting patterns of "white flight."

REACHING ACROSS THE RACIAL DIVIDE

Given the widespread violence of the 1960s, it is sometimes easy to forget that the era also witnessed courageous efforts to reconcile divided black and white communities. On April 7, 1968, one day before rioting broke out on the city's south side, local residents came together to mourn Dr. King's assassination. More than 3,000 people of various backgrounds gathered for an interfaith religious service at Stambaugh Auditorium, an imposing neoclassical building on Youngstown's north side, where they paid tribute to the fallen civil rights leader's life and work. The service, while led by the Reverend Lonnie Simon, the black pastor of New Bethel Baptist Church, featured the participation of a half-dozen area religious leaders.[157] These leaders included Monsignor Breen P. Malone, the white pastor of St. Patrick's Church, a parish situated in the heart of the city's racially divided south side.[158] Monsignor Malone—a tall, balding man who closely resembled the Catholic mystic Thomas Merton—was no stranger to the cause of civil rights. The priest was one of hundreds of white clergy and religious who had marched with Dr. King in Selma, Alabama, in 1965. As a pastor whose commitment to social justice went beyond sermonizing, Monsignor Malone had won a great deal of respect within Youngstown's black community.

At the same time, the pastor's participation in an interfaith ceremony to honor the late Dr. King bore witness to a dramatic sea change that had taken place within the U.S. Catholic Church since the 1950s. This change was especially evident at the leadership level, where the "neutrality" of the past was giving way to strong official support for racial equality. In 1958, American bishops issued a statement condemning racial discrimination, and in the altered climate that ensued, several Louisiana-based segregationists were excommunicated.[159] Then, in 1964, Pope Paul VI, in a departure from his often cautious approach to polarizing issues, took a symbolic stand in favor of the U.S. civil rights movement by agreeing to hold an audience with Dr. King. Soon afterwards, signs appeared that the U.S. Catholic hierarchy's long history of tolerating "local traditions" was coming to an end. In March 1965, as hundreds of white Catholics flooded into Selma to answer Dr. King's call for support, Bishop Thomas Toolen of the Mobile-Birmingham area publicly criticized what he described as "outside agitators." The bishop's pronouncement rang hollow, however, given that the most visible white leader in the local civil rights movement was Father Maurice Ouellet, the pastor of a church based in Toolen's own diocese. Within days, Bishop Toolen faced a more damaging challenge to his leadership. Shortly before Dr. King's march on Selma, Joseph Cardinal Ritter offered his blessing to scores of St. Louis clergy and religious who had "chartered two planes directly to Selma." As

McGreevy wrote, "priests from fifty different dioceses, lay people, and nuns flocked to Alabama to join the marches."[160] This event stunned many Catholics, who were accustomed to clergy and religious who carefully avoided taking stands on potentially divisive political issues. "Issues of social justice took center stage in the 1960s as crusades on behalf of civil rights, women's rights, and peace swept across the landscape," Dolan observed. "These social movements for reform attracted many Catholics, and before long the Catholic religious community became a major player in the reform movements of the 1960s."[161]

Ironically, as U.S. Catholic leaders began to speak out more forcefully against institutional racism, many of them faced challenges that were directly related to urban demographic change. As black non-Catholics replaced white Catholics in center-city neighborhoods, urban parishes and parochial schools lost their most reliable patrons. During this period, the media referred with greater frequency to a Catholic school "bind," which was eventually promoted to a "crisis." Newspaper reports on the plight of urban parochial schools generally focused on factors such as rising per-pupil costs and declining birth rates. By the early 1970s, news reports also cited the effects of falling enrollment, which they attributed to the recent introduction of tuition.[162] The 1971 closure and sale of St. Patrick School's 17-year-old annex on the south side of Youngstown became a stark symbol of the "boom-to-bust" scenario that was unfolding in many urban parish school districts.[163] While all of the trends highlighted in the media contributed in some way to the decline of urban parochial schools, newspaper reports often failed to mention another factor: the demographic shift taking place in neighborhoods where a number of these parish schools operated.

A clear indication of growing diversity within the classrooms of local Catholic schools came in 1973, when the Youngstown Diocesan Board of Education announced its adoption of a resolution to forbid discrimination in diocesan high schools. The board also announced plans to develop a more inclusive secondary school curriculum.[164] As the article pointed out, diocesan Catholic schools—both elementary and secondary—had signed annual compliance forms on nondiscrimination since the Civil Rights Act of 1964, and such compliance was a precondition to receive funding for federal programs. Nevertheless, the board's decision to adopt the resolution to ban discriminatory policies in Catholic high schools, along with steps to redefine the philosophy and objectives of secondary education, signaled a heightened awareness of civil rights issues among local Catholic leaders.

During the early 1970s, a number of financially struggling urban parish schools also benefited from the public and private support of Bishop James Malone, who encouraged wealthy Catholic patrons to fund center-city institutions like Immaculate Conception and St. Patrick's elementary schools. Indeed, Bishop Malone's commitment to urban parish schools was evident from the outset of his tenure as leader of the Diocese of Youngstown. In 1973, the bishop emphasized that the diocese had a moral responsibility to maintain parish schools operating in "poverty areas," and he specifically mentioned St. Patrick's Elementary School, which served a large percentage of nonwhite students. On the bishop's recommendation, the diocesan school board unanimously approved a resolution that St. Patrick's School should remain open for at least three more years, "subject to an annual review of its financial situation and enrollment." The board also passed a resolution that the diocese had "a commitment to provide Catholic education in those schools of the diocese that serve poverty areas and promote this education as a missionary service of the church." Another resolution established a 15-member committee "to determine which schools are in poverty areas, what type of aide might be given and what students are to be served." This committee was charged with recommending policy decisions "regarding schools with increasing proportions of non-Catholics; regarding schools in parishes no longer able to meet all of their financial obligations, and schools serving the poor in increasing numbers."[165]

As the passage of these resolutions suggests, the rising number of non-Catholic, nonwhite students in some urban parish schools presented diocesan administrators with an unprecedented set of financial challenges. The demographic shift that had occurred within the once heavily white, Catholic neighborhoods of the south and east sides ensured that urban parishes would lose members and, by extension, donation dollars. By the late 1970s, this trend was reflected in the growing insolvency of Immaculate Conception Elementary School, located on the city's racially diverse east side. The school, based in a neighborhood once populated by Irish American and Italian American Catholics, now served a substantial percentage of students who did not belong to the parish. Records show that by 1976, 144 of the parish school's 327 students were non-Catholic, and many of them belonged to minority groups.[166] In an effort to offset the school's deepening financial problems, supporters of Immaculate Conception proposed the implementation of a diocesan-wide tax to benefit struggling center-city parish schools. As it turned out, the proposal tested the limits of the diocese's support for such schools and stirred an emotional debate among members of the diocesan school board, who were struggling with the dual challenges of rising expenses and declining enrollment.

In fall 1976, during a meeting held at Immaculate Conception School, the board voted six-to-five against the proposal. Opponents of the proposed tax included Raymond Pelanda, chair of the diocesan finance committee, who argued that the diocese's overwhelming economic difficulties ruled out the possibility of supplemental aid to beleaguered center-city parishes. Pelanda's view triumphed despite the opposition of then Auxiliary Bishop William Hughes, who favored the tax. (This would be neither the first nor the last time that the clergy and laity disagreed on the amount of financial support the diocese should devote to urban parish schools.) Bishop Hughes, a former superintendent of the diocesan school board, framed assistance to struggling urban parish schools as a social "obligation" to the community's underprivileged. Pelanda, however, was unconvinced by this argument and responded that the "poor and minorities can get an education in the public schools."[167] The finance chair (and his supporters) evidently feared that the diocese was ill-equipped to support the growing number of urban parish schools that served nontraditional student populations. In Youngstown alone, two schools served large numbers of non-Catholics. Less than one year later, in April 1977, the *Vindicator* reported that 52 percent of the students at St. Patrick's School were non-Catholic, while almost 60 percent were African American. At Immaculate Conception School, more than 43 percent of the students were reported to be non-Catholic, and almost 38 percent were black.[168] Ultimately, it was only the last-minute intervention of local clerical leaders that prevented the closure of Immaculate Conception Elementary School.[169]

The debate over supplemental aid to urban parish schools was one of many controversial issues the diocese was forced to address in the 1970s. Even as demographic change undermined the viability of certain urban parochial schools, the desegregation of Youngstown's public schools prompted some civic leaders to question whether white-dominated Catholic schools would function as "havens" for European American students seeking to avoid integrated classrooms. In spring 1974, not long after the local NAACP called for the desegregation of Youngstown's public schools, John Augenstein, the diocesan superintendent of schools, issued a public statement. "Some people wanting to avoid desegregation will want to enroll their children in our schools," Augenstein stated. "This we must avoid. We should not become havens for them." At the same time, Monsignor William Hughes, a strong supporter of urban parish schools, spoke on the need to develop registration and enrollment guidelines that would discourage whites from using Catholic schools as a means to avoid desegregation.[170] Several weeks later, the diocese announced the adoption of application guidelines regulating "new and transfer students to Catholic schools."[171] These guidelines required meetings between parents of any student to be transferred and the principal of the parochial school in question. In addition, parish school administrators were expected to contact the principal of the public school from which the student planned to transfer, in an effort to determine possible reasons for the proposed transfer. Amid dwindling enrollment, however, it is questionable whether urban parish schools were in a position to reject applicants their administrators suspected of seeking to avoid integrated public classrooms. Meanwhile, the guidelines may have angered some Catholic parents, who resented having to "prove" that they were not racists.

PARISH SCHOOLS AS A "FOREIGN PRESENCE" IN BLACK NEIGHBORHOODS

Controversies that hinged upon the subject of race multiplied as the decade progressed. Given that urban parish schools played a larger role in the lives of urban black families, some local observers began to raise questions about the dearth of African American leaders in the U.S. Catholic Church, while others pointed to a sharp decline in the percentage of nonwhites among Catholic parishioners. In 1975, critics noted that less than one million black parishioners were reported nationwide.[172] Although this figure represents a modest improvement upon the situation in the early twentieth century (when only 2 percent of African Americans described themselves as Catholics),[173] many black clerical leaders expressed concern by the late 1960s that the Catholic Church was "rapidly dying in the black community."[174] Surprisingly, this perceived downward trend coincided with a sharp rise in the number of black students attending urban parish schools. These apparently divergent developments prompted some observers to question whether the Catholic Church was doing everything in its power to appeal to members of the black community, and a few went so far as to suggest that evangelizing blacks was a low priority among Catholic religious leaders. This view was widely disseminated in the Youngstown area during the mid-1970s. In a series of feature articles published in the *Vindicator* in late summer 1975, Leon Stennis, the newspaper's religion editor, posed a number of searching questions to local Catholic leaders, some of whom were connected to urban parish schools.

Stennis, an African American, often reported on relations between local white Catholic leaders and the black community—a natural inclination, given the area's large white Catholic population and expanding black Protestant population. Following a series of interviews with five local Catholic leaders, the journalist concluded that only two of the interviewees had expressed a strong interest in converting blacks to the Catholic faith. These leaders included Monsignor Breen Malone, whose parish, St. Patrick's Church, recorded the largest percentage of black parishioners in Youngstown—an unprecedented 10 percent. In the course of an interview with Stennis, Monsignor Malone called upon the diocese to "develop a policy that would ensure the future presence of many black people in its membership," adding that "the very presence of blacks and whites, and all colors of men, in the Catholic Church is its best claim to being Catholic or universal." Monsignor Malone's position was evidently shared by Sister Charlotte Italiano, OSU, principal of St. Patrick's Elementary School, who stated that the church was not doing everything in its power to reach out to minority groups. "I . . . just don't feel we can be content when we are in places where what we do and what we believe can be questioned," Sister Charlotte said. "If the church would go outside of its structure we would expose more people to what we are all about and what the Kingdom of God is all about."[175]

Stennis proved more critical of the other three Catholic leaders who participated in interviews, taking them to task for what he described as their "indifference" to the possibility of converting blacks through ministries that included urban parish schools. Two of these Catholic leaders were connected to a parish school that served large numbers of black students. In one article, the journalist suggested that Father John R. Summers, pastor of Immaculate Conception Church, and Sister Teresa Winsen, OSU, principal of Immaculate Conception School, were satisfied with the church's existing level of outreach to blacks. In reaching this conclusion, Stennis referred to their own comments, which appeared to suggest that the church "should not make a special appeal to any specific group."[176] This criticism of local religious leaders probably irritated some area Catholics, along with those black urban dwellers who benefited from the activities of Immaculate Conception Church. The pastor and principal, after all, had earned reputations as advocates of the poor, mostly black families that lived on Youngstown's near east side. Father Summers was a visible proponent of increased diocesan support for center-city parish schools, while Sister Teresa had made headlines five years earlier when she addressed city council members about the need to extend sewage and water lines to some of the poverty-stricken neighborhoods surrounding Immaculate Conception Parish.[177] Stennis's article not only failed to highlight their contributions to the black community; it went on to suggest that Father Summers and Sister Teresa treated African Americans as clients of—rather than as potential leaders within—the local Catholic community.[178]

Father Nathan Willis, a black priest active in the Youngstown area, shared many of Stennis's concerns about the church's relationship with the African American community. The priest suggested the institution's failure to attract blacks was rooted in the fact that it remained "entirely foreign, a closed society enclosed in a black environment." Father Willis also contended that few white pastors working in urban areas had taken steps to modify the liturgy in ways that would appeal to black parishioners. "The blacks have an identity, a culture, and heritage which we value very highly," he said. "And we wish for the day that the church would address itself to these as she has for the literature and history of the European culture."[179] Overall, the series of articles suggested that insensitivity to African American culture was a problem even among those Catholic leaders who provided exceptional service to the black community. "The diocese is not at this time concerned enough with the 'foreign' image of the church in the community in which it serves," Stennis contended. He went on to question the diocese's long-term commitment "to maintaining its two inner-city schools that have large black enrollments"—an apparent reference to Immaculate Conception and St. Patrick's elementary schools.[180]

Leon Stennis's criticism of the Diocese of Youngstown for its failure to turn urban parochial schools into instruments of religious conversion might strike modern-day readers as ironic, given that urban parochial schools, in subsequent decades, earned the praise of secular educators for their understated approach to proselytizing, their high academic standards, and their apparent commitment to broader civic goals. The journalist's complaints, however, paralleled the concerns expressed by black Catholic leaders of the period, even though Stennis himself was not a Catholic. In a curious twist, the church's efforts in the realm of evangelization began to falter at a time when white Catholic leaders were becoming more vocal in their support of racial equality. Prior to the upheavals of the 1960s, the U.S. Catholic Church—despite its failure to seriously address the issue of racial discrimination—took a more activist approach to evangelization within the black community. As McGreevy noted, "One of the most remarkable achievements of the pre-conciliar era had been the development of an African American Catholic community." Given that Catholic parishes were traditionally defined in geographical terms, "parish structures remained even as the original parishioners fled particular areas."[181] McGreevy stressed that, in an era marked by active evangelization, it was hardly inevitable that these urban facilities would sit idle, and indeed, a surprising number of them were transformed into vibrant black parishes. By the late 1950s, McGreevy wrote, "researchers counted 600,000 African-American Catholics, over 3 percent of the African-American population and double the total of 1928."[182] Although he acknowledged that many black Catholics of the early 1960s were "cradle" Catholics (hailing mainly from Louisiana or the West Indies), McGreevy emphasized that "an equal number were converts." He added, "In the first year of that decade, about half of the nation's 700,000 African American Catholics lived in the northern cities, but almost 12,000 converts a year were being added to the rolls." By the close of the 1960s, however, "the mass baptisms of the past slowed to a trickle."[183]

Predictably, many preconciliar black parishes were strictly "Romanist" in their approach to liturgy and made no effort to incorporate elements of African

American spirituality into services and sacraments.[184] Any resentment northern blacks might have felt over the church's cultural insensitivity, however, was mitigated (at least to some extent) by their awareness of the institution's interest in attracting black converts. McGreevy quoted an urban pastor, who described African American neighbors' positive response to the parish's door-to-door outreach efforts: "The reaction to that was wonderful . . . by God, they'd say, you Catholics are really going after us."[185] By the late 1960s, however, it seemed as though many of those white clergy and religious who were most inspired by the civil rights movement showed virtually no interest in building up black membership in urban parishes. "In contrast to their older mentors, and with some opposition from more conservative parishioners," McGreevy wrote, "a corps of young white priests and nuns rejected the 'triumphalist' ethos of African American Catholic parishes." In other words, they were more inclined "to give witness to the Christian faith" than they were to convert blacks to a specific (Catholic) vision of Christianity. For many activist clergy, "the definition of a successful parish became its ability to address social justice issues."[186]

Before long, the declining number of African American Catholics in the postconciliar era drew the worried attention of prominent black Catholics. African American clerical leaders formally expressed their concerns about the decline of the center-city church at a meeting held in Detroit in 1968, just two weeks after the assassination of Dr. King. Shortly before a national conference of clerical leaders on the "interracial apostolate," a black priest invited the nation's 170 African American priests and single black bishop to a "special caucus" to be held during the conference.[187] Consequently, more than 60 black clerical leaders "were meeting as a group for the first time in American history."[188] McGreevy noted that, following "a full day of wrenching debate, and four votes, the priests passed a resolution terming the church 'primarily a white racist institution' and demanding African-American control of inner-city programs." Black religious leaders at the caucus went on to describe their frustration over the steep decline in the number of African American Catholics and complained that they were unable to "provide a ministry for black people in the Church." Finally, in a move that paralleled trends within the larger African American community, black clerical leaders expressed concern that interracial efforts to develop an "overarching religious identity" within the U.S. Catholic community would create an environment in which the church "would become wholly irrelevant to African-American concerns."[189] In the end, these leaders' insistence upon equality in the context of the church did not overshadow their commitment to the maintenance of a distinct identity for black Catholics. Seventeen years later, in 1985, black clerical concerns about flagging evangelical efforts in urban neighborhoods were reiterated once again, in the pastoral letter, "What We Have Seen and

Heard." Significantly, the letter emphasized the role of urban parish schools in proselytizing among African Americans. "The Catholic school has been and remains one of the chief vehicles of evangelization within the Black community," the letter stated. "We even dare to suggest that the efforts made to support them and to insure their continuation are a touchstone of the local Church's sincerity in the evangelization of the Black community."[190]

By the 1970s, younger African Americans' alienation from the U.S. Catholic Church was fueled by many white Catholics' hostile responses to court-ordered school desegregation efforts. Angry reactions to school desegregation were especially evident in heavily Catholic northern cities like Boston, where racial violence stirred up memories of the enmity that had traditionally existed between blacks and white Catholics. Escalating tension between these groups was no doubt compounded by mutual suspicions that had festered beneath the surface for decades. Not only were African Americans embittered over the prejudice they often experienced at the hands of (mostly Catholic) ethnic whites; they were also conditioned by many of their own religious leaders to regard the Catholic Church with an attitude of deep distrust. Anti-Catholic sentiment in the United States, after all, was nowhere more resilient than in the staunchly Protestant South—the ancestral home of many northern blacks. "Membership in the Catholic Church ensured pointed questions, if not open hostility, from African-American Protestants distrustful of Rome, or disillusioned by contact with racist Catholics," McGreevy observed.[191] In Chicago, during the early 1940s, some black ministers, in response to a wave of conversions, organized meetings to "discuss ways and means of saving Protestant youth from the Catholics."[192] Commenting on the rather awkward position of African American Catholics like herself, Beverly Blackshear noted that "a lot of Black people . . . don't appreciate you being Catholic." She added, "They have the Southern Baptist churches . . . and they don't understand what [Catholicism] is all about."[193]

Hence, a potent combination of racially and religiously motivated distrust permeated the atmosphere of many parochial schools that operated in racially diverse neighborhoods. In communities like Youngstown, urban parochial school administrators were often called upon to diffuse misunderstandings that arose between staff members and students and parents. Sister Charlotte Italiano, OSU, recalled that some of her most daunting challenges as an administrator came during her tenure as principal of St. Patrick's Elementary School, which was "turning from an all-White school to a mixed racial environment." By the mid-1970s, she noted, the neighborhoods surrounding the parish school hosted growing numbers of black residents, "who were disenfranchised, and who thought they weren't getting a fair shake . . . and who became very defensive." As a result, teaching black students often involved taking steps to address attitudes of suspicion that "had been passed on from the parents." She noted that, while the school's staff members "did really . . . try to get around that," communication with parents was often limited by the fact that many were unable to attend parent-teacher conferences. "Don't forget, parents also had to work," Sister Charlotte explained. "So, you had the working poor. And then, you had families where the male was not present for whatever reason. So, the mothers were not only working but [also] trying to keep their kids educated and pay for that education, even though they didn't have the real finances to do it."[194]

In this sometimes contentious educational environment, pastoral leadership played an important role in bridge-building efforts. Sister Charlotte noted that St. Patrick's School often benefited from the respect that Monsignor Breen Malone enjoyed within the local black community. "When I worked with people who were very supportive of the changes of the times, I found it very affirming," she recalled. This was the case with Monsignor Malone, who, in Sister Charlotte's words, was "very much at the forefront of this 'let's get along' society." Under his leadership, the parish experienced an emotional turning point in its relationship with the African American residents of the neighborhood. This came in the mid-1970s, when a black student at the school disappeared, only to be found dead in a trash receptacle several months later. "[Monsignor Malone] invited me—and the family invited me—to be part of that funeral service," Sister Charlotte recalled. "It was the very first time I was ever asked to be part of [something like] that." Although apprehensive at first, she found that members of the local black community "were so welcoming, and so happy that a Black pastor and a White pastor and a White principal were taking care of a little eight-year-old child."[195]

REMAINING VIABLE IN A CHANGING CITY

Leaders such as Monsignor Malone, who worked tirelessly to earn the trust of local African Americans, also tried to persuade skeptical whites to provide financial support for struggling urban parish schools. Sister Charlotte recalled that Monsignor Malone constantly sought out patrons "to keep the school going, to keep us running, to support the Black people who were there who wanted to come to school, who were not Catholic."[196] While the diocese tended to rely on the support of wealthy white Catholic philanthropists, it was no less important for pastors and educators to issue broad appeals to the Catholic community. In the course of these fund-raising campaigns, advocates of urban parish schools routinely challenged white, middle-class Catholics to look beyond traditional conceptions of parochial education; and these direct appeals often proved effective. In 1978, for instance, a fund-raising campaign held to benefit Immaculate Conception Elementary School exceeded its $40,000 goal by more than $10,000, ultimately raising $52,000.[197]

The response of mainly Catholic donors remained constant throughout the 1980s, despite the steep economic decline brought on by the collapse of the community's industrial sector. The success of fund-raising efforts during this period was no small achievement. The decade, after all, was characterized by a sharp acceleration of urban depopulation, which contributed to a growing percentage of minority groups in urban neighborhoods. In the wake of serial steel-plant closures, Youngstown's population—recorded at 140,880 in 1970—fell to 115,427 in 1980. Then, between 1986 and 1990, the city's population contracted further, slipping from 104,689 to 95,732.[198] While the number of blacks and whites living in the city noticeably declined, the white population fell even more dramatically. In 1980, Youngstown's black population of 38,473 comprised about 33 percent of the total population. A decade later, however, the black population, which stood at 36,482, constituted about 38 percent of the city's population. In the same decade, Youngstown's white population fell by almost 18,000, slipping from 74,269 to 56,760.[199] A percentage of these former residents probably retreated to neighboring suburbs, while others left the metropolitan area altogether.

Significantly, efforts by pastors, principals, and diocesan administrators to secure funding for urban parish schools that served mainly nonwhite and non-Catholic students occurred against a backdrop of rising tension between urban blacks and whites. This tension was partly a result of the city's growing racial (and economic) diversity, which some white urban dwellers perceived as a threat to their safety and economic well-being. Many urban whites were especially concerned about the expansion of low-income housing projects into neighborhoods that had thus far remained white enclaves. By the late 1970s, such housing developments were a visible presence in every part of the city, with the clear exception of the west side, which retained a large white population. To the surprise of few, the municipal government's 1978 announcement that it planned to build low-income housing on the west side inspired a storm of protests from white residents of the district, highlighting the extent to which the city remained divided along racial lines. In October 1978, during a public hearing on the proposed development, supporters of the Schenley Homes project "felt the brunt of neighboring property owners' criticism." One concerned resident, Mrs. Frances Vernini, predicted that the project would bring about the "destruction" of the district's "stability." She went on to refer to the proposed duplexes as "barracks-type structures." Another west side resident, Eleanor Donatiello, questioned the viability of the project's location, noting that it bordered an expressway. "We don't think the developer has much concern for the people who will live in the area," she said.[200]

The municipal government responded to the project's well-organized opposition by announcing its abandonment. This decision, however, placed the mayor in direct conflict with the U.S. Department of Housing and Urban Development (HUD).[201] HUD promptly informed the city that, in order to remain eligible for funding, it must either allow for the construction of the proposed project on its current site or find another suitable location. By this time, an organization known as the West Side Concerned Citizens Committee was actively distributing a petition to place a referendum on the ballot to halt the project.[202] Meanwhile, the city's efforts to relocate the project to the already racially diverse east side met the opposition of the local NAACP and Urban League.[203] Over the next two years, the municipal government wrangled with HUD, threatening to file a lawsuit against the government agency for "usurping the city's authority to plan the location of housing projects." Nevertheless, in spring 1981, groundbreaking began for the housing development (which was renamed Westview Housing), and opponents of the project were forced to concede defeat.[204] Although the issue of race was never explicitly raised in public debates on the proposed development, references to the project's potentially "destabilizing" effects was probably intended to inspire images of a white exodus from the city's remaining European American enclave. In any event, perceptions of the west side as a white preserve were common among local blacks. Five years earlier, in 1973, African American journalist Leon Stennis wrote: "Blacks have shunned that area of the municipality almost as a tradition. Perhaps, because of some imagined and some real hostilities, or in recent years, because of the cultural and racial identity trends." [205]

It seems unlikely the controversy surrounding the west-side housing development attracted much attention among white suburbanites, who had become largely indifferent to the problems of the city. Few suburban dwellers, apart from those who were employed in Youngstown, found any reason to travel into the city. At this point, residents of the metropolitan area, including many urban dwellers, preferred suburban shopping malls to the city's declining downtown retail outlets; and by the mid-1980s, most of Youngstown's department stores had closed their doors. Likewise, downtown restaurants and drinking establishments, with rare exceptions, failed to draw suburban patrons. In the 1980s, Boardman-based mall developer Edward J. DeBartolo could state with confidence that the suburban township had become "the new downtown."[206] Hence, within less than a decade, a blue-collar community that had taken pride in its egalitarian traditions was transformed into a community of "haves" and have-nots," with most of the former ensconced in surrounding suburbs. The fact that a disproportionate percentage of the area's "have-nots" were people of color only served to deepen the community's longstanding racial divide. Meanwhile, Youngstown's deteriorating downtown district, once a showcase of the city's vitality, underscored the extent to which the community's white elites had written off the center city.

In this climate, urban parish schools fared somewhat better than one might expect. While suburbanites took an increasingly dim view of the city and seemed unconcerned about problems connected to racial inequality, nontraditional urban parochial schools were consistently able to secure the donations needed to keep them open. These schools benefited, at least to some extent, from the fact that they appealed to individuals across the ideological spectrum. Political conservatives, who routinely characterized the public school system as "monopolistic," were inclined to view the success of urban parochial schools as "a prime rationale for school choice."[207] Religious conservatives, meanwhile, pointed to the achievements of urban parish schools when arguing for the efficacy of "faith-based initiatives." Liberal Catholic laypeople and religious, as noted, viewed the schools as a manifestation of the church's commitment to social justice.[208] Finally, urban Catholic schools benefited from the positive attention they had received from certain educational researchers. Beginning in the early 1980s, a flurry of influential empirical studies compared urban Catholic schools favorably to urban public schools, indicating that they were unusually effective at boosting achievement levels among minority, at-risk students.[209]

URBAN CATHOLIC SCHOOLS AS VEHICLES OF SOCIAL UPLIFT

Although beleaguered urban parish schools were usually described as "mission" schools, it was clear that their supporters also regarded them as vehicles of social uplift for disadvantaged groups.[210] The expanded mission of these schools reflected a dramatic sea change within the U.S. Catholic Church. This change was driven, in large part, by the ecumenical spirit of the Second Vatican Council, but it also drew sustenance from the democratic principles that were advocated almost two centuries earlier by John Carroll, the first American bishop.[211] In the 1960s, the American Catholic Church appeared to be moving toward Bishop Carroll's vision of an institution "engaged in contemporary culture and conveying a vision of what society could and should be."[212] In earlier decades, the American church appeared "more concerned about the welfare of its own members, many of them immigrants, than with moulding the national society." After Vatican II, however, Catholics took on a more active role in the public sphere. "An educated and thoughtful laity was thus ready to respond to the new challenges the Second Vatican Council opened up in the early 1960s," noted Robert N. Bellah and his coauthors. "The unprecedented ecumenical cooperation that brought Catholics together with Protestants and Jews in a number of joint endeavors from the period of the Civil Rights movement to the present has created a new atmosphere in American religious life."[213]

Over the years, the nontraditional urban parish schools that grew up in the wake of Vatican II caught the attention of scholars, especially educational researchers, who had once ignored the phenomenon of U.S. Catholic schools. Although much of the earliest research on Catholic education focused on secondary schools, these studies invariably raised the profile of urban parochial elementary schools. In 1982, James S. Coleman, Thomas Hoffer, and Sally Kilgore published their influential study, *High School Achievement: Public and Private Schools,* which concluded that Catholic secondary schools produced relatively high levels of achievement, were less racially segregated, and created an atmosphere in which academic achievement was less dependent on family background.[214] Drawing on the same database employed in the "Coleman Report," Andrew Greeley's 1982 study, *Catholic High Schools and Minority Students,* engaged in a more specialized interpretation. Greeley concluded that achievement levels of minority students enrolled in Catholic schools were significantly higher than those observed among minority students in public schools. In addition, he contended that the most dramatic difference in the effectiveness of private and public schools was found "among students with familial, personal, psychological, and academic disadvantages, and even more among those who have a combination of disadvantages."[215] Such findings led some researchers to conclude that urban Catholic schools were more in line with the "common school" ideal than were their public counterparts.[216]

Growing evidence of superior outcomes among Catholic schools spurred further research designed to highlight relationships between characteristics of effective schools and variables such as achievement. In 1985, for instance, Cornelius Riordan set out to measure the effectiveness of coeducational and single-sex Catholic schools in relation to public schools. After testing his hypothesis that students in single-sex classrooms outperform those in coeducational classrooms because of the reduced effect of adolescent culture, Riordan concluded that, while Catholic schools produced higher levels of achievement than did public schools, single-sex Catholic schools outperformed coeducational Catholic schools.[217] Meanwhile, Anthony S. Bryk and Yeow Meng Thum, in a 1989 study on effective schools, identified a significant negative relationship between absenteeism and the presence of strong normative values in schools: a result that supported earlier findings that organizational aspects of Catholic schools contributed to their effectiveness.[218] In their 1993 study of secondary schools, Stephen W. Raudenbush, Brian Rowan, and Yuk Fai Cheong concluded, among others, that highly bureaucratized environments (such as those found in traditional public school systems) tended to "discourage the pursuit of higher-order instructional goals [among high school teachers], whereas organizational environments characterized by supportive administrative leadership, high levels of teacher collaboration, and strong teacher control over instruction will facilitate the pursuit of such instructional goals."[219]

Perhaps the most comprehensive study on Catholic schools and their apparent effect on urban student populations surfaced in 1993, when Anthony S. Bryk, Valerie E. Lee, and Peter B. Holland published *Catholic Schools and the Common Good*. Among others, the study concluded that the success of Catholic schools in an urban setting was closely related to the fact that contemporary Catholic schools "expose a broad, diverse cross-section of students to a distinctive vision of active participation in a humane society," a vision that "contrasts sharply with the contemporary rhetoric of public schooling that is increasingly dominated by market metaphors, radical individualism, and a sense of purpose organized around competition and the pursuit of individual economic rewards."[220] The study also indicated that lower dropout rates among students enrolled in urban Catholic schools could be attributed to the stronger sense of community engendered in such schools.[221] In 1995, William Sander set out to examine this "Catholic school effect" in the context of elementary schools. He determined that the effect of Catholic elementary schools on minority students could not be attributed to a selection of superior students, that no clear correlation existed between expenditures per students and academic outcomes, and that urban Catholic elementary schools did not have a significant effect on white students, although they had a dramatic effect on black and Hispanic students.[222]

Writing in 1992, Vernon C. Polite argued that urban Catholic schools, in light of their diverse student populations, "most closely resemble the ideal of the common school model." Referring to influential research, Polite challenged "the notion commonly held by the general public that inner-city Catholic schools educate a privileged group of African American students," and reported that "these students have been shown to come predominantly from the African American working class."[223] This research came at a time when many urban public schools appeared to be rapidly resegregating. As Jonathan Kozol observed, urban schools in major metropolitan areas have become, if anything, more segregated than they were at the dawn of the civil rights movement. Kozol noted that, in Chicago, during the 2002–2003 academic year, "87 percent of public-school enrollment was black or Hispanic; less than 10 percent of children in the schools were white." "In Washington,

D.C., 94 percent of children were black or Hispanic; less than 5 percent were white," he continued. Kozol referred to similar statistics in St. Louis (with a population recorded as 82 percent black or Hispanic), Philadelphia (79 percent), Los Angeles (84 percent), Detroit (96 percent), and Baltimore (89 percent). [224] A 2002 report on private schools sponsored by the National Center for Educational Statistics concluded that Catholic schools, as a whole, show higher levels of minority students than other religious schools, and "were much more likely than the other . . . types of private schools to have any students eligible for subsidized lunches (69 percent versus 38–40 percent)."[225] Ironically, in the face of abundant (if contested) research pointing to the effectiveness of urban Catholic schools, these institutions began to decline in cities across the nation—a development that rendered the issue of their "superiority" a moot point for some researchers.[226] In Youngstown, of course, center-city parish schools disappeared completely.

A SYSTEM COLLAPSES

The first signs of waning Catholic support for nontraditional urban parish schools in Youngstown became evident in the 1990s—a decade that seemed to open auspiciously. In 1991, the Diocese of Youngstown announced that special collections would be taken up in churches in Mahoning and Trumbull counties (both located within the Youngstown metropolitan area) to benefit two urban parish schools that served large numbers of nonwhite and non-Catholic students. The diocese also encouraged fund-raising in suburban parochial school classrooms, while benefiting from limited fund-raising among a number of urban Protestant churches whose overwhelmingly black congregants had children attending the schools.[227] Ultimately, the diocese achieved its goal of $115,000, which was needed to maintain the operation of St. Patrick's and Immaculate Conception elementary schools.[228] Subsequent efforts to raise funds for the two schools proved less successful, however. In 1992, for instance, the diocese's efforts to raise $125,000 for the schools fell short by $60,000.[229]

Falling donations coincided with a deepening impression that the city's parochial schools were trapped in a downward spiral. As the urban white population declined, it became evident that many traditionally stable parish schools were experiencing financial difficulties that had long been associated with center-city schools like St. Patrick's and Immaculate Conception. Between 1980 and 1990, enrollment in Youngstown's parish schools fell from 3,921 students to 2,369. Within a decade, fewer than half that number of students attended the schools, as enrollment fell to 1,209 in 2000. Despite a brief surge in 2001, with rolls rising slightly to 1,148 students, the downward trend remained fairly consistent, with enrollment slipping to 764 in 2004. This figure represented a staggering 90 percent decline in enrollment since 1970, when 7,700 students attended the city's parochial schools. For some observers, the departure of Catholics from urban neighborhoods had called into question the long-term viability of Youngstown's pattern of parochial education, as one school after another ceased operation. Moreover, as diocesan fund-raising campaigns experienced chronic shortfalls, urban parish schools like St. Patrick's were forced to make difficult decisions. In 1994, the *Vindicator* reported that students enrolled at St. Patrick's School paid an average of $750 in tuition, a figure considerably less than half the annual cost of educating each child.[230] To make matters worse, St. Patrick's and Immaculate were no longer the sole beneficiaries of diocesan fund-raising campaigns. By 1995, three other urban parish schools were facing imminent closure: St. Anthony's (north side), St. Dominic's (south side), and St. Edward's (north side).[231]

Meanwhile, older urban parishes like St. Patrick's were saddled with huge expenses related to the maintenance of large physical plants. St. Patrick's neo-Gothic church building was (and is) widely regarded as one of Youngstown's architectural treasures, and parishioners—many of whom are white suburbanites—have cited the church's beauty as a major attraction. The preservation of this attractive edifice, however, has come at a steep price. In a 2007 interview, Father Edward Noga, pastor of St. Patrick's Church, recalled that expenses related to the maintenance of the parish complex were overwhelming. "I'd be . . . scared if our bookkeeper took the total of my 21 years here, how much money we've put into that building," he said. "It would probably be a jaw-dropper." The pastor noted that parishioners were asked to make substantial donations toward the repair of the church's massive tile roof (a $200,000 expense), and added that the structure's elaborate stained-glass windows were also in need of repair (a project that was expected to cost $300,000).[232] Other aging urban parishes faced similar expenses as churches, social halls, and school buildings gradually fell into disrepair. St. Brendan's and St. Edward's parishes, for instance, financed extensive interior remodeling of their respective church buildings to reverse the effects of hasty (perhaps ill-conceived) renovations completed in the immediate aftermath of Vatican II. In the end, the refurbishment of cherished liturgical spaces may have done more to bolster these faith communities' collective sense of identity than the maintenance of schools whose students often did not belong to the parish.

A symbolic turning point in the decline of Youngstown's parochial schools came in 1995, when St. Patrick's Elementary School—one of the first institutions of its kind to serve large numbers of minority students—announced that it would close at the end of the school year. The south side school, which had a peak population of 1,057 in 1960, served fewer than 250 students by the mid-1990s. The closure of St. Patrick's School was followed by that of St. Anthony's in 1996, and St. Dominic's in 1999. In the wake of these closures, Immaculate Conception Elementary School briefly became a focal point of Catholic fund-raising efforts in the Youngstown metropolitan area. By 2002, however, the Immaculate was not the only urban parish school facing an uncertain future. Dr. Michael Skube, the new diocesan superintendent, observed that four of the city's parochial schools confronted serious financial difficulties. Immaculate Conception was joined by St. Brendan's (west side), St. Edward's (north side), and St. Matthias's (south side.) Ironically, Immaculate Conception, which the media described as "the most vulnerable," outlived two of the city's three endangered parochial schools.[233]

In 2003, administrators at St. Edward's Elementary School announced the institution's imminent closure, and in June of that year, the 86-year-old parish school held its final graduation ceremony, a development that surprised many former north side residents. One parent of a sixth-grade student enrolled at St. Edward's observed that the school suffered from declining enrollment that "was caused by the out-migration from the Youngstown area of working families with children, the movement of families with children to the suburbs, and the difficulty parents found paying tuition during the troubled economic times."[234] Another shock to the local Catholic community came in February 2005, when news broke that St. Brendan's Elementary School would close at the end of the academic year.[235] Given that the west side school enrolled 119 students—a figure much higher than the number of students enrolled at Immaculate Conception and slightly lower than that of St. Matthias's—the announcement raised questions about the long-term viability of Youngstown's two remaining center-city parish schools. At the time, the south side parish school of St. Matthias's served 124 students, while Immaculate Conception on the east side served 77 students.[236] In each case, demographic change, coupled with urban depopulation, had played a pivotal role in undermining student enrollment.

Within a year, Youngstown's two remaining center-city schools announced that they would cease operation at the close of the academic year. Administrators at St. Matthias's School, which enrolled 63 students in the 2005–2006 school year, revealed that "the most optimistic projection for the 2006–2007 school year is 33 students."[237] Similarly, Immaculate Conception, which enrolled 124 students in the 2005–2006 school year, predicted it would serve only 61 students for the upcoming academic year.[238] At this juncture, the end appeared inevitable, and Monsignor Robert Siffrin, the diocesan administrator, eulogized the two schools, stating that "both the Immaculate Conception and St. Matthias's parish communities have made extraordinary efforts to support and maintain their schools despite declining enrollment and the changing demographics in Youngstown."[239] In the wake of these closures, only one parish school remained open in Youngstown. To the dismay of those who valued urban parochial education, the system's sole survivor, St. Christine's Elementary School, was located in a quasi-suburban district of the west side that was overwhelmingly white and middle class. Thus, the era of Youngstown's nontraditional urban parish schools had come to an end; and with the closure of all but one parochial school within the municipality, the city's pattern of Catholic elementary education had ceased to exist.

CONCLUSIONS ON DEMOGRAPHIC CHANGE AND LOCAL PARISH SCHOOLS

The disappearance of Youngstown's center-city parish schools cannot be attributed entirely to the sweeping demographic changes that occurred in many urban neighborhoods in the decades following World War II. Nor can it be described as the sole consequence of white Catholics' waning support for parish schools that served nontraditional student populations. This support, after all, proved surprisingly resilient, given the cost of maintaining urban schools that no longer benefited from the donations of large numbers of parishioners. Nevertheless, demographic change was a key contributing factor in the decline of urban parochial schools in communities like Youngstown. Among others, this trend ensured that parish schools would lose traditional patrons at a time when they faced myriad economic challenges, including rising costs and declining enrollment. Notably, a few of these urban parish schools substantially altered their mission as they took on more nonwhite and non-Catholic students, a move that probably alienated some prospective Catholic donors, who questioned this nontraditional use of community resources. Considering that many of the Catholic community's most reliable donors were older parishioners, it seems likely that at least some of them were skeptical about nontraditional models of urban parochial education.

Despite the prospect of strong disagreement over the mission of such institutions, however, fund-raising for nontraditional urban parish schools proved relatively successful until the early 1990s. A turning point in the Catholic community's support for nontraditional urban parish schools came with a drastic decline in enrollment—a partial by-product of the rise of charter schools. Catholic donors, who were challenged to reimagine urban parochial schools as instruments of social uplift for non-Catholics, may have felt less inclined to support these schools when they served very few students. Diocesan support for these schools also waned considerably, and parish councils were forced to bow to the realities produced by insufficient funding, declining enrollment, and the rise of highly competitive urban educational alternatives. As Sister Charlotte Italiano, OSU, noted, in the aftermath of Immaculate Conception Elementary School's closure, urban parish schools could not afford to supply the amenities offered by rival charter schools. Furthermore, charter schools had the advantage of being tuition-free, an irresistible bonus for urban parents who were saving money for their children's college education.[240]

The influence of demographic change on Youngstown's urban parish schools was multilayered and often intersected with developments in the political and religious sectors. Tension between African Americans and white Catholics traced back to the early twentieth century, when local industrialists employed southern blacks as "strikebreakers" during periods of labor unrest. This tension was exacerbated by the fact that migrating blacks tended to settle in aging urban neighborhoods where white Catholics were already established. In the same manner that native-born whites viewed recent immigrants as a threat to the existing social order, "new" immigrants tended to perceive blacks as a threat to their own lifestyles. Although the migration of thousands of African Americans to center-city neighborhoods, especially in the postwar era, was bound to transform the city's social, religious, and political landscapes, the discriminatory policies of the FHA played a key role in fueling the white exodus from the city that came later. In the wake of concurrent trends like deindustrialization, urban white Catholics, like other European Americans, came to associate the decline of the city with the advent of demographic change, ignoring the fact that myriad factors had contributed to this phenomenon.

Moreover, the internal debates that divided the Catholic community after Vatican II ensured that white Catholics would have difficulty agreeing upon a common response to the plight of urban parish schools. Diocesan leaders, influenced by the conciliar emphasis on "social justice," stressed the importance of maintaining a Catholic "presence" in the center city, despite the decline of urban parishes. The Catholic laity, on the other hand, was divided on this issue, and many questioned the use of the Catholic community's resources to benefit non-Catholics. In addition, some white Catholics were sensitive to the fact that a large percentage of non-Catholic beneficiaries of urban parish schools were African American—an important factor, given that relations between blacks and urban whites were often less than harmonious in the decades leading up to the 1960s. Indeed, this relationship became more complicated over time.

During the 1970s, race-related conflicts erupted over issues related to the city's growing racial and economic diversity. Many urban whites resented desegregation programs aimed at urban public schools and also resisted

municipal efforts to build low-income housing in districts that were traditional white strongholds. Furthermore, tension between blacks and white
Catholics was exacerbated by misunderstandings arising over confessional
differences, and these religious differences sharply limited opportunities for
interracial interaction. The fact that most African Americans were Protestant
also ensured that it would be difficult for them to become integrated into
urban parishes, and some black parents probably had reservations about sending their children to Catholic schools, despite their reputedly high academic
standards. (Such reservations, which were probably shared by black Protestant leaders, may have played a role in facilitating the shift of black students
from parish schools to charter schools in the late 1990s and early twenty-first
century.) Meanwhile, the low rate of religious conversion among black students at nontraditional urban parish schools raised serious questions about
their long-term efficacy among those Catholics who perceived these schools
as potential instruments of evangelization.

Ironically, low rates of conversion among African Americans contributed
to some civic leaders' perception that Catholic parishes and schools were a
"foreign presence" in black neighborhoods.[241] Ultimately, postconciliar urban
pastors, who were generally more sensitive to the realities of racial injustice, proved less committed than their preconciliar counterparts to the evangelization of blacks. Nevertheless, the black Catholic population experienced
modest growth in the 1980s and 1990s, reaching 1.5 million by the end of
the twentieth century—an expansion that dovetailed with increasingly urgent
calls for black leadership in the Catholic community. In time, a number of
African American Catholic leaders (notably George Stallings, a former priest)
came to support the establishment of "an African American ecclesiastical
jurisdiction" that would grant black Catholics "a separate, semiautonomous
status" within the church.[242] Other leaders continued to push for greater black
control over urban ministries. That said, additional research will be required
to determine whether the absence of black leadership in Youngstown's
Catholic community (until recently) played a role in shaping local African
American attitudes toward urban parish schools. It seems apparent that local
black leaders, the majority of whom were Protestant ministers, did not feel
invested in these schools, though some acknowledged the positive role they
played in urban neighborhoods. In the end, many African American leaders
threw their support behind the charter school movement, whose success may
have sealed the fate of urban parish schools in cities like Youngstown.

Youngstown's parish schools provided quality education to urban youth
(some of whom were disadvantaged) over several decades, often in the face
of extraordinary odds. Nontraditional parish schools not only softened misunderstandings that had long existed between white Catholics and black Prot-

estants; they drew much-needed attention to the problems of the center city. Given the obstacles many of these schools were compelled to overcome, their resilience seems remarkable. The durability of urban parish schools owed much to the shared commitment of a small group that included members of religious orders, educators, philanthropists, and diocesan leaders. Significantly, when urban diocesan leaders placed less emphasis on the maintenance of urban institutions (which may have happened during the tenure of Bishop Tobin), the city witnessed a rapid series of parochial school closures. (The community's last two center-city parish schools closed during the yearlong period when the Diocese of Youngstown was without a bishop.)

There is, of course, no way to determine whether Youngstown's urban parish schools would have fared better under the leadership of Bishop George R. Murry, SJ, an African American who emphasizes the church's obligation to remain a presence in urban neighborhoods. Many contend that Bishop Murray's appointment bolstered the morale of black Catholics throughout the diocese, raising the prospect of the community's revitalization. Shortly after Bishop Murry's appointment, one African American parishioner in Canton, Ohio, predicted the new bishop "could bring back a lot of fallen away Catholics," especially African Americans. "We've lost a lot of black Catholics," he added, "but he will bring a lot of other people back to the Church."[243] Given the dramatic economic setbacks that Youngstown has experienced in recent decades, however, it seems unlikely that one leader could have saved the city's beleaguered parochial school system. The fact that some local Catholics believe that visionary leadership could have made a decisive difference is revealing, however. This perception calls attention to the delicate combination of circumstances that enabled these schools to survive as long as they did.

NOTES

1. Lou Jacquet, "New Bishop of Youngstown Meets the Press: Bishop George Murry Pledges to 'Listen' as He Travels through Diocese," *The Catholic Exponent,* 1, February 9, 2007.

2. Linda M. Lionis, "Bishop Takes Up Fight against Racism: The Bishop Said People of Faith Must Strive to End Racism, and Offered Suggestions of How," *The Vindicator,* A-1, November 21, 2007.

3. Jacquet, *The Catholic Exponent,* February 9, 2007.

4. "Freeborn Columbus Woman Settled in Youngstown in 1831," *The Youngstown Vindicator,* A-1, March 27, 1988.

5. Irene Stewart, "Colored People among City's Best Citizens: Mrs. Malinda Knight, First Colored Resident Hundred Years Ago," *The Youngstown Telegram,* A-41, June 29, 1931.

6. "Birthday," *The Youngstown Vindicator,* A-12, October 29, 1939, birthday announcement and brief biography of William R. Stewart.

7. Leon Stennis, "Trace Blacks' History in Community: Week-Long Observance Begins," *The Youngstown Vindicator,* A-8, February 10, 1974.

8. Ibid.

9. George D. Beelen, "The Negro in Youngstown: Growth of a Ghetto" (seminar paper, Kent State University, November 27, 1967), 7.

10. Herbert L. Armstrong, Clarence E. Barnes, Mary G. Byrd, Otis R. Douglas, and James P. Lottier, *Afro-American Bicentennial Observance: A Rediscovery of Part of the Past* (Youngstown, OH: Afro-American Bicentennial Committee, 1976), 56–68.

11. Mary Ellen Pellegrini, "A Pride in Historic District: Three Groups Work Together to Ensure That the Striking Neighborhoods Will Be Preserved," *The Vindicator,* B-1, December 25, 2006.

12. "Birthday," *The Youngstown Daily Vindicator,* October 29, 1939.

13. Stennis, *The Youngstown Vindicator,* February 10, 1974.

14. David A. Gerber, *Black Ohio and the Color Line, 1860–1915* (Urbana, IL: University of Illinois Press, 1976), 274.

15. Stennis, *The Youngstown Vindicator,* February 10, 1974.

16. David Brody, *Steelworkers in America: The Nonunion Era* (Cambridge, MA: Harvard University Press, 1960), 254–55.

17. *The Youngstown Vindicator,* March 15, 1925, editorial.

18. Sherry Linkon and John Russo, *Steeltown U.S.A.: Work & Memory in Youngstown* (Lawrence, KS: University Press of Kansas), 32.

19. Brody, *Steelworkers in America,* 224.

20. E. Wayne Robinson, "Blacks Once Forced to Work as 'Jack-Legged Craftsmen,'" *The Youngstown Vindicator,* B-3, March 31, 1974.

21. Florita Stubbs, "Blacks Were Once Assigned Most Dangerous Jobs in Mills," *The Youngstown Vindicator,* A-8, March 3, 1974.

22. Robinson, *The Youngstown Vindicator,* March 31, 1974.

23. "1930 Census Statistics: Foreign Born Stock; Youngstown-Campbell-Struthers," The International Institute, Young Women's Christian Association (research paper, Reuben-McMillan Public Library, Youngstown, OH).

24. "Thugs Kill Officer Without Warning: Patrolman Alexander Warren Shot Down in Cold Blood as He Crosses Street to Question Two Men Thought to Have Been Negroes or Whites with Faces Blackened," *The Youngstown Vindicator,* 1, May 4, 1921.

25. "Colored People Indignant over Wholesale Round-ups—Want Policeman's Murderer Punished, but Say Police Go Too Far," *The Youngstown Vindicator,* May 5, 1921, letter to the editor.

26. "The Negro and the Community," *The Youngstown Vindicator,* 2, May 6, 1921, editorial.

27. The Executive Committee of the National Association for the Advancement of Colored People, "Colored People Send Protest: Regret Warren Murder, but Feel Needlessly Embarrassed," *The Youngstown Vindicator,* 3, May 6, 1921, letter to the editor.

28. "Negro Bandits Hold Up Store on South Side: Clerk Intimidated with Pistol and Cash Register Is Looted," *The Youngstown Vindicator,* 1, May 6, 1921.

29. John H. Chase, "Youngstown's Colored People," *The Youngstown Vindicator,* 9, May 8, 1921, letter to the editor.

30. Beelen, "The Negro in Youngstown," 6.

31. "Two Colored Bandits Shoot Man Fatally: Wantonly Shoot Victim When They Secure No Loot," *The Youngstown Vindicator,* 1, March 29, 1921.

32. "Murder Stirs West End: Trouble Feared as Murder Result," *The Youngstown Vindicator,* 1, March 30, 1921.

33. The *Vindicator* reported on April 1, 1921, that police arrested two additional suspects, one of whom was identified as "colored."

34. "'Monkey's Nest' Is Evidence City Needs Police Protection: Citizen of the West End Complains That 'Totin' Liquor Is Worse Crime Here than 'Totin' a Gun—If Scott Were to Get a Hold-Up Call and a Bootleg Call at the Same Time He Would Answer the Bootleg Call First," *The Youngstown Vindicator,* 5, April 1, 1921, letter to the editor.

35. "Letters from the People," *The Youngstown Vindicator,* 1, March 30, 1921, letter to the editor.

36. Ibid.

37. "'Monkey's Nest' Is Evidence City Needs Police Protection," *The Youngstown Vindicator,* April 1, 1921.

38. William D. Jenkins, *Steel Valley Klan: The Ku Klux Klan in Ohio's Mahoning Valley* (Kent, OH: Kent State University Press, 1990), *ix-xi*.

39. Brendan Delap, *Mad Dog Coll: An Irish Gangster* (Dublin: Mercier Press, 2002), 38.

40. Andrew R. L. Cayton, *Ohio: The History of a People* (Columbus, OH: The Ohio State University Press, 2002), 310.

41. Jack L. Warner, *My First Hundred Years in Hollywood* (New York: Random House, 1964), 35–36.

42. Ernest Brown, Jr., "Chic It Wasn't, but Monkey's Nest Was Home, and More, to Its People," *The Youngstown Vindicator,* B-3, August 14, 1977.

43. David J. Goldberg, *Discontented America: The United States in the 1920s* (Baltimore, MD: The Johns Hopkins University Press, 1999), 169–70.

44. "'Monkey's Nest' Is Evidence City Needs Police Protection," *The Youngstown Vindicator,* April 1, 1921.

45. David Brody, *Labor in Crisis: The Steel Strike of 1919* (Philadelphia, PA: J. B. Lippincott Company, 1965), 162–63.

46. Brody, *Steelworkers of America,* 254–55.

47. Jenkins, *Steel Valley Klan,* 20–21.

48. Thomas G. Fuechtmann, *Steeples and Stacks: Religion and Steel Crisis in Youngstown* (Cambridge, UK: Cambridge University Press, 1989), 13.

49. Jenkins, *Steel Valley Klan,* 20–21.

50. Cayton, *Ohio,* 311.

51. Jenkins, *Steel Valley Klan,* 26.

52. A. B. Whiting, "Knowing Youngstown: Youngstown's Population Growth," *The Youngstown Vindicator*, 18, November 25, 1924.

53. Jenkins, *Steel Valley Klan*, 22–23.

54. Ibid., 159–60.

55. Ibid., 52.

56. Ibid.

57. Kevin Boyle, *Arc of Justice: A Saga of Race, Civil Rights, and Murder in the Jazz Age* (New York, NY: Henry Holt and Company, 2004), 9–10.

58. Edward Salt, "Morris Scheibel Named Architect: Eighty New Buildings to Accommodate 600 Families Will Be Erected; Work Started at Once on Plans; Assistants Named," *The Youngstown Telegram*, 1, July 12, 1935.

59. Cayton, *Ohio*, 108.

60. Frederick J. Blue, William D. Jenkins, H. William Lawson, and Joan M. Reedy, *Mahoning Memories: A History of Youngstown and Mahoning County* (Virginia Beach, VA: The Donning Company, 1995), 38.

61. "Birthday," *The Youngstown Vindicator*, October 29, 1939.

62. Beelen, "The Negro in Youngstown," 14.

63. Nicholas Lemann, *The Promised Land: The Great Black Migration and How It Changed America* (New York, NY: Vintage Books, 1991), 31.

64. Ibid., 6.

65. Armstrong et al., *Afro-American Bicentennial Observance*, 60–61.

66. "One-on-One: Lorinda Butler—'The Most Important Thing Is to Do Right and Think Right,'" *The Vindicator*, B-1, December 27, 1999.

67. William H. Watkins, *The White Architects of Black Education: Ideology and Power in America, 1865–1954* (New York, NY: Teachers College Press, 2001), 19.

68. "1930 Census Statistics: Foreign Born Stock," The International Institute.

69. "City's Negro Group Doubles; Colored Population Rises from 6,662 to 14,552; Foreign Group Dwindles; Alien-Born Percentage Decreases from 25.6 to 19.4, Census Reveals," *The Youngstown Vindicator*, B-1, June 8, 1931.

70. Jenkins, *Steel Valley Klan*, 159–60.

71. Mark Sullivan, "Harding for Strict Bar to Immigration: He Long Since Declared in Favor of Limiting Tide from Europe," *The Youngstown Vindicator*, 9, May 6, 1921.

72. Matthew Frye Jacobson, *Whiteness of a Different Color: European Immigrants and the Alchemy of Race* (Cambridge, MA: Harvard University Press, 1998), 8.

73. Ibid., 82–83.

74. Joseph Hill, interview by the author, October 9, 2002, transcript, Hogan-Cullinan Family Collection, #314, Mahoning Valley Historical Society, Youngstown, OH.

75. Jenkins, *Steel Valley Klan*, 38.

76. T. Gordon Welsh, interview by the author, May 1, 2007, transcript, Hogan-Cullinan Family Collection, #314, Mahoning Valley Historical Society, Youngstown, OH.

77. Jenkins, *Steel Valley Klan*, 59–60, 71, 112.

78. Ibid., 85.

79. Boyle, *Arc of Justice*, 9–10.

80. David R. Roediger, *Working Toward Whiteness: How America's Immigrants Became White—the Strange Journey from Ellis Island to the Suburbs* (New York, NY: Basic Books, 2005), 171.

81. "10,382 Migrate Here in 5 Years," *The Youngstown Vindicator*, 7, April 13, 1944.

82. "Population Is 167,720: Complete Census Shows 126,385 Native-born Whites in City," *The Youngstown Vindicator*, A-7, March 22, 1942.

83. "Defense Jobs Bring Migration of 11,431 Nonwhites into Area," *The Youngstown Vindicator*, 5, December 19, 1951.

84. John T. McGreevy, *Parish Boundaries: The Catholic Encounter with Race in the Twentieth-Century Urban North* (Chicago, IL: University of Chicago Press, 1996), 84.

85. Ibid., 18–19.

86. Ibid., 84.

87. Sister Charlotte Italiano, OSU, interview by the author, May 31, 2007, transcript, Hogan-Cullinan Family Collection, #314, Mahoning Valley Historical Society, Youngstown, OH.

88. "Negroes Fight Police Action, Want Chief Thomas Removed," *The Youngstown Vindicator*, 17, October 1, 1945.

89. "The Race Trouble," *The Youngstown Vindicator*, 8, September 25, 1945, editorial.

90. "The Swimming Pool Problem," *The Youngstown Vindicator*, 20, July 7, 1949, editorial.

91. Robert E. Casey, interview by the author, February 13, 2007, transcript, Hogan-Cullinan Family Collection, #314, Mahoning Valley Historical Society, Youngstown, OH.

92. Robert E. Casey, *An Irish Catholic Remembers and Reflects* (New Wilmington, PA: New Horizons Publishing, 2006), 58.

93. Casey, interview.

94. "Negro Catholics' Church Named St. Augustine," *The Youngstown Vindicator*, 3, September 30, 1944.

95. Cyprian Davis, *The History of Black Catholics in the United States* (New York, NY: Crossroad, 1990), 96–121.

96. Ibid., 135–36.

97. Sharon M. Howell, CSJ, "'The Consecrated Blizzard of the Northwest': Archbishop John Ireland and His Relationship with the Black Catholic Community," in *Many Rains Ago: A Historical and Theological Reflection on the Role of the Episcopate in the Evangelization of African American Catholics*, ed. Secretariat for Black Catholics, National Conference of Catholic Bishops (Washington, DC: United States Catholic Conference, 1990), 35–48.

98. David W. Southern, *John LaFarge and the Limits of Catholic Interracialism, 1911–1963* (Baton Rouge, LA: Louisiana State University Press, 1996), 180.

99. Davis, *The History of Black Catholics in the United States,* 228.

100. Southern, *John LaFarge and the Limits of Catholic Interracialism,* 110.

101. Davis, *The History of Black Catholics in the United States,* 227.

102. Southern, *John LaFarge and the Limits of Catholic Interracialism,* xiv.

103. Davis, *The History of Black Catholics in the United States,* 256.

104. Eileen M. McMahon, *What Parish Are You From? A Chicago Irish Community & Race Relations* (Lexington, KY: The University of Kentucky Press, 1995), 126.

105. Ibid., 168.

106. Roediger, *Working Toward Whiteness,* 168–69.

107. McMahon, *What Parish Are You From?* 127.

108. McGreevy, *Parish Boundaries,* 31.

109. "Negro Catholics' Church Named St. Augustine," *The Youngstown Vindicator,* 3, September 30, 1944.

110. Bishop Emmet M. Walsh to Father Cyril Kennedy, CPPS, 21 March 1958, Archives of the Diocese of Youngstown.

111. Naomi Byrd, interview by the author, June 4, 2010, transcript, Hogan-Cullinan Family Collection, #314, Mahoning Valley Historical Society, Youngstown, OH.

112. Beverly Blackshear, interview by the author, March 15, 2011, transcript, Ethnic Heritage Society Collection, #385, Mahoning Valley Historical Society, Youngstown, OH.

113. Dorothy Ann Blatnica, VSC, *"At the Altar of Their Gods": African American Catholics in Cleveland, 1922–1961* (New York, NY: Garland Publishing, Inc., 1995), 172.

114. McGreevy, "Racial Justice and the People of God," 224–25.

115. Donald M. Clark, "Black Priest. Black Parish. White Rite," in *Disciples at the Cross Roads: Perspectives on Worship and Church Leadership,* ed. Eleanor Bernstein, CSJ (Collegeville, MN: The Liturgical Press, 1993), 81.

116. Thomas J. Sugrue, *The Origins of the Urban Crisis: Race and Inequality in Postwar Detroit* (Princeton, NJ: Princeton University Press, 1996), 192.

117. Harold A. Buetow, "The Underprivileged and Roman Catholic Education," *Journal of Negro Education* 40, no. 4 (Autumn 1971): 384.

118. Sugrue, *The Origins of the Urban Crisis,* 192.

119. McGreevy, *Parish Boundaries,* 131.

120. Jay P. Dolan, *In Search of an American Catholicism: A History of Religion and Culture in Tension* (New York, NY: Oxford University Press, 2002), 185.

121. McGreevy, *Parish Boundaries,* 105.

122. Ibid., 84–85.

123. Ibid., 72.

124. Ibid., 118.

125. Ibid., 131.

126. McGreevy, *Parish Boundaries,* 180.

127. Kenneth T. Jackson, *Crabgrass Frontier: The Suburbanization of the United States* (New York, NY: Oxford University Press, 1985), 213.

128. McGreevy, *Parish Boundaries,* 92.

129. "New W. Federal Branch Y. M. C. A.," *The Youngstown Vindicator,* 1, July 15, 1930.

130. Howard C. Aley, *A Heritage to Share: The Bicentennial History of Youngstown and the Mahoning Valley* (Youngstown, OH: The Bicentennial Commission of Youngstown and Mahoning County, Ohio, 1975), 372.

131. Casey, interview.

132. "Challenge . . . to the People of Youngstown," (Youngstown, OH: Royal Printing Company, 1958), 4–5.

133. McGreevy, *Parish Boundaries,* 105–6.

134. Mel Watkins, *Dancing with Strangers: A Memoir* (New York, NY: Simon & Schuster, 1998), 142.

135. Ibid., 146.

136. Jackson, *Crabgrass Frontier,* 213.

137. Ida Carter, interview by the author, May 4, 2007, transcript, Hogan-Cullinan Family Collection, #314, Mahoning Valley Historical Society, Youngstown, OH.

138. Ibid.

139. Brown, *The Youngstown Vindicator,* August 14, 1977.

140. Watkins, *Dancing with Strangers,* 133.

141. Ibid., 128.

142. Richard Bruno, *Steelworker Alley: How Class Works in Youngstown* (Ithaca, NY: Cornell University Press, 1999), 72–74.

143. Linkon and Russo, *Steeltown U.S.A.,* 42.

144. Matthew Frye Jacobson, *Whiteness of a Different Color: European Immigrants and the Alchemy of Race* (Cambridge, MA: Harvard University Press, 1998), 247.

145. Stefano Luconi, "Frank Rizzo and the Whitening of Italian Americans in Philadelphia," in *Are Italians White? How Race Is Made in America,* eds. Jennifer Guglielmo and Salvatore Salerno (New York, NY: Routledge, 2003), 179.

146. T. Gordon Welsh, interview by the author, May 1, 2007, transcript, Hogan-Cullinan Family Collection, #314, Mahoning Valley Historical Society, Youngstown, OH.

147. Sister Margaret Ann Traxler, "American Catholics and Negroes," *Phylon* 30, no. 4 (1969): 357.

148. Sugrue, *The Origins of the Urban Crisis,* 6.

149. Fuechtmann, *Steeples and Stacks,* 22–23.

150. Ibid., 25.

151. "Shift to Suburbs Shown in Population Figures," *The Youngstown Vindicator,* A-6, August 1, 1954.

152. George R. Reiss, "Predicts City Will Grow Horizontally," *The Youngstown Vindicator,* A-1, October 16, 1955.

153. "Shift to Suburbs Shown in Population Figures," *The Youngstown Vindicator,* August 1, 1954.

154. Linkon and Russo, *Steeltown U.S.A.,* 42.

155. Patricia Meade, "Remembering the Rage: Angry Blacks Were 'Emulating What Their Peer Groups Were Doing in Bigger Cities,' One Official Said," *The Vindicator,* 1, April 6, 2008.

156. "City Curfew Stands, Guard Curbs Disorder: 2 Officers Are Shot in Hillman St.," *The Youngstown Vindicator,* 1, April 9, 1968.

157. "3,000 Attend Service for Dr. King Here," *The Youngstown Vindicator,* 1, April 8, 1968.

158. "Clergy, Civic Leaders Attend Memorial for Dr. King," *The Youngstown Vindicator,* 8, April 8, 1968, photographic spread with captions.

159. McGreevy, *Parish Boundaries,* 133.

160. Ibid., 155.

161. Dolan, *In Search of an American Catholicism,* 198.

162. "2,000 to Leave Catholic Schools," *The Youngstown Vindicator,* August 30, 1971.

163. "St. Patrick School Sold for $325,000," *The Youngstown Vindicator,* July 27, 1971.

164. "Anti-Discrimination Policy Approved by Diocese Board," *The Youngstown Vindicator,* 48, December 5, 1973.

165. "Says Diocese Owes Poor Schools Aid," *The Youngstown Vindicator,* 1, February 28, 1973.

166. Marie Aikenhead, "Board Refuses School Funding: Votes Against Inner City Aid," *The Youngstown Vindicator,* 1, November 17, 1976.

167. Ibid.

168. Marie Aikenhead, "Diocesan Schools Reveal Ethnic Makeup: 8.2% of 10,408 Students Are from Minorities," *The Youngstown Vindicator,* B-7, April 3, 1977.

169. "School to Remain Open 1 More Yr.," *The Youngstown Vindicator,* 40, January 19, 1977.

170. "Catholic Schools in Youngstown Won't Be Havens," *The Cleveland Plain Dealer,* A-12, May 11, 1974.

171. "Diocese OKs New Enrollment Rules," *The Youngstown Vindicator,* 10, May 22, 1974.

172. Leon Stennis, "Leadership's View on Diocese's Approach Toward Blacks Differ," *The Youngstown Vindicator,* 7, September 6, 1975.

173. McGreevy, *Parish Boundaries,* 7.

174. Davis, *The History of Black Catholics in the United States,* 257–58.

175. Stennis, *The Youngstown Vindicator,* September 6, 1975.

176. Ibid.

177. "School Principal Urges Northeast Sewer Action," *The Youngstown Vindicator,* 5, February 12, 1970.

178. Stennis, *The Youngstown Vindicator,* September 6, 1975.

179. Leon Stennis, "Church Should Recruit Black Priests, Nuns for Leadership, Clergyman Says," *The Youngstown Vindicator,* B-5, August 30, 1975.

180. Leon Stennis, "Status Quo for 'Church of St. Peter': Catholic Diocese Should Lead the Way to Stronger Ties in Black Community," *The Youngstown Vindicator,* 5, September 20, 1975.

181. John T. McGreevy, "Racial Justice and the People of God: The Second Vatican Council, the Civil Rights Movement, and American Catholics," *Religion and American Culture* 4, no. 2 (Summer 1994): 224.

182. McGreevy, *Parish Boundaries,* 59.

183. McGreevy, "Racial Justice and the People of God," 224–25.

184. Ibid., 225.

185. McGreevy, *Parish Boundaries,* 59.

186. McGreevy, "Racial Justice and the People of God," 226.

187. Ibid, 224.

188. Davis, *The History of Black Catholics in the United States,* 257.

189. McGreevy, *Parish Boundaries,* 224–25.

190. The Confraternity of Christian Doctrine, *"What We Have Seen and Heard":* *A Pastoral Letter on Evangelization from the Black Bishops of the United States* (Washington, DC: St. Anthony Messenger Press, 1984), 28.

191. McGreevy, *Parish Boundaries,* 61.

192. Ibid., 59.

193. Blackshear, interview.

194. Italiano, interview.

195. Ibid.

196. Ibid.

197. Chris Amatos, "A Look at the Past and Future of Catholic Schools," *The Youngstown Vindicator,* B-3, January 29, 1978.

198. "Valley Population," *The Vindicator,* January 22, 1995, illustrated chart.

199. Demographics Now, "Youngstown City: Census Trend 1980–2000 Summary Report with Charts," library.demographicsnow.com/OnX_WriteReport.srct (Retrieved on May 14, 2008).

200. Tim Yovich, "West Siders Hit Housing Project," *The Youngstown Vindicator,* 1, October 26, 1978.

201. "Faces HUD Cuts over Housing," *The Youngstown Vindicator,* 1, December 6, 1978.

202. "Project Vote Petitions Filed," *The Youngstown Vindicator,* 1, January 20, 1979.

203. Tim Yovich, "E. Side Blacks Oppose Project," *The Youngstown Vindicator,* 1, December 7, 1978.

204. Bertram de Souza, "Groundbreaking for Westview Housing Is Expected This Month," *The Youngstown Vindicator,* 4, April 2, 1981.

205. Leon Stennis, "Blacks Face City Problems: Present 25 Pct. Ratio Will Grow," *The Youngstown Vindicator,* 5, March 28, 1973.

206. Tom Bagsarian, "DeBartolo: Faith, Values Stand Out; Politicians, Business Leaders and Longtime Friends Remember the Business Legend," *The Vindicator,* 1, December 20, 1994.

207. James Youniss and John J. Convey, *Catholic Schools at the Crossroads,* 1.

208. Anthony S. Bryk, Valerie E. Lee, and Peter B. Holland, *Catholic Schools and the Common Good* (Cambridge, MA: Harvard University Press, 1993), 51–53.

209. Ibid., 57.

210. Ibid.

211. Ibid., 21–22.

212. Ibid., 34.

213. Robert N. Bellah, James Madsen, William M. Sullivan, Ann Swidler, and Steven M. Tipton, *Habits of the Heart: Individualism and Commitment in American Life* (Berkeley, CA: University of California Press, 1985/1996), 238.

214. Bryk et al., *Catholic Schools and the Common Good,* 57.

215. Andrew M. Greeley, *Catholic High Schools and Minority Students* (New Brunswick, NJ: Transaction Publishers, 2002), xiv.

216. Vernon C. Polite, "Getting the Job Well Done: African American Students and Catholic Schools," *The Journal of Negro Education* 61, no. 2 (Spring 1992): 213.

217. Cornelius Riordan, "Public and Catholic Schooling: The Effects of Gender Context Policy," *American Journal of Education* 93, no. 4 (August 1985): 535–37.

218. Anthony S. Bryk and Yeow Meng Thum, "The Effects of High School Organization on Dropping Out: An Exploratory Investigation," *American Educational Research Journal* 26, no. 3 (Fall 1989): 374–77.

219. Stephen W. Raudenbush, Brian Rowan, and Yuk Fai Cheong, "Higher Order Instructional Goals in Secondary Schools: Class, Teacher, and School Influences," *American Educational Research Journal* 30, no. 3 (Autumn 1993): 525.

220. Bryk et al., *Catholic Schools and the Common Good,* 11.

221. Ibid., 272–73.

222. William Sander, "Catholic Grade Schools and Academic Achievement," *The Journal of Human Resources* 31, no. 3 (Summer 1996): 544–46.

223. Polite, "Getting the Job Well Done," 213.

224. Jonathan Kozol, "Still Separate, Still Unequal: America's Educational Apartheid," *Harpers,* September 1, 2005, 41.

225. Martha Naomi Alt and Katharin Peter, *Private Schools: A Brief Portrait* (Washington, DC: U.S. Department of Education, 2002), 7–11.

226. Youniss and Convey, *Catholic Schools at the Crossroads,* 2.

227. Marie Shellock, "Fund-raiser Begins for Two Catholic Schools, *The Vindicator,* A-8, March 16, 1991.

228. John Goodall, "Fund Drive Spares 2 Catholic Schools," *The Vindicator,* A-1, April 9, 1991.

229. "Bishop: Catholic Schools Stay Open; The Fund-Raising Efforts Didn't Bring In Enough Money, but Three Diocesan Schools Will Still Be Open," *The Vindicator,* B-2, April 7, 1992.

230. "St. Brendan's Elementary: Declining Numbers Led to School Closing," *The Vindicator,* 1, March 1, 2005.

231. Ron Cole, "Catholic Schools Launch Fund Drive: Diocese Officials Hope to Know by March 15 If They Can Raise the Money. If Not, a School Could Close," *The Vindicator,* B-1, February 12, 1995.

232. Noga, interview.

233. Ron Cole, "Immaculate Conception: Does Bell for Pupils Also Toll for School? The School Has Opened Early; the New Principal's Attitude Is That It Won't Be Closed," *The Vindicator,* B-1, August 14, 2002.

234. Peter H. Milliken, "Many Bid Farewell as St. Edward School Closes: St. Edward's Graduates Serve This Community Well, the Speaker Said," *The Vindicator,* 1, June 6, 2003.

235. "St. Brendan's in Final Year: The Diocese Says an Official Announcement Will Be Released Monday," *The Vindicator,* 1, February 26, 2005.

236. "St. Brendan's," *The Vindicator,* March 1, 2005.

237. "Declining Enrollment Closes Youngstown IC, St. Matthias Schools," *The Catholic Exponent,* April 21, 2006, www.doy.org/viewpast.asp?ID=1965 (accessed May 8, 2011).

238. Harold Gwin, "Final Bell Tolls for Two Schools: There Were Some Long Faces As Children Left St. Matthias on Tuesday," *The Vindicator,* B-1, June 7, 2006.

239. "Declining Enrollment Closes Youngstown IC, St. Matthias Schools," *The Catholic Exponent,* April 21, 2006.

240. Italiano, interview.

241. Stennis, *The Youngstown Vindicator,* September 6, 1975.

242. Davis, *The History of Black Catholics in the United States,* 260.

243. Joanne Malene, "Black Catholics Excited about New Bishop's Appointment," *The Catholic Exponent,* 42, March 28, 2007.

Chapter 6

Out of These Ashes: Vatican II and Catholic Identity

For five decades, the granite, neo-Gothic edifice of St. Columba's Church dominated a bluff overlooking Youngstown's central retail district. The parish, which operated the city's oldest parochial school, was described by locals as a "fortress of the faith," a name that reflected (perhaps unconsciously) the defensive mentality prevalent among the white Catholic working classes at the time the building was completed in 1903.[1] The Catholic community's insularity was encouraged, in part, by the highly centralized and Romanized model of American Catholicism that emerged from the internal controversies of the late nineteenth century. This mentality was reinforced by the distrust and intolerance that held sway among "old stock" European Americans during the late nineteenth and early twentieth centuries. Indeed, examples of anti-Catholic sentiment are well documented. In the 1910s, a *Vindicator* editorial condemned the widespread dissemination of rumors that local Catholics "were drilling for civil war in St. Columba's church, that they had guns and ammunition stored in the Phelps street parish school and . . . finally . . . that on the night before the city elections all Catholic servant girls in the city will assassinate their employers."[2] By the 1920s, the growth of the local chapter of the Ku Klux Klan was stimulated by factors including "a rapid influx of numerous southern and eastern European immigrants."[3] Significantly, a large percentage of these newcomers were Catholic.

By the time St. Columba's was designated as a cathedral in 1943, interreligious tensions had largely subsided, and most area residents—regardless of religious background—viewed the building as one of the community's architectural treasures. Yet, for some middle-aged Catholics, the wounds of the past remained fresh, and more than a few were sensitive to any hint of religious discrimination. Some local Catholics went so far as to question the motives behind the municipal government's refusal to relocate high-voltage wires that stretched across the cathedral's rose-petal window like a ragged scar, marring the structure's beauty. On the evening of September 2, 1954, these high-voltage wires posed a challenge that transcended aesthetic considerations. Their presence hampered—perhaps even doomed—local firefighters' efforts to contain a blaze that swept the cathedral. Firefighters believed the fire broke out in the cathedral's choir loft around 9:30 p.m., shortly after the building was struck by lightning during a violent storm.[4] There were no witnesses to the outbreak of the fire, with the possible exception of Mary Clarke, an elderly parishioner who resided at a nearby boarding house. Mrs. Clarke, however, was widely seen as "confused," and her landlady ignored her warning.[5] The fire that Mrs. Clarke all but predicted blazed undetected for an hour and a half before a passerby noticed the flames and contacted the municipal fire department.

By the time firefighters arrived on the scene, flames had engulfed the cathedral's organ and choir loft, eerily illuminating the building's massive rose-petal window. Those on hand were disturbed by evidence that the fire was creeping along a catwalk and loft that ran the length of the cathedral's nave. Firefighters recognized that, if the massive timbers of the ceiling and roof were to catch fire, the blaze would burn out of control, reducing the cathedral to a shell. The department's fire hoses, however, were unable to reach the top of the building. Youngstown Fire Chief John R. Lynch later explained that the department could not "get the aerial ladder to its full height because of high-voltage wires, which carried 2,000 volts." The firefighters' efforts to contain the blaze in the choir loft ultimately failed, and they watched helplessly as the blaze "spread across the roof toward the rear of the building." As the fire progressed, the cathedral's northern spire burst into flames and collapsed onto Elm Street, which ran to the immediate west of the building. Meanwhile, the structure's stately twin spires, which soared 98 feet above Wood Street, to the south, showed signs of structural damage and instability. At one point, the western spire veered dangerously close to the high-voltage wires that stretched before the edifice. By the time the blaze was contained, at around 2:30 a.m., St. Columba's Cathedral was ruined and presumed to be a total loss.[6]

The following morning, Youngstown Bishop Emmett M. Walsh calculated damage to the cathedral at "more than $1,250,000," adding that insurance would cover just $940,000 of rebuilding expenses.[7] An able administrator and effective fund-raiser, Bishop Walsh quickly launched a drive for contributions; and on April 12, 1959, less than five years after the destruction of the old cathedral, a new structure was dedicated on the site. For many Catholics around the diocese, however, the new cathedral came as nothing less than a second shock. Overall, the structure could not have been more different in design and dimension than the one it replaced. A 1997 anniversary booklet for the cathedral parish described the building as follows: "The new cathedral was noteworthy for its simplicity of design. Statues were replaced with bas-reliefs over the altar. Pastels and neutral tones in mosaic and marble make for a bright and airy structure. More modest dimensions called for a central aisle of 102 feet as opposed to the 130-foot long Gothic church. The sanctuary was significantly smaller, 44 x 49 feet, as opposed to the 78-foot wide sanctuary in the old cathedral. The exterior of the new cathedral was a cream Mankato stone."[8]

The new building's most salient quality was its self-consciously modern style, which stood in stark contrast to the neo-Gothic style of its predecessor. Unsurprisingly, local Catholics, who viewed the former cathedral as a cherished icon, showed mixed reactions to the new building, whose appearance struck many as unfamiliar, even alienating. On a Sunday morning in fall 1958, when Father Glenn W. Holdbrook sang the first high mass in the new cathedral, he appeared to speak to these reservations as he compared the new edifice to the reconstructed temple of King Solomon in the Old Testament. "On the day of the viewing . . . the young men and women stood in amazement and open awe at the beauty of the new building," Father Holdbrook told the assembled congregants. "But the old men and women sat down and cried because the temple did not compare to the old place of worship."[9] Paula McKinney, a longtime parishioner of St. Columba's, recalled her own impressions of the new building. "We didn't like it," she said. "It's like 'The Emperor's New Clothes.' You were afraid to admit that you didn't like it. And then, all of a sudden, it would come out in conversation that nobody liked it."[10]

In fact, the designer's decision to eschew the medievalist aesthetic that characterized much of U.S. Catholic architecture before World War II reflected a sea change that had occurred within the American church itself. This shift became more apparent in the wake of the Second Vatican Council, a decade later. Thus, in certain ways, the destruction and rebuilding of St. Columba's Cathedral presaged the theological and liturgical changes of the postconciliar era that helped transform American Catholicism. These changes, in combination with the social and political developments of the 1960s, undermined the brand of Catholicism that had thrived in America since the mid-nineteenth century.[11] Given that many U.S. Catholics took a decidedly unhistorical view of their Church, a position consistent with official characterizations of the institution as "eternal and unchanging," many of them failed to grasp that American Catholicism's "love affair" with medievalism was a relatively recent development. As Philip Gleason, SJ, pointed out, the brand of medievalism eventually embraced by U.S. Catholics had its origins in the nineteenth-century Romantic Movement. Although Catholics were not conspicuously involved in the romantics' sympathetic reevaluation of the Middle Ages, "the Church could not fail to be positively affected by this reversal of feeling toward the period in which she had been the dominant spiritual and cultural force in Europe."[12] What Gleason termed as "antirevolutionary romantic medievalism" captured the imagination of conservative European intellectuals, many of whom converted to Catholicism. A subsequent wave of conversions within the German intelligentsia witnessed its counterpart in England's Oxford Movement; and within a few decades, a number of English "convert-medievalists," notably August Welby Pugin and Ambrose Phillips de Lisles, exerted an influence on American Catholics.[13]

Perhaps the most tangible manifestation of American Catholic medievalism was the rise of neo-Gothic cathedrals in northeastern urban centers like New York City. In 1858, New York Bishop John Hughes laid the cornerstone for what became the country's most famous Catholic house of worship, a massive, twin-towered structure that set a new standard for U.S. Catholic religious architecture. In 1879, when St. Patrick's Cathedral was finally dedicated, the ceremony harked back to the pomp and pageantry of the medieval church.[14] The impact of medievalism was not limited to architecture and ritual, however. As Gleason observed, medievalism had, by the mid-nineteenth century, "become thoroughly mixed up with the critique of individualism and industrial capitalism, with efforts to restore the sense of community, with anti-urbanism, with the 'arts and crafts' approach, and with various philosophies of the dignity of work and the importance of good workmanship."[15] In a Catholic context, a medievalist critique of the modern world was most apparent in the "social encyclicals" of the late nineteenth and early twentieth centuries. American Catholics gravitated to medievalism mainly because it was "the obverse of Catholic anti-modernism and its intensity [reflected] the degree of uneasiness felt by Catholics about the dominant tendencies of the modern world." During a period of sweeping change and interminable social conflict, Catholics admired what they regarded as the most salient feature of the Middle Ages—its emphasis on social unity.[16]

Well into the 1950s, the corporatist underpinnings of American Catholic thought were reflected in a Catholic community that focused on tight-knit neighborhoods, vibrant parishes, and replicated organizations. "Underlying this institutional and local sensibility were particular conceptions of both the human person and the sacred," McGreevy noted. "Crucially, the natural law tradition so central to Catholic thought in the modern period described humans as fundamentally social." U.S. Catholic leaders "deliberately created a Catholic counterpart for virtually every secular organization," and most Catholics believed that their religion "could not flourish independent of a Catholic milieu;

the schools, parish societies, and religious organizations were seen as pieces of a larger cultural project."[17] Indeed, the Catholic parish became such an essential ingredient of neighborhood identity that urban Catholics, when asked, "Where are you from?" routinely responded with the name of the parish to which they belonged.[18] In Rome, Pope Pius XII gazed with approval on this thriving subculture and "warned against a public school system from which religion was excluded."[19] Clerical observers of the American scene, after all, had long recognized that the "great instrument of Catholic separatism was the parochial school."[20] Firmly traditional in his educational views, Pope Pius "valued Latin in the curriculum" and observed "that one of the great values of Catholic schools was that they inculcated religious vocations."[21] A large percentage of Catholic schools were attached to urban parishes. Through their sponsorship of religious processions and other events, many of these parishes claimed surrounding neighborhoods as "sacred ground."[22]

Beginning in the late 1950s, a tide of events culminating in the Second Vatican Council began to erode the theological, philosophical, and material foundations of this urban "cultural project." Once thriving urban ethnic enclaves gradually fell into decline as more Catholics relocated to the suburbs—a trend briefly masked by the postwar baby boom. During the same period, parish schools were deprived of a vital source of "cheap labor" as teaching nuns retreated from the classroom and moved into other service-oriented fields. Buetow noted that "by 1960 the number of lay teachers increased by 537% over the 7,422 lay teachers in the Catholic schools of 1948."[23] Then, in the 1960s, the combined influence of Vatican II and the civil rights movement placed "the Catholic struggle over race and religion at the center of the nation's cultural turmoil." As McGreevy observed, the well-organized Catholic neighborhoods that were "admired by contemporary intellectuals at one historical moment . . . proved unable to separate 'community' from racial mythology at another."[24] As Catholics retreated from the "ghetto" and entered the American mainstream, their leaders expressed concern about a loss of Catholic "distinctiveness." Less than two decades after the council, theologian Frans Jozef Beeck, SJ, warned that, whenever the Catholic Church "finds itself in the *diaspora* of a modern, open, secular society, she will also feel the subtle impact of the tendency to level and equalize, which is the dark side of the prevailing atmosphere of toleration and civil liberty."[25]

THE CALM BEFORE THE STORM

At the close of World War II, most American Catholics were connected to territorial parishes, "whose borders were strictly defined and whose churches were permanent fixtures on the cityscape."[26] After decades of institution building, the U.S. church had successfully established "a virtual state-within-a-state so Catholics could live almost their entire lives within a thick cocoon of Catholic institutions."[27] Faced with a well-organized, robust, and seemingly permanent subculture, observers of American Catholicism in this period could hardly have anticipated the ruptures and controversies that came with the 1960s. As Gabert noted, for a decade and a half following the end of the war, the growth of Catholic parish schools reached a high-water mark. The number of Catholic schools in the country grew by 50 percent between 1940 and 1960, rising from 7,597 to 9,897. Enrollment practically doubled, jumping from 2,108,892 to 4,195,781.[28] During this same period, the U.S. Catholic community "grew from twenty-one million to an astounding forty-two million members."[29] Surprisingly, the growth rate of Catholic schools exceeded that of public schools. Buetow observed that "between 1950 and 1960, public elementary schools grew by 142 percent, while their Catholic counterparts grew by 171 percent."[30] According to Gabert, the number of parochial schools in the United States rose from 7,914 to 9,897 between 1950 and 1960.[31]

In Youngstown, as elsewhere in the northeastern United States, parochial schools were attached to parishes that served as focal points of Catholic social life, especially for young people. During the 1940s and 1950s, young parishioners participated in church-sponsored field trips, youth organizations, and fund-raising activities. Many of these young people were members of families whose connections to a particular parish spanned several generations. Elizabeth Fleisher Fekety, a Youngstown-area resident who recalls the postwar era, described the "homey" atmosphere she enjoyed at St. Joseph's Church, a German American national parish on the city's north side. "It wasn't like just people walking in and out," Mrs. Fekety said. "Every generation sent their kids there . . . Everybody knew somebody [in your family], from two years before, or four years before." Most members of St. Joseph's Church were involved, in some capacity, in the maintenance of parish institutions. The parish, in turn, provided schooling, religious ceremonies, limited forms of social welfare, and scores of social events. "Catholic schools at the time were always trying to make money," Mrs. Fekety recalled. Parishioners attempted to sustain the parish school by organizing paper collections and raffles, including an annual lottery for a Thanksgiving turkey. Like other former parishioners of St. Joseph's Church, Mrs. Fekety retained pleasant memories of the pastor, Father John H. Lenz, who passed out boxes of candy to students every Christmas and "made sure that everybody always had what they needed."[32]

The quasi-communal arrangements Mrs. Fekety described at St. Joseph's were typical of the era. Robert Casey, who attended Immaculate Conception

Elementary School in the 1950s, recalled an institutional ethos that stressed cooperation and orderliness. He noted that "students swept the classroom floors and hallways every day," an activity that reinforced the prevailing impression that the students themselves were stakeholders in the parish school. "Since Immaculate was our school, there was no graffiti on its exterior," he recalled in a memoir. "Students did not jam up toilets so they would overflow and cause damage to the school. There were no holes punched in the walls. The students were no more likely to cause damage to Immaculate than they would in their own homes."[33] Indeed, many of the city's parochial school students participated in parish communities that were cohesive and all-encompassing. Father Joseph Rudjak, raised in the shadow of St. Casimir's Church, a Polish American national parish in the Brier Hill district, spent much of his early childhood in the environs of parish and parochial school, where he was exposed to religious indoctrination on an almost daily basis. Besides attending weekly mass, Father Rudjak joined his family at religious devotions three times a week. "And then, we'd go to daily Mass at school," he added.[34] Meanwhile, diocesan employee Carla J. Hlavac recalled that Slovak language and culture were actively promoted at St. Matthias's Elementary School, an institution attached to a national parish on the city's south side. "We had some kind of a little band . . . where we all had a little instrument that we played," she recalled. "And I remember a Christmas play in first grade; we all had dressed as angels, and we were dusting the throne for Mary . . . and we all had to sing some kind of a Slovak song called . . . 'Sleep, Sleep, Little Jesus.'"[35]

Postwar urban parish schools attracted even those "solitary" ethnic groups, especially Italian Americans, who had once avoided them. "The traditional rancor that had existed between the newcomers and 'Americanized' parish was largely a thing of the past," Gabert observed. It seemed as though a parish school system once characterized by ethnic tension had "survived and was entering into a time of expansion."[36] As shrewd observers recognized, however, the vitality of urban parish schools depended on the viability of neighborhoods in which they operated. By the 1950s, a growing number of urban Catholic neighborhoods were in transition. McGreevy noted that the enforcement of highly restrictive immigration quotas in the 1920s "and the lack of economic mobility (at least upward) during the Depression imposed a false sense of stasis on Catholic life." While many of the replicated institutions of the Catholic ghetto "remained, and even flourished, much of what made the Catholic experience of the early twentieth century distinctive faded into the larger American kaleidoscope."[37] Significantly, the decline of urban Catholic culture kept pace with the growth of urban black neighborhoods and the retreat of whites to the suburbs.[38] By the mid-1960s, the traditional mission of urban schools had fallen under close scrutiny, as Catholics confronted urban change, the civil rights movement, theological reform, the polarizing debate over the Vietnam War, and other developments that challenged their community's traditional insularity.

THE ROAD TO VATICAN II

In the late 1940s and early 1950s, most establishment liberals would not have described Catholics as a group on the threshold of assimilation. Respected scholars railed against the "antidemocratic" influence of "Catholic power," and critics complained that Catholics were immune to the currents of progressive change then sweeping the country.[39] In the wake of the unprecedented human rights violations committed during World War II, "an enhanced sense of individual autonomy emerged from the world of politics and law." Activists and members of the legal community, "working in the shadow of the Holocaust" transformed the decade after World War II into "a golden age for those devoted to human and civil rights." This new emphasis on personal autonomy not only galvanized the civil rights movement in the South; it also raised questions about longstanding legal restrictions on abortion and assisted suicide.[40] Meanwhile, the war undermined traditional Catholic domestic values by driving six million women into the U.S. workforce. Significant portions of these women chose to remain employed after the war, and by the late 1940s, they comprised 31 percent of the labor force. "As the trend of working women grew stronger," Dolan wrote, "the objection to it from Catholic voices became louder, intensifying the contrast between the ideal and the reality."[41]

The church's critique of liberal postwar trends drew a withering response from progressives; and by the late 1940s and early 1950s, many liberal intellectuals described the U.S. Catholic subculture as a veritable "ministate" that eschewed democratic principles. Influential monographs criticized Catholics for their "separatist" habits and "collectivist" values, while defining "Catholicism and Soviet Communism as parallel threats to American democracy." McGreevy observed that critical examinations of U.S. Catholicism, "along with criticism of racial segregation and opposition to fascism and communism, helped define the terms of postwar American liberalism." Postwar liberals held that "religion, as an entirely private matter, must be separated from the state, and that religious loyalties must not threaten intellectual autonomy or national unity." For many liberals, the Catholic Church posed a problem of "integration," because its insularity was believed to prevent Catholics from participating in a "culture" of democracy.[42] Although liberals and Catholics crossed swords earlier in the twentieth century—on issues ranging from the legalization of birth control to the merits of the Mexican Revolution—it is unlikely that many Catholics were prepared for Paul Blanshard's *American Freedom and Catholic Power* when it appeared in 1949. Blanshard's book referred to the U.S. Catholic hierarchy as "antidemocratic," "blamed Catholics for producing the bulk of white criminals," and warned of the "divisive" influence of Catholic schools.[43]

Yet, while the church drew the wrath of establishment liberals, the U.S. popular media was practically celebrating American Catholic values. Former *Commonweal* editor Peter Steinfels observed that during the postwar era, "the Catholic Church was to morality and uplift what General Motors was to industry and the Yankees were to baseball." Films ranging from *Boys' Town* to *On the Waterfront* portrayed priests as "virile, wise, good-humored, compassionate, and in emergencies possessed of a remarkable knockout punch." Oddly enough, the quality of apartness that "once made the church so suspect now enabled it to step forward as a repository of the old-fashioned, tried-and-true American values that had lost some of their grip on the rest of the culture."[44] Celluloid images of a harmonious, fervently patriotic Catholic subculture left some viewers unmoved, however. For many liberals, the American clergy bore less resemblance to the jovial parish priests in Hollywood films than to right-wing prelates like Francis Cardinal Spellman, the powerful archbishop of New York. Secular and Protestant leaders alike were alarmed at Cardinal Spellman's apparent disregard for the principle of church-state separation, which the archbishop dismissed as a "shibboleth."[45]

Liberal anxieties about the political instincts of Catholics gained wider currency during the anticommunist "witch hunts" that were led by Joseph R. McCarthy, a Catholic senator from Wisconsin who enjoyed the support of many of his coreligionists, including Cardinal Spellman. McCarthy's strong connections to the Catholic community weren't lost on Reverend Robert McCracken, pastor of New York's Riverside Church. In a widely publicized 1954 sermon, the minister compared McCarthy's tactics to those of the Catholic Church, an institution that had "never disavowed the Inquisition, that makes a policy of censorship, that insists on conformity." The "implications were ominous" for Protestant and secular liberals, observed McCarthy biographer David M. Oshinsky. "More Catholics meant more Catholic power," he wrote. "More Catholic power meant more pressure for federal aid to parochial schools, more campaigns to censor objectionable books and movies, and more votes for politicians like Joe McCarthy."[46] Survey results lent credibility to liberal claims that McCarthy enjoyed disproportionate support among Catholics. Indeed, Catholic support for the senator "ran 7 to 9 points ahead of national and Protestant support"—a disparity that widened in September 1954, after the televised "Army-McCarthy" hearings that resulted in McCarthy's censure. At

the nadir of McCarthy's public career, Catholic support for the Wisconsin senator was recorded at 40 percent, while Protestant support, following a "drastic
nosedive," stood at just 23 percent.[47]

Most of the church's sharpest critics were secularists, but a significant
number of liberal Protestant leaders (along with Reverend McCracken)
expressed reservations about Catholic political power and its implications.
This group included Methodist Bishop G. Bromley Oxnam, who in 1947
helped organize Protestants and Other Americans United for the Separation
of Church and State. Three years later, in 1950, the Protestant establishment's reservations about Catholicism surfaced in a less overt manner, when
the Federal Council of Churches "yielded . . . to a more vigorous National
Council of Churches," which "incorporated Orthodox bodies" while largely
ignoring Catholics. As James Hennesy, SJ, put it, liberal Protestant ecumen-
ists who reached out to Orthodox Christians proved "less anxious to relate
to Roman Catholicism." Nevertheless, Catholic scholars like John Courtney
Murray viewed the U.S. liberal establishment's rising hostility to Catholicism
as a symptom of something beyond resurgent "nativism." Murray wrote that
this new species of anti-Catholicism "was not so much Protestant as it was
naturalist, operating on the premise that democracy demanded a naturalist,
secularist philosophy."[48]

While Murray's concerns about "creeping secularism" in American society
intensified over the years, he found a good deal to criticize in the Catholic
Church's official position on church-state relations. His carefully worded
articles on the subject rankled influential churchmen, and in the 1950s, the
Holy Office (once known as the Inquisition) officially silenced Murray for his
views: a standard procedure since Pius X's condemnation of the Modernists
in the early twentieth century. "The ordeal of these men is hard to describe,"
wrote Wills, "since they were disciplined in secret, under orders to keep silent
about being silenced." In Murray's case, the Holy Office's decision to impose
silence came partly in response to an act of political imprudence. In 1954,
while speaking at Catholic University, Murray criticized a speech delivered
a year earlier by Cardinal Alfredo Ottaviano, the presiding officer of the
Holy Office. During the speech, Ottaviano "restated the traditional position
on church-state relations—that only the true religion should be recognized,
since all others are subject to the rule that 'error has no rights.'" Murray's
criticism of Ottaviano's speech suggested that it "was inconsistent with a later
speech delivered by Pope Pius XII, *Ci Riesce,* an address to Italian jurists."
Although he strongly denied that he perceived the constitutional separation of
church and state in the United States as a universal ideal, a position Pope Leo
XIII condemned in the late nineteenth century, the American theologian's
defiance of a powerful member of the Roman Curia evidently sealed his fate.

For the duration of the 1950s, Murray found "his outlets for publishing and lecturing cut off."[49]

Murray's cautious critique of the Vatican's official stance on church-state issues reflected a liberal trend among American Catholic intellectuals, who—decades behind their European counterparts—began to develop "their own criticisms of Catholic conformity." In 1955, Catholic historian John Tracy Ellis, SJ, provoked controversy by "castigating American Catholics for neglect of the intellectual life" and criticizing U.S. Catholic universities for their "betrayal of the West's most distinguished intellectual tradition." During this period, thousands of Catholic graduate students enrolled at the nation's top universities, against the advice of conservative clerical leaders, who dismissed secular colleges as "hot-beds of anti-Catholicism."[50] By the late 1950s, a growing number of "emancipated" Catholics "were embarrassed by, or openly ridiculed the largely Irish Catholic folkways that still permeated their Church."[51] These developments dovetailed with a gradual softening of anti-Catholic sentiment in liberal circles, where earlier comparisons of the church to totalitarian movements like fascism and Communism lost favor. In this climate of growing acceptance, and accelerated integration, liberal Catholic intellectuals like Murray (though officially forbidden to write on religious freedom) "continued to urge Catholics to strike a more temperate balance between Catholic principles and public consensus."[52]

Then, in 1960, Murray's fortunes revived in a way that his opponents could hardly have imagined. When John F. Kennedy launched his presidential campaign, "all the charges of Paul Blanshard were renewed," and a growing number of U.S. Catholics came to regard the church's official position on church-state relations (which few had closely examined) as an "embarrassment." Murray, the onetime theological outcast, emerged as a useful "defender of the faith." One month after Kennedy's election as the first Catholic president of the United States, the theologian's image appeared on the cover of *Time* magazine.[53] Murray won liberal plaudits for his attempt to reconcile Catholic ideals with American principles of religious freedom in his landmark treatise, *We Hold These Truths*. "It remains only to insist that in regarding the religious clause of the First Amendment as articles of peace and in placing the case for them on the primary grounds of their necessity, one is not taking low ground," Murray wrote. "Such a case does not appeal to mean-spirited expediency nor does it imply a reluctant concession to *force majeure*. In the science of law and the art of jurisprudence the appeal to social peace is an appeal to a high moral value. Behind the will to social peace stands a divine and Christian imperative."[54] By 1962, even Murray's powerful enemies in Rome, who had prevented him from attending the first session of Vatican II, were unable to block his participation in the second session.[55] The dramatic alteration of Murray's status, while profoundly influenced by events in America, was also facilitated by unexpected developments in Rome.

More than two years before President Kennedy assumed office, the Vatican had set a course that "radically altered the parameters by which the American Catholic community measured itself and the world around it."[56] The 1958 papal election of Angelo Roncalli marked the beginning of a new era in the history of the Catholic Church. At the outset of his brief pontificate, Pope John XXIII "stunned the world by calling an ecumenical council" that was intended to "throw open the windows of the church to the modern world."[57] Traditionalists in the U.S. hierarchy recoiled from Pope John's appeal for *aggiornamento* ("updating"), in much the same way they later retreated from the prospect of a Kennedy presidency. Cardinal Spellman, particularly hostile, snapped to aides that Roncalli was "no pope" and added sarcastically, "He should be selling bananas."[58] As Catholic writer James Carroll observed, Spellman, in the wake of Roncalli's election, "commissioned a life-size wax dummy of Pius XII," which he "displayed . . . in a case at the rear of St. Patrick's Cathedral—the image of the real pope." Nevertheless, Pope John's call for openness in the church proved irresistible. Through small gestures and acts of inclusion, he "undercut what had been taken to be Catholic absolutes," including perceptions "that Protestants and Jews are doomed, that priests are ontologically superior beings, that error has no rights, that the pontiff himself, no mere 'bridge,' is a kind of God."[59] The international mass media "beamed" Pope John's "joyful, avuncular presence . . . around the world" as he "embraced Orthodox patriarchs and Jewish rabbis."[60] Jewish leaders "rejoiced that the head of a church that had seemed to them Christ-killers would remove the most odious anti-Semitism of the Christian liturgy and speak to them as brothers." In addition, communists and nonbelievers, who instinctively "assumed that the Catholic faith was their antagonist, found themselves drawn to the humanity of Pope John."[61]

These developments failed to impress Pope John's powerful detractors in the Roman Curia, and conservative Catholics in the United States became increasingly concerned about the "sea change occurring in the papacy's appreciation of world problems and its prescriptions for them."[62] The first ideological skirmish in the U.S. Catholic community occurred in 1961, when Pope John's social encyclical, *Mater et Magistra* ("Mother and Teacher"), "signaled the divisions between so-called liberals and conservatives that would intensify after 1968 over the legacy of Vatican II."[63] A commentary in the conservative *National Review*—irreverently titled "Mater, si; Magistra, no," a riff on the popular maxim of Cuban refugees: "Cuba, si; Castro, no"—criticized Pope John for stressing the inequalities that arose in capitalist economies while downplaying the abuses committed by authoritarian powers like the Soviet Union. "The most obtrusive social phenomena of the moment are surely the continuing and demonic successes of the Communists, of which there is scant mention," wrote the magazine's founding editor, William F. Buckley, Jr., a conservative Catholic. Buckley argued that the pope's encyclical took "insufficient notice" of "the extraordinary material well-being that such free economic systems as Japan's, West Germany's and our own are generating." [64] Buckley's commentary precipitated a firestorm among Catholics, and some liberals went so far as to brand him as "anti-Catholic."[65] Overall, the controversy seemed inevitable, given that John's encyclical represented a sharp departure from the insistent anticommunism of Pope Pius XII. At this point, a "pattern" had been set that "marked the social teaching of John XXIII and his successor, Paul VI." While both spiritual leaders "continued to challenge the atheistic materialism and totalitarianism ways of world communism," they also "abandoned ritual denunciation and initiated dialogue with communists," while directing criticism "with greater force at western cultural imperialism and liberal capitalism." Hennesey noted that, for those Americans who "expressed their Catholicism largely in terms of emotional anti-communism or uncritically accepted the assumptions of the American and Western economic system, an era had ended even before the Second Vatican Council began."[66]

Although criticism of unfettered capitalism had been part of the Vatican's stock-in-trade since the late nineteenth century, papal leaders before Pope John tended to attract more attention for their condemnation of modern trends than for any pronouncements that could be interpreted as liberal. This was true even for the late-19th- and early-20th-century popes, whose social encyclicals drew uncharacteristic praise from liberals. After the long, reactionary reign of Pope Pius IX, who openly criticized democracy, liberal Catholics in the United States took comfort in the "social justice" rhetoric of his successor, Pope Leo XIII, who assumed the papacy in 1878. Popular among working-class American Catholics, Pope Leo earned a reputation as a liberal because of his 1891 encyclical *Rerum Novarum* ("Of New Things"), which affirmed the dignity of work and insisted that each worker had a right to a decent wage. Although these positions dovetailed with liberal views of the era, Pope Leo's outlook was shaped by his profound admiration for the Middle Ages. Even the pope's laudatory assessment of labor unions was based "on the misconception that they resemble medieval guilds."[67] By 1899, the medievalist sensibilities that inspired Leo to criticize laissez-faire capitalism drove him to condemn a vaguely defined "heresy" he termed as "Americanism." Pope Leo's irritation with U.S. churchmen who sought to accommodate the Church's teachings with liberal democratic values reflected his distaste for republics that relegated religion to the private sphere. "The union of church and state with the church ruling over the state had been a key Catholic doctrine since at least the Middle Ages," Dolan wrote. To praise the American model of church-state relations "was to challenge the legitimacy of an ancient, and indeed seemingly immutable, Catholic doctrine."[68]

Pope Leo XIII's distrust of the modern world was reflected in his support for the neo-Thomist philosophical revival launched during the reign of his predecessor. In 1879, Pope Leo's encyclical *Aeterni Patris* ("On the Restoration of Christian Philosophy") "enjoined on the Church universal the study of St. Thomas Aquinas."[69] Central to neo-Thomism was a "doctrine of revealed truths essential to salvation and entrusted to the church," which justified the institution's hierarchal structure and authority, and belief in "a universal moral law that is embedded in nature and accessible to rightly ordered reason."[70] The church's philosophical adherence to neo-Thomist principles was reaffirmed in Pope Pius X's 1907 encyclical *Pascendi Dominici Gregis* ("On the Doctrine of the Modernists"), which condemned the so-called Modernist "heresy." The targets of this searing encyclical were European Catholic intellectuals who "resemble in some way the American Transcendentalists."[71]

It is unsurprising that Pope Pius discerned a threat in the Modernist movement, given that many of its theological propositions anticipated the guiding principles of Vatican II. According to *The Encyclopedia of American Catholic History,* "the Modernists taught that God revealed divine truth through, and not apart from, history and the experience of ordinary people," a position that could be seen as a challenge to a strictly hierarchal model of the church. Although the handful of American clerics influenced by European Modernists "did not see themselves as radicals bent on revolutionizing the Church according to the demands of modernity," they aspired "to fashion a new Catholic apologetic that would speak more effectively to the democratic, scientific worldview of their fellow Americans."[72] Like their European counterparts, Catholic Modernists in America undertook "the critical study of the Bible; the historical study of the development of Christian doctrines, practices and institutions, and the comparative study of religions." Their opponents criticized these activities, advocating a largely sacramental approach to spiritual wisdom. Anti-Modernists emphasized the "sacerdotal power" of the ordained priesthood, defined the Church in clerical terms, and understood the sacred "to be utterly transcendent—remote from ordinary experience and inaccessible apart from the mediation of the Church."[73] When the Vatican officially condemned Modernism in 1907, William L. Sullivan, an American Paulist priest, was among those who sensed the presence of a "political" motive. Sullivan contended that Modernism was denounced not because it "violated biblical or spiritual truths," but because its "major tenets . . . undermined the absolutist claims of the Roman Catholic hierarchy."[74]

Yet, in a dramatic break with the past, the council initiated by Pope John XXIII welcomed the contributions of liberal thinkers who had been forced into "ecclesiastical exile" for their unorthodox views. These scholars and theologians "infused" the documents of the Second Vatican Council "with biblical and patristic emphases, a sensitivity to diverse liturgical forms, and a focus on laypeople." In addition, their efforts imbued Catholicism with "a new sense of the church moving through history . . . and directly addressing the problems of the current age."[75] Among the most relevant documents for U.S. Catholics was the council's *Declaration on Religious Liberty*, which was "framed to a significant degree by Father Murray." This declaration "explicitly affirmed what American Catholics had long held: there should be no coercion of conscience on matters of religious belief; the state need not profess or privilege the one true church; all faiths, rather, could enjoy civil tolerance." From a liberal Catholic perspective, the document—which drew on the American tradition of church-state separation—effectively "rescued American Catholics from the equivocal position in which they had always been placed . . . by older church teachings."[76]

The Second Vatican Council's apparent resolution of the church-state issue was one of its many achievements. As John W. O'Malley observed, one of Vatican II's most distinctive characteristics "was the broad scope of the issues it addressed."[77] Under the council's influence, the church softened its focus on individual eternal salvation and stressed the need to witness "to God's love and compassion by striving to bring justice and healing to the world right here." In addition, the council modulated the church's position on modernity, "from one of almost blanket suspicion and antagonism to one of critical sympathy and engagement."[78] Consequently, the Catholic Church "not only recognized the importance of culture in shaping religion, but it also underscored the need for religion to transform culture."[79] Still more surprising was the council's drastic redefinition of the church's relationship with other branches of Christianity. As Steinfels wrote, the conciliar documents "acknowledged the need for church reform, emphasized the place of scripture in the church's life and liturgy, stressed the calling for the laity and the need for collegial structures in church governance—all implicit bows to features of Protestant Christianity."[80] This spirit of openness, however, created new challenges as Catholics struggled to redefine their collective religious identity. "Catholic identity no longer excluded a positive approach to ecumenism and evangelization," wrote theologian Frans Jozef van Beeck, SJ. "But this change in focus . . . called for the elaboration of a new, very precarious balance between Catholic identity and openness."[81]

The reforms of Vatican II, while they "sounded a death knell for prickly apartness," also smoothed the path for the U.S. church's participation in the controversies of the 1960s.[82] The postconciliar church, as Dolan noted, "did an about-face, abandoned its sectarian posture, and sought to become a major force in American public life."[83] American clergy and religious, inspired by the council's message of social justice, became participants in the civil rights movement, and religiously motivated antiwar activists "put a distinctly Catholic stamp on the seizure and burning of draft records and other dramatic nonviolent protests." As Steinfels wrote, "Radical sixties Catholicism left a permanent mark on the church's presence in the public square. It melded the imperatives of the Council with the civil rights movement's techniques of civil disobedience and nonviolent direct action and with the antiwar movement's nearly apocalyptic mood of urgency."[84] Unsurprisingly, the church's decision to address divisive social and political issues generated internal conflict that "spread through the entire community, dividing families and parishes, bishops and priests."[85]

Significantly, many changes later described as factors contributing to the "crisis" in the U.S. Catholic Church actually helped create conditions similar to those found in other religious communities. If, for instance, U.S. Catholics were widely known for their "knee-jerk" anticommunism in the 1950s, their political attitudes became more difficult to predict in the late 1960s. As Dolan noted, "Catholics in the United States were becoming more like the rest of the American population." On political issues, American Catholics often "described themselves as more liberal and less conservative than the rest of white America." According to a survey conducted in 1967, "24 percent of the Catholic population opposed the war, while only 16.5 percent of the Protestants adopted such a position."[86] While this result was not duplicated in every study conducted during the Vietnam War, influential research on Catholic attitudes toward the war suggests that their views did not differ substantially from those of Protestants. William L. Lunch and Peter W. Sperlich, in their analysis of data concerning public attitudes on the Vietnam War between 1964 and 1973, concluded that U.S. Catholics were "less troubled by the general justification for the war" but no less likely than U.S. Protestants to support policy alternatives.[87] In short, Catholics were no less divided than Protestants were on what was arguably the most polarizing issue of the day. Unsurprisingly, the "liberalization" of the U.S. Catholic community coincided with a dramatic upsurge in social and economic mobility. Dolan noted that by the 1960s, Irish American Catholics "were especially successful educationally and economically."[88]

During the 1960s, many American Catholics watched closely as reforms were promulgated at Vatican II—a significant departure from the past, when few eyes were turned toward Rome. In 1870, for instance, U.S. Catholics were practically oblivious to the First Vatican Council, mainly because they were still "struggling with the question of what it meant to be an American." By 1965, most Catholics seemed comfortable with their American identity. As Catholics discovered, however, the moment they "had solved one half of the riddle—what it meant to be American—the other half came unraveled." Vatican II not only challenged U.S. Catholics "to rethink the meaning of Catholicism in the modern world"; it also "sanctioned" and "accelerated" reform. Hence, U.S. Catholics were pressured to "solve the riddle of religion and modernity overnight"—a goal that some Protestant leaders regarded as overly ambitious. Protestant theologian Langdon Gilkey noted that Protestantism, unlike Catholicism, had been trying "for 200 years or more to deal with, absorb, and reinterpret the culture of modernity—a modernity that has developed more and more radically over those two centuries." Yet, the Catholic Church, in the wake of the council, "tried to absorb the effects of this whole vast modern development from the Enlightenment to the present in the short period between 1963 and 1973." Consequently, the political, social, and economic forces "that had structured and transformed the modern history of the West have suddenly, and without much preparation, impinged forcefully on her life" and therefore needed "to be comprehended, reinterpreted, and dealt with by Catholicism in one frantic decade."[89] In the process, Catholics were treated to the extraordinary spectacle of episcopal leaders engaged in "verbal duels" that resembled parliamentary debates.[90]

THE "CATHOLIC MOMENT"

The 1960 election of President John F. Kennedy, as one observer wrote, "suggested more than any proclamation could that Catholics at long last were comfortably integrated into American society."[91] Nowhere did the election results elicit greater enthusiasm than in Youngstown, a working-class community with a substantial Catholic population. By fall 1960, the presidential candidate was no stranger to the city. Kennedy had first visited Youngstown in 1946, while attending the funeral of former PT-109 crew member Leonard Thom, who died in an automobile accident, leaving behind a pregnant wife and a child. Kennedy was asked to serve as a pallbearer at the funeral, which was held at St. Edward's Church on the north side. He remained in Youngstown for several days. As his political career gained momentum, Kennedy kept in touch with Thom's widow, Catherine Jane Thom Kelley, who developed friendships with other members of the Kennedy family.[92] Then, in 1959, the Massachusetts senator served as the keynote speaker at a testimonial dinner for influential Youngstown congressman Michael J. Kirwan, an event held at the city's Idora Park Ballroom.[93] Kennedy's final visit to Youngstown came in October 1960, when he addressed a huge crowd in the main square of the city's downtown.[94] Apart from his personal decision to attend a friend's funeral in the 1940s, however, Kennedy's awareness of Youngstown probably reflected little more than the city's political and economic importance. Youngstown, after all, was viewed as a crucial northeastern Democratic stronghold until well into the 1970s.[95]

Hundreds of those who gathered in Youngstown's central square in 1960, however, were drawn to Kennedy for reasons that may have seemed personal, given their connection to deeply rooted religious and ethnic identities. Despite the candidate's wealth and glamour, many ethnic whites viewed Kennedy as "one of them"—a descendant of immigrants who belonged to a marginalized religion.[96] Later in the day, thousands of local young people, many of whom were enrolled at Catholic schools, rushed to catch a glimpse of Kennedy as his motorcade moved along Belmont Avenue on the city's north side. Among the "scads of kids" who gathered along the main artery that October afternoon was Father Edward Noga, then a student at a local parish school. Like most of his classmates, Noga took pride in the presidential candidate: a Catholic, a war hero, and a "debonair-looking fellow." Yet, the future priest was also aware of the controversy that swirled around the prospect of a Catholic president. "Some people were ecstatic," Father Noga said. "But there was also that fear among people [who] kind of felt if he won, the pope was going to run America—all that unfounded stereotypical talk. But nevertheless, it was real."[97]

Conservative prelates like Cardinal Spellman shared none of the Catholic laity's enthusiasm for Kennedy's candidacy. Spellman, who supported the Republican candidate, Richard M. Nixon, was concerned about Kennedy's public statements indicating that "if he were elected President there would be strict separation of Church and State on all issues."[98] Indeed, in March 1959, 15 months before the Democratic Convention, Kennedy took preemptive measures to neutralize critics who warned of the dangers of a Catholic president. Kennedy, in an interview with *Look* magazine, said that, "for an office holder, nothing takes precedence over the oath to uphold the Constitution and all its parts—including the First Amendment and the strict separation of church and state." At one point, the youthful senator "bluntly" dismissed the option of public aid for parochial schools, terming it "unconstitutional under the First Amendment as interpreted by the Supreme Court." He added that "fringe matters" such as transportation and lunches were "primarily social and economic concerns and not religious." "With this one bold statement," Walch observed, "Kennedy dashed the hopes of millions of Catholics who had prayed that one of their own would champion public aid for parochial schools."[99]

Kennedy's unyielding position on church-state issues could be seen as a product of political expedience, given that the issue of religion loomed large in the 1960 presidential campaign. The religiously motivated "distrust" Kennedy confronted "spanned the cultural spectrum," ranging from "a crude prejudice against 'micks,' pressed by hooded 'patriots' who burned crosses in the night, to highly literate, liberal concerns, voiced by some of the most respected seminary professors in the nation, about the hegemonic designs of a religious institution that had held, for many centuries, that 'error has no rights.'" Yet, it seemed "ironic" that Kennedy's religion had become an issue at all, given that he had "never been accused of being overly pious at any point in his life."[100] Discerning Protestant critics of the "Catholic candidate" rejected the idea that Kennedy was "constitutionally suspect," and several of them voiced "reservations on opposite grounds." As Hennesy observed, "Presbyterian scholar Robert McAfee Brown thought the *Look* article revealed 'a rather irregular Christian,' and Lutheran Martin Marty feared Kennedy was 'spiritually rootless and almost disturbingly secular.'"[101] James Pike, the Episcopal bishop of California, made a similar observation in a book published several months after the *Look* interview. Bishop Pike described Kennedy as "a thorough-going secularist, who truly believes that a man's religion and his decision-making can be kept in watertight compartments."[102]

Meanwhile, Kennedy's detractors in the Catholic community were hardly limited to Cardinal Spellman, whose views reflected those of many other American prelates. Some bishops regarded the senator as "soft" on Communism, and future conservative political leader James Buckley argued, in an "open letter" to U.S. Catholics, that Kennedy had "chosen to identify himself with that segment of American society which is either unwilling or unable to regard Communism as more than a childish bugaboo." Kennedy's public comments on church-state issues raised eyebrows even in Rome, where influential observers resented the candidate's vow that "he would never appoint an American ambassador to the Vatican." On the heels of one of Kennedy's speeches on church-state relations, an editorial in the Vatican's official newspaper, *L'Osservatore Romano,* asserted that the church was obliged "to tell Catholics how to vote." Shortly after the editorial's publication, Kennedy snapped to a confidant, "Now I understand why Henry VIII set up his own church." In the course of his campaign, the candidate distanced himself from the church and vigorously attacked every attempt to portray him as "a Catholic candidate for president."[103]

Most U.S. Catholic voters were unaware of John Kennedy's contentious relationship with the Catholic hierarchy, and some anticipated a chief executive who would share their particularistic concerns. After Kennedy's inauguration in January 1961, the new president disappointed these coreligionists when he resisted all efforts to reopen the debate on public assistance for parochial schools: a response that underlined the fundamental sincerity of his public statements on the issue. "In retrospect it is not surprising that Kennedy would hold a position so at odds with the Catholic community," wrote Walch. "The president was a millionaire's son who had gone to private preparatory schools and then on to Harvard. He had never attended parochial or Catholic schools and had only a few friends who were Catholic."[104] Notably, even Murray—whose writings on church-state issues helped ease public concerns about a Catholic president—strongly advocated public tax support for parochial schools. Murray, in his famed treatise *We Hold These Truths,* argued that the resolution of "the School Question reached in the nineteenth century reveals injustice, and the legal statutes that establish the injustice are an abuse of power."[105]

If Kennedy's position on "the School Question" troubled some of his coreligionists, it also emboldened the rising number of Catholics who regarded religious schools as divisive (and increasingly expensive) relics of the past. Most Catholic critics of parochial schools conceded that such institutions might have been necessary in the past, when public school textbooks often reflected an anti-Catholic bias. Indeed, public schools in earlier decades often promoted Protestant religious values. Historian Joseph Moreau observed that, as late as the 1870s, a U.S. history textbook "classed Catholics as papists and lamented the lack of 'pure' religion before the Reformation."[106] Anti-Catholic sentiment reached another high point in the 1920s, when a resurgent Ku Klux Klan promoted public schools as "agents for Americanization," while arguing that Catholicism was "actually and actively alien, un-American and usually anti-American."[107] By the early 1960s, however, most Catholics believed that anti-Catholicism had ceased to be a potent force in American society. "The Roman Catholic Church . . . is certainly not under siege from Protestantism," asserted Mary Perkins Ryan, in a book published four years after Kennedy's election to the presidency. "We no longer need to learn Catholic teaching 'against' Protestantism."[108] As Thomas C. Hunt and Timothy Walch observed, "The justification for maintaining a separate, very costly school system seemed less compelling."[109]

Despite Kennedy's indifference to "Catholic" issues, his presidency benefited many of the nation's Catholics. The election of a Roman Catholic as president "lessened the psychological defensiveness that had historically marked the Catholic American."[110] Kennedy's landmark speech to Baptist ministers in Houston blunted the edge of traditional allegations that Catholics were "hostile to freedom."[111] No less important was Kennedy's endorsement of civic-minded voluntarism, enshrined in his inaugural address, which pointed to new outlets for the idealism of younger Catholics. Although large numbers of American Catholics continued to enter the religious life, "a growing number . . . became secular American missionaries in the Peace Corps and later in VISTA and similar programs."[112] Significantly, the timing of Kennedy's election coincided with the first rumblings of reform in Rome, which enabled Catholics to "claim the best of both worlds." As Wills put it, "Balancing the secular respectability of Kennedy in office, there was the added joy, for Catholics, of a very religious man on the chair of Peter, restoring an air of saintly love to an office that had looked too harsh—authoritarian, doctrinally imperialist—under Pius XII."[113] Steinfels observed that, during the early 1960s, "all the residual stress points between Catholicism and America's public ethos seemed to collapse."[114] Kennedy's truncated presidency, in particular, became a powerful symbol of this development, in large part because it coincided with the deterioration of the old U.S. Catholic subculture.[115] Morris contended that "Kennedy's election—the moment that was hailed as the Church's greatest triumph—was an unmistakable signal that the old separatist, ethnic wellsprings of Catholic power were finally running dry."[116] As Catholics moved "into the mainstream of the culture," many assumed a "dramatically new identity," one that helped "unleash a traumatic identity crisis for American Catholics by the end of the twentieth century."[117]

FIRST SUNDAY OF ADVENT 1964

For many U.S. Catholics, the most obvious symbol of change in the postconciliar era was the vernacular mass, introduced in churches across the country on the first Sunday of Advent in 1964. While the impact of the liturgical changes is often downplayed, the new liturgy "helped to shape new cultural nuances of 'being Catholic' in America." Along with the social encyclicals of Pope John, the introduction of the "new Mass" contributed to a situation in which "American Catholics could now be labeled as 'liberal' or 'conservative' . . . based on (among other things) their reception of the mandated liturgical changes."[118] Thomas Day made this point in his controversial meditation on Catholic culture, *Where Have You Gone, Michelangelo?* "Meteorologists should investigate a very bizarre phenomenon," Day wrote. "During a polite, ordinary conversation among a group of Catholics, someone casually slips in two words, 'Latin Mass.' Suddenly, there is a chill in the room." If older Catholics were to describe "the inexpressible beauties" of a Latin mass they recalled from their past, Day added, "that drift of the conversation will be quickly halted by someone who, with cold reasoning, denounces the utter wickedness of worship in Latin."[119]

The controversy that surrounded liturgical reform should not have surprised anyone. As Wills noted, the liturgy "was the one point where religion touched most Catholics, where they communicated not only with God but with their fellow believers and their own past."[120] While the Vatican Instruction of September 26, 1964, outlined a "gradualist timetable" for what it called the "restoration" of the mass, "the nature of the changes mandated held the seeds for both a liturgical and ecclesial revolution." The instruction granted wide latitude to individual celebrants on the details of the mass—a flexibility that paved the way for innovation and experimentation.[121] By the early 1970s, the mass "had become unrecognizable to many—a thing of guitars instead of the organ, of English instead of Latin, of youth-culture fads instead of ancient rites."[122] The experimental nature of liturgical reform at the parish level often obscured the fact that the internal debate over the Latin mass was centuries old. Catholic scholars had discussed the possibility of a vernacular mass well before the Reformation; and in the sixteenth century, the Council of Trent's edict on the liturgy merely stated that the mass could "rightly and properly continue to be celebrated in Latin"—a far cry from condemning all usages of the vernacular.[123]

In Youngstown, as elsewhere, the liturgical changes were carefully explained and aroused little initial resistance. On October 23, 1964, Bishop Emmett M. Walsh announced that English-language services would be held in diocesan churches on Sunday, November 29. Bishop Walsh summarized "a series of eight sermons on liturgical reform to be preached each Sunday preceding the change." The bishop also noted that classes had been scheduled for the 1,700 lay commentators of the diocese who were to "lead the responses of the congregation"—a move that heralded a new level of lay participation.[124] Father Edward Noga, a junior high school student at the time, recalled that his co-parishioners were "curious" about the "new" mass. "They were surprised," he said. "There were some things that made their jaws drop a bit, their eyes open." Noga himself was largely unfazed by the changes, however. "When I first starting serving Mass [as an altar boy], everything was in Latin," he said. "And I loved it. I was in the choir. I sang a lot of songs in Latin. I can still hum and sing many of them." He did not recall being unsettled by the introduction of a "transitional card" that featured translations of four Latin hymns into English, and he indicated that he was equally receptive to the vernacular mass introduced some time later. "I didn't ever look upon it as some kind of liberal-conservative, pre-Vatican II-post-Vatican II issue," he said. "It was just like: 'I'm an American. We speak English. Our prayers now are in English, and we're going to sing in English.'"[125]

The liturgical changes, of course, involved more than the translation of prayers and songs from Latin into the vernacular. The reforms also played a critical role in expanding the Catholic laity's understanding of the Bible. After November 29, 1964, U.S. Catholics were exposed to readings presented in English rather than in Latin, a reform that highlighted "the biblically based nature of the worship." Furthermore, assigned readings became "the basis for the homily preached by the celebrant, thus sponsoring a more scriptural (as opposed to doctrinal, 'disciplinary,' or financial) weekly application of the Tradition to the lives of the faithful."[126] Kathleen Zimmerman, an administrator at a Catholic social service agency in Youngstown, recalled her openness to this aspect of the "new" mass. A native of Renton, Pennsylvania, a coal-mining town about 85 miles east of Youngstown, Mrs. Zimmerman described her impressions of a newly assigned pastor who "started to truly teach." "It was just so stimulating to me, to be listening to theology coming from homilies," she said. She could not help but notice, however, that most parishioners did not seem to share her enthusiasm for the pastor's homilies. "Coal-mining people in the pews didn't like him," she recalled. "And they really didn't want to know more." During sermons, older parishioners "were saying their Rosary, or else reading out of their . . . missalettes." Mrs. Zimmerman, on the other hand, welcomed these biblically grounded homilies as a refreshing alternative to the brief, moralizing sermons she recalled from her early childhood. "The old church was labeled as 'pray, pay, and obey,'" Mrs. Zimmerman said. "And I think . . . they're still people who feel more comfortable in a 'pay, pray, and obey' environment. It's easier."[127]

While the introduction of the English-language mass appeared uneventful, Catholics were deeply divided in their responses to liturgical reform. As Massa noted, a large percentage of Catholics "welcomed the 'reformed' liturgy introduced at the end of 1964 like water in an arid desert," while others "used 'betrayal' language to describe their new worship—betrayal language often of a particularly fierce kind."[128] Among those parishioners who found themselves alienated by the reforms was Jack O'Connell, a Youngstown-area labor leader, who argued that the Tridentine (Latin) mass "had a mystique to it that was taken away by Vatican II." O'Connell was shocked by the elimination of Latin, and he disliked the fact that the congregation was forced to rely on hymnals. "All the old songs disappeared: 'Pange Lingua,' and all the rest of the old ones," O'Connell said. "In fact, after Vatican II, we started to learn [from] a whole new hymn book. And to tell you the truth, I resented it." O'Connell's dissatisfaction with the postconciliar liturgical changes remained evident four decades later. "I will not . . . pick up the hymnal book," he insisted. "I won't pick up that book. I grew up knowing, memorizing every song that was done in the Catholic Church, and it isn't the same today."[129]

O'Connell's concerns were shared by a small, often vocal, minority of his coreligionists who also preferred the Latin mass. Paula McKinney, a longtime parishioner at St. Columba's Cathedral, argued that, in the wake of reform, the liturgy had "lost its sparkle." Although Mrs. McKinney indicated that she welcomed Pope John's call to "update" the church, she nevertheless regretted that church leaders "threw out all of the lovely devotions." The Latin mass, she said, was more "dignified" than its reformed counterpart. "And we did know what we were saying," Mrs. McKinney added. "I mean the prayer book was in two sections—Latin on one side and English on the other."[130] Other local parishioners mourned the loss of something less tangible: a liturgical space that offered refuge from the pressures of everyday life. Elizabeth Fekety, who did not criticize the vernacular mass, still looked back with nostalgia on the liturgical atmosphere of the preconciliar era. "You weren't allowed to talk in church," Mrs. Fekety said. "And so, the serenity of [the Mass] was what kind of drew you to it."[131] For communicants "accustomed to the familiar and comforting world of Catholic popular devotions to the Virgin Mary and one's 'household saints' . . . the sudden 'intrusion' of congregational singing appeared foreign, even suspiciously Protestant."[132] Feminist theologian Denise Lardner Carmody, writing about her own mother, indicated that the older woman would probably agree with psychologists that her commitment to devotional Catholicism was "a way to console herself." Carmody added, however, that her mother would also insist that "God's therapy . . . was much cheaper and more highly recommended" than the services of a psychologist.[133] As Dolan observed, the liturgical changes "had touched the very soul of Catholic devotional life, and many people openly rebelled."[134]

The introduction of the vernacular liturgy was one of several potentially off-putting changes that awaited traditionalists on the first Sunday of Advent in 1964. A detail that caught parishioners' attention "on just entering the church building" was the repositioning of the altar. The high altar "which formed the locus of attention of all present for the celebration was now to be 'pulled away' from the wall, so that the priest would face the congregation rather than stand with his back to the people—a simple logistical move that, while restoring liturgical practice of the twentieth century to the tradition of the early church, overturned the style of worship that had obtained for over a thousand years." The new arrangement presented a "theological conundrum" to some parishioners. "Who, many Catholics would soon ask, was being 'addressed' in the rite?" Massa wrote. "And on 'whose side' was the priest: representing the congregation before God, or standing in *persona Christi* (and thus on the 'side' of God) before the gathered people?"[135]

Meanwhile, the renovation of church interiors offended some Catholics for reasons that had little to do with theology. Ornate, well-kept church buildings were a source of pride for many parishioners, who gave generously to maintain parish physical plants. These quaint interiors were not valued by everyone, of course. Wills, writing in 1971, observed that, upon entering a preconciliar church, "one might think history was a rummage sale, and this place had been fitted out after a visit to the sale."[136] James Carroll, as a young campus priest in the 1960s, felt a need to drastically remodel the student chapel at Boston University, with its "grim Stations of the Cross, dull smoked-glass windows . . . and formal altar raised on a small pyramid of stairs."[137] Even Thomas Day, an occasional critic of the postconciliar renovations, acknowledged that some churches erected before World War II were "half-baked imitations" of European monuments.[138] Traditionalists, however, were "poorly prepared" for changes such as the streamlining of elaborately furnished church interiors; and they watched in dismay as high altars were dismantled, communion rails were removed, and statuary and paintings disappeared.[139]

In Youngstown, the renovation of church interiors was carried out on a sweeping scale after Vatican II. In spring 1969, the already uncluttered interior of Youngstown's rebuilt cathedral was further simplified when Bishop James W. Malone ordered "removal of the heavy marble altar, bronze reredos screen and baldachino." Monsignor Glenn Holdbrook, the cathedral rector, said it was "doubtful that the marble altar can be removed without destroying it," and the *Vindicator* reported that there were "no plans to salvage or retain these art treasures."[140] Some local Catholics complained that such renovation projects were destructive and also showed a lack of respect for older parishioners. "If you remember the remodeling of the churches, we had to throw out all the gold," O'Connell stated. "These were brought in as monuments and remembrances of people, and we threw them out and replaced them with wood."[141] Burdened by similar feelings of loss, Paula McKinney looked back on the fire that destroyed "old" St. Columba's Cathedral a full decade before the liturgical reforms. She suggested that the neo-Gothic building's destruction was "for the best." "It would have been painful to see them strip down the interior in the wake of Vatican II," McKinney said. "It would have been like seeing Ethel Barrymore in toreador pants."[142]

Despite the myriad controversies generated by liturgical reform, a substantial number of Catholics treated the elimination of the Latin mass as evidence of the church's newfound openness and flexibility. McGreevy observed that the preconciliar church prided itself on "its ability to unify various cultures across the globe into one set of liturgical rituals and practices." Likewise, the U.S. hierarchy's intolerance for "immigrant practices," along with its insistence that black parishes adopt "a rigidly Romanist style," reflected a "pervasive confidence in 'integration' broadly conceived." Vatican II's "openness to a variety of liturgical forms," on the other hand, conveyed the bishops' desire "to create a pluralistic institution, one more deeply rooted in local cultures."[143] Notably, the liturgical changes created new opportunities in the African American community, where even those who had converted to Catholicism often expressed "great difficulty with some of its rituals and use of Latin." One Cleveland-area black Catholic admitted that she did not feel "part of her religion" until the implementation of the postconciliar liturgical changes.[144] In a similar vein, a Chicago-based Catholic interracialist praised the reforms and characterized "traditional pietistic practices" as "odd and rather occult."[145]

Nevertheless, the potential benefits of liturgical reform were lost on most traditionalists, who experienced the disappearance of the Tridentine mass as a personal tragedy. "The laymen, coming home, found it a strange house, cluttered with signs of an alien occupancy," Wills noted, writing seven years after the council. "He was asked to do things against which elaborate inhibitions had been built up all his life—touch the communion wafer, *chew* it, receive it standing instead of kneeling, even drink from the chalice."[146] Such changes troubled conservatives, who struggled to retain a meaningful connection to the values and practices of their religious upbringing. "The only thing I . . . have left of the heritage that I grew up with in the Catholic Church [is] going to Communion," said Jack O'Connell. "And to this day, if the priest is there, I'll take Communion by mouth [rather than by hand]. It's the only thing that I have left of the Catholic Church that I grew up with."[147] Amid the protests of those traditionalists who objected to the changes, Pope Paul VI made the reformed vernacular liturgy official in 1969.

As church officials discovered, however, resistance to the liturgical changes was not limited to traditionalists among the laity. On the international stage, schismatics like French archbishop Marcel Lefebvre, contended that the Latin mass was "the fullest if not the only expression of Catholic faith"—a view shared by a small number of American Catholics.[148] In the Diocese of Youngstown, the most serious case of clerical resistance to liturgical reform emerged in Vienna Township, a semirural community about 20 miles north of Youngstown. Through much of the 1970s, Bishop James Malone engaged in a battle of wills with Father John F. Roach, the traditionalist pastor of St. Vincent de Paul Church. Father Roach, over the complaints of liberal parishioners and diocesan officials, "continued to say the old Latin Mass, which he termed 'The Liturgy,' as opposed to the 'new Mass.'" After years of conflict, Father Roach appeared to capitulate to diocesan pressure, and he reluctantly agreed to retire. When a new pastor arrived at St. Vincent de Paul Church, however, he was shocked to discover that the altar, statuary, and Stations of the Cross had all been removed.[149] Within days, a group of former parishioners announced their plan to build a new church that would host Latin masses celebrated by the "retired" Father Roach. Bishop Malone, who acknowledged he could not prevent the group from building the church, warned them against identifying with the diocese.[150]

In the early 1990s, a relatively mild controversy involving liturgy surfaced in neighboring Girard, Ohio, where supporters of the Tridentine mass had established an "independent" parish. In February 1991, Our Lady of Sorrows Parish hosted a confirmation ceremony officiated by Bishop Tissier de Mallerais, a schismatic French churchman. "It's the American Catholic Church," one parishioner said. "It's not the Roman Catholic Church—the Diocese of Youngstown. . . . They've left the church. We haven't left the church."[151] This stubborn resistance to the vernacular mass mystified erstwhile liturgical reformers, who expected all Catholics to welcome a liturgy that addressed them in their own language. As Morris noted, "Theologians blithely assumed that if people didn't *understand* the Latin liturgies, they couldn't be attached to them, missing the ritualistic significance that the liturgies had acquired."[152]

Pope Paul VI's 1968 decision to "replace" the Tridentine mass was rooted in his conviction that "two forms of the Roman or Latin rite within the one church would bring disunity." Indeed, the church's emphasis on liturgical conformity grew stronger in subsequent decades. Since the 1978 papal election of Karol Wojtyla, the Vatican has taken bold measures to reimpose "theological order and central control." Consequently, Pope John Paul II's decision, in 1984, to permit the Latin mass "to be more widely celebrated" precipitated an outcry among international bishops, who feared a rollback of the council's liturgical reforms. The papacy's conservative position on the liturgy came into play, once again, in 2003, when the Vatican shelved a 1998 missal that had been prepared over a 13-year period by the International Commission on English in the Liturgy (ICEL), established in the late 1960s to oversee the English translation of the reformed liturgy. Critics of the Vatican's decision to suppress the ICEL's missal praised its gender-inclusive language as well as its fluid, elevated prose, which avoided the colloquialisms of the widely criticized 1973 missal.[153] This conservative trend gained momentum in 2007, when Pope Benedict XVI approved wider use of the Latin mass, a move followed up by his 2009 decision to revoke the excommunication of four schismatic bishops, including one who denied the Holocaust. While the Vatican presented the latter move as a step toward "reconciliation," liberal critics contended that Pope Benedict's "decision to welcome the Lefebvrists showed that he was more willing to embrace schismatic conservatives than wayward leftists."[154] It remains unclear whether conservatives intend a complete restoration of the Tridentine mass, but there is little doubt that opponents of the liturgical reforms of Vatican II have taken heart from the policies of Pope John Paul II and his successor.

Overall, the debate concerning the postconciliar liturgical reforms crystallized the conflict between liberal and conservative Catholics. In the mid-1960s, a majority of American Catholics embraced the reformed liturgy as a more authentic form of worship than the Latin mass, and most of them still

do. As Steinfels noted, even "highly vocal critics of the liturgical reform seldom deny its popularity."[155] While liberal Catholics welcomed the fact that
the new liturgy reflected "a degree of diversity and adaptability unknown in
the recent past," traditionalists mourned the loss of a heritage and clung to
vestiges of the preconciliar church.[156] If liberals reveled in the church's new
openness to mainstream culture, conservatives were more likely to lament
the erosion of a well-defined religious identity that distinguished them from
other Americans. Whatever the outcome of the ongoing debate over liturgy,
there is little doubt that American Catholicism was irrevocably altered by
the reforms that came in the wake of Vatican II.[157] Writing in the late 1990s,
Massa referred to a scene from Charles Dickens's *Great Expectations* to
describe the momentous impact of liturgical reform: "Like the opening of the
windows to let the streaming sunlight into Miss Haversham's house, which
instantaneously destroyed the timeless, death-defying world of her jilted
wedding day decades before, all of that former world was now gone."[158]
Naturally, the replicated institutions that were an integral part of that "former
world" experienced transformation in the wake of the conciliar reforms.

POSTCONCILIAR REEVALUATIONS OF CATHOLIC SCHOOLING

Despite its wealth of scholarly output, the council produced no groundbreaking documents that dealt specifically with education. Buetow noted that the
council's "relatively weak and traditional" *Declaration on Christian Education* essentially reaffirmed "the special status of the Catholic school" and
emphasized parents' "duty to entrust their children to Catholic schools."[159]
While the declaration did not directly endorse the (mainly American) fight
for public aid to parochial schools, it nevertheless affirmed the principle of
subsidiarity "as a guiding policy in education." This principle, formulated in
Pope Pius XI's encyclical letter, *Quadragesimo Anno* (translated as "In the
Fortieth Year," a reference to the fact that it was issued 40 years after *Rerum
Novarum*), was defined by the council as follows: "Just as it is wrong to
withdraw from the individual and commit to the community at large what
private enterprise and endeavor can accomplish, so it is likewise unjust and a
gravely harmful disturbance of right order to turn over to a greater society of
higher rank functions and services which can be performed by lesser bodies
on a lower plane." In the context of education, the principle of subsidiarity
suggested that governmental bodies should "aid private schools so that they
do not have to price themselves out of existence"—a situation that would
produce "an undesirable 'school monopoly' . . . where there would be only

public schools." As Gabert noted, however, the principle of subsidiarity led to a rather flawed, even "dangerous," argument in support of state aid to private religious schools. "The pivotal question rests with the word 'can,'" he wrote. "If the family 'can,' the state should not. If the state 'can,' the federal government should not." Gabert questions whether the financial difficulties facing U.S. parochial schools reflected the Catholic community's inability to "foster an independent school system." "If Catholics 'can' but simply 'will' not pay the costs of a separate school system," he continued, "then the *Declaration on Christian Education* itself, drawing on a long series of traditional writings, condemns plans for state aid."[160]

The relative conservatism of the *Declaration on Christian Education* was overshadowed by the general impact of the council, however. As Walch noted, the drastic reforms "in doctrine and liturgy mandated by Vatican II seemed to transform Catholicism into a new religion."[161] Moreover, the council's central document, *Guadium et Spes* ("The Church in the Modern World"), "evidenced a positive concern for the whole world" that encouraged Catholic educators to broaden their mission. On the one hand, *Guadium et Spes* asserted that any assistance the church "offers to society is based on her religious role, in this role transcending the political, economic, and social orders." On the other, it stressed that every Catholic should live up to "his temporal duties . . . toward his neighbor." It was, therefore, the council's enveloping theme, rather than its specific educational recommendations, that inspired Catholic educators to reconsider the mission of religious schools. Buetow noted that among the "tangible results of Vatican II as applied to the United States Catholic education" was the 1968 revision of the National Catholic Education Association (NCEA) constitution. The altered constitution placed the organization "at the service of *society* through Catholic education, rather than only at the service of Catholic schools." This subtle shift in focus was important, because it inspired the NCEA to expand its goals "to promote Christian ideals, encourage educational cooperation, and contribute to the national educational effort."[162]

Significantly, the influence of Vatican II contributed to the rise of nontraditional urban parish schools that served the needs of the underprivileged. In 1972, the National Conference of Catholic Bishops issued a directive called *To Teach as Jesus Did,* which "fleshed out the council's themes of active, publicly engaged schools." The directive outlined "a threefold educational ministry: to teach the message of hope contained in the gospel; to build community 'not simply as a concept to be taught, but as a reality to be lived'; and 'service to all mankind which flows from a sense of Christian community.'" In the wake of the directive, U.S. Catholic leaders took steps to prevent their urban schools from becoming "havens" of racial segregation in "changing" neighborhoods. Amid sweeping demographic change, many U.S. dioceses "moved firmly and aggressively, in many cases against its own members, in resisting a tide of racially motivated enrollments." In addition, parish schools in changing neighborhoods resisted pressure to relocate, despite the migration of traditional clients to the suburbs. Anthony S. Bryk and his coauthors noted that, if Catholic educators had obeyed "economic logic," they would have closed "all fast-emptying inner-city institutions" and shifted their resources to suburban schools, "but often this course was not followed."[163]

Such decisions were made by diocesan officials in cities like Youngstown beginning in the late 1960s and early 1970s. In 1973, the Diocese of Youngstown publicly affirmed its commitment to urban parish schools, especially those that served large numbers of minority students. To illustrate this commitment, the diocese established a committee to recommend policies for schools based in "poverty areas."[164] Alert to the possibility that Catholic schools could become "havens" for whites seeking to avoid integrated urban public schools, the diocese initiated guidelines in 1974 to prevent this development. The diocese observed that, when a student attempted to transfer from a local public school "to the Catholic school of the attendance area in which their parents reside," the following provisions would need to be met: (1) parents would be required to complete an application for admission; (2) the principal of the "receiving" Catholic school would be required to confer with the principal of the "sending" public school to discuss "his or her knowledge of the transfer"; and (3) a conference regarding the reason for the transfer would need to be held among the parents, the pastor, and the principal of the "receiving" Catholic school. Moreover, the diocesan school board's policy on registration and transfer of students was amended to include the following statement: "It is of utmost importance that principals and pastors of diocesan schools must refuse admission to anyone who is, in their opinion, attempting to circumvent the laws or court orders affecting the integration of public schools."[165] Given the difficulty of discerning parents' motivations for transferring their children from one school to another, however, it is questionable whether these policies did much to prevent urban parish schools from serving as havens. Meanwhile, the efficacy of such policies may have been undermined by the fact that many urban parish schools were struggling with the effects of declining enrollment—a situation that limited their capacity to turn away prospective students.

That said, a policy of fostering support for nontraditional urban parish schools (those serving primarily nonwhite and non-Catholic students) continued for decades. In the late 1960s, Immaculate Conception Elementary School, located on the city's east side, was among the first of Youngstown's parish schools to accept large numbers of nonwhite, non-Catholic students.

By 1976, about 44 percent of Immaculate Conception's 327 students were non-Catholics, and many of these were members of minority groups.[166] Likewise, St. Patrick's Elementary School, located on the south side of Youngstown, served an increasingly diverse student population. By the early 1970s, diocesan leaders cited St. Patrick's as one of two urban parish schools based in Youngstown that enrolled large numbers of nonwhite, non-Catholic students.[167] In 1976, after a heated debate, the diocesan school board rejected a proposed diocesan-wide tax to assist struggling urban parish schools like Immaculate Conception. Some board members apparently rejected the proposed tax because the beneficiaries were schools that served primarily nonwhite and non-Catholic students. This position was articulated by Raymond Pelanda, chair of the diocesan finance committee. "If there were no public schools in Youngstown, I would think differently," Pelanda said. "The poor and minorities can get an education in the public schools. We are backed up to the wall."[168] However, several months later, in January 1977, the board succumbed to pressure from local clerical leaders to secure alternative funding that would help to keep these schools operational. Among others, the board drew resources from the home mission fund of the Youngstown Society for the Propagation of the Faith, which was designed to support evangelical ventures.[169] As late as the early 1990s, two of Youngstown's eight remaining parish schools served a majority of black students.[170]

While the U.S. church's stated commitment to maintain a presence in urban neighborhoods drew plaudits from liberal Catholics, this period in the history of American Catholic education was characterized by setbacks and disappointments. Indeed, many Catholic observers have traced the decline of parish schools to the tumultuous period following Vatican II.[171] Amid deepening internal conflict, U.S. Catholics began to question the efficacy of institutions that were once considered beyond reproach, especially parish schools. The first salvo in the battle over the relevance of Catholic education was fired in 1964 by Mary Perkins Ryan, who wrote, "the parochial school system does not and cannot answer present needs."[172] Ryan, a layperson with no previous experience as a researcher, criticized an unwieldy "alternative" school system that could be sustained only through an enormous outlay of resources. Drawing on figures taken from the *Official Catholic Directory*, Ryan noted that, in 1963, "an estimated 4,524,393 children would be attending 10,322 parochial elementary schools and institutional schools and an additional 84,636 would be in private Catholic elementary schools under a total of 111,091 teachers." She added that another 623,897 "would be attending 1,537 diocesan and parochial high schools," while "an additional 381,048 would be attending 895 private Catholic schools, all these staffed by 46,625 teachers." Ryan concluded that, despite the enormous expenditures needed to support

Catholic education (almost $1 million in 1958 alone to maintain, operate, and refurbish U.S. parochial schools), religious schools were not used by a significant percentage of American Catholics. Only 55 percent of Catholics patronized religious elementary schools, she noted, and this percentage would likely decrease as the cost of maintaining these schools became untenable.[173]

Inspired by liberal theologians who reinterpreted church history to justify institutional reform, Ryan also argued that the church had persisted for centuries without relying on a system of separate schools. Her book had an immediate—and profound—impact on U.S. Catholic opinion. "Ryan was not a sociologist or educator and her book at times seemed shrill and wrongheaded," Walch wrote. "Yet like the child questioning the emperor's new clothes, Ryan caused something of a panic."[174] An adherent to the preconciliar Liturgical Renewal movement that promoted congregational participation, Ryan "argued that Christians should be formed by the liturgy, not by classroom teaching." By the early 1970s, she had abandoned this position, dismissing it as "astoundingly naïve."[175] Her dramatic reversal on the issue made little impact, however. In the face of influential research suggesting that urban Catholic schools were especially beneficial to the underprivileged, these institutions continued to decline.

In 1985, Greeley described the postconciliar condition of Catholic schools as "paradoxical." "On the one hand, the evidence is overwhelming that the schools are remarkably successful both religiously and academically," Greeley wrote. "On the other hand, enrollment in the schools is dwindling and Catholic leadership does not appear to be committed to Catholic schools as it was before the Vatican Council."[176] Greeley appeared uncertain about the connection between the conciliar reforms and flagging support for Catholic schools. In his 1985 report, *American Catholics Since the Council*, he noted that many U.S. Catholic leaders cited the conciliar document *Guadium et Spes* when they sought to justify the nontraditional mission of certain urban parish schools. He added that the U.S. church, while publicly affirming its "obligations to the poor," had "phased out as quickly as it could much of the most effective service it has ever done for the inner-city poor in the Catholic schools."[177] Naturally, this trend raises questions about the depth of U.S. Catholic leaders' commitment to the preservation of urban parish schools, despite the prevalence of public statements affirming the church's responsibility to maintain a presence in the cities.

Not all observers agree with Greeley that a failure of leadership at diocesan and parish levels was a primary factor in the decline of parish schools. Some point to other developments, especially the exodus of religious teaching orders from parochial school classrooms after Vatican II. Former *New York Times* religion editor Kenneth Briggs, in his journalistic account of the decline of women's religious orders in the U.S. church, argued that the virtual disappearance of the teaching nun was an unintended consequence of conciliar reforms. "The resolve with which sisters proclaimed and practiced their imperative in the years following the Council fueled their incentive to fulfill the highest aims of Gaudium et Spes for justice and service to the world," Briggs wrote. Many religious communities, he continues, turned "their energies away from certain kinds of activities such as teaching in Catholic schools in favor of projects to combat racism, feed the hungry, and find shelter for the homeless."[178] Briggs added that the council's emphasis on civic engagement coincided with a decisive shift away from a traditional hierarchal model of the church that once minimized the role of the laity. This model was displaced by a more inclusive vision of the church as "the people of God," which diminished the "special" status previously accorded clergy and religious. Thus, Vatican II "flattened the playing field regarding vocations, lowering the status of a nun or upgrading the vocation of marriage, depending on one's perspective."[179] (The author did not take into account that many former nuns pursued alternatives to religious life that did not involve marriage.) In Briggs's view, this alteration in status, along with other controversies of the postconciliar era, facilitated the sharp decline in religious vocations that began in the late 1960s. Consequently, religious orders, who were already starting to focus on service-oriented activities outside of the classroom, found themselves dealing with a drastic reduction in membership. Between 1966 and 1976, the number of women living and working in religious communities fell from 181,421 to 130,995.[180] This trend profoundly affected urban parochial schools, especially as it gained momentum over time. James Youniss noted that, between 1965 and 1995, the number of religious teachers in the nation's Catholic schools fell from 114,000 to 15,600.[181] A 2004 study of urban parochial elementary schools revealed that only 8 percent of their staff members were connected to religious communities, while 80 percent were laywomen. The report noted that the "figures remain relatively stable across poverty indicators."[182]

In Youngstown, the decline of teaching religious orders was underscored by the final departure of nuns from the classrooms of St. Christine's Elementary School in the late 1980s. Located in a relatively affluent district of the city's west side, the parish school achieved its peak enrollment in 1964, when 18 religious instructors served 1,554 students. By February 1988, however, only two nuns were included on a staff of 25 administrators and teachers, who served 600 students ranging from preschool to eighth grade. That year, Sister Mary Stella Aquilina, principal of St. Christine's, announced that she, along with her coworker, Sister Cecilia Ann West, would leave the school at the end of the academic year. Their departure, she explained, came at the request of their religious order, the Daughters of Charity. As the *Vindicator* noted, events at St. Christine's parish school reflected a larger trend of laicization among the community's parochial elementary schools. In a statement, Sister Nancy Dawson, OSU, then general superior of the Ursuline Sisters of Youngstown, one of the area's largest teaching orders, placed the departure of nuns from local classrooms in the context of recent trends. "Our institutions were built and staffed to respond to the needs of an immigrant church," she said. "Today . . . religious [orders] with fewer, aging members and limited financial resources simply cannot afford to own or staff the institutions. However, we have nurtured and trained competent lay teachers and administrators with Catholic, Christian values, to replace us." In a more pessimistic assessment, Sister Mary Stella described the decline of teaching orders as "another phase in the church that will not be without pain."[183]

For Catholic schools, this "phase" yielded more difficulty than many observers could have predicted. The retreat of thousands of teaching nuns from the classroom not only diluted the religious atmosphere of parish schools; it substantially drove up the cost of maintaining these institutions. Members of religious orders were gradually replaced by lay teachers who required—and soon demanded—greater remuneration. To make matters worse, these economic demands overlapped with a steep decline in church-related donations by U.S. Catholics, which prevented dioceses around the country from offering teachers "adequate salaries and benefits."[184] Few communities were immune to this dilemma, and reports of salary disputes involving lay teachers at parochial schools surfaced in Youngstown as early as the mid-1980s. In February 1985, teachers opted for union representation at eight diocesan parish schools, including four that were based in Youngstown—St. Dominic's (south side), St. Christine's (west side), Holy Name (west side), and St. Patrick's (south side). Diocesan officials responded cautiously to this news. On the one hand, they emphasized that the diocese was "not bound by the National Labor Relations Act" to engage in collective bargaining. On the other, they "affirmed the Catholic Church's support for the right of workers to unionize."[185] The diocese's response offered little comfort to parochial schoolteachers, who had reason to question the church's commitment to offer them a livable wage. Earlier, in December 1984, Superintendent John Augenstein told parish teachers that "they would no longer receive a county-wide salary base, but would need to negotiate with principals and pastors of individual schools." One lay instructor described the policy as a "power play" and complained that it worked to the disadvantage of teachers at poorer parishes. "And if the power play doesn't work," the teacher added, "they pull out their spirituality and make you feel like you are someone with less faith." [186] Naturally, as teacher salaries became less competitive, parish schools had more difficulty securing qualified staff.

In 2000, educational researcher Maryellen Schaub noted that "Catholic school teachers are, on average, less educated and less likely to be certified in either their main or any other teaching field."[187]

The virtual disappearance of teaching nuns also raised questions about the possibility of maintaining a satisfactory religious atmosphere at parish schools. To meet this challenge, diocesan leaders developed policies that would assist them in evaluating the "fitness" of lay teachers to serve in Catholic schools. Unlike the past, when religious orders comprised the bulk of the teaching staff, diocesan officials felt they could no longer assume that teachers held "appropriate" religious views. Therefore, in the 1980s, diocesan officials in Youngstown introduced a policy on the "religious development" of teachers. Superintendent Nicholas Wolsonovich, who stressed the need for such a policy, reaffirmed that the primary purpose of Catholic schools was "to teach the Catholic faith." Given the central importance of religious instruction, Wolsonovich argued, it was essential "that the teachers and administrators have a thorough understanding of the Catholic faith so that they can pass it on to younger people." The superintendent's comments echoed those of Sister Patricia McNicholas, OSU, diocesan director of religious education, who suggested that the new policy was "based on the diocese's belief that a teacher's actions in the classroom have an impact on students' faith."[188] As a later newspaper account revealed, the policy featured a "provision in the contracts of diocesan teachers" that required them "to abide by church law."[189]

Subsequent critics of the diocesan policy complained that it was applied to issues that did not necessarily affect a teacher's ability to serve in a religious educational setting. In January 1988, an emotional controversy erupted over the diocese's dismissal of a longtime elementary school instructor who was accused of violating the policy. Parents and faculty alike were shocked to discover that Kathy Koker Doslovik, a teacher at St. Patrick's Elementary School in nearby Hubbard, Ohio, had lost her job because "she married a Yugoslavian man whose previous marriage ended in divorce." Within days of Doslovik's dismissal, a protest petition was signed by 300 people, "representing 97 percent of all parents who have children enrolled in the school." One parent described Doslovik, a fourth-grade teacher with 13 years of experience, as "a very loving person" who was popular with students. In the face of widening opposition, Wolsonovich defended the dismissal of Doslovik, insisting that Catholic school teachers "are required to abide by the laws of the church, which does not recognize marriages in which one person is divorced."[190]

The controversy stretched on for weeks. Angry parents in Hubbard noted that Doslovik "had sought advice from a diocesan tribunal before getting married" and fully believed that "the diocese understood the unusual circumstances of her situation and would work with her through the annulment process here."[191]

In February 1988, the St. Patrick Home and School Association in Hubbard threatened to picket the offices of the Diocese of Youngstown in the event that Doslovik was "not allowed back in the classroom."[192] Although concerned parents protested outside the diocesan offices for five hours on February 4, 1988, they agreed to suspend their activities on the following day, while attorneys representing Doslovik and the diocese worked out the "final details" of an "agreement."[193] The parents did not remain silent, however. On February 8, 1988, the *Vindicator* published a letter signed by two of the concerned parents that questioned whether "parents of children enrolled at St. Patrick School in Hubbard" were true partners in Catholic education "when we, who are paying for our children to attend this school, are not notified or consulted about the advisability of dismissing one of our teachers." The letter appeared on the same day that Doslovik announced her resignation as an instructor at St. Patrick Elementary School, where she had taught for 10 years. Doslovik indicated to a reporter that she "wanted to explain to her students why she was forced to leave but was nearly at a loss of words." She noted that the details of her agreement with the diocese were expected to remain "confidential."[194] Two days later, on February 10, Doslovik and her husband, Mladen, suggested in an interview that recent events had "strengthened their faith in God but undermined their confidence in the hierarchy of their church."[195]

Significantly, the laicization of the parish school staff coincided with a drastic narrowing of differences between Catholic and public education that displeased some Catholic parents. In 1971, the diocesan school board faced a storm of protests when it announced plans to introduce a sex education program in elementary and secondary schools. Superintendent Monsignor William A. Hughes told the *Vindicator* that the 15-member board had already approved the diocese's "Family Life" education program. He added, however, that board members would "consider the objections." Among those who opposed the program was James O'Connell, a policeman from nearby McDonald, Ohio, who predicted "if this program is introduced, you will not have a Catholic school in McDonald." O'Connell's concerns were shared by several local Catholic physicians who questioned the need for any kind of sex education program. Dr. C. E. Pichette recommended that the diocese "go back to teaching parents to teach children [about] sex as [they] did 15 years ago." Dr. William Moskalik, another opponent, predicted that the program would "not be implemented in Byzantine Catholic schools in Youngstown and Warren."[196]

Similar events unfolded within the borders of Youngstown itself. In March 1972, the Youngstown chapter of Catholics United for the Faith (CUF), a lay organization, took issue with the diocese's "Becoming a Person" program, which sought to integrate sex education and Catholic moral teaching. Attorney Edward Sobnosky, president of the CUF's local chapter, announced that his organization supported Parents for Responsible Education of Youngstown (PREDY), an advocacy group, in its opposition to the program's implementation. Sobnosky indicated that his organization would do everything "it possibly can to help PREDY make area Catholics aware of the serious consequences and effects this program will have on their children and their faith." Sobnosky stated that teacher manuals used in the program contained "articles on sex education written by the Rev. Walter Imbiorski, a priest affiliated with the Sex Information and Education Council of the United States (SIECUS)," a secular organization that promoted the teaching of sex education in schools. The attorney added that several articles for the program's teacher manual were written by "noted dissenters against the teaching of the church on contraception."[197]

The introduction of a diocesan-wide sex education program was one of many developments that blurred the distinction between public and parochial schools in the Youngstown area. Two years earlier, in 1969, guidance counseling programs had been set up at the diocese's 78 schools.[198] By the late 1970s, many diocesan schools benefited from psychologists, who were provided "under the auxiliary services provision of the Ohio Revised Code."[199] Still more surprising was the introduction of innovative curricula such as the Individually Guided Education (IGE) program, which was implemented at several of the city's parish schools in the mid-1970s.[200] Such developments were generally opposed by conservatives, who believed that Catholic schools should focus on the transmission of traditional religious values. For some of them, postconciliar Catholic schools suffered from serious deficiencies, because in their view, they did "not foster the firm commitment to the faith that students in previous generations had."[201]

By the 1980s, many traditionalists had concluded that Catholic schools offered a diluted version of church doctrine, and a vocal minority lobbied for the reinstitution of the widely criticized *Baltimore Catechism.* Debates over classroom "catechetics," more often than not, pitted liberals against conservatives. Walch observed that "progressive educators pushed for a religious education that centered on issues of war and peace, social justice, and the environment," while traditionalists promoted the unembellished transmission of Catholic doctrine. Conservatives and liberals "often talked past each other in promoting specific changes in Catholic school religious education."[202] Such controversies unfolded in dioceses throughout the country. Officials of the Diocese of Youngstown were forced to intervene when "irreconcilable differences" over the "new" catechism resulted in the removal of three teaching nuns from Holy Trinity Elementary School, in nearby Struthers, Ohio. In April 1985, Sister Mary Regis, superior of the Vincentian Sisters of Charity, said she decided to withdraw the nuns after learning that the pastor, a traditionalist, prevented them from teaching the postconciliar catechism. Sister Mary Regis ignored diocesan requests to reconsider the move and carefully outlined her position. "Our concern is the religious foundation for the children," she said. "We are not at liberty to train the children in the religion the way they should be trained; therefore, our presence is divisive rather than cohesive."[203]

As noted, parents were frequently involved in debates over catechetics, and efforts to promote a postconciliar model of religious education elicited strong feedback. At the center of some disputes was theologian Karl Rahner's concept of "theological anthropology," which influenced conciliar documents on cat- echetics. A firm believer in the church's need to engage with the modern world, Rahner encouraged an approach to religious education that was grounded in social realities. As early as the 1960s, parents accustomed to "a traditional presentation" began to criticize many of the religious textbooks used in parish schools. Buetow, writing in 1970, observed that such "complaints had similar patterns: pictures of the Rev. Martin Luther King, modern art illustrations, 'political' issues included in the text, the recommendation of folk songs by Pete Seeger, and a de-emphasis of the question-and-answer approach."[204] Changes in religious instruction came under heightened criticism in 1981, when a National Opinion Research Center survey revealed that Catholic schools, while they reinforced some traditional Catholic practices, "had no effect on student attitudes toward prayer and sexual morality." Vocal conservatives called for "a return to old-fashioned moral education." Catholic educators, in response, argued that only the "method" of moral instruction had changed; the "content" remained the same. They asked traditionalists "to concentrate on substance, not on form." Meanwhile, amid rising concerns over "religious illiteracy" among parochial school students, William D. Kelly, executive director of the NCEA's religious education department, launched a 12-year plan that encouraged "more testing of students' knowledge of religious content" as well as "the direct involvement of parents in the catechetical process."[205]

The protracted debate over curricular changes in Catholic schools left many traditionalists disillusioned, and some even questioned the long-term relevance of parochial schools. One conservative Catholic, a product of par- ish and diocesan schools, outlined his reasons for transferring his own chil- dren to public schools. Post–Vatican II religious education programs, in his opinion, failed to provide parochial school students with an adequate moral compass. "Although conscience plays a role in your daily life, the rules when I was growing up were bigger," said T. Gordon Welsh, a parishioner at St. Patrick's Church. "So, you weren't permitted to make decisions about behav- ior. It was too clear." For traditionalists like Welsh, the unraveling of this sort of moral conditioning, which often occurred in parochial school classrooms, can be traced to the council. "In my world, [Catholic education] was the strictest, most rigid approach to education," he said. "When it stopped, so did parochial school education. John XXIII . . . a loving man, screwed it up." Welsh recalled that, in the late 1960s, he was pressured to transfer his eldest son to a public school when the boy complained to his mother about the strict discipline maintained at the neighborhood parish school. When he ignored his wife's request to transfer their son to another school, she contacted the parish pastor and asked him to intervene. "[The pastor] said to me on the phone, 'Hey, let your kid come out of the school,'" recalled Welsh. "John XXIII . . . Vatican II . . . Imagine [former St. Patrick's Church pastor] Father [Maurice] Casey saying that? Father Casey would say, 'Knock his block off.'"[206]

Overall, there is strong evidence that parish schools—especially those in urban areas—experienced sharp decline during a period that many liberals described as an era of "restructuring." What's more, these schools have seen little in the way of a comeback during the conservative retrenchment that began in the Catholic Church during the late 1970s and early 1980s. "Catholic schools simply are no longer as important to the ecclesiastical institution as they were at the time of the Vatican Council," wrote Greeley, more than 20 years after its fourth and final session. He suggested that the U.S. Catholic community had lost its "confidence in Catholic schools even though they are now more important both to Catholics and to disadvantaged non-Catholics than they used to be."[207] In recent decades, even episcopal support for urban parish schools has weakened. O'Keefe and his coauthors noted that, while U.S. bishops "gave firm and unequivocal support to inner-city schools" in their 1979 pastoral letter on racism, this commitment "can be eroded by competing demands, personnel problems, and serious financial constraints."[208]

As urban parish schools continue to close, a growing number of educators have lamented the so-called eliting of Catholic education.[209] David P. Baker and Cornelius Riordan observed that, in the wake of sharp tuition hikes, almost 50 percent of students attending Catholic elementary schools "come from wealthy, upper-middle-class homes." This average holds true, they pointed out, "for students in both the city and the suburbs." Baker and Riordan interpreted these averages as a by-product of the sweeping demographic changes that occurred in urban neighborhoods after World War II.[210] Similarly, O'Keefe and his coauthors reported that urban parish schools, which once "created a non-elitist, egalitarian-type institution," have been adversely affected by "the strain of serving students, regardless of their family's ability to pay."[211] According to Baker and Riordan's research, those seeking to identify the causes of decline among urban parochial schools should examine the altered realities of U.S. urban life rather than concentrating exclusively on the "failures" of Catholic educators.[212]

There is little doubt that administrators charged with maintaining urban parish schools have faced overwhelming challenges. Trends negatively affecting these institutions have ranged from urban demographic change, to deindustrialization, to the impact of internal religious reform. Under such circumstances, even exceptionally talented administrators have been unable to prevent mass closures. In 2001, when Dr. Nicholas Wolsonovich ended his 16-year tenure as superintendent of schools for the Diocese of Youngstown, he was praised for his effectiveness. At no point was the administrator criticized for the fact that 5 of the 10 parish schools operating in Youngstown in 1985, the year of his appointment, had closed their doors by the time he resigned in 2001. Indeed, evidence suggests that Dr. Wolsonovich's supervision of diocesan schools was rated an overall success. After all, he moved on to become superintendent of schools for the Archdiocese of Chicago, the largest Catholic school system in the country.[213] Although his responsibilities at the Diocese of Youngstown extended beyond the boundaries of Youngstown itself, the city's beleaguered pattern of parish schools posed a singular challenge. Some observers evidently interpreted his success in keeping half of the community's parish schools open as a remarkable accomplishment.

THE DECLINE OF TRADITIONAL CATHOLIC IDENTITY AND URBAN PARISH SCHOOLS

The pressures that came to bear on U.S. Catholic educators in the aftermath of Vatican II were hardly the exclusive by-product of changes that occurred within the church. Nevertheless, the reforms of the council inspired U.S. Catholics to become more engaged with mainstream American society, a development that represented a significant departure from the separatist tendencies of the past. Furthermore, under the influence of the council, the corporatist values that permeated the Catholic subculture subsided, giving way to a new emphasis on personal autonomy. These developments overlapped with external trends that dampened the vitality of urban Catholic neighborhoods, while undermining the cohesiveness of the U.S. Catholic community. Significantly, many changes connected to the council were amplified—even foreshadowed—by urban trends that contributed to the breakup of Catholic enclaves and led many Catholics to relocate to ethnically and religiously diverse suburban neighborhoods.

Meanwhile, the election of President Kennedy alerted Catholics to the fact that they were no longer perennial outsiders in American society. Under these circumstances, U.S. Catholics were more likely to be drawn into the polarizing national debates that surrounded issues including the civil rights movement and the Vietnam War. Ultimately, they were no less divided than were American Protestants on many of these issues, and internal ideological disagreements were exacerbated by the fact that many religious leaders took public stands on issues that were once regarded by the church as political rather than moral concerns. Such developments, in concert, worked against the conformity (and apparent uniformity) that traditionally characterized the U.S. Catholic community. In this period of accelerated integration, many Catholics began to question the need for replicated institutions such as parish schools, which some of them dismissed as insulating and divisive.

Given that the broader social commitment encouraged by Vatican II inspired many Catholic educators to envision urban parish schools as vehicles of social uplift for disadvantaged students (many of whom were non-Catholic), the role that the conciliar reforms played in the decline of these schools seems ironic. Apparently, the council's reevaluation of the "special" status of priests and nuns contributed (albeit inadvertently) to a precipitous decline in religious vocations, as idealistic Catholics chose other (often secular) ways to be of service to their communities. In turn, the virtual disappearance of teaching nuns from the classroom was a substantial factor in rising costs among parish schools, given that members of religious orders were invariably replaced by laypeople with greater financial requirements. At the same time, postconciliar debates regarding the efficacy of Catholic schools may have encouraged some Catholic leaders (including bishops) to reconsider their commitment to these institutions, especially in the wake of trends including soaring costs, dwindling enrollment, and the Catholic laity's growing ambivalence about the maintenance of parish schools that served mainly non-Catholics. As a result, many urban parish schools are dealing with severe challenges. Walch observed that, despite the well-documented contributions of these schools, they "face a troubled future." The cost of maintaining these institutions, he added, is "much higher than the spreadsheets reveal," and the poverty confronting urban parish schools "is an obstacle that has been almost insurmountable, even for the most dedicated Catholic educator."[214] In the absence of decisive support from Catholic leaders and members of the laity, many patterns of parochial education throughout the country could suffer the fate of Youngstown's system of parish schools.

NOTES

1. Lou Jacquet, "The Cathedral: New St. Columba's Rose from Ruins of the Old: After Fire Destroyed a Youngstown Landmark the Demolition and Rebuilding Were a Story in Themselves," *The Catholic Exponent*, 5, May 7, 1993, supplement for fiftieth anniversary of the Diocese of Youngstown.

2. "Hogan and Religious Freedom in Youngstown," *The Youngstown Daily Vindicator*, 6, October 30, 1914, editorial.

3. William D. Jenkins, *Steel Valley Klan: The Ku Klux Klan in Ohio's Mahoning Valley* (Kent, OH: Kent State University Press, 1990), 56.

4. Stephen L. Ritz and Clarence T. Sheehan, "$1,250,000 Fire Ruins St. Columba's: Lightning Sets Cathedral Ablaze," *The Youngstown Vindicator,* 1, September 3, 1954.

5. Paula (Lehnerd) McKinney, interview by the author, June 14, 2007, transcript, Hogan-Cullinan Family Collection, #314, Mahoning Valley Historical Society, Youngstown, OH.

6. Ritz and Sheehan, *The Youngstown Vindicator,* September 3, 1954.

7. Ibid.

8. *The Cathedral Parish of St. Columba, Youngstown, Ohio: 150 Years of Faith, 1847–1997* (Youngstown, OH: Diocese of Youngstown), 11.

9. Anna Jean Schuler, "Rev. Holdbrook Sings First Mass at Cathedral," *The Youngstown Vindicator,* A-1, November 10, 1958.

10. McKinney, interview.

11. Charles R. Morris, *American Catholic: The Saints and Sinners Who Built America's Most Powerful Church* (New York, NY: Vintage, 1997), 281.

12. Philip Gleason, *Keeping the Faith: American Catholicism, Past and Present* (Notre Dame, IN: University of Notre Dame Press, 1987), 15.

13. Ibid., 16–22.

14. Morris, *American Catholic,* 13–14.

15. Gleason, *Keeping the Faith,* 22.

16. Ibid., 22–29.

17. John T. McGreevy, *Parish Boundaries: The Catholic Encounter with Race in the Twentieth-Century Urban North* (Chicago, IL: University of Chicago Press, 1996), 24.

18. Ibid., 21.

19. Glen Gabert, Jr., *In Hoc Signo? A Brief History of Catholic Parochial Education in America* (Port Washington, NY: Kennikat Press, 1972), 95.

20. Morris, *American Catholic,* 110.

21. Gabert, *In Hoc Signo?* 95.

22. McGreevy, *Parish Boundaries,* 22.

23. Harold A. Buetow, *Of Singular Benefit: The Story of Catholic Education in the United States* (New York, NY: McMillan Company, 1970), 347.

24. McGreevy, *Parish Boundaries,* 5.

25. Frans Jozef van Beeck, *Catholic Identity After Vatican II: Three Types of Faith in the One Church* (Chicago, IL: Loyola University Press, 1985), 41.

26. Thomas J. Sugrue, *The Origins of the Urban Crisis: Race and Inequality in Postwar Detroit* (Princeton, NY: Princeton University Press, 1996), 192.

27. Morris, *American Catholic,* vii.

28. Gabert, *In Hoc Signo?* 131.

29. James Hennesy, SJ, *American Catholics: A History of the Roman Catholic Community in the United States* (New York, NY: Oxford University Press, 1981), 283.

30. Buetow, *Of Singular Benefit,* 285.

31. Gabert, *In Hoc Signo?* 131.

32. Elizabeth (Fleisher) Fekety, interview by the author, April 19, 2007, transcript, Hogan-Cullinan Family Collection, #314, Mahoning Valley Historical Society, Youngstown, OH.

33. Robert E. Casey, *An Irish Catholic Remembers and Reflects* (New Wilmington, PA: New Horizons Publishing, 2006), 59–60.

34. Father Joseph S. Rudjak, interview by the author, June 22, 2008, transcript, Hogan-Cullinan Family Collection, #314, Mahoning Valley Historical Society, Youngstown, OH.

35. Carla J. (Haiser) Hlavac, interview by the author, July 15, 2009, transcript, Hogan-Cullinan Family Collection, #314, Mahoning Valley Historical Society, Youngstown, OH.

36. Gabert, *In Hoc Signo?* 93.

37. McGreevy, *Parish Boundaries,* 79.

38. Jay P. Dolan, *In Search of an American Catholicism: A History of Religion and Culture in Tension* (New York, NY: Oxford University Press, 2002), 185.

39. John T. McGreevy, *Catholicism and American Freedom: A History* (New York, NY: W. W. Norton & Company, 2003), 166–68.

40. Ibid., 252–53.

41. Dolan, *In Search of an American Catholicism,* 177.

42. McGreevy, *Catholicism and American Freedom,* 166–69.

43. Ibid., 166.

44. Peter Steinfels, *A People Adrift: The Crisis of the Roman Catholic Church in America* (New York, NY: Simon & Schuster, 2003), 71.

45. John Cooney, *The American Pope: The Life and Times of Francis Cardinal Spellman* (New York, NY: Times Books, 1985), 117.

46. David M. Oshinsky, *A Conspiracy So Immense: The World of Joe McCarthy* (New York, NY: The Free Press, 1983), 305.

47. Hennesy, *American Catholics,* 292–93.

48. Ibid., 295.

49. Garry Wills, *Why I Am a Catholic* (Boston, MA: Houghton Mifflin Company, 2002), 215–16.

50. McGreevy, *Catholicism and American Freedom,* 212–13.

51. Morris, *American Catholic,* 276–77.

52. McGreevy, *Catholicism and American Freedom,* 211–12.

53. Wills, *Why I Am a Catholic,* 218–19.

54. John Courtney Murray, SJ, *We Hold These Truths: Catholic Reflections on the American Proposition* (New York, NY: Sheed & Ward, 1960), 60.

55. Wills, *Why I Am a Catholic,* 219.

56. Hennesy, *American Catholics,* 308–9.

57. R. Scott Appleby, Patricia Byrne, and William L. Portier, eds., *Creative Fidelity: American Catholic Intellectual Traditions* (New York, NY: Orbis Books, 2004), 285.

58. John Cooney, *The American Pope: The Life and Times of Francis Cardinal Spellman* (New York, NY: Times Books, 1985), 261.

59. James Carroll, *An American Requiem: God, My Father, and the War That Came between Us* (Boston, MA: Houghton Mifflin Company, 1996), 73.

60. Appleby et al., *Creative Fidelity,* 285.

61. Denise Lardner Carmody, *The Double Cross: Ordination, Abortion, and Catholic Feminism* (New York, NY: Crossroad, 1986), 22.

62. Hennesy, *American Catholics,* 309.

63. Appleby et al., *Creative Fidelity,* 166.

64. Appleby et al., *Creative Fidelity,* 177.

65. Wills, *Why I Am a Catholic,* 43–44.

66. Hennesy, *American Catholics,* 309.

67. Wills, *Why I Am a Catholic,* 198.

68. Dolan, *In Search of an American Catholicism,* 108.

69. Gleason, *Keeping the Faith,* 23.

70. Appleby et al., *Creative Fidelity,* 247.

71. Wills, *Why I Am a Catholic,* 209.

72. Michael Glazier and Thomas J. Shelley, eds., *The Encyclopedia of American Catholic History* (Collegeville, MN: The Liturgical Press, 1997), 969.

73. Appleby et al., *Creative Fidelity,* 247–48.

74. Glazier and Shelley, *The Encyclopedia of American Catholic History,* 972.

75. McGreevy, *Catholicism and American Freedom,* 237.

76. Steinfels, *A People Adrift,* 74.

77. John W. O'Malley, *What Happened at Vatican II* (Cambridge, MA: The Belknap Press of Harvard University Press, 2008), 5.

78. Steinfels, *A People Adrift,* 74.

79. Dolan, *In Search of an American Catholicism,* 194.

80. Steinfels, *A People Adrift,* 74.

81. van Beeck, *Catholic Identity After Vatican II,* 18.

82. Steinfels, *A People Adrift,* 74–75.

83. Dolan, *In Search of an American Catholicism,* 194.

84. Steinfels, *A People Adrift,* 75.

85. Dolan, *In Search of an American Catholicism,* 195.

86. Jay P. Dolan, *The American Catholic Experience: A History from Colonial Times to the Present* (Garden City, NY: Image Books, 1985), 426–27.

87. William L. Lunch and Peter W. Sperlich, "American Public Opinion and the War in Vietnam," *The Western Political Quarterly* 32, no. 1 (March 1979): 41.

88. Dolan, *The American Catholic Experience,* 426.

89. Ibid., 427–28.

90. Carl Bernstein and Marco Politi, *His Holiness: John Paul II and the History of Our Time* (New York, NY: Penguin Books, 1996), 92.

91. Dolan, *In Search of an American Catholicism,* 192.

92. William K. Alcorn, "On Friendship and War: JFK Left Lasting Impression on Valley Woman," *The Vindicator,* 1, May 25, 2008.

93. Howard C. Aley, *A Heritage to Share: The Bicentennial History of Youngstown and the Mahoning Valley* (Youngstown, OH: The Bicentennial Commission of Youngstown and Mahoning County, Ohio, 1975), 449.

94. Clingan Jackson, "Thousands Hail Kennedy at Valley Talks: Hits Mill Output, UN China Vote," *The Youngstown Vindicator,* 1, October 10, 1960.

95. Thomas G. Fuechtmann, *Steeples and Stacks: Religion and Steel Crisis in Youngstown* (Cambridge, UK: Cambridge University Press, 1989), 29.

96. Colleen Carroll Campbell, "The Enduring Costs of John F. Kennedy's Compromise," *The Catholic World Report*, retrieved on July 7, 2008, www.ignatius.com/Magazines/CWR/campbell.htm

97. Father Edward P. Noga, interview by the author, June 18, 2007, transcript, Hogan-Cullinan Family Collection, #314, Mahoning Valley Historical Society, Youngstown, OH.

98. Cooney, *The American Pope*, 265–66.

99. Timothy Walch, *Parish School: American Catholic Parochial Education from Colonial Times to the Present* (Washington, DC: The National Catholic Educational Association, 2003), 209.

100. Mark S. Massa, *Catholics and American Culture: Fulton Sheen, Dorothy Day, and the Notre Dame Football Team* (New York, NY: W. W. Norton & Company, 1999), 129.

101. Hennesy, *American Catholics*, 308.

102. Massa, *Catholics and American Culture*, 135.

103. Cooney, *The American Pope*, 266–71.

104. Walch, *Parish School*, 211.

105. Murray, *We Hold These Truths*, 18.

106. Joseph Moreau, *Schoolbook Nation: Conflicts over American History Textbooks from the Civil War to the Present* (Ann Arbor, MI: The University of Michigan Press, 2006), 102.

107. Douglas J. Slawson, *The Department of Education Battle, 1918–1932* (Notre Dame, IN: University of Notre Dame Press, 2005), 152.

108. Mary Perkins Ryan, *Are Parochial Schools the Answer? Catholic Education in the Light of the Council* (New York, NY: Holt, Rinehart and Winston, 1964), 96.

109. Thomas C. Hunt and Timothy Walch, eds., *Urban Catholic Education: Tales of Twelve American Cities* (Notre Dame, IN: Alliance for Catholic Education Press at the University of Notre Dame, 2010), 4.

110. Hennesy, *American Catholics*, 308–9.

111. Garry Wills, *Bare Ruined Choirs: Doubt, Prophecy, and Radical Religion* (Garden City, NY: Doubleday, 1972), 79–83.

112. Hennesy, *American Catholics*, 309.

113. Wills, *Bare Ruined Choirs*, 81–83.

114. Steinfels, *A People Adrift*, 73.

115. McGreevy, *Parish Boundaries*, 79–80.

116. Morris, *American Catholic*, 281.

117. Massa, *Catholics and American Culture*, 5.

118. Ibid., 155.

119. Thomas Day, *Where Have You Gone, Michelangelo? The Loss of Soul in Catholic Culture* (New York, NY: Crossroad, 1993), 39.

120. Wills, *Bare Ruined Choirs*, 64.

121. Massa, *Catholics and American Culture*, 160.

122. Wills, *Bare Ruined Choirs*, 64.

123. John W. O'Malley, "Trent and Vernacular Liturgy: Evenhanded Restraint Marked the Council's Approach to Controversies," *America*, January 29, 2007, 18–19.

124. "Catholics Will Begin English Masses Nov. 29," *The Steel Valley News*, 3, October 23, 1964.

125. Noga, interview.

126. Massa, *Catholics and American Culture*, 162.

127. Hank and Kathleen Zimmerman, interview by the author, February 19, 2007, transcript, Hogan-Cullinan Family Collection, #314, Mahoning Valley Historical Society, Youngstown, OH.

128. Massa, *Catholics and American Culture*, 155.

129. Martin "Jack" O'Connell, interview by the author, April 13, 2007, transcript, Hogan-Cullinan Family Collection, #314, Mahoning Valley Historical Society, Youngstown, OH.

130. McKinney, interview.

131. Fekety, interview.

132. Massa, *Catholics and American Culture*, 161.

133. Carmody, *The Double Cross*, 3.

134. Dolan, *The American Catholic Experience*, 430.

135. Massa, *Catholics and American Culture*, 160.

136. Wills, *Bare Ruined Choirs*, 17.

137. Carroll, *American Requiem*, 243.

138. Day, *Where Have You Gone, Michelangelo?* 98.

139. Dolan, *The American Catholic Experience*, 430.

140. "Plan Cathedral Renovation," *The Youngstown Vindicator*, April 11, 1969.

141. O'Connell, interview.

142. McKinney, interview.

143. McGreevy, *Parish Boundaries*, 223.

144. Dorothy Ann Blatnica, VSC, *"At the Altar of Their Gods": African American Catholics in Cleveland, 1922–1961* (New York, NY: Garland Publishing, 1995), 47.

145. McGreevy, *Parish Boundaries*, 206.

146. Wills, *Bare Ruined Choirs*, 65.

147. O'Connell, interview.

148. Steinfels, *A People Adrift*, 173.

149. Emily Webster, "Conflict over 'New' Mass Greets Priest at Vienna," *The Youngstown Vindicator*, A-1, November 6, 1977.

150. Leon Stennis, "Bishop Won't OK Vienna Latin Rite," *The Youngstown Vindicator*, A-2, December 8, 1977.

151. Marie Shellock, "Our Lady of Sorrows Keeps Latin Tradition," *The Vindicator*, B-16, February 16, 1991.

152. Morris, *American Catholic*, 404.

153. John Wilkins, "Lost in Translation: The Bishops, the Vatican & the English Liturgy," *Commonweal*, December 2, 2005, 12–20.

154. Rachel Donadio, "Healing Schism, Pope Risks Another," *The New York Times*, January 25, 2009, www.nytimes.com/2009/01/26/world/europe/26pope.html (accessed June 5, 2010).

155. Steinfels, *A People Adrift,* 173.

156. Dolan, *The American Catholic Experience,* 430.

157. Judith Kubicki, "More than Words: The Many Symbols of the Liturgy," *America,* May 26–June 2, 2008, 17–19.

158. Massa, *Catholics and American Culture,* 170.

159. Buetow, *Of Singular Benefit,* 302–4.

160. Gabert, *In Hoc Signo?* 104–5.

161. Walch, *Parish School,* 175.

162. Buetow, *Of Singular Benefit,* 302–5.

163. Anthony S. Bryk, Valerie E. Lee, and Peter B. Holland, *Catholic Schools and the Common Good* (Cambridge, MA: Harvard University Press, 1993), 51–52.

164. "Says Diocese Owes Poor Schools Aid," *The Youngstown Vindicator,* 1, February 28, 1973.

165. "Diocese OKs New Enrollment Rules," *The Youngstown Vindicator,* 10, May 22, 1974.

166. Marie Aikenhead, "Board Refuses School Funding: Votes Against Diocese Inner City Aid, *The Youngstown Vindicator,* 1, November 17, 1976.

167. "Says Diocese Owes Poor Schools Aid," *The Youngstown Vindicator,* February 28, 1973.

168. Aikenhead, *The Youngstown Vindicator,* November 17, 1976.

169. "School to Remain Open 1 More Yr.," *The Youngstown Vindicator,* 40, January 19, 1977.

170. "Bishop: Catholic Schools Stay Open," *The Vindicator,* B-2, April 7, 1992.

171. Andrew M. Greeley, *American Catholics Since the Council: An Unauthorized Report* (Chicago, IL: The Thomas More Press, 1985), 130.

172. Ryan, *Are Parochial Schools the Answer?* vii.

173. Ibid., 8–9.

174. Walch, *Parish School,* 177.

175. Gleason, *Keeping the Faith,* 189.

176. Greeley, *American Catholics Since the Council,* 130.

177. Ibid., 141.

178. Kenneth Briggs, *Double Crossed: Uncovering the Catholic Church's Betrayal of American Nuns* (New York, NY: Doubleday, 2006), 79.

179. Ibid., 121.

180. Ibid., 117.

181. James Youniss and John T. Convey, eds., *Catholic Schools at the Crossroads: Survival and Transformation* (New York, NY: Teachers College Press, 2000), 2.

182. Joseph M. O'Keefe, Jessica A. Greene, Susan Henderson, Moira Connors, Erik Goldschmidt, and Katherine Schervish, *Sustaining the Legacy: Inner-City Catholic Elementary Schools in the United States* (Washington, DC: The National Catholic Educational Association, 2004), 36.

183. Ellen J. Sullivan, "Nuns Leaving Teaching Positions to Take Greater Roles in Ministry," *The Vindicator,* 8, February 1, 1988.

184. Dirk Johnson, "Catholics Giving Less to Church, Report Says," *The New York Times,* 22, June 10, 1987.

185. "Parochial Teachers Vote for Union at Eight Schools, Says No at Six Others," *The Youngstown Vindicator,* 2, February 13, 1985.

186. "Elementary Teachers Miffed by Shift of Talks to Parishes," *The Youngstown Vindicator,* 10, December 5, 1984.

187. "Maryellen Schaub, "A Faculty at a Crossroads: A Profile of American Catholic School Teachers," in *Catholic Schools at the Crossroads,* eds. James Youniss and John T. Convey (New York, NY: Teachers College Press, 2000), 84.

188. Norman Leigh, "Diocese Adopts New Policy to Teachers' Faith," *The Youngstown Vindicator,* 10, June 3, 1987.

189. "Hubbard Group Will Picket Diocese If Dismissed Teacher Is Not Reinstated," *The Vindicator,* 6, February 2, 1988.

190. David Hosansky and Ellen J. Sullivan, "Marriage Puts Teacher out of Work," *The Vindicator,* 1, January 29, 1988.

191. Ellen J. Sullivan, "Students' Parents Defend Diocese Teacher's Actions," *The Vindicator,* 1, January 30, 1988.

192. "Hubbard Group Will Picket Diocese If Dismissed Teacher Is Not Reinstated," *The Vindicator,* February 2, 1988.

193. "Parents Vow to Keep Pressuring Diocese over Teacher," *The Vindicator,* 6, February 5, 1988.

194. Ellen J. Sullivan, "Teacher Who Wed Divorced Man Quits School Post," *The Vindicator,* 2, February 8, 1988.

195. Ellen J. Sullivan, "Shaken: Couple Keep Faith, Question Decision," *The Vindicator,* 1, February 10, 1988.

196. "Calls Board to Reconsider Sex Program," *The Youngstown Vindicator,* 2, June 29, 1971.

197. Ibid.

198. "78 Diocese Schools Have Total Guidance Program," *The Youngstown Vindicator,* A-5, November 23, 1969.

199. Marie Aikenhead, "Says Catholic Schools Lack Psychologists," *The Youngstown Vindicator,* 6, February 23, 1977.

200. "Parochial Rolls Dropping: Down to 27,690 Students," *The Youngstown Vindicator,* September 3, 1972.

201. Walch, *Parish School,* 234.

202. Ibid., 233.

203. "Ask Superior Reconsider Recalling Nuns," *The Youngstown Vindicator,* 2, April 8, 1985.

204. Buetow, *Of Singular Benefit,* 319–20.

205. Walch, *Parish School,* 232–35.

206. T. Gordon Welsh, interview by the author, May 1, 2007, transcript, Hogan-Cullinan Family Collection, #314, Mahoning Valley Historical Society, Youngstown, OH.

207. Andrew M. Greeley, *The Catholic Myth: The Behavior and Beliefs of American Catholics* (New York, NY: Charles Scribner's Sons, 1990), 172.

208. O'Keefe et al., *Sustaining the Legacy,* 68–69.

209. David P. Baker and Cornelius Riordan, "The Eliting of the Common American Catholic School and the National Education Crisis," *Phi Delta Kappan*, 80, no. 1 (September 1998): 16–23.

210. David P. Baker and Cornelius Riordan, "It's Not About the Failure of Catholic Schools: It's About Demographic Transformations," *Phi Delta Kappan* 80, no. 6 (February 1999): 462–63.

211. O'Keefe et al., *Sustaining the Legacy*, 3.

212. Baker and Riordan, "It's Not About the Failure of Catholic Schools," 462–63.

213. Ron Cole, "Catholic Schools Superintendent Takes Same Position in Chicago: Youngstown's Bishop Said a Search for a New Superintendent Will Begin Soon," *The Vindicator*, 1, May 4, 2001.

214. Walch, *Parish School*, 245.

Chapter 7

A House Divided: Conclusions

In May 2008, Pope Benedict XVI delivered a homily to American clergy and religious who had gathered at St. Patrick's Cathedral in New York City. In an address that one reporter described as the "most effective" of his American tour, Pope Benedict "brilliantly used the metaphor of the cathedral for the entire Catholic Church." The pope gestured to the building's elaborate stained-glass windows, "which on the outside are dark, but which on the inside 'reveal their splendor.'" Pope Benedict then spoke to the challenge of drawing people "into the church who see only its darkness," a reference to the growing skepticism toward organized religion that characterized the era. At that point, the pope encouraged the gathering to view the neo-Gothic cathedral itself as a "symbol of church unity." He noted that the massive structure had been "born of the dynamic tension of diverse forces." The pope concluded by describing the cathedral's spires, which soared 330 feet above midtown Manhattan, as a "reminder" of the "constant craving of the human spirit to rise to God."[1]

Pope Benedict's address, while effective, may have drawn unwanted attention to the fact that the church he led failed to conform to any definition of unity, particularly its American branch. Liberals and conservatives disagreed on issues ranging from sexual ethics to the church's response to U.S. immigration policies; and since the 1970s, the American hierarchy's public stance against legalized abortion has sharply divided Catholics, many of whom "still expect their religious leaders to speak out on public issues."[2] The abortion debate, in particular, has taken on heavy political overtones, and in 2008, one priest observed, "Any American bishop today who comes out publicly to identify with a Democratic candidate would be shunned by his fellow bishops."[3] Naturally, the church's public stance on certain political issues has inspired criticism from observers outside the Catholic community, and a few have leveled charges echoing those that Paul Blanshard presented in the late 1940s. On the one hand, critics of the religious right, notably Damon Linker, have identified a strong Catholic influence in what appears to be a well-orchestrated political effort to elide America's longstanding distinction between church and state.[4] On the other hand, conservatives have routinely questioned the U.S. hierarchy's defense of the "basic human rights" of illegal immigrants. In April 2008, several weeks before Benedict's visit, Congressman Tom Tancredo, a Colorado Republican, remarked sarcastically that it was not in the pope's "job description to engage in American politics."[5] These controversies have closely paralleled strong disagreements within the Catholic community; and in the face of widening ideological divisions, it would appear that U.S. Catholics do not even agree on what it means to be Catholic. "We're all in a boat that has been rocked," wrote Kerry Kennedy, in her 2008 book, *Being Catholic Now.* "Everyone is struggling to find the proper balance; for comfort, for truth."[6]

Amid the array of internal conflicts that have arisen since the late 1960s, the U.S. Catholic community has struggled to come to terms with a clergy abuse scandal that "has compromised the credibility of the Church leadership."[7] Writing in 2002, six years before Pope Benedict's visit, Dolan noted that, despite the church's myriad "good works," the abuse scandal had "shaken to its foundation the sacred trust between priests and their parishioners."[8] The widening scandal has been among many factors that have contributed to the erosion of the church's public image. Greeley concluded that, in the decades that have elapsed since the final session of Vatican II, a church "so attractive during the time of Pope John" has "lost much of its respect and esteem."[9] Naturally, the U.S. church's loss of prestige has had negative consequences for parochial schools. Writing in 2005, Joseph O'Keefe, SJ, noted that "[dis-enchantment in the wake of the recent sexual-abuse scandal" contributed to "a drop not only in enrollment, but in the number of teachers and donations."[10] Then, in 2008, shortly before Pope Benedict's arrival in the United States, an article released by the Associated Press reported that "huge payouts to settle sex abuse lawsuits" were a likely factor in the closing of many urban Catholic schools in the six years since the scandal had broken. The article quoted a report by the National Catholic Education Association (NCEA) indicating that 1,267 Catholic schools had closed since 2000, while "enrollment nationwide . . . dropped by 382,125 students, or 14 percent."[11]

These figures surprised few people acquainted with the challenges confronting urban parish schools, which include dwindling donations, aging physical plants, the high cost of technology, and declining enrollment.[12] In a 2004 report on urban parish schools, O'Keefe and his coauthors acknowledged the extent of these difficulties and suggested that they "have not only persisted, but have arguably gained vigor."[13] At the same time, they contended that U.S. Catholics are well equipped materially to "sustain the legacy of inner-city schools." The report, sponsored by the NCEA, stated that 43 percent of Catholics recorded an income of $25,000 or more, while only 37 percent of Protestants showed a comparable income. Yet, according to the report, the material well-being of U.S. Catholics offered no guarantee that these belea-guered institutions would be preserved. O'Keefe and his colleagues ques-tioned whether Catholics had the "will" to support parish schools that were "totally reliant on resources beyond themselves, either in diocesan structures or among philanthropists."[14] A major source of such skepticism: the relatively low patterns of church-related giving among American Catholics.[15]

This trend came to the public's attention in the late 1980s, when Andrew Greeley released a study showing that Catholics contributed "half as much of their income to the church as they did 25 years ago." The study, which was based on six national surveys taken between 1960 and 1984, showed that "contributions to Catholic churches have fallen to 1.1 percent of parishioners' income, as opposed to 2.2 percent for Protestants." Significantly, the study revealed that, during the same period, Catholic contributions to nonchurch charities "kept pace" with those of Protestants. "People thought that Catholics would either 'knuckle under' or leave the church," Greeley stated. "But nei-ther happened. And the result is a protest through money."[16] The trends Gree-ley highlighted have remained constant. In 2000, Charles E. Zech reported that Catholics continued to give "at about half the rate of Protestants." According to some research, material losses related to this decline have been staggering. Zech referred to a 1994 study that estimated "low Catholic giving in the United States costs the Church $1.934 billion a year"—a figure that reflected the amount the church could collect annually "if Catholics gave at the average rate for all Americans."[17]

Catholics tend to disagree on the reasons for this dramatic decline in giv-ing, and some theories reflect strongly held ideological convictions. Greeley, for instance, argued that lower rates of giving have reflected "resentment about what Catholics perceive as insensitive church teachings and authority," especially regarding birth control.[18] In other words, an angry laity "was show-ing its displeasure by withholding contributions."[19] Greeley's theory, while controversial, is not without merit. Liberals, after all, have experienced their share of disappointments in recent decades. Many assert that the Second Vati-can Council was compromised by conservative members of Paul VI's cabinet, who took "drastic steps to stop the revolution that was taking place before their eyes."[20] According to this view, the first casualty of the conservative backlash was the concept of collegiality, "the notion of [bishops'] shared responsibility," which "tempered the papal spiritual monarchy which had reached its peak in the century after Vatican I." [21] In the first of many interventions on behalf of the assembly's conservative minority, Pope Paul took steps to ensure that the document on collegiality would include an "explanatory note" that diluted its impact. Other papal measures to shore up preconciliar policies and practices followed.[22]

A momentous turning point came in July 1968, when Pope Paul issued *Humanae Vitae,* an encyclical letter that upheld the church's ban on "artificial" birth control. Released only two years after a papal commission found no justification to continue the ban, *Humanae Vitae* has been called "the Vietnam War of the Catholic Church."[23] News of Pope Paul's encyclical met an outcry in the United States, where a letter of protest was signed by more than 600 Catholic scholars.[24] In 1969, a lone, prominent theologian Charles E. Curran edited two works highly critical of *Humanae Vitae.*[25] At the same time, surveys conducted in "country after country showed Catholics overwhelmingly in disagreement with the papal position—and more and more so as time went on."[26] Within a decade, the damage the encyclical had inflicted on the U.S. church became evident, as scores of disillusioned clergy and religious opted for secular life. Throughout the 1970s, the institution "saw the number of priests leaving their ministry swell, church attendance drop, and financial contributions decrease."[27] As Steinfels observed, the encyclical "only spurred questioning by the clergy as well as by the laity of the church's moral competence in matters of sexuality." In time, the church's vast network of parallel institutions was adversely affected "as nuns shed not only their peculiar head-to-foot garb, but, in many cases, their traditional roles as schoolteachers and nurses, and not a few left their strife-ridden orders altogether."[28] The extent to which this exodus was precipitated by the ideological divisions of the postconciliar era remains unclear. Briggs, for instance, has pointed out that many sisters reconsidered their vocations when Vatican II reevaluated the elevated status of priests and nuns, a development that led some to pursue "comparable goals in service and holiness as a woman outside religious life."[29] Nevertheless, the timing of many of these departures raises the possibility that disillusionment over the reversal of conciliar reforms helped to fuel this trend.

Further efforts to rein in the liberalizing influence of the council were to come. In 1978, following the short pontificate of Pope John Paul I, the College of Cardinals elected a decisive leader, whose position on the conciliar reforms betrayed none of Pope Paul's ambivalence. "Paul VI seemed to yearn back, beyond the intervening council, to a more settled time, a kind of blissful status quo ante," Wills wrote. "John Paul II was ready to *take* people back there."[30] Pope John Paul II promoted a vision of the church that was strictly hierarchal, far removed from the conciliar model, which envisioned the church as "the people of God." He appointed "extremely conservative" bishops to the church's far-flung dioceses, and he "rarely engaged in serious consultation" with episcopal leaders.[31] The pope's cabinet, above all, reflected his stringently conservative agenda. As head of the Congregation for the Doctrine of the Faith (the former Holy Office), Joseph Cardinal Ratzinger (the future Pope Benedict XVI) condemned "the conciliar emphasis on the 'People of God,'" claiming that the concept had been "transformed into a Marxist myth" that introduced a "false democracy" into the church.[32] These reversals were accompanied by what Steinfels described as the Vatican's growing "fundamentalism" on issues related to "sexual morality and . . . the role of women" in the church.[33] As Catholic sociologist Michele Dillon noted, even some of those theologians who sympathized with the pope's opposition to the ordination of women criticized his "faulty theology." In their view, he should have called attention to "the differences in women's equality cross-nationally" and appealed to "the communal unity of the global church," rather than asserting that the church lacked the authority to ordain women because Jesus did not do so.[34]

Meanwhile, liberals, who were already acutely aware of the Vatican's conservative "domestic policy," became increasingly alert to a rightward tilt in its "foreign policy," as Pope John Paul II forged close ties with Western powers to undermine Soviet Communism and curb Communist influence in Latin America.[35] Some observers complained that the pope's failure to identify with the victims of right-wing regimes in Latin America was inconsistent with his outspoken support for the Solidarity labor movement in his native Poland.[36] By the mid-1980s, a growing number of U.S. bishops expressed concern about the pope's close ties with the administration of President Ronald Reagan. Although Pope John Paul II "didn't hesitate to confront the excesses of capitalism or materialism in global terms," he consistently refrained from attacking the Reagan administration's economic policies and "prevailed on the U.S. bishops to water down their criticism of Reaganomics."[37] President Reagan, for his part, even quoted the pope when he condemned "certain economic theories that use the rhetoric of class struggle to justify injustice," and his own rhetoric took on "religious cadences" that made him "*sound* like the pope."[38]

Liberal U.S. bishops were especially concerned about Pope John Paul II's apparent desire to roll back the reforms of Vatican II. Among the more outspoken critics of the Vatican's conservative policies was Youngstown Bishop James W. Malone, who served as president of the U.S. Conference of Catholic Bishops from 1983 to 1986. "The prophets of gloom, of whom Pope John XXIII spoke, are still very much with us," announced Bishop Malone in the mid-1980s. "They would have it that the last two decades have witnessed nothing but dissolution and collapse and that the church can be saved only by returning to some earlier, fictitious, golden age."[39] While even critics of Pope John Paul II acknowledged his "global stature" as a leader "who had shaken the foundations of the Soviet empire," some feared that his approach to "internal leadership had given new life to the old conservatism and only put off the day of reckoning with necessary changes that the Council had prefigured."[40] Unsurprisingly, criticism of the pope continued to mount, and in the waning years of his pontificate, Pope John Paul II's popularity among American Catholics plunged. This was markedly evident after 2002, when his response to the burgeoning clergy abuse scandal seemed "to many to be less vigorous than was appropriate."[41] Although the ailing pope publicly professed his "sorrow" over the incidents, he also "laid the blame on homosexual priests, who he said had 'deviations in their affections,' suggesting they experienced great difficulty in honoring their commitment to celibacy."[42] Those who looked forward to the Vatican's symbolic acknowledgment of the victims' collective trauma would need to wait until spring 2008, when Pope Benedict XVI met with a group from the Archdiocese of Boston while visiting the United States.[43]

In the face of the conservative policies of Pope John Paul II and his successor, Pope Benedict XVI, most U.S. Catholics have remained faithful to the legacy of Vatican II. As Wills wrote, "One indication of the popular attitude toward the council is the way the Vatican has had to deplore it as a major crisis."[44] Some critics of the conservative retrenchment have questioned whether, at this point, it is even possible to restore preconciliar policies and practices. "No one person or no collection of people would be able to shut the windows that Pope John XXIII had opened to *aggiornamento*—the letting in of fresh air," observed the late Catholic novelist William X. Kienzle. "To try to close the windows of change would be to try to put the toothpaste back in the tube."[45] Greeley, along with other liberal observers, has argued that the Vatican's emphasis on centralized authority has alienated Catholics, and this dissatisfaction has been reflected in falling donations. Moreover, Greeley's 1987 study suggested that the decline of church-related contributions that began in the 1960s exacerbated the "crisis" in Catholic schools. In an epilogue to Greeley's study, Bishop William McManus, formerly of the Diocese of Fort Wayne-South Bend, Indiana, noted that the sharp decrease in contributions was "especially ominous" for the thousands of lay workers employed by the church, particularly those working in schools. "We've got lay workers with family obligations living on a pittance," Bishop McManus wrote. He added that "the wages of most Catholic lay teachers were far below those of their counterparts in the public schools." Bishop McManus estimated that, if "salaried" parishioners "paid 2 to 3 percent of their salary income for the support of their parish and dioceses, the church would have more than enough to pay all employees adequate salaries and benefits." Like many critics of the church's vertical power structure, McManus urged parishes "to allow lay people a larger role in the administration of church funds."[46] Since then, lay control has remained a relevant issue for many American Catholics. Dr. Frank Butler, in an address delivered at a 2004 conference on church leadership at Boston College, complained that "despite a Vatican II understanding of the church as a communion of people . . . clericalism has prevailed and is robbing the church of the rich sense of belonging to and being responsible for one another."[47]

Interestingly, not all researchers attribute the steady decline in church-related giving to ideological disagreements within the Catholic community. Charles E. Zech suggested that this trend is connected to generational differences rather than ideological ones. Zech wrote that today's U.S. Catholic Church "is really composed of three generations: the pre-Vatican II generation; the Vatican II generation; and the post-Vatican II generation." He argued that those Catholics who came of age before the council were exposed to a "hierarchal church, where the emphasis was on tradition." According to this theory, when Catholics of the pre–Vatican II generation "speak of the Church, they are most likely referring to the magisterium." Such Catholics are inclined "to regard the Church as an institution, and are more likely to support it financially." On the other hand, members of the post–Vatican II generation "were raised in a Church with a decreased emphasis on tradition and an increased emphasis on democratic processes and the primacy of individual conscience." Zech argued that members of this generation, who envision the church as "the people of God," show "less of an institutional commitment to the Church, and are more reluctant to support it financially." Finally, those who came of age when the reforms of Vatican II were being implemented seem to be "caught in [the] middle," though they tend to show giving patterns comparable to those found among the post–Vatican II generation.[48]

If Zech emphasized generational differences in his study, it is nevertheless difficult to ignore that ideological perspectives affected the trends he described. In light of his conclusion that models of the church influence levels of giving, Zech's study seems to complement Greeley's position that flagging donations reflect the presence of ideological differences among parishioners. At one point, Zech's study actually drew a correlation between lower patterns of giving and disagreement with official church positions. Using data collected in 1993 for the Lilly Endowment's American Congregational Giving Study, a survey of five U.S. religious denominations, Zech attempted "to analyze religious giving only in the Catholic Church."[49] He found that Catholics who took issue with the church's position on abortion contributed far less on an annual basis than those who supported this position, with the former contributing about $588 and the latter giving about $790. Similarly, those who disagreed with the church's position on contraception contributed somewhat less annually than those who concurred, with the former giving about $643 and the latter contributing about $778. The study highlighted one unexpected departure from this trend, however. Parishioners who disagreed with the church's ban on the ordination of women actually tended to contribute more than those who accepted it, with the former contributing about $719 and the latter giving about $644.[50] Curiously, this pattern suggests that Catholics who take a more progressive stand on this particular issue tend to show a greater material commitment to the church.

Liberals are hardly alone in their frustration with the institutional church. Many conservatives mourned the loss of cherished symbols and traditions in the wake of Vatican II, and some left the church altogether. Traditionalists who blame the council for many of the church's difficulties stress that some conservative dioceses record exceptionally large numbers of religious vocations. As Charles R. Morris wrote, "The commitment to strict orthodoxy and to obedience comes bundled with a very exalted view of the priesthood."[51] Although it is difficult to establish a clear connection between declining donations and the reforms of the postconciliar era, there is little doubt that conservatives found the changes jarring. As Day observed, many parishioners—regardless of ideology—resented shouldering the cost of expensive church renovations, especially when they were granted no role in the decision-making process. He cited the example of an unnamed cathedral parish, a "massive neo-Gothic extravaganza" that "needed repairs and a more 'postconciliar look.'" Day noted that the cathedral staff, after consulting with a decorator, presented a plan for "a spaceship modern interior so artistically bare that it looked as if it had been sterilized for surgery." The renovation plan called for the removal of an elaborate marble altar, the replacement of stained-glass windows with clear-glass panels, and the "obliteration" of a religious mural that ran along the interior of the building. "The altar would stand alone and bare, at the crossing, the architectural center of the building, and behind it, at the focal point of the worshiper's attention, would be the priest's chair." When publicized, the plan was widely criticized. "The parishioners and the people of the diocese, who had to pay for this Star Wars throne room, were not impressed," Day wrote. "In fact, some of them screamed bloody murder."[52] Ironically, pastoral efforts to bring church interiors into conformity with postconciliar liturgical standards often called attention to the fact that "the people of God" had little control over funds that were largely comprised of their own donations. Once again, amid widespread lip service to a Vatican II model of the church, it appeared that clericalism "prevailed."

Yet, the decline of urban parish schools cannot be entirely attributed to dwindling donations in the Catholic community. In Youngstown, as elsewhere, parish schools were affected by a combination of urban trends—including demographic change, deindustrialization, and depopulation—that eroded the traditional Catholic enclaves that supported these institutions. The disappearance of these neighborhoods ensured that urban parishes would lose many of the patrons needed to maintain their schools. Meanwhile, thousands of U.S. Catholics suddenly found themselves separated from their traditional urban milieu. For decades, U.S. parochial schools had served as centerpieces of an insular subculture that encouraged (and was sustained by) the growth of replicated institutions. During the late 1950s and 1960s, however, the removal of Catholics to religiously and ethnically diverse suburbs overlapped with destabilizing societal trends as well as sweeping reforms within the Catholic Church. These developments coalesced to undermine the seemingly static, separatist model of American Catholicism that inspired the building of the nation's largest parallel school system. Postwar urban trends not only starved parish schools materially; they also contributed to the erosion of a "ghetto" that exemplified the U.S. church's "stiff-necked resistance to the great American assimilationist engine."[53]

Postconciliar efforts to broaden the mission of urban parish schools drew mixed responses from Catholics. While liberal Catholics were initially receptive to the idea of supporting parish schools that served nonwhite, non-Catholic students, the political landscape became increasingly complicated during the 1980s. As Baker and Riordan observed, Catholic schools, in the wake of contested research claiming they were more effective than public schools at boosting achievement levels among at-risk minority students, became implicated in a conservative agenda to undermine public education. Baker and Riordan observed that "the once moribund Catholic schools had become the darlings of the political Right and of influential social scientists bent on 'saving public schools.'" The researchers asserted that "the whole movement toward the privatization of schools gained momentum largely as a result of studies of Catholic schools."[54] Catholic educational researcher James Youniss agreed, noting that "the work of Coleman and others was drawn into a larger assault on public schools and the philosophy behind them."[55] This development not only ensured that debates on school vouchers (and other issues connected to the "school choice" agenda) would become increasingly contentious, but it also precipitated the creation of charter schools, which posed a lethal challenge to urban parish schools.[56]

While these controversies undoubtedly dampened the enthusiasm of some Catholics for urban parish schools, many of these institutions were hobbled by some of the very forces that had facilitated their transformation into vehicles of social uplift for disadvantaged urban youth; regardless of religious background. Ironically, the conciliar reforms that enabled Catholic educators to broaden the mission of many urban parish schools also contributed to the decline of America's religious teaching orders. These teaching orders had served as the backbone of America's parallel system of Catholic schools, and their virtual disappearance had consequences for parish schools. Amid a precipitous decline in vocations, the Ursuline religious community, one of the largest and most influential of America's religious teaching orders, revised their constitution after Vatican II, allowing sisters "to negotiate or propose their own work situations."[57] The Ursuline community was one of many religious communities whose dwindling number of members redirected their efforts toward forms of community service that did not necessarily involve classroom teaching.

When analyzing developments in Youngstown, a community that lost all but one of its 18 parish schools between 1960 and 2006, it is often tempting to consider what Catholic educators could have done differently. Some local observers have suggested that popular resistance to diocesan consolidation efforts in the 1980s may have doomed the city's remaining parish schools. A smaller number have questioned whether local Catholic leaders took full advantage of opportunities in the areas of interracial outreach and evangelization. Is it possible that a more aggressive program of evangelization could have resulted in thriving black urban parishes and parish schools? Naturally, this question is tinged with controversy. One aspect of urban parish schools that made them palatable to many secular observers was that they were not envisioned as instruments of conversion. Indeed, after Vatican II, many priests and nuns involved in urban ministry "rejected the 'triumphalist' ethos of African American Catholic parishes."[58] More than a few of them eschewed proselytizing in favor of activities that conformed to their ideas of social justice. As admirable as this behavior might appear, it led some black leaders to question the church's seemingly tepid approach to evangelization. In the mid-1970s, African American observers in Youngstown interpreted the low rate of conversion within the black community as evidence of the church's "indifference" to minority groups. These critics also suggested that the dearth of black leaders in the Catholic community, and the inability of African Americans to assume "ownership" of urban parish schools, ensured that Catholic institutions would remain a "foreign presence" in many center-city neighborhoods.[59] Questions about the "outsider" status of some urban parochial schools that operated in black neighborhoods could provide the impetus for further research.

Youngstown's pattern of parish schools was seemingly the victim of a "perfect storm" scenario, one involving a formidable combination of social, political, economic, and religious trends. Moreover, all of these trends contributed to a steep decline in traditional conceptions of Catholic identity, which tended to place a strong emphasis on the parish structure and replicated institutions such as parish schools. Although the reforms of Vatican II contributed to the transformation of many urban parochial schools, as they broadened their mission to include more non-Catholic students, these changes also facilitated the decline of traditional religious teaching orders. During the same period, the council's emphasis on engagement with the world inspired many American Catholics to question their commitment to a system of private religious schools that limited their contact with non-Catholics. In the wake of these developments, the traditional parish school—still regarded as the most reliable provider of Catholic elementary education—appears unlikely to experience resurgence within the city limits, at least within the foreseeable future.

Evidence of the system's deterioration is plentiful. Vacant parish school buildings dot many of Youngstown's declining neighborhoods, and the Ursuline Motherhouse, built in the early 1960s on 100 acres of undeveloped land in Canfield Township, now sits practically empty. The vast majority of the sprawling complex's 80 rooms are vacant, and a small—and shrinking—community of elderly nuns occupies an infirmary located on the second floor. The facility's chapel, designed to seat about 400 people, rarely draws more than a handful of worshippers for weekly services, though sizable crowds still gather for funerals or jubilee celebrations. Younger members of the religious order generally choose to live in private apartments or vacant diocese-owned properties, a development that has caused some residents of the motherhouse to lament a "loss of community." One of those residents is Sister Julia Baluch, OSU, a vibrant septuagenarian who once worked as a principal and teacher in local parish schools. During a 2007 interview, Sister Julia recalled that, in the recent past, communication among members of the order routinely occurred "at table," while camaraderie among the nuns was strengthened by their collective participation in classroom teaching. "We were strictly education," the nun recalled. "I would liken it to Youngstown being strictly [steel mills]." Sister Julia, then serving as a pastoral minister at local hospitals, pointed out that since the community's vocational diversification, the sisters no longer had "much time with each other." She predicted that, if current trends continued, the Ursulines would have difficulty maintaining a cohesive community. "I think the big adjustment is that with diversified missions and not having enough community, we can't hold it [together] any longer . . . only in smaller groups."[60]

Nevertheless, Sister Julia, like other Ursuline nuns who embraced the post-conciliar reforms, seemed convinced that her order was moving steadily closer to its original purpose. Established in the sixteenth century by St. Angela de Merici, the Ursuline religious order was initially dedicated to protecting exploited women who were living in the vicinity of Brescia, Italy; and Sister Julia indicated many of the order's younger members were engaged in work that harkened back to that mission. "We're going back to what Angela really and truly wanted her daughters to do," she said. "It was to live the gospel, be a witness to the gospel, [by protecting the women] from the soldiers living up in the garrison about half a mile from where they were."[61] The order's early history, which the community's leaders began to explore in the 1950s, appeared consistent with the postconciliar church's emphasis on social justice; and a growing number of Ursuline sisters began to question their order's overwhelming emphasis on formal teaching. Indeed, by the end of the 1980s, nuns of all orders were virtually absent from the classrooms of Youngstown's parish schools.[62] When asked about the vocational choices of the community's active members, Sister Julia indicated that one of them worked at a local food bank, while another served as the diocesan director of religious education; several others were employees of Catholic Charities, a faith-based philanthropic organization. Meanwhile, a number of Ursuline sisters are involved in the operation of two local transitional homes for disadvantaged women and children. "*Very few are classroom teaching,*" Sister Julia added.[63]

The vocational diversification she described represented a sharp departure from the order's recent past. In 1961, when construction began on the Ursuline Motherhouse, more than 10,000 students in Youngstown were "under instruction by the Ursulines."[64] Yet, by 2007, most of the facility's residents were retired, and a large percentage were physically disabled, including 92-year-old Sister Virginia McDermott, OSU, a former elementary and secondary school teacher. Confined to a motorized wheelchair, Sister Virginia proved to be lucid and lively; and she spoke philosophically about the decline of the Catholic school, an institution she believed had run its course. "Everything says something about that—the economic situation, the social situation," she said in a 2007 interview. "Everything contributes to the fact that the public schools probably better be the schools that people turn to." It was difficult to ignore that Sister Virginia was calmly predicting the demise of a system to which she had devoted two decades of her life. She began her teaching career in the 1940s, at Immaculate Conception Elementary School, on the city's east side; and when she retired from the classroom in the 1960s, Sister Virginia was working as a journalism instructor at Ursuline High School, the older of the city's two Catholic secondary schools. In the years since her retirement, she had watched parochial school enrollment fall precipitously; and amid dwindling vocations, she was forced to acknowledge that the area's Ursulines might be compelled to "have a union with some other community." Sister Virginia appeared to recognize that the community's altered mission reflected a need to adapt to changing circumstances, but she nevertheless reflected nostalgically on an era when Ursuline sisters staffed many of the city's Catholic schools. "When we were all in education, you wished that it would be passed along to somebody else," she said. Her desire to bestow a legacy of teaching to a new generation of Ursuline sisters, however, did not prevent Sister Virginia from coolly assessing the likely future of parish schools. "It isn't going to be again for Catholic schools, I don't think," she said. "Maybe our work in teaching is finished."[65]

While a growing number of Catholic leaders have questioned the long-term viability of the traditional parish school model, not all of them are prepared to abandon the project of Catholic education. Bishop George V. Murry, SJ, who is acutely aware of developments that contributed to the decline of parochial education in Youngstown, has taken steps to support the 32 Catholic elementary schools that still operate within his six-county diocese. The bishop noted in an interview that schools in Mahoning and Stark counties have been working with a consultant to develop a regional school system "so that they can share resources and work more closely together to promote Catholic education at a reasonable price for the people." He stressed that a regionalized system of Catholic schooling is already in place in neighboring Trumbull County, where regional committees have worked to develop guidelines for the maintenance of schools. Moreover, the diocese is exploring ways to encourage cooperation among emerging regional systems, while also providing support to "those schools that don't fit into (or aren't in) a defined region." Notably, Bishop Murry has stressed a need for Catholics "to shift our mentality away from the idea that the financing of Catholic schools is the responsibility of the parish on whose property the school happens to sit." Echoing an approach considered (but ultimately rejected) by diocesan administrators more than three decades earlier, the bishop added, "Catholic education is a mission of the entire diocese, and all entities of the diocese need to be actively involved in supporting Catholic education."[66]

As part of his response to the ongoing depopulation of the diocese, Bishop Murry has ordered the merging of parish schools that have recorded exceptionally low enrollment. The first of these mergers occurred in 2009, in the suburb of Austintown Township, where St. Joseph and Immaculate Heart of Mary elementary schools were consolidated—a move framed as an effort to prevent the closing of both institutions.[67] More recently, in 2011, St. Luke's Elementary School, located in the outlying community of Boardman Township, became an early childhood learning center for children between the ages of 2 and 10. In a development that may signal a move toward regionalization in Mahoning County, the facility's transformation was overseen by the newly formed Mahoning Valley Catholic School Collaborative, a consortium of local parishes that operate (or recently operated) elementary schools. St. Luke's pastor, Father Joseph Fata, explained to a *Vindicator* reporter that he approached the collaborative "after researching innovative early childhood programs."[68] The pastor's decision probably prevented the facility from closing altogether, given that, as early as 2009, media reports indicated St. Luke's Elementary School would most likely consolidate with another parochial school in nearby Struthers, Ohio.[69]

Although the Diocese of Youngstown's plan to regionalize parochial elementary schools remains a work in progress, Bishop Murry has stressed the importance of Catholic education more vigorously than did his predecessor. In statements both public and private, the bishop has argued that Catholic schools are practically unique in their promotion of religious values that tend to reinforce civic values, and he emphasized that many of Youngstown's leaders (regardless of religious background) attended Catholic schools, where "they learned to be men and women for others." This conditioning, he added, is not always a salient feature of educational programs offered by even well-regarded private institutions, especially those with a more secular orientation. "I have friends who send their kids to very expensive, very high-powered private schools," Bishop Murry said. "And when you talk to those kids about sharing their gifts with others, being part of a program to build up the community, they have blank stares on their faces, because they don't learn that in school." Too often, he added, exclusive private schools do little more than inspire students to "get ahead" in a competitive marketplace, an approach unlikely to stem the ongoing erosion of service-oriented values. "Catholic schools, from the very beginning, have said: 'You are standing here on the shoulders of other people. You are standing here because of other people's generosity, and you need to give back to society to repay all the gifts that you have,'" Bishop Murry stated. "And I think that's a great value."[70] The bishop's comments are consistent with observations made by those educational researchers who conclude that Catholic schools play an important civic role in U.S. society. It remains to be seen, however, whether the policies the bishop has advocated will protect the diocese's remaining parochial elementary schools from the powerful forces arrayed against them.

NOTES

1. James Martin, "Benedict in America: Message of Joy," *America*, May 12, 2008, 8.
2. Jay P. Dolan, *In Search of an American Catholicism: A History of Religion and Culture in Tension* (New York, NY: Oxford University Press, 2002), 202–3.

3. The Rev. Emmett Coyne, "Are Bishops Making Democratic Catholics Choose?" *The Vindicator,* A-8, October 5, 2008, editorial.

4. Damon Linker, *The Theocons: Secular America under Siege* (New York, NY: Anchor Press, 2006/2007), 3.

5. Drew Christiansen, "Immigration's Dark Moments," *America,* October 13, 2008, www.americamagazine.org/content/article.cfm?article_id=11126 (accessed June 5, 2010).

6. Kerry Kennedy, *Being Catholic Now: Prominent Americans Talk About Change in the Church and the Quest for Meaning* (New York, NY: Crown Publishers, 2008), xvii.

7. Andrew M. Greeley, *The Making of the Pope 2005* (New York, NY: Little, Brown and Company, 2005), 115.

8. Dolan, *In Search of an American Catholicism,* 257.

9. Greeley, *The Making of the Pope 2005,* 115.

10. Joseph O'Keefe, "How to Save Catholic Schools: Let the Revitalization Begin," *Commonweal,* March 25, 2005, 15.

11. Matt Sedensky, The Associated Press, "More Catholic Schools Closing Across US: Dwindling Enrollment a 'Vicious Cycle,'" April 12, 2008, transfigurations .blogspot.com/2008/04/more-catholic-schools-closing-across-us.html (accessed June 5, 2011).

12. O'Keefe, "How to Save Catholic Schools," 15.

13. Joseph M. O'Keefe, SJ, Jessica A. Greene, Susan Henderson, Moira Connors, Erik Goldschmidt, and Katherine Schervish, *Sustaining the Legacy: Inner-City Catholic Elementary Schools in the United States* (Washington, DC: National Catholic Educational Association, 2004), 2–3.

14. Ibid., 71–72.

15. Charles E. Zech, *Why Catholics Don't Give . . . and What Can Be Done about It* (Huntington, IN: Our Sunday Visitor Publishing, 2000), 7.

16. Dirk Johnson, "Catholics Giving Less to Church, Report Says," *The New York Times,* A-22, June 10, 1987.

17. Zech, *Why Catholics Don't Give,* 13.

18. Johnson, *The New York Times,* June 10, 1987.

19. Zech, *Why Catholics Don't Give,* 15.

20. Garry Wills, *Why I Am a Catholic* (Boston, MA: Houghton Mifflin Company, 2002), 231–32.

21. James Hennesy, SJ, *American Catholics: A History of the Roman Catholic Community in the United States* (New York, NY: Oxford University Press, 1981), 312.

22. Wills, *Why I Am a Catholic,* 232–33.

23. Peter Steinfels, *A People Adrift: The Crisis of the Roman Catholic Church in America* (New York, NY: Simon & Schuster, 2003), 257.

24. Charles E. Curran, *Loyal Dissent: Memoir of a Catholic Theologian* (Washington, DC: Georgetown University Press, 2006), x.

25. Philip Gleason, *Keeping the Faith: American Catholicism, Past and Present* (Notre Dame, IN: University of Notre Dame Press, 1987), 192.

26. Steinfels, *A People Adrift,* 255.

27. Ibid., 256.

28. Ibid., 6–7.

29. Kenneth Briggs, *Double Crossed: Uncovering the Catholic Church's Betrayal of American Nuns* (New York, NY: Doubleday, 2006), 121.

30. Wills, *Why I Am a Catholic,* 243.

31. Greeley, *The Making of the Pope 2005,* 115.

32. Wills, *Why I Am a Catholic,* 261.

33. Steinfels, *A People Adrift,* 305.

34. Michele Dillon, *Catholic Identity* (Cambridge, UK: Cambridge University Press, 1999), 228–29.

35. Carl Bernstein and Marco Politi, *His Holiness: John Paul II and the History of Our Time* (New York, NY: Penguin Books, 1996), 10–13.

36. Ibid., 462.

37. Ibid., 474.

38. Ibid., 309–10.

39. Ibid., 429.

40. Steinfels, *A People Adrift,* 35.

41. Greeley, *The Making of the Pope 2005,* 115.

42. Ibid., 506.

43. James Martin, "Pastor of the Victims," *America,* May 12, 2008, 10.

44. Wills, *Why I Am a Catholic,* 272.

45. William X. Kienzle, *The Gathering* (Kansas City, MO: Andrews McMeel Publishing, 2002), 223.

46. Johnson, *The New York Times,* June 10, 1987.

47. O'Keefe et al., *Sustaining the Legacy,* 72.

48. Zech, *Why Catholics Don't Give,* 43–45.

49. Ibid., 23.

50. Ibid., 53–54.

51. Charles R. Morris, *American Catholic: The Saints and Sinners Who Built America's Most Powerful Church* (New York, NY: Vintage, 1997), 385.

52. Day, *Where Have You Gone, Michelangelo?* 133–34.

53. Morris, *American Catholic,* vii.

54. David P. Baker and Cornelius Riordan, "The Eliting of the Common American Catholic School and the National Education Crisis," *Phi Delta Kappan,* 80, no. 1 (September 1998): 16–23.

55. Youniss and Convey, *Catholic Schools at the Crossroads,* 1.

56. Scott J. Cech, "Catholic Closures Linked to Growth of City Charters," *Education Week,* February 16, 2008, 1.

57. Briggs, *Double Crossed,* 16.

58. John T. McGreevy, "Racial Justice and the People of God: The Second Vatican Council, the Civil Rights Movement, and American Catholics," *Religion and America* 4, no. 2 (1994): 226.

59. Leon Stennis, "Leadership's View on Diocese's Approach toward Blacks Differ," *The Youngstown Vindicator,* 7, September 6, 1975.

60. Sister Julia Baluch, OSU, interview by the author, April 24, 2007, transcript, Hogan-Cullinan Family Collection, #314, Mahoning Valley Historical Society, Youngstown, OH.

61. Ibid.

62. Ellen J. Sullivan, "Nuns Leaving Teaching Positions to Take Greater Roles in Ministry," *The Vindicator,* February 1, 1988.

63. Baluch, interview.

64. "Open Drive for $1,000,000 Ursuline Motherhouse," *The Youngstown Vindicator,* April 25, 1961.

65. Sister Virginia McDermott, interview by the author, May 31, 2007, transcript, Hogan-Cullinan Family Collection, #314, Mahoning Valley Historical Society, Youngstown, OH.

66. Bishop George V. Murry, SJ, interview by the author, April 5, 2011, transcript, Ethnic Heritage Society Collection, #385, Mahoning Valley Historical Society, Youngstown, OH.

67. Marly Kosinski, "Austintown Merger, New Principals Top 'Elementary' News," *The Catholic Exponent,* August 21, 2009, .cathexpo.org/ articledetails.aspx?articleid=359# (accessed April 28, 2011).

68. Sarah Floor, "St. Luke to Offer Early Childhood Center," *The Vindicator,* March 5, 2011, boardman.vindy.com/news/2011/mar/05/st-luke-to-offer-early-child-hood-center/ (accessed April 28, 2011).

69. Harold Gwin, "Parochial Schools in Boardman, Struthers Consider Consolidation," *The Vindicator,* February 24, 2009, vindy.com/news/2009/feb/24/parochial-schools-in-boardman-struthers-consider/ (accessed April 28, 2011).

70. Murry, interview.

Epilogue

Last Mass

On the morning of January 30, 2011, Youngstown Bishop George V. Murry, SJ, presided over the final mass at Immaculate Conception Parish, whose brick steeples had marked the entrance to the city's east side since 1890. The parish itself predated the neo-Gothic edifice by eight years. Founded in 1882, "the Immaculate," as it was known to longtime parishioners, served generations of families, some of whom retained connections to the center-city parish, even though they had since relocated to suburban communities. Those who returned were drawn back, in part, by the beauty of the parish's main building, whose smoke-darkened exterior offered visitors no preparation for the bright, airy worship space contained within. That space had changed over the years, but not in ways that longtime parishioners found disconcerting. Starting in the 1960s, a series of interior renovations were carried out, though often with an eye toward preserving cherished remnants of the past. At one point, a talented parishioner removed a section of the wooden reredos screen that once stretched across the back of the sanctuary and refashioned it into an elegant altarpiece—a gesture that typified the sense of commitment many people felt toward the parish.[1] When the service ended, Boardman Township resident Julia Palazzo, a member of Immaculate Conception for more than six decades, conveyed an attitude of mournful resignation. "It's difficult, but we knew it was inevitable," she said, in an interview with a local newspaper reporter. Others expressed cautious optimism about the future. "It's a sad day, but something dies and something starts up living again," said Cosmo Pecchia, a parishioner who had also driven in from Boardman. Pecchia's comment echoed the theme of Bishop Murry's homily, which focused on the parish's enduring legacy. "[Immaculate Conception] has a future," the bishop said to the gathered crowd, "and the future is you."[2] The future to which

Bishop Murry referred was inextricably bound up with the newly created parish of Immaculate Conception–Sacred Heart of Jesus, the product of a recent merger between two established east side churches.

Feelings of hope and resignation may not have been the only emotions at play among those who attended the final mass. Some parishioners probably felt a twinge of resentment over the imminent loss of a beloved icon. For many of them, the choice of Sacred Heart as the home of the merged parish appeared no less "inevitable" than the closing of the Immaculate itself. Months before a decision was announced, unsettling rumors had circulated among Immaculate Conception's parishioners. "Early on . . . there were statements made that kind of indicated it was . . . a foregone conclusion that Immaculate would close," recalled Father Kevin Peters, pastor of Immaculate Conception–Sacred Heart of Jesus Parish. "That was really unfair to the people at the Immaculate . . . because the decision had not been made." Although Father Peters took steps to discredit such rumors, many parishioners at the Immaculate found Sacred Heart's attributes difficult to ignore, and some fell into a "despairing mode." Unlike Immaculate Conception, whose surrounding neighborhood had been destroyed by a combination of highway construction and commercial development, Sacred Heart was ensconced within a stable, mostly Latino neighborhood; and more than 30 percent of Sacred Heart's parishioners resided within the parish boundaries, a figure that compared to less than 10 percent at the Immaculate. Moreover, Sacred Heart's granite, Norman-style physical plant, which comprised three buildings arranged in a U-shaped pattern, did not lend itself to a wide range of reuses. Meanwhile, all three of Immaculate Conception's buildings could be leased or sold, independently. Indeed, the parish's former school building, located across the street from the church, had served as the site of a charter school for almost five years. Some observers pointed out that the stately rectory would be an ideal site for an inn catering to out-of-town guests, while others later suggested that the church's spacious edifice would make a natural home for the diocesan archives, whose contents are currently spread across a number of sites.[3] In certain ways, the parish complex of Immaculate Conception had become a victim of its own versatility.

The final decision regarding the site of the merged parish, however, rested with the parish councils of Immaculate Conception and Sacred Heart of Jesus, an arrangement that reflected the diocese's determination to avoid some of the tensions and misunderstandings that had accompanied parish consolidations in other communities. Youngstown, as the last Catholic diocese in Ohio to engage in parish downsizing, benefited from hard lessons meted out elsewhere; and there was no shortage of cautionary tales for those anxious to avoid the controversies of the past. In 2004, for instance, a sweeping parish reconfiguration plan implemented in the Archdiocese of Boston inspired a backlash among parishioners, many of whom resisted orders to close their churches. In one high-profile case, parishioners of St. Frances Xavier Cabrini Church, based in Scituate, Massachusetts, occupied the parish complex and, over the next six years, maintained a 24-hour vigil to prevent the building from being closed. Parishioners at St. Frances were among representatives of nine parishes in the archdiocese who appealed directly to the Vatican, which upheld the archdiocese's right to close the parishes a few months later.[4]

More recently, in March 2009, Cleveland Bishop Richard G. Lennon's decision to close 29 of his diocese's 224 parishes, while merging 41 others, met similar resistance. Twelve days after the bishop's announcement, the *Cleveland Plain Dealer* reported that representatives of no fewer than 11 parishes were appealing the decision.[5] As *U.S. Catholic* reported in 2010, three of those appeals yielded encouraging results, when St. Colman, St. Ignatius of Antioch, and St. Stephen parishes "were given a four-year directive to prove their viability." Meanwhile, embittered parishioners of St. Peter Parish, whose appeal had been rejected, set out to establish an unauthorized congregation, a move that prompted Bishop Lennon to threaten them with excommunication.[6] In a particularly surprising development, the Diocese of Cleveland's decision to close churches that were regarded as urban landmarks drew expressions of concern from members of Cleveland City Council, who moved to strengthen the city's historical landmark law.[7] "We think of these churches as houses of worship, but they're also part of the basic foundations of our community," Councilman Michael Polensek said. "They have a great impact on neighborhood stability. We need to protect these structures."[8]

Consolidation was bound to come to Youngstown, and few residents should have been surprised when, on May 29, 2010, Bishop Murry announced there would be 25 fewer parishes in the diocese, bringing their number from 112 to 87. The planned consolidation was framed as a necessary response to trends including demographic change, economic difficulties, and a chronic shortage of priests.[9] So far, the consolidation process in Youngstown has been relatively smooth, which may owe something to careful planning. "When we started this process, I deliberately spent time looking at how it was done in other dioceses," Bishop Murry explained in an interview. "Then, we tried to monopolize on the strengths and minimize the weaknesses." The bishop stressed that his primary concern was to ensure that "plans came from the local level."[10] In 2008, within months of his installation, Bishop Murry recommended that each of the diocese's 115 parishes organize a planning committee, whose first order of business would be to conduct an assessment of the parish. Guided by a survey developed at the diocesan level, parish planning committees composed a detailed overview of their parish that included estimates of attendance at Sunday services, the average age of parishioners, the overall condition of the physical plant, and (in cases where parishes maintained schools) the general direction of enrollment. Each parish was then asked to select two representatives of its planning committee to serve on a larger deanery planning committee. The deaneries, for the most part, corresponded to the diocese's six counties—Mahoning, Trumbull, Columbiana, Portage, Stark, and Ashtabula—but given the size of Mahoning County, it comprised two deaneries: Mahoning North and Mahoning South. At that point, the deanery planning committees were instructed to select two representatives to serve on an executive (or diocesan) planning committee.

The planning stage of the process was overseen by Monsignor John Zuraw, former diocesan director of clergy and then administrator of Immaculate Conception Parish.[11] In a move that underscored the diocese's investment in the process, Bishop Murry appointed another diocesan priest, Father Nicholas R. Shori, to oversee the implementation of the consolidation plan, on a full-time basis. Apparently, one of the bishop's goals was to ensure that lines of communication between the diocese and pastors and parishioners would remain open. "We've seen how other dioceses did this," Father Shori explained in an interview. "My position is a full-time position and, technically, the bishop didn't want me to have any contacts with parishes, as far as assignment is [concerned] so that there was no indication of preference or favor." Father Shori recognized that, if he were appointed to the position, he would be required to step down as pastor of St. Paul Parish, in New Middletown, Ohio, where he had served for 17 years.[12]

Even some of those with misgivings about the consolidation plan have praised the diocese for treating the matter seriously. Richard Scarsella, a Youngstown area writer and preservationist, is one of them. "I have to give the diocese credit," Scarsella said in a recent interview. "They are [addressing] parish councils. They have encouraged regular meetings. They have a consolidation-merger-suppression-collaboration facilitator with . . . Father Shori. So, that much I will give them credit for." In other areas, Scarsella has found much to criticize. He argued, for instance, that the diocese placed strict limits on dialogue when it determined beforehand that a certain number of buildings would need to be closed. "Yes, [parishioners] attended these meetings," he said. "But they were told in no uncertain terms that these things were going to be done. There might've been a menu of things that were going to be done, but many of them—all of them, really, for the most part—were unpalatable." When the diocese presented the options of merger, collaboration, and closure, few parishioners were able to discern much of a difference, he argued. From the outset, Scarsella warned that the diocese's decision to close churches poses a threat to the community's architectural heritage, given that older parishes will be disproportionately affected.[13] In spring 2010, his concern about the fate of local religious landmarks inspired him to launch a program called the "Sacred Places Dialogue."[14] Since then, he has met with a number of groups to discuss strategies for the preservation of threatened religious landmarks; and in recent months, he has worked closely with parishioners of St. Casimir's Church, a Polish national parish that is set to merge with St. Columba Cathedral within the next two years. The parishioners, who recently established a nonprofit organization, are attempting to purchase the parish complex from the diocese, with the long-term goal of turning it into a multipurpose community center and museum. Scarsella suggested that the predicament of parishes like St. Casimir's highlights the church's insensitivity to ethnic institutions, and he went on to question the diocese's apparent failure to enlist the support of potential donors, especially those connected to ethnic communities. "I think the Catholic Church is looking at . . . demographics, but I think they're ignoring some other demographics . . . because your . . . Europeans are very well heeled," Scarsella said. "They have deep pockets, even though they may be of a certain age."[15]

Bishop Murry denies that he is indifferent to the plight of many of the community's national parishes, and he contends that the parish reconfiguration plan will ultimately strengthen local ethnic communities. "I made it clear from the very beginning that I wanted to maintain the ethnic heritage, ethnic traditions, and cultures," he said in an interview. "My point to these various groups was that, if we try to maintain all of these buildings, what is going to happen is, all the money that you have is going to be spent on building maintenance, and you're going to reach a point where you can't afford to maintain these building, and they will simply disappear." Bishop Murry indicated that, by reducing the number of ethnic parishes, the diocese will contribute to the survival of those that remain. "Do we need to have three Slovak parishes in the city of Youngstown?" he asked. "Can we come together and maintain culture, history, and tradition in fewer buildings, so that we can do more outreach and evangelization, attract young people, and maintain this into the future?"[16] Yet, it is difficult to ignore that the consolidation plan has struck ethnic parishes harder than most others, and few groups have been more adversely affected than Youngstown's Polish American community, given that the city's two Polish national parishes, St. Casimir and St. Stanislaus Kostka, are scheduled to merge with St. Columba Cathedral.[17] The impending demise of these institutions, in particular, has fueled questions about steps that can, and should, be taken to preserve the memory of churches that were once repositories of Old World culture. In December 2010, Father Shori addressed this issue in a meeting with the Ethnic Heritage Society, an organization established by another diocesan priest, Father Joseph Rudjak, who currently serves as the pastor of three ethnic parishes—Sts. Peter and Paul (Croatian), Our Lady of Hungary, and St. Stephen of Hungary. The organization's stated mission is to support local ethic communities.[18] More recently, in March 2011, Father Shori indicated that he intends to form a committee of scholars, preservationists, and representatives of ethnic communities that would examine strategies to preserve the history of ethnic churches that are scheduled to close.[19]

As the consolidation process unfolds, other critical observers have warned that the closing of urban parishes could send an unintended message regarding the diocese's commitment to the cities, especially in the wake of serial school closures that have left one parochial elementary school operating in Youngstown. Bishop Murry indicated that, while he appreciated such concerns, the consolidation plan should be understood as part of a larger effort to bolster urban parishes that remain viable. "In the three years since I've been here, I have spoken on a number of occasions . . . about the commitment of the diocese to the cities," he said. "And I've said over and over again, 'We are not going to abandon the cities.'" The bishop added that he is often advised by Catholic business leaders "to just let the cities crumble and focus [our] energies in the suburbs," a course that he claimed to reject. "We're not going to do that," he said. "What I see as a result of these consolidations is to create stronger urban parishes that can do the outreach . . . that can do the ministry that is needed for people who are sometimes on the edge." The maintenance of urban parishes, he said, enables Catholics (many of whom live in suburban communities) "to make that commitment to walk with the city" and to address its problems in a more direct manner. At the same time, however, the diocese has been compelled to respond to demographic shifts that have resulted in smaller urban Catholic populations.[20] This development was underscored by the findings of the 2010 U.S. Census, which revealed that Youngstown's population had fallen by 18.4 percent since 2000, a loss of 15,044 residents.[21] The census report showed that, during the same period, the population of Mahoning County, as a whole, fell by 7.3 percent, a figure suggesting that the city's losses were disproportionate.[22] While the census data failed to specify the religion of those residents who had migrated from the city, the findings point to a further decline in Youngstown's Catholic population.

Similar trends elsewhere have encouraged some episcopal leaders to shift their base of operations to the suburbs, as Boston's archbishop, Sean Cardinal O'Malley, did in 2007, when he moved the archdiocesan offices to the outlying community of Braintree.[23] Bishop Murry has taken a decidedly different path. In April 2009, he announced plans to sell the five-bedroom suburban residence that was purchased by his predecessor, Bishop Thomas J. Tobin, and promptly relocated from Liberty Township to Youngstown.[24] "When I moved into the city," the bishop recalled, "I got letters from people saying: 'Don't move into the city. Move to the suburbs.'" For the bishop, who resided for a time in the Detroit area, the church's responsibility to maintain a relationship with urban communities is not just a matter of ethics; it is a practical necessity. "The church in Detroit, in many ways, simply became disconnected from the city, because the Catholics were all in the suburbs," he said. "The African American Methodists were in the city, and the Catholics were out in the suburbs; and so, understandably, the churches were serving their own people." Bishop Murry stressed, however, that U.S. church leaders have become increasingly sensitive to the fact that "you can't have a strong, stable economy in the suburbs if you don't have a strong, stable economy in the city." He added that there must be "fluidity and interaction between both" if the metropolitan area, as a whole, is to prosper. While this may be true, the demographic challenges facing the Diocese of Youngstown at this juncture are by no means limited to the flow of Catholics from the cities to the suburbs, as the bishop readily acknowledged.[25] The six-county diocese is feeling the impact of regional depopulation, as more people migrate from the northeastern United States to the South and the West; and reports indicate that the number of registered Catholics in the diocese has fallen from 256,071 in 2000 to 201,857 in 2009.[26] This population decline has plunged many diocesan parishes into "severe financial straits," making the merger and closure of some inevitable.[27] As Father Shori noted, the situation in the Diocese of Youngstown reflects challenges facing much of the state of Ohio. "The only diocese in Ohio that hasn't had to do this . . . reconfiguration is Columbus," Father Shori said, "and that's because [the Catholic] population in Columbus is increasing."[28]

These sweeping demographic changes have overlapped with a worsening priest shortage, which has made it difficult for the diocese to staff parishes. "At this point in the history of the diocese, we have approximately a hundred priests, with fifty priests who are retired," Bishop Murry explained. "Of that 100 active priests, the majority of those priests are over the age of sixty; and between 2011 and 2014, thirty-five of those active 100 priests will reach the retirement age of seventy." The bishop noted that this sobering figure does not take into account the possibility that some priests will become disabled or will die prematurely. "We, physically, cannot continue to maintain 115 parishes," Bishop Murry said. "That's why we had to make a change, because we want to be able to provide a full range of services to the people in our parishes."[29] The priest shortage in the Diocese of Youngstown is consistent with a national trend. According to the Center for Applied Research in the Apostolate at Georgetown University, the number of priests in the United States fell from almost 60,000 in 1965 to almost 50,000 in 1995, to slightly more than 40,000, in 2009.[30] Over the past decade, the central role the priest

Epilogue

shortage has played in the trend toward parish consolidation has stirred questions about the viability of the so-called one-priest, one-parish model. Indeed, those parishes who resisted consolidation in the Archdiocese of Boston publicly urged the archdiocese to employ "parish life coordinators or lay or religious administrators to circumvent closures." The consolidations have also rekindled the debate over priestly celibacy. "We don't believe the priest shortage is a valid reason to close parishes," stated Sister Chris Schenk, CSJ, a parish-based activist. "We're closing parishes rather than opening ordination. Why couldn't we open the conversation to the married priesthood?"[31]

Bishop Murry acknowledged that the priest shortage has forced the diocese to consider a range of models for parish administration. "One alternative to the one-priest, one-parish model, of course, is to bring parishes together, as we have in a number of places in the dioceses," he said. "You have one priest who is pastor of two smaller parishes, and he works with the parish council, the finance council, [and] also a lay administrator." There has been some resistance to this approach, however, and most of it has come from parishioners who insist on access to a priest. The bishop noted that, in cases where a priest is able to travel back and forth between parishes (celebrating a Saturday Mass at one site and a Sunday Mass at the other), the arrangement tends to work well. "When he can't do that, that's when the people will write me and say, 'Would it be possible to assign another priest, or could we restructure in such a way that we have a priest available to us?'" he added. Apparently, some parishes in the diocese have fared well under the management of administrators, including St. Patrick's Church, based in Leetonia, Ohio. The current administrator, Sister Joan Franklin, OP, addresses most responsibilities connected to the parish's daily management, while sacramental duties are handled by Father Robert Edwards, the pastor of St. Paul's Parish, in nearby Salem, Ohio. "Father [Edwards] comes over and celebrates Mass and the other sacraments," Bishop Murry explained. "But if someone needs baptismal records, if someone needs counseling, if someone needs to be visited in the hospital, Sister Joan does that." The bishop stressed, however, that the use of parish administrators has done nothing to relieve the financial difficulties that have arisen at many parishes amid regional depopulation, and a growing number of these institutions are no longer equipped to cover the cost of their operation.[32]

In the face of these challenging trends, a handful of center-city parishes in Youngstown have managed to flourish, even though their parish boundaries are depopulated or include few Catholics. Bishop Murry indicated such parishes share three fundamental characteristics. "First and foremost, the parish has to be . . . an evangelizing parish," he said. "When a parish starts thinking in terms of, 'What we want to do is maintain what we have,' that is the death knell." He added that those parishes that have remained vibrant reflect a "commitment, a dedication, a thirst for growth." The second characteristic Bishop Murry associated with thriving parishes was a vibrant liturgical life "that reaches out to younger people, to middle-aged people, and to older people." Unsurprisingly, the third characteristic was financial stability. "You can't run a stable parish if, year after year, the parish is in debt," he noted. When asked to identify an urban parish that exemplified these qualities, the bishop singled out St. Patrick's, located on the city's south side. "They do an excellent job in all three of those areas," the bishop said. "If we had more parishes like St. Patrick's, I think we would have a strong church."[33] Carla Hlavac, former director of faith formation at the parish, stressed that St. Patrick's reputation is the product of continuous effort. "Since I've been on staff here, I have felt like we have to compete with the big parishes," she said in a 2009 interview. "Not only do we have to do it well, but we have to do it better." She added that the church's pastor, Father Edward P. Noga, consistently reminded staff members and parishioners alike that, if they weren't "cutting edge," they would die. Although a significant percentage of St. Patrick's members are older suburbanites who have sentimental ties to the neighborhood, the parish maintains an active youth program, offers a special liturgy for children (held in the parish social hall during the regular mass), and provides a family-based religious education program. Hlavac observed that many families who have joined St. Patrick's were once associated with suburban "mega-parishes." "What they told me is that they felt like numbers there," she said. "And they wanted their kids to grow up in a parish that was a real community, where they would know one another."[34] The strong sense of community Hlavac described has inspired many parishioners to be generous with their time and their resources. Over the years, the parish has not only remained afloat financially, but it also has sponsored benefits for a range of charitable causes. In the wake of Hurricane Katrina, St. Patrick's parishioners contributed in various ways to the rebuilding of Our Lady of Lourdes Parish, in Slidell, Louisiana, which was completely destroyed in the disaster.[35] Bishop Murry has expressed confidence that at least some of Youngstown's consolidated parishes will move in this positive direction.[36]

This is the hope of urban priests like Father Kevin Peters, who said he is encouraged by recent developments at the merged parish of Immaculate Conception–Sacred Heart of Jesus. Father Peters noted that the vast majority of parishioners who belonged to Immaculate Conception have chosen to join the merged parish, even though some of them expressed misgivings about the consolidation. The pastor recalled that, when the two parishes were formally joined on January 9, 2011, he requested that parishioners at the Immaculate specify whether or not they planned to join the new parish; and to his aston-ishment, about 80 percent of the respondents indicated they would become part of Immaculate Conception–Sacred Heart of Jesus. "I was figuring . . . that, if we got a handful of people, we'd be lucky," he said. Shortly after the closing of Immaculate Conception's edifice, the pastor arranged for workers to remove three items from the vacant building and transport them to the site of the merged parish. These included the reconfigured altarpiece, the pulpit, and a Schantz organ that had been installed at Immaculate Conception a century earlier. "Well, as soon as it was announced that we were going to move [these items] to the Sacred Heart church . . . that started this process of people thinking, 'Okay, well, we're moving physically and emotionally to this new place,' and that kind of brought it together for them." More refresh-ing surprises were in store, including the almost pastoral environment of the merged parish's surrounding neighborhood, a district stigmatized as a locus of crime. "We can talk about how dangerous it is," Father Peters said. "But the reality is . . . on any given day, there are elderly couples walking down toward Lincoln Park. There're kids riding bikes." The pastor recalled that on one afternoon as he sat at his desk in the parish rectory, he saw a young boy riding his bike up the street. As the boy approached the church complex, he paused and made the sign of the cross. "Now, where do you see that?" Father Peters asked. "And I think that is more descriptive of the east side than we give the east side credit for." The priest went on to describe a parish com-munity that seems committed to improving the neighborhood. One group of parishioners had announced plans to establish a communal vegetable garden, he noted, while another had volunteered to remove debris from a dry-bed creek that flows near the parish complex. Father Peters indicated that much of this energy is a by-product of the merger. "I don't know how this would happen, but it seems to make sense to me that . . . mergers and collaborative efforts should be general maintenance of the church," he said.[37]

For some of the city's older Catholics, however, the past tends to hold more allure than the future. Fred and Josephine Ross, lifelong members of St. Anthony's Parish, are having difficulty coming to terms with the scheduled merger of their church with its north side neighbor, Our Lady of Mt. Carmel Parish, Youngstown's "other" Italian national parish. The couple appeared to slip into a reverie as they recalled the days when St. Anthony's Parish was the center of a bustling Italian American enclave. Each dawn, the men, on their way to the nearby steel mills, fired up the district's communal brick ovens; as their wives, mothers, and sisters took turns baking their allotment of dough, the smell of bread permeated the neighborhood. In the decades before World War II, the annual highlight of the district was the St. Anthony religious procession, held on July 13. Led by a brass band, the men of the neighborhood carried a plaster image of the saint through the cobblestone streets of Brier Hill, while a clutch of elderly women followed close behind. "The old women, imagine them, marching in the parade, carrying their shoes," Fred Ross recalled. "That was their devotion to St. Anthony. That was their penance." Meanwhile, his wife, Josephine, looked back with surprising nostalgia on the harsh years of the Depression, when neighbors in the district refused to allow her and her widowed mother to "go without." "My mother would get up in the morning, and there'd be crackers in the door," she recalled. "Somebody just dropped them off, but you don't know who. They never wanted you to feel that they were giving you something, but they didn't want us to go hungry." When the conversation turned to the present, however, the couple became noticeably reserved, though Fred Ross eventually agreed to discuss the plight of his long-time parish. "I feel, and a lot us feel . . . that this new bishop was brought here to straighten out this diocese from a financial viewpoint," he said. "And all this change is dollars and cents. St. Anthony's probably has 200 parishioners. . . . We can't even pay our utilities." Fred Ross struggled to put a positive spin on St. Anthony's merger with Our Lady of Mt. Carmel, noting that many of its parishioners are "doing their best" to make the prospective newcomers feel at home. While he claimed to bear no grudge against the diocese, he admitted that he could not fully accept the imminent closure of his parish. "We are letting our hearts control what we think should be done, and I think we're going to get hurt," he said. "We of St. Anthony's are going to get hurt."[38]

NOTES

1. Father Kevin Peters, interview by the author, March 22, 2011, transcript, Ethnic Heritage Society Collection, #385, Mahoning Valley Historical Society, Youngstown, OH.

2. Sean Barron, "Tears, Hopes Mesh at Last Mass at East Side Church," *The Vindicator*, 1, January 31, 2011.

3. Peters, interview.

4. J. D. Long-Garcia, "The Need for Closure: Parishes Should Have an Exit Strategy Before Shutting Their Doors," *US Catholic*, October 2010, 12–13.

5. Michael O'Malley and Robert L. Smith, "Parishioners Rally to Keep Churches Open: 'Selected' Ones Appeal Their Cases to Bishop," *The Plain Dealer*, 1, March 27, 2009.

6. Long-Garcia, "The Need for Closure," 16.

7. O'Malley and Smith, *The Plain Dealer*, March 15, 2009.

8. "City Council Aims to Protect Churches Slated for Closure," *The National Catholic Reporter*, 3, March 20, 2009.

9. Michael O'Malley, "Youngstown Diocese Closes Building, but Merges Congregations, *The Plain Dealer,* May 29, 2010, blog.cleveland.com/metro/2010/03/youngstown_diocese_closes_buil.html (accessed April 20, 2011).

10. Bishop George V. Murry, SJ, transcript, interview by the author, April 5, 2011, Ethnic Heritage Society Collection, #385, Mahoning Valley Historical Society, Youngstown, OH.

11. Lou Jacquet, "Process Gears Up as Diocese Launches Parish/Schools Study: Monsignor John Zuraw Has Been Chosen to Direct the 'Comprehensive' Undertaking," *The Catholic Exponent,* 3, October 17, 2008.

12. Father Nicholas R. Shori, interview by the author, March 10, 2011, transcript, Ethnic Heritage Society Collection, #385, Mahoning Valley Historical Society, Youngstown, OH.

13. Richard S. Scarsella, interview by the author, March 11, 2011, transcript, Ethnic Heritage Society Collection, #385, Mahoning Valley Historical Society, Youngstown, OH.

14. "Presentation to Focus on Preserving Houses of Worship," *The Vindicator,* September 24, 2010, www.vindy.com/news/2010/sep/24/presentation-to-focus-on-preserving-hous/ (accessed April 20, 2011).

15. Scarsella, interview.

16. Murry, interview.

17. Sean Barron, "End of Special Liturgy at St. Stan Has Some Poised to Exit Church," *The Vindicator,* December 27, 2010, www.vindy.com/news/2010/dec/27/polish-masssflbexodus/ (accessed April 20, 2011).

18. Sean Barron, "Diocese Implementation Plan: Community Outreach Must Be Main Focus," *The Vindicator,* December 12, 2010, www.vindy.com/news/2010/dec/12/diocese-implementation-plan-outreach-mus/ (accessed April 2, 2011).

19. Shori, interview.

20. Murry, interview.

21. David Skolnick, "2010 Census Results," *The Vindicator,* March 10, 2011, www.vindy.com/news/2011/ mar/10/2010-census-results/ (accessed April 18, 2011).

22. "Census: Youngstown Population Drops 18.3 Percent," *The Vindicator,* March 9, 2011, www.vindy.com/news/2011/mar/09/census-youngstown8217s-population-drops-/ (accessed April 18, 2011).

23. Michael Paulson, "Boston Archdiocese to Sell Headquarters for $65 Million, Move to Braintree," *The Boston Globe,* May 24, 2007, www.boston.com/news/globe/city_region/breaking_news/2007/05/boston_archdioc_1.html (accessed April 18, 2011).

24. "Youngstown Catholic Bishop Sells Residence to Cut Costs," The Associated Press, April 29, 2009, www.journalgazette.net/article/20090428/NEWS11/904289971/-1/NEWS09 (accessed April 18, 2011).

25. Murry, interview.

26. Bob Coupland and Joshua Flesher, "Plan: Close, Merge Parishes: Diocese Cites Changing Attitudes, Demographics," *The Tribune Chronicle,* February 26, 2010, 1.

27. Murry, interview.

28. Shori, interview.

29. Murry, interview.

30. Long-Garcia, "The Need for Closure," 13.

31. Ibid., 15–16.

32. Murry, interview.

33. Ibid.

34. Carla J. (Haiser) Hlavac, interview by the author, July 15, 2009, transcript, Hogan-Cullinan Family Collection, #314, Mahoning Valley Historical Society, Youngstown, OH.

35. Amanda Garrett, "St. Pat's Helps Out Ruined La. Church," *The Vindicator,* November 6, 2006, www4.vindy.com/content/local_regional/303521855015346.php (accessed April 20, 2011).

36. Murry, interview.

37. Peters, interview.

38. Fred and Josephine Ross, interview by the author, April 9, 2010, transcript, Center for Working-Class Studies at Youngstown State University, Youngstown, OH.

Bibliography

Aikenhead, Marie. "Board Refuses School Funding: Votes against Diocese Inner City Aid." *Youngstown Vindicator,* November 17, 1976, A-1.

————. "Catholic School Enrollment Dips." *Youngstown Vindicator,* January 12, 1975, A-13.

————. "Diocesan Schools Reveal Ethnic Makeup: 8.2% of 10,408 Students Are from Minorities." *Youngstown Vindicator,* April 3, 1977, B-7.

————. "Family of 4 Teachers Gets Involved: Winsens Tackle Inner City Problems." *Youngstown Vindicator,* January 16, 1972, A-3.

————. "Says Catholic Schools Lack Psychologists." *Youngstown Vindicator,* February 23, 1977, 6.

Alcorn, William K. "Of Friendship and War: JFK Left Lasting Impression on Valley Woman." *Vindicator,* May 25, 2008, A-1.

Aley, Howard C. *A Heritage to Share: The Bicentennial History of Youngstown and the Mahoning Valley.* Youngstown, OH: The Bicentennial Commission of Youngstown and Mahoning County, Ohio, 1975.

Alt, Martha Naomi, and Katharin Peter. *Private Schools: A Brief Portrait.* Washington, DC: U.S. Department of Education, 2002.

Amatos, Chris. "Immaculate Conception Pupils Love Their School: Join with Pastor, Parents in Effort to Save Facility." *Youngstown Vindicator,* December 11, 1977, A-24.

————. "A Look at the Past and Future of Catholic Schools." *Youngstown Vindicator,* January 29, 1978, B-3.

Appleby, R. Scott, Patricia Byrne, and William L. Portier, eds. *Creative Fidelity: American Catholic Intellectual Traditions.* New York, NY: Orbis Books, 2004.

Armstrong, Herbert L., Clarence E. Barnes, May Byrd, Otis R. Douglas, and James P. Lottier. *Afro-American Bicentennial Observance: A Rediscovery of Part of the Past.* Youngstown, OH: Afro-American Bicentennial Committee, 1976.

Bagsarian, Tom. "DeBartolo: Faith Values Stand Out; Politicians, Business Leaders and Longtime Friends Remember the Business Legend." *Vindicator,* December 20, 1994, A-1.

Baker, David P., and Cornelius Riordan. "The Eliting of the Common American Catholic School and the National Education Crisis." *Phi Delta Kappan* 80, no. 1 (September 1998): 16–23.

———. "It's Not about the Failure of Catholic Schools: It's about Demographic Transformations." *Phi Delta Kappan* 80, no. 6 (February 1999): 462–63, 478.

Barron, Mary. "The Return of the Communion Wars: Prominent Catholic Democrat Targeted for Obama Support." *National Catholic Reporter,* 10, May 30, 2008. findarticles.com/p/articles/mi_m1141/is_20_44/ai_n25495213/ (accessed June 7, 2010).

Barron, Sean. "Diocese Implementation Plan: Community Outreach Must Be Main Focus." *Vindicator,* December 12, 2010. www.vindy.com/news/2010/dec/12/diocese-implementation-plan-outreach-mus/ (accessed April 2, 2011).

———. "End of Special Liturgy at St. Stan Has Some Poised to Exit Church." *Vindicator,* December 27, 2010. www.vindy.com/news/2010/dec/27/polish-mass flbexodus/ (accessed April 20, 2011).

———. "Tears, Hopes Mesh at Last Mass at East Side Church." *Vindicator,* January 31, 2011, A-1.

Beauregard, Robert A. *When America Became Suburban.* Minneapolis, MN: University of Minnesota Press, 2006.

Beelen, George D. "The Negro in Youngstown: Growth of a Ghetto." (seminar paper, Kent State University, Kent, OH, November 27, 1967).

Bellah, Robert N., James Madsen, William M. Sullivan, Ann Swidler, and Steven M. Tipton. *Habits of the Heart: Individualism and Commitment in American Life.* Berkeley, CA: University of California Press, 1985/1996.

Benson, Peter L. "Catholic Education and Its Impact on the Value System of Low Income Students." In *American Catholic Identity: Essays in an Age of Change,* edited by Francis J. Butler, 185–203. Kansas City, MO: Sheed & Ward, 1994.

Bernstein, Carl, and Marco Politi. *His Holiness: John Paul II and the History of Our Time.* New York, NY: Penguin Books, 1996.

Blatnica, Dorothy Ann. *"At the Altar of Their Gods": African American Catholics in Cleveland, 1922–1961.* New York, NY: Garland Publishing, 1995.

Blue, Frederick J., William D. Jenkins, H. William Lawson, and Joan M. Reedy. *Mahoning Memories: A History of Youngstown and Mahoning County.* Virginia Beach, VA: Donning, 1995.

Boyle, Kevin. *Arc of Justice: A Saga of Race, Civil Rights, and Murder in the Jazz Age.* New York, NY: Henry Holt, 2004.

Briggs, Kenneth. *Double Crossed: Uncovering the Catholic Church's Betrayal of American Nuns.* New York, NY: Doubleday, 2006.

Brody, David. *Labor in Crisis: The Steel Strike of 1919.* Philadelphia, PA: J. B. Lippincott, 1965.

———. *Steelworkers in America: The Nonunion Era.* Cambridge, MA: Harvard University Press, 1960.

Brown, Ernest Jr. "Chic It Wasn't, but Monkey's Nest Was Home, and More, to Its People." *Youngstown Vindicator,* August 14, 1977, B-3.

_____. "Continued Area Population Drop Likely." *Youngstown Vindicator,* September 12, 1985, 1.

Bruno, Richard. *Steelworker Alley: How Class Works in Youngstown.* Ithica, NY: Cornell University Press, 1999.

Bryk, Anthony S., Valerie E. Lee, and Peter B. Holland. *Catholic Schools and the Common Good.* Cambridge, MA: Harvard University Press, 1993.

Bryk, Anthony S., and Yeow Meng Thum. "The Effects of High School Organization on Dropping Out: An Exploratory Investigation." *American Educational Research Journal* 26, no. 3 (1989): 353–83.

Buetow, Harold A. *Of Singular Benefit: The Story of Catholic Education in the United States.* New York, NY: Macmillan, 1970.

_____. "The Underprivileged and Roman Catholic Education." *Journal of Negro Education* 40, no. 4 (Autumn 1971): 373–89.

_____. "The United States Catholic School Phenomenon." In *Perspectives on the American Catholic Church,* edited by Stephen J. Vecchio and Virginia Geiger, 197–222. Westminister, MD: Christian Classics, 1989.

Buss, Terry F., and Stearns Redburn. *Shutdown in Youngstown: Public Policy for Mass Unemployment.* Albany, NY: State University of New York Press, 1983.

Butler, Francis J., ed. *American Catholic Identity: Essays in an Age of Change.* Kansas City, MO: Sheed & Ward, 1994.

Campbell, Colleen Carroll. "The Enduring Costs of John F. Kennedy's Compromise." *Catholic World Report,* February 2007. www.ignatius.com/Magazines/CWR/campbell.htm (accessed July 7, 2008).

Carmody, Denise Lardner. *The Double Cross: Ordination, Abortion, and Catholic Feminism.* New York, NY: Crossroad, 1986.

Carroll, James. *An American Requiem: God, My Father, and the War That Came between Us.* Boston, MA: Houghton Mifflin, 1996.

Casey, Robert E. *An Irish Catholic Remembers and Reflects.* New Wilmington, PA: New Horizons Publishing, 2006.

Cayton, Andrew R. L. *Ohio: The History of a People.* Columbus, OH: Ohio State University Press, 2002.

Cech, Scott. "Catholic Closures Linked to Growth of City Charters." *Education Week,* February 12, 2008, 1–2.

Chase, John H. "Youngstown's Colored People." *Youngstown Vindicator,* May 8, 1921, 9.

Christiansen, Drew. "Immigration's Dark Moments." *America,* October 13, 2008. www.americamagazine.org/content/article.cfm?article_id=11126 (accessed June 5, 2010).

Cibulka, James Gerald, Timothy O'Brien, and Donald Zewe. *Inner-City Private Elementary Schools.* Milwaukee, WI: Marquette University Press, 1982.

Cizmar, Paula L. "Steelyard Blues." *Mother Jones,* April 1978, 36–42.

Clark, Donald M. "Black Priest. Black Parish. 'White' Rite?" In *Disciples at the Crossroads: Perspectives on Worship and Church Leadership,* edited by Eleanor Bernstein, 81–91. Collegeville, MN: Liturgical Press, 1993.

Cole, Ron. "At Princeton, Reading, Writing and Religion Rule." *Vindicator,* August 6, 1995, A-1.

_____. "Catholic Schools Launch Fund Drive: Diocese Officials Hope to Know by March 15 If They Can Raise the Money. If Not, a School Could Close." *Vindicator,* February 12, 1995, B-1.

_____. "Catholic Schools Superintendent Takes Same Position in Chicago: Youngstown's Bishop Said a Search for a New Superintendent Will Begin Soon." *Vindicator,* May 4, 2001, A-1.

_____. "Charter School Gets Set to Open: Private Donors Have Given $400,000 to Renovate the Old High School, the Board President Said." *Vindicator,* June 30, 1998, A-1.

_____. "Diocese to Launch Drive to Keep 2 Schools Open: The Survival of Two Youngstown Catholic Schools Could Turn on a Special Collection Next Weekend." *Vindicator,* January 2, 1992, A-1.

_____. "Finances Close St. Dominic's School." *Vindicator,* April 10, 1999, B-1.

_____. "Fund-Raiser Falls Thousands Short of Goal." *Vindicator,* March 16, 1995, A-1.

_____. "Immaculate Conception: Does Bell for Pupils Also Toll for School? The School Has Opened Early; the New Principal's Attitude Is That It Won't Be Closed." *Vindicator,* August 14, 2002, B-1.

_____. "Immaculate Redemption: Urban School Rebounds." *Vindicator,* October 2, 1994, A-1.

_____. "In a Class by Itself: Parochial School 1st with Year-Round Plan." *Vindicator,* April 5, 1998, A-1.

Coleman, James, and Thomas Hoffer. *Public and Private Schools: The Impact of Communities.* New York, NY: Basic Books, 1987.

Coleman, James, Thomas Hoffer, and Sally Kilgore. *Public and Private Schools.* Washington, DC: National Center for Educational Statistics, 1982.

Cooney, John. *The American Pope: The Life and Times of Francis Cardinal Spellman.* New York, NY: Times Books, 1985.

Cornwell, John. *Breaking Faith: Can the Catholic Church Save Itself?* New York, NY: Viking Press, 2001.

Coupland, Bob, and Joshua Flesher. "Plan: Close, Merge Parishes: Diocese Cites Changing Attitudes, Demographics." *Tribune Chronicle,* February 26, 2010, A-1.

Coyne, Emmett. "Are Bishops Making Democratic Catholics Choose?" *Vindicator,* October 5, 2008, A-8.

Curran, Charles E. *Loyal Dissent: Memoir of a Catholic Theologian.* Washington, DC: Georgetown University Press, 2006.

Davis, Claire. "St. Columba's Climaxes 90-Year History Here." *Youngstown Vindicator,* July 21, 1943, 14.

Davis, Cyprian. "God of Our Weary Years: Black Catholics in American Catholic History." In *Taking Down Our Harps: Black Catholics in the United States,* edited by Diana L. Hayes and Cyprian Davis, 17–46. New York, NY: Orbis Books, 1998.

_____. "God's Image in Black: The Black Community in Slavery and Freedom." In *Perspectives on the American Catholic Church, 1789–1989,* edited by Stephen

J. Vicchio and Virginia Geiger, 105–22. Westminster, MD: Christian Classics, 1989.

———. *The History of Black Catholics in the United States.* New York, NY: Crossroad, 1990.

Day, Thomas. *Where Have You Gone, Michelangelo? The Loss of Soul in Catholic Culture.* New York, NY: Crossroad, 1993.

———. *Why Catholics Can't Sing: The Culture of Catholicism and the Triumph of Bad Taste.* New York, NY: Crossroad, 1990.

Delap, Brendan. *Mad Dog Coll: An Irish Gangster.* Dublin, UK: Mercier Press, 2002.

De Souza, Bertram. "Groundbreaking for Westview Housing Is Expected This Month." *Youngstown Vindicator,* April 2, 1981, 4.

Dick, Denise. "Smoky Hollow Revitalization Plan Taking Shape." *Vindicator,* October 8, 2010. www.vindy.com/news/2010/oct/08/8216it8217s-a-beginning8217/ (accessed April 29, 2011).

Dillon, Michele. *Catholic Identity.* Cambridge, UK: Cambridge University Press, 1999.

Dolan, Jay P. *The American Catholic Experience: A History from Colonial Times to the Present.* Garden City, NY: Image Books, 1985.

———. *In Search of an American Catholicism: A History of Religion and Culture in Tension.* New York, NY: Oxford University Press, 2002.

———. *The Irish Americans: A History.* New York, NY: Bloomsbury Press, 2008.

Donadio, Rachel. "Healing Schism, Pope Risks Another." *The New York Times,* January 25, 2009. www.nytimes.com/2009/01/26/world/europe/26pope.html (accessed June 5, 2010).

Donovan, Daniel. *Distinctively Catholic: An Exploration of Catholic Identity.* New York, NY: Paulist Press, 1997.

Fisher, Ian. "Some Muslim Leaders Want Pope to Apologize for Remarks." *New York Times,* September 16, 2006, A-6.

Fitzpatrick, Timothy. "Council at Sacred Heart Hits Merger of Schools." *Youngstown Vindicator,* May 7, 1982, A-1.

———. "Parents Protest Diocesan Move." *Youngstown Vindicator,* April 30, 1982, A-19.

Flanigan, James. "The Priests, the Nuns and the People: Changes in the Church and Religious Life Are Reflected in the Bronx Neighborhood of 'Doubt.'" *National Catholic Reporter,* February 20, 2009, 14a.

Floor, Sarah. "St. Luke to Offer Early Childhood Center." *Vindicator,* March 5, 2011. boardman.vindy.com/news/2011/mar/05/st-luke-to-offer-early-childhood-center/ (accessed April 28, 2011).

Formisano, Robert P. *Boston against Busing: Race, Class, and Ethnicity in the 1960s and 1970s.* Chapel Hill, NC: University of North Carolina Press, 1991.

France, David. *Our Fathers: The Secret Life of the Catholic Church in an Age of Scandal.* New York, NY: Broadway Books, 2004.

Fuechtmann, Thomas G. *Steeples and Stacks: Religion and Steel Crisis in Youngstown.* Cambridge, MA: Cambridge University Press, 1989.

Gabert, Glen Jr. *In Hoc Signo? A Brief History of Catholic Parochial Education in America.* Port Washington, NY: Kennikat Press, 1972.

Gans, Herbert J. *The Urban Villagers: Group and Class in the Life of Italian-Americans.* New York, NY: Free Press, 1962.

Garrett, Amanda. "St. Pat's Helps Out Ruined La. Church." *Vindicator,* November 6, 2006. www4.vindy.com/content/local_regional/303521855015346.php (accessed April 20, 2011).

Gaustaud, Edwin S. *Proclaim Liberty throughout the Land: A History of Church and State in America.* New York, NY: Oxford University Press, 1999/2003.

Gerber, David A. *Black Ohio and the Color Line, 1860–1915.* Urbana, IL: University of Illinois Press, 1976.

Gibson, David. *The Rule of Benedict: Pope Benedict XVI and His Battle with the Modern World.* New York, NY: HarperSanFrancisco, 2006.

Gillis, Chester. *Roman Catholicism in America.* New York, NY: Columbia University Press, 1999.

Giura, Shirley Ann. "Youngstown St. Patrick Marks 85th Anniversary." *Catholic Exponent,* March 8, 1996, 12.

Glazer, Nathan, and Daniel P. Moynihan. *Beyond the Melting Pot: The Negroes, Puerto Ricans, Jews, Italians & Irish of New York City.* Boston, MA: MIT Press, 1963.

Glazier, Michael, and Thomas J. Shelley, eds. *The Encyclopedia of American Catholic History.* Collegeville, MN: Liturgical Press, 1997.

Gleason, Philip. *Keeping the Faith: American Catholicism, Past and Present.* Notre Dame, IN: University of Notre Dame Press, 1987.

Goldberg, David J. *Discontented America: The United States in the 1920s.* Baltimore, MD: Johns Hopkins University Press, 1999.

Goodall, John. "3 Counties Lose Young Workers: The Drain of 18-to-24-Year-Olds Will Spell Problems for the Valley's Job Market, Said a Labor Analyst." *Vindicator,* June 3, 1991, A-1.

———. "Fund Drive Spares 2 Catholic Schools." *Vindicator,* April 9, 1991, A-1.

Goulder, Grace. "Youngstown's Catholic Cathedral Has European Air." *Cleveland Plain Dealer Picture Magazine,* April 20, 1947.

Greeley, Andrew M. *American Catholics since the Council: An Unauthorized Report.* Chicago, IL: Thomas More Press, 1985.

———. *Catholic High Schools and Minority Students.* New Brunswick, NJ: Transaction Publishers, 1982/1996.

———. *The Catholic Myth: The Behavior and Beliefs of American Catholics.* New York, NY: Charles Scribner, 1990.

———. *The Catholic Revolution: New Wine, Old Wineskins, and the Second Vatican Council.* Berkeley, CA: University of California Press, 2004.

———. "How Conservative Are American Catholics?" *Political Science Quarterly* 92, no. 2 (Summer 1977): 208–9.

———. *The Making of the Pope 2005.* New York, NY: Little, Brown, 2005.

Gwin, Harold. "Final Bell Tolls for Two Schools: There Were Some Long Faces As Children Left St. Matthias on Tuesday." *Vindicator,* June 7, 2006, B-1.

_____. "Parochial Schools in Boardman, Struthers Consider Consolidation." *The Vindicator,* February 24, 2009. vindy.com/news/2009/feb/24/parochial-schools-in -boardman-struthers-consider/ (accessed April 28, 2011).

_____. "Plan to Save Schools: The Diocese Had 10,868 Pupils Last Year." *Vindicator,* August 20, 2006, A-1.

Hallinan, Maureen T. "Conclusion: Catholic Education at the Crossroads." In *Catholic Schools at the Crossroads: Survival and Transformation,* edited by James Youniss and John T. Convey, 201–24. New York, NY: Teachers College Press, 2000.

Hamilton, Albert. *The Catholic Journey through Ohio.* Columbus, OH: Catholic Conference of Ohio, 1976.

Hamilton, Esther. "Death Takes Msgr. Kenny: Was Pastor of Immaculate Conception Here from 1910 to 1925." *Youngstown Vindicator,* March 31, 1943, A-1.

Harris, Joseph Claude. "The Funding Dilemma Facing Catholic Elementary and Secondary Schools." In *Schools at the Crossroads: Survival and Transformation,* edited by James Youniss and John T. Convey, 55–71. New York, NY: Teachers College Press, 2000.

Heffernan, Joseph L. "City's Oldest Irishman Is Interviewed by Former Mayor on St. Patrick's Day: John Slavin, 97, Says He Was Born during Year of 'the Big Wind.'" *Youngstown Telegram,* March 17, 1934, 1.

Hennesy, James. *American Catholics: A History of the Roman Catholic Community in the United States.* New York, NY: Oxford University Press, 1981.

Hitchcock, James. *The Decline and Fall of Radical Catholicism.* New York, NY: Herder & Herder, 1971.

Hosansky, David, and Ellen J. Sullivan. "Marriage Puts Teacher out of Work." *Vindicator,* January 29, 1988, A-1.

Houk, George Francis. *The Church in Northern Ohio and in the Diocese of Cleveland, from 1749 to September, 1887.* Cleveland, OH: Short & Forman, 1889, c1887.

Hunt, Thomas C., and Norlene M. Kunkel. "Catholic Schools: The Nation's Largest Alternative School System." In *Religious Schooling in America,* edited by James C. Carper and Thomas C. Hunt, 1–34. Birmingham, AL: Religious Education Press, 1984.

Hunt, Thomas C., and Timothy Walch, eds. *Urban Catholic Education: Tales of Twelve American Cities.* Notre Dame, IN: Alliance for Catholic Education Press, 2010.

Hynes, Michael J. *History of the Diocese of Cleveland: Origin and Growth (1847–1952).* Cleveland, OH: Diocese of Cleveland, 1953.

Ilg, Timothy J., Joseph D. Massucci, and Gerald M. Cattaro. "Brown at 50: The Dream Is Still Alive in Urban Catholic Schools." *Education and Urban Society* 36, no. 3 (2004): 355–67.

Ingham, John. *The Iron Barons: A Social Analysis of an American Elite, 1874–1965.* Westport, CT: Greenwood Press, 1978.

Jackson, Clingan. "Thousands Hail Kennedy at Valley Talks: Hits Mill Output, UN China Vote." *Youngstown Vindicator,* October 10, 1960, A-1.

Jackson, Kenneth T. *Crabgrass Frontier: The Suburbanization of the United States.* New York, NY: Oxford University Press, 1985.

Jacobson, Matthew Frye. *Whiteness of a Different Color: European Immigrants and the Alchemy of Race.* Cambridge, MA: Harvard University Press, 1998.

Jacquet, Lou. "The Cathedral: New St. Columba's Rose from Ruins of the Old: After Fire Destroyed a Youngstown Landmark the Demolition and Rebuilding Were a Story in Themselves." *Catholic Exponent,* May 7, 1993, 5.

_____. "IC Dinner Speaker: Laity Have Responsibility to Serve Those in Need—John Carroll University President Praises Work of Those Who Teach at, Support the School." *Catholic Exponent,* March 12, 2004, 9.

_____. "New Bishop of Youngstown Meets Press: Bishop George Murry Pledges to 'Listen' in Travels through Diocese." *Catholic Exponent,* February 9, 2007, 1.

_____. "Process Gears Up as Diocese Launches Parish/Schools Study: Monsignor John Zuraw Has Been Chosen to Direct the 'Comprehensive' Undertaking." *Catholic Exponent,* October 17, 2008, 3.

_____. "Youngstown St. Anthony School to Close in June." *Catholic Exponent,* March 8, 1996, 3.

Jenkins, Philip. *The New Anti-Catholicism: The Last Acceptable Prejudice.* New York, NY: Oxford University Press, 2003.

Jenkins, William D. *Steel Valley Klan: The Ku Klux Klan in Ohio's Mahoning Valley.* Kent, OH: Kent State University Press, 1990.

Johnson, Dirk. "Catholics Giving Less to Church, Report Says." *New York Times.* June 10, 1987, 22.

Kahn, Roger. *The Boys of Summer.* New York, NY: Harper and Row, 1972.

Kennedy, Kerry. *Being Catholic Now: Prominent Americans Talk about Change in the Church and the Quest for Meaning.* New York, NY: Crown Publishers, 2008.

Kenny, J. R. "Ireland at Valley Forge: A Series Specially Compiled for Information of Students and Respectfully Submitted to the Thinking, Scholarly Readers of This Paper." *Youngstown Daily Vindicator,* March 24, 1921, 5.

Kienzle, William X. *The Gathering.* Kansas City, MO: Andrews McMeel Publishing, 2002.

Knight, Jerry. "Dedication of 154-Unit Project Will Be Held by City Wednesday." *Youngstown Vindicator,* October 11, 1959, B-1.

Kohl, Herbert R. *The Open Classroom: A Practical Guide to a New Way of Teaching.* New York, NY: New York Review, 1969.

Kosinski, Marly. "Austintown Merger, New Principals Top 'Elementary' News." *Catholic Exponent,* August 21, 2009. cathexpo.org/articledetails.aspx?articleid=359# (accessed April 28, 2011).

Kozol, Jonathan. "Still Separate, Still Unequal: America's Educational Apartheid." *Harpers,* September 1, 2005, 41–54.

Kubicki, Judith. "More than Words: The Many Symbols of the Liturgy." *America,* May 26–June 2, 2008, 17–19.

Küng, Hans. *The Catholic Church: A Short History.* New York, NY: Random House, 2003.

LaRue, Dennis. "National City Commits $1 Million to Charter School: Bank CEO on Hand to Greet Voinovich as Governor Defends His Education Initiatives." *Youngstown-Warren Business Journal,* October, 1998, 3.

Leavy, Mary Jerome. "The Catholic Incarnation of America's One Best System: The Relationship of the Catholic and Public School Systems in the United States." PhD diss. University of South Florida, Tampa, 1989.

Leigh, Norman. "Diocese Adopts New Policy to Teachers' Faith." *Youngstown Vindicator,* June 3, 1987, A-10.

Lemann, Nicholas. *The Promised Land: The Great Black Migration and How It Changed America.* New York, NY: Vintage Books, 1991.

Leone, Carmen J. *Rose Street: A Family Story.* Youngstown, OH: Carmen John Leone, 1996/1998.

Linker, Damon. *The Theocons: Secular America under Siege.* New York, NY: Anchor Press, 2006/2007.

Linkon, Sherry, and John Russo. *Steeltown U.S.A.: Work & Memory in Youngstown.* Lawrence, KS: University Press of Kansas, 2002.

Linonis, Linda M. "Bishop Murry Seeks Orderly Downsizing of the Diocese." *Vindicator,* February 6, 2009, 1.

_____. "Bishop Takes Up Fight against Racism: The Bishop Said People of Faith Must Strive to End Racism, and Offered Suggestions of How." *Vindicator,* November 21, 2007, A-1.

_____. "Diversity and Friendliness Make Immaculate Conception Special: The Church, Which Is Marking Its 125th Anniversary Dec. 9, Remains Committed to City." *Vindicator,* November 24, 2007, A-1.

_____. "Politically Active Pastor Dies at 75: The Pastor's 'Love and Mentorship Will Be Missed.'" *Vindicator,* May 28, 2008, B-1.

Long-Garcia, J. D. "The Need for Closure: Parishes Should Have an Exit Strategy before Shutting Their Doors." *US Catholic,* October, 2010, 12–17.

Luconi, Stefano. "Frank L. Rizzo and the Whitening of Italian Americans in Philadelphia." In *Are Italians White? How Race Is Made in America,* edited by Jennifer Guglielmo and Salvatore Salerno, 177–91. New York, NY: Routledge, 2003.

Lunch, William L., and Peter W. Sperlich. "American Public Opinion and the War in Vietnam." *The Western Political Quarterly* 32, no. 1 (March 1979): 21–44.

Lynd, Staughton. *The Fight against Shutdowns: Youngstown's Steel Mill Closings.* San Pedro, CA: Singlejack Books, 1983.

Macedo, Stephen. *Diversity and Distrust: Civic Education in a Multicultural Society.* Cambridge, MA: Harvard University Press, 2000.

Malene, Joanne. "Black Catholics Excited about New Bishop's Appointment." *Catholic Exponent,* March 28, 2007, 42.

Martin, James. "Benedict in America: Message of Joy." *America,* May 12, 2008, 8–9.

_____. "Pastor to the Victims." *America,* May 12, 2008, 10.

Massa, Mark S. *Catholics and American Culture: Fulton Sheen, Dorothy Day, and the Notre Dame Football Team.* New York, NY: W. W. Norton, 1999.

McBride, Paul W. "The Solitary Christians: Italian Americans and Their Church." *Ethnic Groups* 3, no. 4 (1981): 333–54.

McFadden, James A. *The March of the Eucharist from Dungannon.* Youngstown, OH: Diocese of Youngstown, 1951.

McGirr, Lisa. *Suburban Warriors: The Origins of the New American Right.* Princeton, NJ: Princeton University Press, 2001.

McGreevy, John T. *Catholicism and American Freedom: A History.* New York, NY: W. W. Norton, 2003.

_____. *Parish Boundaries: The Catholic Encounter with Race in the Twentieth-Century Urban North.* Chicago, IL: University of Chicago Press, 1996.

_____. "Racial Justice and the People of God: The Second Vatican Council, the Civil Rights Movement, and American Catholics." *Religion and American Culture* 4, no. 2 (1994): 221–54.

McMahon, Eileen M. *What Parish Are You From? A Chicago Irish Community & Race Relations.* Lexington, KY: University Press of Kentucky, 1995.

McNichol, Dan. *The Roads That Built America: The Incredible Story of the U.S. Interstate System.* New York, NY: Barnes & Noble, 2003.

Meade, Patricia. "Remembering the Rage: Angry Blacks Were 'Emulating What Their Peer Groups Were Doing in Bigger Cities,' Official Said." *Vindicator,* April 6, 2008, 1.

Miller, Kerby A. *Emigrants and Exiles: Ireland and the Irish Exodus to North America.* Oxford, UK: Oxford University Press, 1985.

Milliken, Peter H. "Many Bid Farewell as St. Edward School Closes: St. Edward's Graduates Serve This Community Well, the Speaker Said." *Vindicator.* June 6, 2003, A-1.

_____. "Parish the Thought: Can St. Pat's Be 85?" *Vindicator,* May 19, 1996, B-2.

Moreau, Joseph. *Schoolbook Nation: Conflicts over American History Textbooks from the Civil War to the Present.* Ann Arbor, MI: University of Michigan Press, 2006.

Morris, Charles R. *American Catholic: The Saints and Sinners Who Built America's Most Powerful Church.* New York, NY: Vintage, 1997.

Murray, John Courtney. *We Hold These Truths: Catholic Reflections on the American Proposition.* New York, NY: Sheed & Ward, 1960.

Nelson, M. Sheila. "Black Catholic Schools in Inner-City Chicago: Forging a Path to the Future." In *Catholic Schools at the Crossroads: Survival and Transformation,* edited by James Youniss and John T. Convey, 157–77. New York, NY: Teachers College Press, 2000.

O' Keefe, Joseph. "How to Save Catholic Schools: Let the Revitalization Begin." *Commonweal,* March 25, 2005, 15–18.

O'Keefe, Joseph M., Jessica A. Greene, Susan Henderson, Moira Connors, Erik Goldschmidt, and Katherine Schervish. *Sustaining the Legacy: Inner-City Catholic Elementary Schools in the United States.* Washington, DC: National Catholic Educational Association, 2004.

O'Malley, John W. "Trent and Vernacular Liturgy: Evenhanded Restraint Marked the Council's Approach to Controversies." *America,* January 29, 2007, 16–19.

_____. *What Happened at Vatican II.* Cambridge, MA: Belknap Press, 2008.

O'Malley, Michael. "Youngstown Diocese Closes Building, but Merges Congregations." *Plain Dealer,* May 29, 2010. blog.cleveland.com/metro/2010/03/youngstown _diocese_closes_buil.html (accessed April 20, 2011).

O'Malley, Michael, and Robert L. Smith. "Parishioners Rally to Keep Churches Open: 'Selected' Ones Appeal Their Cases to Bishop." *Plain Dealer,* March 27, 2009, 1.

Oshinsky, David M. *A Conspiracy So Immense: The World of Joe McCarthy.* New York, NY: Free Press, 1983.

O'Toole, James M. *The Faithful: A History of Catholics in America.* Cambridge, MA: Belknap Press, 2008.

Ott, Thomas. "Dr. Wosonovich Promises Direct Involvement in Schools." *Youngstown Vindicator,* May 25, 1985, 53.

Owen, William. "Board Votes to Close Sts. Cyril and Methodius." *Youngstown Vindicator,* March 30, 1983, 13.

Paulson, Michael. "Boston Archdiocese to Sell Headquarters for $65 Million, Move to Braintree." *Boston Globe,* May 24, 2007. www.boston.com/news/globe/city_region/breaking_news/ 2007/05/boston_archdioc_1.html (accessed April 18, 2011).

Pellegrini, Mary Ellen. "A Pride in Historic District: Three Groups Work Together to Ensure That the Striking Neighborhoods Will Be Preserved." *Vindicator,* December 25, 2006, B-1.

Phelps, Jamie T. "Black Spirituality." In *Taking Down Our Harps: Black Catholics in the United States,* edited by Diana L. Hayes and Cyprian Davis, 179–98. New York, NY: Orbis Books, 1998.

Polite, Vernon C. "Getting the Job Well Done: African American Students and Catholic Schools." *Journal of Negro Education* 61, no. 2 (Spring 1992): 211–22.

Raudenbush, Stephen W., Brian Rowan, and Yuk Fai Cheong. "Higher Order Instructional Goals in Secondary Schools: Class, Teacher, and School Influences." *American Educational Research Journal* 30, no. 3 (Autumn1993): 523–53.

Reiss, George R. "Predicts City Will Grow Horizontally." *Youngstown Vindicator,* October 16, 1955, A-1.

Riordan, Cornelius. "Public and Catholic Schooling: The Effects of Gender Context Policy." *American Journal of Education* 93, no. 4 (August 1985): 518–40.

Ritz, Stephen L., and Clarence T. Sheehan. "$1,250,000 Fire Ruins St. Columba's: Lightning Sets Cathedral Ablaze." *Youngstown Vindicator,* September 3, 1954, A-1.

Roberts, Tim. "Population Drops in District Counties: Mahoning Hit Hardest with Exodus of 13,257 Residents." *Youngstown Vindicator,* March 31, 1987, 19.

Robinson, E. Wayne. "Blacks Once Forced to Work as 'Jack-Legged Craftsmen.'" *Youngstown Vindicator,* March 31, 1974, B-3.

Roediger, David R. *Working toward Whiteness: How America's Immigrants Became White—the Strange Journey from Ellis Island to the Suburbs.* New York, NY: Basic Books, 2005.

Rowland, John R. "Youngstown's Purse: Growth of Population in Youngstown Pictured from U.S. Census Record." *Youngstown Telegram,* March 7, 1930, 9.

Ryan, Mary Perkins. *Are Parochial Schools the Answer? Catholic Education in the Light of the Council.* New York, NY: Holt, Rinehart and Winston, 1964.

Safford, Sean. *Why the Garden Club Couldn't Save Youngstown: The Transformation of the Rust Belt.* Cambridge, MA: Harvard University Press, 2009.

Salt, Edward. "Morris Scheibel Named Architect: Eighty New Buildings to Accommodate 600 Families Will Be Erected; Work Started at Once on Plans; Assistants Named." *Youngstown Telegram,* July 12, 1935, 1.

Sander, William. "Catholic Grade Schools and Academic Achievement." *Journal of Human Resources* 31, no. 3 (Summer 1996): 540–48.

Scarnecchia, H. J. "First Italians Settled in Coalburg." *Youngstown Vindicator.* February 7, 1932, 3 (magazine supplement).

Schaub, Maryellen. "A Faculty at a Crossroads: A Profile of American Catholic School Teachers." In *Catholic Schools at the Crossroads: Survival and Transformation,* edited by James Youniss and John T. Convey, 72–86. New York, NY: Teachers College Press, 2000.

Schmitt, Angie. "Hope and Gloom: Some 24,000 Jobs Have Been Lost in the Mahoning Valley Since 2000. What Does the Contracting Economy Mean for the Youngstown Revitalization Plan?" *Vindicator,* February 13, 2008, A-1.

_____. "Taking Back Our Neighborhoods: Fifty Percent of Youngstown Residents Feel Unsafe in Their Neighborhoods at Night, a 2004 Study Said." *Vindicator,* February 11, 2008, A-1.

Schuler, Anna Jean. "Parochial Schools Found 1959 Big Year; Enrollment at Record." *Youngstown Vindicator,* January 10, 1960, E-10.

_____. "Rev. Holdbrook Sings First Mass at Cathedral." *Youngstown Vindicator,* November 10, 1958, A-1.

Sease, Douglas R. "Closing of a Steel Mill Hits Workers in U.S. with Little Warning: Though They Keep Getting Income, Retraining Aid, Creation of New Jobs Lag." *Wall Street Journal,* September 23, 1980, 1.

Sedensky, Matt. "More Catholic Schools Closing Across US: Dwindling Enrollment a Vicious Cycle.'" The Associated Press, April 12, 2008. transfigurations.blogspot.com/2008/04/more-catholic-schools-closing-across-us.html (accessed June 5, 2011).

Sheehan, Mary Claire. "St. Columba School Ends 112 Years of Education." *Youngstown Vindicator,* June 4, 1972, B-1.

Sheeran, Thomas J. "YSU Student Fatally Shot at Ohio Frat House." Associated Press, February 7, 2011. www.usatoday.com/news/nation/2011–02–07-ysu-student _N.htm (accessed April 28, 2011).

Shellock, Marie. "Fund-Raiser Begins for Two Catholic Schools." *Vindicator,* March 16, 1991, A-8.

_____. "Our Lady of Sorrows Keeps Latin Tradition." *Vindicator,* February 16, 1991, B-16.

_____. "Parishioners at St. Edward's Have Good Reason to Celebrate: Refurbishment Is Part of a $750,000 Project." *Vindicator,* January 8, 1994, B-4.

Shilling, Don. "Dare to Dream? City's Potential Noted." *Vindicator,* July 18, 2009. www.vindy.com/news/2009/jul/18/dare-to-dream-city8217s-potential-noted/ (accessed April 27, 2011).

Skolnick, David. "2010 Census Results." *Vindicator,* March 10, 2011. www.vindy .com/news/2011/ mar/10/2010-census-results/ (accessed April 18, 2011).

_____. "Sealing the Deal on the Chevrolet Centre: The City and County Will Make a 'Good-Faith' Effort to Buy GM Vehicles." *Vindicator,* November 18, 2005, A-1.

Slawson, Douglas J. *The Department of Education Battle, 1918–1932.* Notre Dame, IN: University of Notre Dame Press, 2005.

Smith, Roger, David Skolnick, and Peter H. Milliken. "Despite City's Loss, Valley Sees Growth: Several Communities—Including Canfield, Cortland, Columbiana and Calcutta—Grew Significantly in the '90s." *Vindicator,* March 17, 2001, A-1.

Soos, Elaine Polomsky. "Catholic Schools Prepare Students for Real World." *Catholic Exponent,* May 9, 1993, 11 (supplement).

Southern, David W. *John LaFarge and the Limits of Catholic Interracialism, 1911–1963.* Baton Rouge, LA: Louisiana State University Press, 1996.

Starzyk, Edith. "Catholic Schools Facing Pressure to Consolidate: Parish Classrooms' Conversion, However, Not Strictly Paired with Church Closings." *Plain Dealer,* March 30, 2009, 1.

Steinfels, Margaret O'Brien. "Are Catholics Active Enough in Church?" In *American Catholic Identity: Essays in an Age of Change,* edited by Francis J. Butler, 25–38. Kansas City, MO: Sheed & Ward, 1994.

Steinfels, Peter. *A People Adrift: The Crisis of the Roman Catholic Church in America.* New York, NY: Simon & Schuster, 2003.

Stennis, Leon. "Bishop Won't OK Latin Rite." *Youngstown Vindicator,* December 8, 1977, A-2.

_____. "Blacks Face City Problems: Present 25 Pct. Ratio Will Grow." *Youngstown Vindicator,* March 28, 1973, 5.

_____. "Church Should Recruit Black Priests, Nuns for Leadership, Clergyman Says." *Youngstown Vindicator,* August 30, 1975, B-5.

_____. "Leadership's View on Diocese's Approach toward Blacks Differs." *Youngstown Vindicator,* September 6, 1975, A-7.

_____. "St. Ann Reunion Planned in July." *Youngstown Vindicator,* November 29, 1981, A-16.

_____. "Status Quo for 'Church of St. Peter': Catholic Diocese Should Lead the Way to Stronger Ties in Black Community." *Youngstown Vindicator,* September 20, 1975, A-5.

_____. "Trace Blacks' History in Community: Week-Long Observance Begins." *Youngstown Vindicator,* February 10, 1974, A-8.

Stewart, Irene. "Colored People among City's Best Citizens: Mrs. Malinda Knight, First Colored Resident Hundred Years Ago." *Youngstown Telegram,* June 29, 1931, A-41.

Stubbs, Florita. "Blacks Were Once Assigned Most Dangerous Jobs in Mills." *Youngstown Vindicator,* March 3, 1974, B-3.

Sugrue, Thomas J. *The Origins of the Urban Crisis: Race and Inequality in Postwar Detroit.* Princeton, NJ: Princeton University Press, 1996.

Sullivan, Ellen J. "Nuns Leaving Teaching Positions to Take Greater Roles in Ministry." *Vindicator,* February 1, 1988, 8.

_____. "Shaken: Couple Keep Faith, Question Decision." *Vindicator,* February 10, 1988, A-1.

_____. "Students' Parents Defend Diocese Teacher's Actions." *Vindicator,* January 30, 1988, 1.

_____. "Teacher Who Wed Divorced Man Quits Post." *Vindicator,* February 9, 1988, 2.

Sullivan, Mark. "Harding for Strict Bar to Immigration: He Long Since Declared in Favor of Limiting Tide from Europe." *Youngstown Vindicator,* May 6, 1921, 9.

Taft, Robert F. "Return to Our Roots: Recovering Western Liturgical Traditions." *America,* May 26–June 2, 2008, 10–13.

Tracy, Grace. "Old Immaculate Conception Pupils Recall '93 Honors: Work from Little Frame School Won World's Fair Award—to Mark 50 Years." *Youngstown Vindicator,* January 22, 1933, A-7.

Trautman, Donald W. "How Accessible Are the New Mass Translations?" *America,* May 21, 2007, 9–11.

Traxler, Sister Margaret Ann. "American Catholics and Negroes." *Phylon* 30, no. 4 (Winter 1969): 355–66.

Trevas, Dan. "2 Charter Schools OK'd for the City: The New Schools, Along with Eagle Heights Academy and Youngstown Community School, Have a Total Enrollment of About 1,200 Pupils." *Vindicator,* April 14, 1999, A-1.

Trolio, Tony. *Brier Hill USA.* Poland, OH: Ciao Promotions, 2001.

Van Beeck, Frans Jozef. *Catholic Identity after Vatican II: Three Types of Faith in the One Church.* Chicago, IL: Loyola University Press, 1985.

Varley, Sara. "Catholic Churches and Schools Take Big Part in Life of Youngstown: Had Beginning in One of the First Log Cabins Built in Forest of Mahoning Valley—First Mass at Dungannon." *Youngstown Telegram,* June 29, 1931, A-37.

Vecoli, Rudolph J. "Cult and Occult in Italian-American Culture: The Persistence of a Religious Heritage." In *Immigrants and Religion in Urban America,* edited by Randall M. Miller and Thomas D. Marzik, 25–47. Philadelphia, PA: Temple University Press, 1977.

_____. "Prelates and Peasants: Italian Immigrants and the Catholic Church." *Journal of Social History* 2, no. 3 (Spring 1969): 217–68.

Vinyard, JoEllen McNergney. *For Faith and Fortune: The Education of Catholic Immigrants in Detroit, 1803–1925.* Chicago, IL: University of Illinois Press, 1998.

Walch, Timothy. *Parish School: American Catholic Parochial Education from Colonial Times to the Present.* Washington, DC: National Catholic Educational Association, 2003.

Warner, Jack L. *My First Hundred Years in Hollywood.* New York, NY: Random House, 1964.

Watkins, Mel. *Dancing with Strangers: A Memoir.* New York, NY: Simon & Schuster, 1998.

Watkins, William H. *The White Architects of Black Education: Ideology and Power in America, 1865–1954.* New York, NY: Teachers College Press, 2001.

Weakland, Rembert G. *All God's People: Catholic Identity after the Second Vatican Council.* New York, NY: Paulist Press, 1985.

Webster, Emily. "Conflict over 'New' Mass Greets Pastor at Vienna." *Youngstown Vindicator,* November 6, 1977, A-1.

Welsh-Huggins, Andrew. "Despite Spotty Growth, Population Will Drop: The Mahoning County Planning Commission Director Disputes This Picture of a Slowly Deflating Population." *Vindicator,* May 26, 1996, A-1.

Whiting, A. B. "Knowing Youngstown: No. 50, Youngstown's Population Growth." *Youngstown Vindicator,* November 25, 1924, 18.

Wilkins, John. "Lost in Translation: The Bishops, the Vatican & the English Liturgy." *America,* December 2, 2005, 12–20.

Wills, Garry. *Bare Ruined Choirs: Doubt, Prophecy, and Radical Religion.* Garden City, NY: Doubleday, 1972.

———. *Head and Heart: American Christianities.* New York, NY: Penguin Press, 2007.

———. *Why I Am a Catholic.* Boston, MA: Houghton Mifflin, 2002.

Wilson, William Julius, and Richard P. Taub. *There Goes the Neighborhood: Racial, Ethnic, and Class Tensions in Four Chicago Neighborhoods and Their Meaning for America.* New York, NY: Alfred A. Knopf, 2006.

Winter, Ralph E. "Crumbling Wall: Public Aid to Schools Operated by Churches Increases Despite Foes." *New York Times,* November 10, 1970, 1.

Wirtz, William. "East Side Church Marks 75th Year." *Youngstown Vindicator,* September 29, 1957, A-15.

Wolf, B. David. "Enrollment Doubles at Area's 'Christian Schools': 18 Here Teaching 2,000." *Youngstown Vindicator,* August 30, 1981, A-10.

Yovich, Tim. "E. Side Blacks Oppose Project." *Youngstown Vindicator,* December 7, 1978, 1.

———. "West Siders Hit Housing Project." *Youngstown Vindicator,* October 26, 1978, A-1.

Youniss, James, and John T. Convey, eds. *Catholic Schools at the Crossroads: Survival and Transformation.* New York, NY: Teachers College Press, 2000.

Zech, Charles E. *Why Catholics Don't Give . . . and What Can Be Done about It.* Huntington, IN: Our Sunday Visitor Publishing, 2000.

Addendum

Since this manuscript's completion, three significant developments have occurred in Youngstown. Despite tentative plans to establish a diocesan archive at the former site of Immaculate Conception Church, the Diocese of Youngstown elected in July 2011 to sell the physical plant (including church, school, and rectory) to Atlanta and New York-based Mosaica Education, Inc., a company that operates elementary, middle, and secondary school programs throughout the world. On August 8, 2011, Mosaica opened the STEAM (Science, Technology, Engineering, Arts, and Math) Academy of Youngstown, one of two schools that the company currently operates within the city limits. During that same month, Dr. Nicholas M. Wolsonovich, who retired in June 2011 after a three-year stint as secretary of faith formation and superintendent of Catholic schools for the Diocese of Orlando, returned to Youngstown to serve as acting superintendent of Catholic schools. (The previous school superintendent, Dr. Michael Skube, assumed a new position as assistant to the bishop for regional school planning and high school board development.) Dr. Wolsonovich presided over the relocation of St. Joseph the Provider Elementary School, then based in neighboring Campbell, Ohio, to the former site of St. Anthony Elementary School, located in Youngstown's Brier Hill district. In a move that reflected a diocesan shift to the president and principal model of Catholic schooling, Father Michael A. Swierz, former pastor of St. Joseph the Provider Church, was appointed as president of the school. The diocese indicated that the school's relocation was intended to enhance its ability to serve its students, most of whom reside in Youngstown. The move also had the effect of re-establishing a Catholic parochial elementary school within Youngstown's central city, where none had operated since June of 2006.

Index

Index 319

Rerem Novarum ("Of New Things"), 102, 223, 238
Riordan, Cornelius, 192, 249, 269
Rising Star Baptist Church, 126
Ritter, Joseph Cardinal, 166, 168
Roach, Father John F., 236
Robinson, E. Wayne, 147
Roediger, David R., 161
Roman Curia, 220
Rose Street: A Family Story (Leone), 40
Rowan, Brian, 193
Rudjak, Joseph, 51, 74, 217
Rummel, Archbishop Joseph F., 168
Russo, Dr. John, 52, 107, 119, 177
"Rust Belt" phenomenon, 10, 176
Ryan, Mary Perkins, 230, 241, 242
Rzendarski, Father Aloysius, 74

Sacred Heart of Jesus: Parish, 15; School, 65, 73, 75, 76, 77.
Safford, Sean, 105, 106, 107, 116
salaries, and laicization of staff, 54–56
Sander, William, 193
Scarazzo, Lianna, 80
Schaub, Maryellen, 245
Schenley Homes, 189
Schrembs, Archbishop Joseph, 26
Scott, David J., 150–51
Sebelius, Kathleen, 7
Second Plenary Council of Baltimore, 165
Second Vatican Council, 4–5, 13, 14, 15, 59, 102–103, 104, 191–92, 198, 215, 225, 226, 263. *See also* liturgy reform
Secular counterparts, 214, 269
Sex Information and Education Council of the United States (SIECUS), 247
Sheehy, Daniel, 21
Shuba, George "Shotgun," 122
SIECUS. *See* Sex Information and Education Council of the United States (SIECUS)
Siffrin, Monsignor Robert, 196
Skube, Dr. Michael, 85, 86, 196

Slovak Americans, 122
Smith, Reverend Lonnie, 80–81, 179
Smoky Hollow, 23, 133, 177
social justice: commitment to, 191; parishes and, 185; schools as instruments of, 14, 69; wages as, 14; and women, 272
Southern, David W., 166
Spalding, Martin J., 165
Spellman, Francis Cardinal, 219, 222, 228
Stallings, George, 199
St. Ann's Parish, 23, 25
St. Anthony's: Parish, 24, 103, 109, 111; School, 195, 196
Starks, Pete, 57
St. Augustine's Church, 24, 167
St. Brendan's: Parish, 23; School, 123, 128, 196
St. Casimir's: Church, 217; Parish, 24; School, 74, 114
St. Christine's: Church, 32; School, 129, 197, 243, 244
St. Columba's Church, 22, 23, 24, 33, 42, 144, 211, 235; fire and reconstruction, 212–13; Parish, 23, 43; School, 59, 60, 111
St. Cyril's: Parish, 23; School, 121
St. Dominick's: Parish, 23, 109; School, 127, 244
Steadman, Marion, 56
St. Edward's: Parish, 23; School, 60, 127–28, 195, 196
Steele, Dr. James, 58
Steel Strike of 1919, 152
"Steel Valley" job losses, 118
Steelworkers Organizing Committee (SWOC), 147
Steinfels, Peter, 7, 219, 225, 226, 238
Stennis, Leon, 144, 183–84, 185
Stewart, Lemuel, 144, 145, 149
Stewart, William R., 157
St. Francis Parish, 24
Stilson, Kelly, 44
St. John's Episcopal Parish, 158